CRITICAL ISSUES IN CURRICULUM
John Willinsky, EDITOR

Reading and Writing the Self:
Autobiography in Education and the Curriculum
Robert J. Graham

Understanding Curriculum as Phenomenological
and Deconstructed Text
William F. Pinar and William M. Reynolds, Editors

Sexuality and the Curriculum:
The Politics and Practices of Sexuality Education
James T. Sears, Editor

SEXUALITY AND THE CURRICULUM

The Politics and Practices of Sexuality Education

EDITED BY
James T. Sears

TEACHERS
COLLEGE
PRESS

Teachers College, Columbia University
New York and London

Published by Teachers College Press, 1234 Amsterdam Avenue, New York, NY 10027

Copyright © 1992 by Teachers College, Columbia University

Chapter 2 copyright © 1991 by the Board of Trustees of the University of Illinois

Library of Congress Cataloging-in-Publication Data

Sexuality and the curriculum : the politics and practices of sexuality
    education / edited by James T. Sears.
        p.   cm.—(Critical issues in curriculum)
    Includes bibliographical references and index.
    ISBN 0-8077-3153-6.—ISBN 0-8077-3152-8 (pbk.)
    1. Sex instruction—United States. 2. Sex instruction—United
States—Curricula.   I. Sears, James T. (James Thomas), 1951–
II. Series.
HQ57.5.A3S489   1992
    305.3'07'073—dc20   91-43984

Printed on acid-free paper
Manufactured in the United States of America
97 96 95 94 93 92   8 7 6 5 4 3 2 1

Contents

Foreword: Sexuality Education in Policy and Practice   vii
    Debra W. Haffner

Foreword: Border Anxiety and Sexuality Politics   ix
    Peter McLaren

Introduction   1
    James T. Sears

PART I: Foundations for Sexual Inquiry   5

1   Dilemmas and Possibilities of Sexuality Education:
    Reproducing the Body Politic   7
    James T. Sears

2   Ideological Conflict and Change in the Sexuality Curriculum   34
    Dennis L. Carlson

3   Sexuality and Censorship in the Curriculum:
    Beyond Formalistic Legal Analysis   59
    James Anthony Whitson

    Commentary: Whose Sexuality Is It Anyway?   78
    Mariamne H. Whatley

PART II: Gender and Sexuality   85

4   Learning to Be the Opposite Sex: Sexuality Education
    and Sexual Scripting in Early Adolescence   89
    Mara Sapon-Shevin and Jesse Goodman

5   Bitter Lessons for All: Sexual Harassment in Schools   106
    Eleanor Linn, Nan D. Stein, and Jackie Young, with Saundra Davis

6   Talking About Talking About Sex: The Organization of
    Possibilities   124
    Christine LaCerva

7   The Impact of Culture and Ideology on the Construction of
    Gender and Sexual Identities: Developing a Critically
    Based Sexuality Curriculum   139
    James T. Sears

  8   Teaching College Students About Sexual Identity
      from Feminist Perspectives   157
      Mary Margaret Fonow and Debian Marty

      Commentary: Why Should We Care About Gender and
      Sexuality in Education?   171
      Susan Shurberg Klein

PART III: Making Meaning of Sexuality in the Schools   181

  9   Sexuality Education for Immigrant and Minority Students:
      Developing a Culturally Appropriate Curriculum   183
      Janie Victoria Ward and Jill McLean Taylor

 10   Inside a Ninth-Grade Sexuality Classroom: The Process of
      Knowledge Construction   203
      Bonnie K. Trudell

 11   Discussing Sexuality in a Language Arts Class: Alternative
      Meaning-Making and Meaning-Making as an Alternative   226
      Diane D. Brunner

      Commentary: What's "Left" in Sexuality Education?   242
      Lynn Phillips and Michelle Fine

PART IV: Problematics of Change   251

 12   Integrating Cognitive, Affective, and Behavioral Approaches
      into Learning Experiences for Sexuality Education   253
      Patricia Barthalow Koch

 13   School-Based HIV/AIDS Education: Is There Safety
      in Safer Sex?   267
      Jonathan G. Silin

 14   Ill-Structured Problems: Reconsidering Teenage Sexuality   284
      Diane Lee and Louise M. Berman

 15   Sexuality Education—In Whose Interest? An Analysis of
      Legislative, State Agency, and Local Change Arenas   300
      Ruth F. Earls, Joanne Fraser, and Bambi Sumpter

      Commentary: Administrators as Barriers to Change?   328
      Charol Shakeshaft

Annotated Resources   337
About the Contributors   347
Index   355

Sexuality Education in Policy and Practice

Ideally, sexuality education encompasses sexual knowledge, beliefs, attitudes, values, and behaviors. Classrooms address anatomy, physiology, and biochemistry of the sexual response system, gender roles, identity, and personality, and thoughts, feelings, behaviors, and relationships. Students discuss and debate ethical and moral concerns, and group and cultural variations. At its best, sexuality education is about social change—about helping to create a world where all people have the information and the rights to make responsible sexual choices—without regard to age, gender, socioeconomic status, or sexual orientation.

Sexuality education classes in the United States do not begin to realize this ideal. Less than 10% of American children receive comprehensive sexuality education from kindergarten through adulthood. Although most young people receive some type of sexuality education before they graduate from high school, what is labeled sexuality or family life education is often little more than teaching about biology, reproduction, and virology.

Sexuality and the Curriculum is a very exciting book. This collection of 15 essays will inspire you, provoke you, and maybe even disturb you. Each of the authors challenges the current status of sexuality education and offers new perspectives on educating children about their sexuality.

The authors decry current sexuality education curricula. Sexuality education classes often focus on disaster prevention—in the early primary grades, they begin with sexual abuse. HIV/AIDS is then introduced, and in high schools, date rape is added. The powerful message is that sexuality is dangerous. Almost all programs in the United States are designed to promote abstinence from sexual behaviors. Young people are taught to control their sexuality rather than affirm it. Many state laws specifically require the emphasis on abstinence, and only a few require balanced presentations of safer sex. As several of the authors in this volume note, the official curriculum teaches a reproductive heterosexuality, removed from discussions of gender politics, violence, economics, and even pleasure. Programs are often based on a model that assumes all children live in two-parent family middle-class homes and will grow up to be monogamous, married for life, heterosexual adults.

The authors ask us to examine the "hidden sexuality education curriculum" that exists in schools. In the average American high school, the hidden curriculum teaches teenagers that in order to be popular, one has to be attractive, physically fit and able-bodied, heterosexual, conform to gender-role expectations, and dress according to school norms. The institutional bureaucracy in most schools urges conformity, promotes homophobia, and reinforces gender inequity. Teenagers learn much more powerful messages about sexuality in the halls, locker rooms, and playing fields than they do in their health classes.

The authors of the essays in this volume raise disturbing questions about sexuality education programs. They ask the educator to address gender issues, cultural issues, ideological conflict, sexual orientation, and pleasure and desire. They insist that educators address sexuality education in ways that promote gender equity. They summon us to look beyond the formal curriculum, to the hidden curriculum of sexuality from preschool through college and the messages it imparts about sexuality and gender roles.

The authors dare us to focus on the desired outcomes of sexuality education. Going beyond the avoidance of behaviors and diseases, they challenge us to educate about sexual health, sexual pleasure, and sexual diversity. They raise disturbing questions about sexuality education as an instrument of social control, often reinforcing patriarchal, antisexual norms.

As several authors in this volume note, it makes little sense to simply offer up ideal visions about sexuality education in today's world. The political reality of the 1980s and 1990s has meant increased conservatism and attempts at sexual repression. Although the HIV/AIDS epidemic led to an increase in the number of states mandating sexuality education, these newer programs are often limited by restrictive legislation, inadequate funding, and poorly prepared teachers.

The opposition to sexuality education has become increasingly sophisticated. Recognizing that they have lost the battle to prevent sexuality education, opposition groups now focus on promoting their own brand of sexuality education based on teaching moral absolutes and withholding information from children. Too many communities are accepting these programs as a way to provide this desired education without invoking community controversy. The authors of these essays remind the reader that sexuality education is inherently political, and that efforts to improve curricula must take place in a political context.

This book is designed to encourage a dialogue between sexuality educators and curriculum developers. I wished as I read the essays that I was participating in a seminar where I could discuss and debate its exciting ideas. I hope that readers will use this book to challenge themselves to develop truly model sexuality education programs. Our children's future sexual health depends on it.

Debra W. Haffner, MPH
Executive Director
Sex Information and Education
Council of the U.S.

Border Anxiety and Sexuality Politics

Lexical distinctions surrounding the term "sex" and "sexuality" give people a general means to discuss and evaluate the consequences of sexual activity and sexual knowledge, but through this process ontologies of moral absolutism often develop that divide people into perverts/queers and straights/innocents. This is especially true today, given the vast sweep of multiple readings surrounding the meaning of sexuality that are available and the contemporary cult of terror that associates sexual practice in the age of AIDS with demonic desire and moral contagion. If we are to challenge the self-righteousness that encysts moral ontologies built upon repression, displacement, guilt, and fear, far-reaching questions need to be asked that extend beyond the debilitating Manichean obsession with "decent/perverse" sexual practices. These questions include: In what way do our views and proclamations about sexuality constitute a social bond, a social contract, a political project? And whose interest do they serve? In what ways do large public constituencies find their objective counterpart in a single system of explanation that can be used as a defense against what its adherents see as ever-increasing, contradictory threats to prevailing ideologies (local, regional, national) surrounding sexuality? To what extent is the current struggle to define the limits, meaning, and purpose of sexuality education actually a struggle against what some see as the sinister malevolence of an increasingly indeterminate and ambiguous moral agency that is linked to the breakdown of the traditional American family. To what degree does the way in which we name sexuality both reflect and contribute to the virulently homophobic orthodoxy of psychoanalytic theory that anchors itself to an ideology of reproductive heterosexuality as both a cultural norm and prescription of psychic health (Friedman, 1988)? In what ways are the oppressions of racism, sexism, heterosexism, ageism, and ableism representative of a larger border anxiety that is territorialized by patriarchal discourse and irrevocably linked to a fear of the Other, connecting the culture of Otherness to death (Kristeva, 1982; Young, 1990)?

Questions of these kinds are crucial to what we define as the problem of sexuality and schooling and point to the increasing importance of recognizing the role of language in gender formation. Post-structuralist theory has advanced our understanding of the relationship between language and gender formation by asserting that identity is constituted through the retroactive effect of naming itself (Laclau, 1989; Zizek, 1989). Naming is a process through which our reality becomes socially constructed. For instance, the performative character of naming "sexual" and "gender" identity amounts to the very act of their constitution. Unless we want to adhere to a descriptivist approach to sexuality and gender that discounts the possibility of any discursive hegemonic variation (since the sexual/gendered subject under descriptivism would be pre-constituted and then attributed objective features), we can look to the process of renaming sexuality and gender as a way to destabilize their current descriptive features and open their patriarchal and heterosexist anchor points to hegemonic rearticulations. As Jeanne Brady Giroux (1990) notes, "To ask teachers to be attentive to language does not merely suggest that they be able to identify how sexist interests are embedded in discourse; at stake here is recognizing that language actively constructs reality and as such must be seen as playing a central pedagogical and political role in any theory of gender formation." This suggests that we can alter the way power and discourse are currently related by re-naming oppression, by providing teachers and students with a new vocabulary for understanding their sexual and social construction as gendered, desiring body/subjects, and by exploring how students and teachers are themselves implicated in existing power/ knowledge relations and how the differential privileges of race, class, sexual preference, and age that exist at both local and global levels can be transformed.

Teachers need a critical language for engaging issues of sexuality and gender that takes into account the complexity of contemporary social life. The world of contemporary gender theory is one that is populated by meanings already colonized by patriarchy's Law of the Father. Despite the ongoing need to de-capitalize the registers of Patriarchy, Manhood, and Truth, it nevertheless remains a terrain of political struggle that has urgent importance for understanding how we desire, why we desire, and in what direction we are able to and should desire.[1] By renaming sexuality and gender construction, teachers and students can enter into a process of desemanticization: detaching such constructions from prior meanings and realigning them with new meanings that have implications for emancipatory practices. As James Sears has so acutely pointed out, it is truly tragic that given the work being accomplished in sexuality and gender theory, teacher educators have, for the most part, been denied the opportunity to critically engage its strengths, limitations, and theoretical tensions. Student teachers have not been encouraged to survey the terrain of contemporary theories of sexuality and gender and to respond to questions currently being raised: Is sexuality the crisis of a universal semiosis? Is our desire for and dependence on a unitary identity a means of excluding multiple subjectivities we cannot or choose not to confront? Are our gendered identities forms of social writing—inscriptions? Is sexual identity linked to the excess or remainder of linguistic systems, as many of Lacan's interpreters would have us believe (see Flax, 1990)? Or does sexuality have its roots in pre-discursivity, in the gaps within the orders of discourse? Why does the power of the phallus govern so many contemporary readings—even feminist readings—where desire is mapped in terms of semiotic algorithms or turned into a linguistic grid or psycho-linguistic ontology (Levin, 1991)? Is it the autonomous ego as an archic site of consciousness that thinks about the body, or does the body as an intentional agent use the "I" as a discursive conduit to reflect upon its own desire? Is meaning primarily a cognitive function or is all meaning transcoded through the body—through forms of enfleshment?[2]

It is in the body that the most profound moral and social dilemmas take on flesh. The concept of the body as a site of social and cultural inscription—"the factored product of the unequal and differential effects of intersecting antagonistic forces" (Feldman, 1991, p. 176)—is growing in prominence as a topic of investigation among contemporary social theorists. The analysis of desire is also gathering increased interest, especially among those who follow semiotic and post-structuralist analysis. Efforts are being made to uncouple the idea of the feminine body/subject from the negative and unspoken Other and to recognize the body as a site of enfleshment—that is, as a site where the body is historicized and congealed by social practices and where epistemic codes grip bodies in social norms. Recent post-structuralist investigations of the body have revealed it to be a product of the carceral machine of corporate capitalism—that is, of situating bodies "incorporally" through the commodification of signs with social formations that serve to regulate the production of desire and that organize and align the heterogeneous regimes of discourses of the flesh. This has made it impossible to return to a simple vitalism that reduces human nature to repressed libidinal energy biologically housed in the glandular system or to psychic energy whose transmutation into pathological complexes is kept in check by various forms of cultural panopticism and convergent social practices we know in the literature by the term "hegemony" (and gays and lesbians know from experience as "queer bashing").

The material density of our subjectivities are inscribed in our bodies through the enfleshment of social relations. As educators, we have divorced knowledge from the body to the detriment of our pedagogies and to our own peril as potential producers of historical agency. This is most damagingly evident in "official" school practices where we witness in oppositional student behavior what Terry Eagleton (1990) calls "the body's long inarticulate rebellion against the tyranny of the theoretical" (p. 13). My concern is that sexuality education in the schools needs to draw upon the affective economies situated within what Paul Willis (1990) calls "common culture," to render such economies problematic, and eventually to find ways to transform them into a larger political project and social vision. In this way, pedagogies of sexuality education can be developed that enable students to construct knowledge that is lived in the body, felt in the bones, and situated within a larger commitment to social justice and emancipation. This requires a critical social theory that stresses the mutual implication of race, class, gender, and sexual preference and that refuses to be recontained within the boundaries of hegemonic cultural discourses by simply reversing patriarchy's terms (de Lauretis, 1990). Also needed is a critical pedagogy of sexuality education that moves beyond the (albeit important) domain of relevance and into the arena of a transformative social practice in the struggle against patriarchal oppression. The problem is that male social theorists have either failed to pay attention to or have diminished the importance of feminist currents in contemporary debates over race, class, and gender oppression and in constructing pedagogies of liberation. This means, following Teresa de Lauretis (1990), "giving up a place that is safe, that is 'home'—physically, emotionally, linguistically, epistemologically—for another place that is unknown and risky, that is not only emotionally but conceptually other; a place of discourse from which speaking and thinking are at best tentative, uncertain, unguaranteed" (p. 138). This is "theory in the flesh," "a constant crossing of the border," and "a remapping of boundaries between bodies and discourses, identities and communities" (p. 138).

Unless a curriculum of sexuality education addresses the issues of sexuality and gender as they are lived throughout multiple forms of subjectivity, as they are constructed within the domain of enfleshed popular culture, students will find little use for it because it will simply be received as yet another form of the official culture imposing itself on them (Giroux, 1990). The task of developing an emancipatory and counter-hegemonic curriculum of sexuality education has been the impetus for this impressive volume.

Sexuality and the Curriculum, edited by James T. Sears, constitutes both a reterritorialization of the relationship between sexuality and schooling and a challenge to the current state of sexuality illiteracy in this country.[3] It is designed specifically to help students, parents, teachers, and administrators better understand the complex issues surrounding current debates over sex education, to shed a new critical understanding on the construction of male and female sexual identity as it has been mapped by sovereign regimes of patriarchal scientific discourses and colonized by phallic desire, and to challenge regressive and insidiously harmful myths about gay and lesbian sexuality. In this volume, Sears has brought together an impressive list of contributors, each of whom manages to reveal in different ways what is politically, ethically, and pedagogically at stake in naming ourselves as gendered, sexual, and desiring body/subjects. *Sexuality and the Curriculum* not only warns us of the dangers of constructing educational and social practices that enforce misogynous, homophobic, and patriarchal acts of naming, it also provides us with the basis of undermining such oppressions and for constructing the grounds for both a radically enfleshed pedagogy and a transformative and egalitarian politics of difference. In addition, it is a book that sounds an important and timely challenge to critical social theorists to engage the topic of education in their work and make it one of the pivotal points of their analysis. Reading *Sexuality and the Curriculum* leads one to think that it is in the domain of gender research and sexuality education that the florescence of future liberatory struggles will take root.

Peter McLaren
Associate Director
Center for Education and Cultural Studies
Miami University of Ohio

NOTES

1. For an excellent discussion of critical pedagogy from a feminist perspective, see bell hooks, "bell hooks speaking about Paulo Freire the man—his work," in P. McLaren & P. Leonard (Eds.), *Paulo Freire: A critical encounter* (New York: Routledge, in press).

2. Enfleshment refers to the mutually constitutive (enfolding) of social structure and desire; that is, it constitutes the dialectic relationship between the material organization of interiority and the cultural forms and modes of materiality we inhabit subjectively. Enfleshment also refers to the "quilting point" that results when the radical externality of the body/subject as independent of and resistant to our volition joins the interiority of our own subjectivity, our own politics of location. See McLaren, 1990.

3. For a brilliant analysis of the relationship between education and literacy, see Kathleen Rockhill, "Dis/connecting literacy and education: Speaking the unspeakable in the classroom," in C. Lankshear & P. McLaren (Eds.), *Critical literacy: Politics, praxis, and the postmodern* (Albany: SUNY Press, in press).

REFERENCES

De Lauretis, T. (1990). Eccentric subjects: Feminist theory and historical consciousness. *Feminist Studies, 16,* (1), 115–150.

Eagleton, T. (1990). *The ideology of the aesthetic.* London: Basil Blackwell.

Feldman, A. (1991). *Formations of violence: The narrative of the body and political terror in Northern Ireland.* Chicago: University of Chicago Press.

Flax, J. (1990). *Thinking fragments: Psychoanalysis, feminism, and postmodernism in the contemporary west.* Berkeley: University of California Press.

Friedman, R. (1988). *Male homosexuality: A contemporary psychoanalytic perspective.* New Haven, CT: Yale University Press.

Giroux, H. A. (1990). Modernism, postmodernism, and feminism. In H. A. Giroux (Ed.), *Postmodernism, feminism, and cultural politics* (pp. 1–59). Albany: SUNY Press.

Giroux, J. B. (1990). *Schooling, sex education, and the discourse of desire.* Unpublished manuscript.

Kristeva, J. (1982). *Powers of horror: An essay in abjection* (L. S. Roudiez, Trans.). New York: Columbia University Press.

Laclau, E. (1989). Preface. In S. Zizek, *The sublime object of ideology* (pp. ix–xv). New York: Verso.

Levin, C. (1991). Lacanian psychoanalysis and feminist metatheory. In A. Kroker & M. Kroker (Eds.), *The hysterical male: New feminist theory* (pp. 235–252). New York: St. Martin's Press.

McLaren, P. (1990). Schooling the postmodern body: Critical pedagogy and the politics of enfleshment. In H. A. Giroux (Ed.), *Postmodernism, feminism, and cultural politics* (pp. 144–173). Albany: SUNY Press.

Willis, P. (1990). *Common culture.* Boulder and San Francisco: Westview Press.

Young, I. M. (1990). *Justice and the politics of difference.* Princeton, NJ: Princeton University Press.

Zizek, S. (1989). *The sublime object of ideology.* New York: Verso.

Acknowledgments

While there seems to be no end to the commercialization and commodification of sexuality in our society, there has been little willingness on the part of publishers to address critically sexuality and sexuality education in our schools' curriculum. As publisher at Teachers College Press, Carole Saltz's commitment to and enthusiasm for this controversial project has been unwavering. I was also buoyed by the editorial support and advice of Sarah Biondello and, most particularly, by the hands-on editorial skills of Susan Liddicoat. I salute three talented and committed women who well reflect the tradition of excellence and integrity that has become the trademark of Teachers College Press.

During the initial stage of reviewing abstracts of potential contributors, I was assisted greatly by a group of curriculum scholars, sexuality educators, and sex-equity specialists. They were Bill Ayers, Barbara Bitters, Patt Dodds, Noreen Garman, Lucile Jordan, Pat Hulsebosch, Melissa Keyes, Susan Klein, Suzanne Kutsch, Janet Miller, Pam Miller, Carlos Ovando, Norm Overly, Marian Schoenheit, William Sweigart, Elizabeth Vallance, Lynn Wallich, and Robert Zeigler. In the latter stages of this manuscript, the sage advice of Janet Miller, Patti Lather, and Mariamne Whatley was particularly welcomed. Of course, it was the willingness of this volume's contributors to revise their manuscripts, to communicate with one another, and to trust my vision for how their chapters would eventually fit into this book for which I am most thankful.

Finally, in this writing endeavor there was a small group of people with whom I had very different relationships but without whom I would not have been able to complete this book: Tara Fulton, Pat Lindler, J. Dan Marshall, and, of course, Bob Williamson.

This book is dedicated to the talented and committed women and men at Teachers College Press and to the memory of Ron Galbraith, whose editorial skills and personal charm will be missed by us all.

SEXUALITY AND THE CURRICULUM

*The Politics and Practices
of Sexuality Education*

Introduction

Sexuality and the Curriculum brings together curriculum scholars and developers, sexuality educators, and sex-equity specialists to explore the explicit and hidden curriculum of sexuality from preschool through college. In recent years there has been significant scholarship and discourse within the field of sexuality education (e.g., Children's Defense Fund, 1987; Fine, 1988; Kirby, 1984; Klein, 1989; Myerson, 1986) as well as in the curriculum field (e.g., Apple, 1988; Giroux, 1988; Pinar, 1988; Schubert, 1986; Sears & Marshall, 1990). However, little communication occurs *between* sexuality educators or sex-equity specialists and curriculum scholars or developers. *Sexuality and the Curriculum* is the beginning of what will hopefully become a long and fruitful dialogue between these two fields.

THE THEORETICAL FRAMEWORK

This collection of 15 interrelated essays challenges conventional assumptions regarding sexuality and the curriculum while proposing specific curricular strategies and alternatives. All of the authors share a discomfort with conventional approaches to the teaching of sexuality in the schools; all reject the technocratic design and implementation of the conventional sexuality curriculum.

Overly technocratic in its development, expressly behavioristic in its design, and generally cognitive in content, sexuality education in the United States reproduces social divisions and categories existing within the body politic. Even in those communities that have experienced a reduction in the rate of sexually transmitted diseases or teenage pregnancies, students' felt experiences remain ungrounded, and linkages to structural relations are absent. Operating from a techno-rational worldview that prizes instrumental control and linear thinking, sexuality education minimizes community dialogue and avoids community conflict. However, sexuality education is an important, though neglected, part of the contested terrain in the battle to expand democracy and improve schooling in the United States. While our social understandings may be technocratically premised, the highly charged issue of sexuality is fertile terrain for critical discourse about our fundamental social and political assumptions.

In rethinking sexuality and the curriculum, the authors in this volume borrow from feminist thought, critical social theory, and existential phenomenology. Though these contributors do not represent a singular theoretical voice, *Sexuality and the Curriculum* challenges conventional sexual discourse and curriculum design by bringing nontraditional perspectives to traditionally unresolved problems.

THE ORGANIZATIONAL FRAMEWORK

A call for abstracts was sent to more than 1,000 sexuality educators, sex-equity specialists, and curriculum scholars and developers in North America and overseas in May 1989. Reviews of prospective authors' abstracts were prepared by persons familiar with the human sexuality and/ or the curriculum field. Based upon those reviews, about two dozen potential authors were invited to submit a more detailed outline of their proposed chapter. Ultimately, 15 chapters were selected for inclusion in this book.

Each chapter in *Sexuality and the Curriculum* presents one critical topic that sex-equity specialists, educators, curriculum developers, and scholars should acknowledge as they address this long taboo subject. In arguing the importance of this topic, the author provides analytical, theoretical, historical, empirical, and ethnographic evidence to support her or his position and suggests strategies the reader might employ in order to address this particular topic.

Sexuality and the Curriculum is divided into four parts. Part I, "Foundations for Sexual Inquiry," provides the reader with an interdisciplinary understanding of sexuality and its placement in the school curriculum. Part II, "Gender and Sexuality," includes essays that explore the integral relationship between gender and sexuality and its relationship to sexuality education. Part III, "Making Meaning of Sexuality in the Schools," allows the reader to peer below the curricular surface to understand the sexual meanings, messages, acts, and thoughts of students and their implications for what is formally taught in the school curriculum. The authors contributing to Part IV, "Problematics of Change," discuss the difficulties in conventional curricular approaches to sexuality education while revealing the dynamics of institutional, curricular, and personal change. Preceding each part is a brief introduction; following each section is a longer, scholarly commentary. At the end of the book, readers will find annotations of outstanding materials and resources relating to topics addressed in this book.

The commentaries coupled with the 15 essays provide an interdisciplinary and critical perspective to sexuality and the curriculum. Of course, the most important voice—that of you, the reader—is about to join this chorus of reflective practitioners raising provocative issues and suggesting innovative solutions.

REFERENCES

Apple, M. (1988). *Teachers and texts*. New York: Routledge, Chapman and Hall.

Children's Defense Fund. (1987). *Adolescent pregnancy: An anatomy of a social problem in search of comprehensive solutions*. Washington, DC: Author.

Fine, M. (1988). Sexuality, schooling and adolescent females: The missing discourse of desire. *Harvard Educational Review, 58*(1), 29–53.

Giroux, H. (1988). *Teachers as intellectuals*. Granby, MA: Bergin and Garvey.

Kirby, D. (1984). *Sexuality education: An evaluation of programs and their effects*. Santa Cruz, CA: Network Publications. (ERIC Document No. ED 277955)

Klein, S. S. (Ed.). (1989). Sex equity and sexuality in education [Special issue]. *Peabody Journal of Education, 64*(4).

Myerson, M. (1986). The politics of sexual knowledge: Feminism and sexology textbooks. *Frontiers, 9*(1), 66–71.

Pinar, W. (1988). *Contemporary curriculum discourses*. Scottsdale, AZ: Gorsuch Scarisbrick.

Schubert, W. (1986). *Curriculum: Perspective, paradigm, and possibility*. New York: Macmillan.

Sears, J., & Marshall, J. (1990). *Teaching and thinking about curriculum: Critical inquiries*. New York: Teachers College Press.

Part I

FOUNDATIONS FOR SEXUAL INQUIRY

The taken-for-granted understanding that accompanies the phrase "sexuality and the curriculum" is the sequence and scope of sexuality content and the methods for presenting that knowledge in the schools. Should the school curriculum include information about contraceptives, masturbation, or homosexuality? At what grade level should discussions occur about human physiology, the birth process, or sexually transmitted diseases? What mode of instructional delivery is most effective in reducing adolescent sexual experimentation or promoting safer sex?

Before we can generate a meaningful answer to any of these questions, we must understand the history of sexuality education in the United States and the various ideological bases for sexuality curricula. There must also be a realistic appraisal of the extensiveness and relevance of existing sexuality curricula, the consequences—intended and unintended—of such curricula, and the integral relationships between politics and sexuality. Finally, curriculum developers and sexuality educators must be apprised of the legal issues surrounding sexuality and the curriculum as well as constitutional issues relating to First Amendment rights. These areas comprise Part I of *Sexuality and the Curriculum*.

In Chapter 1, I discuss the shortcomings of conventional curriculum design and discourse on sexuality education through a careful review of studies on its effectiveness. Overly technocratic in its development, expressly behavioristic in its design, and generally cognitive in content, sexuality education in the United States reproduces the gender, racial, and social class divisions within the body politic. Even in those communities that have experienced a reduction of the rate of sexually transmitted diseases or teenage pregnancies, there is little grounding to students' felt experiences, and linkages to structural relations are absent. Setting the theme for this book, I conclude that sexuality education is an important, though long neglected, territory of the contested terrain for democratic education within the schools and the communities they serve.

Dennis Carlson, in Chapter 2, critically examines the cultural and historical context of four ideologies, each of whose influence and scope has varied during this century. In his analysis of selected books and authors representative of the traditionalist, progressive, radical Freudian, and libertarian ideologies, Carlson discusses the limitations and possibilities of each in a holistic approach to sexuality education within a democratic state. Following his examination of the works of Reich, Marcuse, Kinsey, and Masters and Johnson, Carlson concludes that the sexuality curriculum must be "re-conceptualized" by removing it from the domain of physiology and placing it firmly in the domains of cultural studies, liberal arts, and history.

In the final chapter within this part, James Whitson explores the relationship between sexuality and the curriculum by examining the ideology behind First Amendment interpretations. While Whitson examines cases, statutes, and administrative regulations, his focus differs from that found in mainstream law texts. In Chapter 3, he considers how the legalistic analysis of censorship cases has distorted the significance and value of addressing sexuality in the curriculum, how this distortion has been institutionalized on the basis of a false ideological theory of curriculum that has emerged from the legal process, and how this theory—used to justify the censorship of sexuality—undermines the integrity of other essential aspects of the curriculum.

In the commentary to Part I, Mariamne Whatley documents that the problem in sexuality education is that "learning activities seem driven not by theories of education but by the fear of attack." She goes on to discuss prospects for a "thoughtful," comprehensive sexuality curriculum. Working in the area of feminist approaches to health and sexuality education, her writing represents groundbreaking scholarship, wedding curriculum thinking to sexuality education.

CHAPTER 1

Dilemmas and Possibilities of Sexuality Education

Reproducing the Body Politic

JAMES T. SEARS

During recent years we have seen increasing interest in providing sexuality education in the public schools. Given the AIDS crisis, the efforts of former Surgeon General Everett Koop, and the tactics of groups such as Planned Parenthood and Citizens for Decency, sexuality is no longer an easily hidden part of the school curriculum. Prodded by some state legislatures, many schools are addressing sexual topics at levels of specificity and at school grades considered inappropriate only a generation ago. Further, a national poll found that an overwhelming majority of Americans—themselves ill-informed about the topic—favor sexuality education, including AIDS education endorsing the value of condoms for prevention; three fourths favor integrating sexuality education into the elementary school curriculum (Kahn, 1990).

Despite the more extensive discussion of sexual topics and the expansion of sexuality education into early and preadolescent years, sexual discourse and sexuality education remain conventional. The conceptual framework of sexuality education, the organization and delivery of sexual content to students, and the criteria by which such programs are judged effective reflect a techno-rational worldview.

There are several important elements to this worldview. Sexuality education is first and foremost an *instrument* of sexual and social control in which the effectiveness of such programs is judged on the basis of sexual *behavior* and its observable consequences: adolescent pregnancy rate, per capita abortions, and rate of sexually transmitted disease (STD) infection. The sexuality curriculum is generally a series of content-based units (e.g., physiology, sexual decision making) taught to a homogeneous set of students. Conventional curriculum design rests on a model of sexual decision making that places priority on *rationality:* the ability to weigh the costs and benefits of particular sexual behavior. Viewed primarily in cognitive terms, sexual knowledge—like knowledge of geometry or history—can be reduced to definable curricular modules for teacher presentation and student consumption. Decisions about the scope and sequence of this curriculum are *technical*, hiding sexual ideology beneath a veneer of scientism.

Those involved in sexuality education seldom address fundamental curricular questions such as

> What sexual knowledge is of most worth (and consequently included or excluded in sexuality education)?
> How do educators incorporate that knowledge into the school curriculum?
> How do students interpret it?
> Who has access to what types of sexual information?

THE STATE OF SEXUALITY CURRICULUM

The reemergence of political and religious conservatism in the United States combined with the abortion controversy and the twin crises of AIDS and teenage pregnancy have catapulted sexuality education into tens of thousands of classrooms. Twenty-two states and the District of Columbia now mandate the teaching of sexuality in the public schools; only three states did in 1980 (Haffner, 1990). An estimated 50,000 public school teachers provide sexuality instruction in grades 7 to 12 (Forrest & Silverman, 1989). Two thirds of the nation's largest school districts now require instruction in sex education (Kenney, Guardado, & Brown, 1989), and most (80%) provide AIDS education; less than 2% discourage or prohibit sexuality education. But how extensive is this curriculum? How relevant is this curriculum to adolescents' needs and concerns? And what are the hidden messages conveyed in this curriculum?

Extensiveness

What different states prescribe or proscribe for sexuality in the curriculum varies significantly. In South Carolina, for example, sexuality education legislation prohibits teaching about abortion or homosexuality; in Utah it is a Class B misdemeanor for school personnel to discuss condoms with students without parental consent. In contrast, New Jersey mandates comprehensive sexuality education that includes methods of contraception and discussion about homosexuality. In their evaluation of state-developed sexuality curriculum and training requirements for teachers, researchers at the Alan Guttmacher Institute concluded that only three states (New Jersey, New York, and Wisconsin) and the District of Columbia have "what can be construed as a program on sex education and AIDS education" (Kenney, et al., 1989, p. 61).

The scope of sexuality education also varies widely among school districts within states. The Guttmacher researchers found *no* relationship between state and school district policies on sex education (Kenney et al., 1989). While students in some school districts within a state may experience a comprehensive health education curriculum, the formal curriculum for students attending other school districts in that state may consist of little more than lessons on sexual hydraulics or admonitions for "sex respect."

Most sexuality education is presented as a separate unit in health, home economics, science, or physical education (Sonenstein & Pittman, 1984)—most commonly at the 9th- or 10th-grade levels (Forrest & Silverman, 1989). A study conducted by the National Institute of Education found that schools that integrate some form of sexuality content into the curriculum provide an average of 41.7 hours of instruction to students in grades 7 to 12 (Marsiglio & Mott, 1986). Nevertheless, less than one third of metropolitan school districts provide at least 75% of the student body with sexuality education for at least one class period before the ninth grade (Sonenstein & Pittman, 1984). Further, the most likely sexuality-related topics discussed in schools are anatomy and physiology (e.g., changes at puberty, physical differences), sexually transmitted diseases, and sexual decision making (issues relating to dating, marriage, and parenthood) with particular emphasis on sexual abstinence (de Mauro, 1990; Forrest & Silverman, 1989; Sonenstein & Pittman, 1984). Studies have consistently found that the topics least discussed are homosexuality, gynecologic examinations, birth control, abortion, and masturbation and other safer sex practices (Forrest & Silverman, 1989; Orr, 1982; Sonenstein & Pittman, 1984). The Guttmacher researchers concluded that state educational agencies "place greater emphasis on the negative outcomes of sex (such as STDs and AIDS) and on abstinence than on the prevention of pregnancy" (Kenney et al., 1989, p. 59).

Relevance

Although a majority of women and men report having taken a sexuality education course by the age of 19 (Marsiglio & Mott, 1986), the placement of sexuality in the school curriculum does *not* parallel students' needs and concerns. For example, a substantial number of youth are sexually active *before* their first formal encounter with this subject (Marsiglio & Mott, 1986). One study of nearly 1,700 inner-city students reported that 92% of the ninth-grade males and 54% of the females were sexually active (Zabin, Hirsch, Smith, Street, & Hardy, 1986b); another study of 758 eighth-grade students from three rural counties found that nearly two thirds of the boys and 4 out of 10 girls had engaged in sexual intercourse (Alexander et al., 1989). Simply stated, the integration of sexuality education in the curriculum has *no* relationship to the adolescent's decision to engage in heterosexual intercourse (Dawson, 1986; Kirby 1989; Marsiglio & Mott, 1986). If that decision is made, however, the adolescent female who has had a unit in sexuality is more likely to seek birth control services—particularly if health clinic services supplement their basic sexuality education program (Zabin et al., 1986b).

Beyond the issue of "timing" lies a significant gap between the sexual interests and concerns of students and what is provided to them in the formal sexuality curriculum. For example, children entering adolescence are interested in physiology, which many sexuality teachers cover. But they also want an explanation of slang terms, and these are generally not discussed because of their obscenity and teachers' fear of class disruption or parental objection. High school age students express most interest in contraception, pregnancy, and health risks (Campbell & Campbell, 1986). A survey of Chicago teens ages 15 to 18 found that the three most important topics that both males and females wanted the school to discuss were birth control, abortion, and how to handle sexual feelings; sexual decision making—dating, pregnancy and parenthood, and marriage—was less often cited (Juhasz, Kaufman, & Meyer, 1986). But three fourths of the sexuality teachers surveyed by Forrest and Silverman (1989) believed that students should be taught *not* to have sex; and another recently published study found that teachers place "diminished importance" on birth control and student sexual behavior compared to the more conventional topics in the sexuality curriculum (Gingiss & Hamilton, 1989, p. 431). Not surprisingly,

> many teachers list student reactions or lack of interest as one of their most important problems. . . . It could reflect a discrepancy between the importance teachers place on the abstinence message and the fact that many of their students have already had sex. . . . The finding that about one-quarter of the teachers who discuss birth control methods in class do so only in response to student questions suggests that tension exists between what teachers teach and what their students want to know. (Forrest & Silverman, 1989, p. 72)

Another factor relating to students' disinterest in a conventional sexuality education program is its white, middle-class content—principally directed at female students. Following a careful examination of photographic images of African-Americans in 16 college-level sexuality textbooks, Whatley (1988) noted the "presence of certain *dominant* meanings in cultural texts and photographs" (p. 140). Among these are images of blacks as sexually dangerous—"in all four cases in which there were pimps pictured, the pimps were Black" (p. 147)—and blacks as asexual—"there are more than 30 photographs of individuals, couples, or small groups who are identified as lesbians or gay men. All these individuals are white" (p. 150). Whatley concludes:

> The emphasis is on the Black man, much more than the Black women, who becomes nearly invisible. The possibilities for the sexuality of the Black man become polarized into the dangerous pimp, or the good, loving father, without allowing for the full range of sexual expression allowed to whites. (pp. 152–153)

The level of sexual knowledge is low among adolescents—even those who have had instruction in sexuality—and it is particularly low among minority youth (Scott-Jones & Turner, 1988; Marsiglio & Mott, 1986). For example, in a study of inner-city seventh- and eighth-grade students, researchers found that though most students knew of the existence of contraceptive methods and the importance of their use in sexual activity, fewer than half could specify the least or most effective contraceptive methods; fewer than 15% knew when pregnancy was most likely to occur during the menstrual cycle (Herz & Reis, 1987).

Further, regardless of their formal instruction, twice as many women as men are knowledgeable about the likelihood of pregnancy, and white women are significantly more knowledgeable than women of color (Marsiglio & Mott, 1986). Though contraceptive use correlates positively with taking a unit in sexuality education, this relationship exists only for *white* women. For African-Americans and Hispanics, there is no relationship between sexuality instruction and contraceptive behavior (Dawson, 1986; Marsiglio & Mott, 1986).

The lack of contraceptive knowledge, greater sexual activity, and higher teenage pregnancy rates among African-Americans may stem partly from poverty, disillusionment, school failure—which result in a disproportionate number of minorities discontinuing school beyond the age of 16 (an age at which many schools implement their sexuality programs)—living in a disruptive family or community environment, and the differing meanings associated with sexual experiences (Alexander et al., 1989; Furstenberg, 1987).

Most research and evaluation on sexuality education programs, operating from a techno-rational perspective, fail to study the meanings adolescents attach to sexual activity. Ethnographic research is the most appropriate method for gaining such an understanding. A distillation of one such study is included in this volume. In Chapter 10, Bonnie Trudell takes the reader into a ninth-grade sexuality education classroom from a perspective that "conceptualizes school knowledge as socially constructed by teachers and students whose historical, social, and biographical relationships intersect with a particular set of school and social conditions." She portrays the dilemmas faced by Mrs. Warren, a hard-working, middle-aged, white teacher struggling to teach sexuality to a diverse group of 27 adolescents. Trudell also explores how students interpret and reinterpret, resist, and acquiesce to the sexual knowledge presented by Mrs. Warren. Mrs. Warren represents the conventional approach to teaching sexuality and the problems of school-based sexuality programs directed at white, middle-class students.

In Chapter 11 Diane Brunner examines the possibilities of dialogical teaching using a language-arts-based curriculum in a nonformal educational setting. Allowing inner-city black adolescents to "make meaning" of their lived experiences through the critical reading of story texts, according to Brunner, "can enhance possibilities for students' sexual learning that authenticates cultural knowledge and diversity as it challenges existing systems of power." Both the Brunner and Trudell chapters enable us to enter into the realm of sexual meanings constructed by black and white students under the rubric of sexuality education.

The differences in perspectives between adolescent males and females of different cultural groups has been infrequently studied. In one study comparing pregnant Mexican- and Anglo-American adolescents, the most striking cultural differences were that the Mexican-Americans received less information about birth control measures from their parents, their pregnancies generally followed a long-term relationship, and there was close emotional bonding between the teenage mother and the baby's father (de Anda, Becerra, & Fielder, 1988). In another study comparing Anglo-American, Native-American, and Mexican-American adolescents, males, in general, had less sexual knowledge and interest than females, and Anglo-Americans were the most knowledgeable (and most frequently communicated with parents on sexual issues), while Native-American adolescents had the least sexual knowledge (Davis & Harris, 1982). In chapter 9 Janie Ward and Jill Taylor detail cultural differences in family communication and adolescent understanding of sex education, contraception, gender, and sexual decision making. These authors conclude that conventional sexuality education ignores multicultural populations, "and because sexuality education fails to incorporate the issues and concerns teens themselves say are important, their needs are not being met."

Another contributing factor to the ineffectiveness of the contemporary sexuality curriculum is its emphasis on the cognitive area. Though sexuality education appears under various titles (most commonly, "family life education," "human growth and development," "sex education," "health education"), the two principal goals articulated by most sexuality teachers are to promote rational and informed decision making about sexuality and to increase a student's knowledge of reproduction (Forest & Silverman, 1989). The assumption, of course, is that knowledge about sexuality (and particularly the consequences of heterosexual intercourse) will result in changes in behavior (sexual abstinence, the use of safer-sex techniques).

There is little evidence, however, to suggest a relationship between students' knowledge and their sexual behaviors (Zabin, Hirsch, Smith, & Hardy, 1984). This is partly a result of adolescent egocentrism and inability to perceive cause-effect relations (Cvetkovish, Lieberman, & Miller, 1978). As one researcher noted, "Early adolescents will believe they cannot get pregnant while standing up, and the like; and providing them with correct information, before their emotional development allows them to assimilate it, is not likely to turn them into contraceptors" (Shornack, 1986, p. 318). The implications, as a leading educational policy analyst suggests, are obvious:

> Among teenagers, the decision to become pregnant is seldom rational. Rather, it tends to be shaped by personal and cultural traits. Schools traffic quite effectively in information and skills, but they tend to be weak when it comes to altering emotionally based and culturally conditioned responses. (Cuban, 1986, p. 321)

Hidden Curriculum

Sexuality education, of course, takes place in many forums other than the school's formal sexuality curriculum, yet the hidden curriculum of sexuality in the schools remains a potent, generally unaddressed phenomenon. One example of this hidden curriculum is the overemphasis on rational decision making and the failure to explore the eroticism associated with sexuality and the language of intimate sexual communication.

> Sexuality, while having a certain structure that confines it, can take any number of forms. It is a language we first learn on the borderlines of sex, in shaking hands, standing with our hands on our hips, letting a cigarette droop from our lips in Junior High School. . . . Like dancing, sexuality is an extension and fine development of everyday movements, capable of open-ended refinement and individual variation, as poetry of the body. (Solomon, 1975, pp. 281–282)

Formal sexuality curricula define the range of legitimate sexual options and depict sexuality as an "adult" activity with grave consequences for those adolescents who "play with fire." The language of sexual intimacy, the fluidity of sexuality, and the creativity of human sexual responses is not part of the sexual curriculum that emphasizes the prevention of adolescent heterosexual coital activity. Expression of sexuality to another human being, of course, can range from homosexual or heterosexual oral or anal intercourse, to mutual masturbation and genital fondling, to whole body massages and deep kisses, to erotic glances and sensuous language. Yet, the sexual curriculum often "turns out to be nothing more than a brief bout with a swimming-sperm and Fallopian-tube course that has put students to sleep for generations" (Leo, 1987, p. 139).

The theme of the 1988 annual meeting of the Society for the Scientific Study of Sex (SSSS) was "sexual literacy," which the Society defined as

> the basic sexual information and skills to thrive in a modern world; a comprehensive knowledge of sex and sexuality; the ability to understand alternative sides of a sexual issue; tolerance for ambiguity and paradox; and understanding of the advantages and limitations of different methodologies used in the study of sex. (Scales, 1989, p. 172)

While appearing to be an enlightened, liberal statement, this organization's use of the term "sexual literacy" (like "cultural literacy") is expressly rational. Devoid of the language of pleasure, pain, and intimacy, "sexual literacy" is a checklist of knowledge, skills, and information with no invitation for the adolescent to explore sexual feelings or express sexual authenticity. This definition reflects conventional sexuality education that emphasizes the mind and the libido at the expense of body and the spirit. With the language of science supplanting the poetics of intimacy, it should come as no surprise that such a curriculum has little impact on today's adolescents. As Robert Solomon (1975) astutely observes: "Sexuality conceived of as a language of intimacy and feeling that calls for ever new variation and inventiveness has as its worst violators those who, unimaginative and illiterate themselves, attempt to force others to accept their limited and impoverished vocabulary" (p. 284).

As I discuss in the next section, the hidden curriculum of sexuality education also has a political element. The privatization of sex and the placement of its study within the natural science of sexology through formal organizations such as SSSS, both of which are hidden aspects of sexuality curriculum, serve to depoliticize sexuality by removing it from the contested terrain of public discourse and enveloping it within a veneer of "scientific objectivity."[1]

This use of scientific theories to support a biological determinist approach to sexuality has been examined by scholars, most notably feminists[2] (e.g., Bleier, 1984; Fausto-Sterling, 1985; Irvine, 1990). Mariamne Whatley has clearly and cogently explored the impact that this mode of thinking has upon sexuality education. From her extensive analysis of sexuality education, Whatley (1987) acknowledges that "providing a good, solid, biological and physiological base for understanding many issues associated with sexuality, such as reproduction and disease transmission, is essential in sexuality education" (p. 29). At the same time, she cautions sexuality educators that

> the reliance upon scientific explanations . . . often reduces very complex concepts, which involve social, cultural, and psychological factors, such as gender role behavior and sex drive, to simple biological determination. . . . The scientific approach to sexuality can easily lead to a view in which the "laws of nature" neatly coincide with a political agenda. (p. 29)

REPRODUCING THE BODY POLITIC

Ideology is a constellation of beliefs and values, often held unreflectively by individuals, embedded in a particular social and historical context. Sexual ideology is more than the observance of certain sexual mores or the expression of particular sexual beliefs; sexual ideology reflects the hegemonic power that dominant social groups have to control the body politic, and also reflects the limits of this power.

Institutions such as the church, the family, the media, and the school are important agents for the transmission of sexual beliefs and values. Fundamental curricular questions such as what sexual knowledge is of most worth, how is that knowledge translated into the school curriculum, and who has access to what types of sexual information yield insights about the role of the school in the sexual socialization of youth.

Following a brief discussion of the shared ideology of proponents and opponents of sexuality education, I will illustrate how this sexual ideology manifests itself in the reproduction of social relations through the sexual curriculum in three areas: sexual arrangements predicated on gender, teenage pregnancy, and child sexual abuse.

Shared Ideology Between Competing Groups

Opponents and proponents of sexuality education reflect differences within the ideological mainstream of American politics and culture. Beginning with the origins of the "social hygiene" movement in 1905, the public debate in sexuality education has largely centered on the role played by the public schools in the battle against venereal disease. Like their latter-day disciples, early social hygiene leaders such as Prince Morrow, a New York physician, and Charles Elliott, president of Harvard, believed the twin goals of any sexuality education were the reduction of venereal disease and the promotion of sexual morality. Like their contemporary counterparts, they asserted that sexuality education in the schools was an unfortunate necessity due to the failure of adequate home instruction (Imber, 1984; Strong, 1972).

Though modern-day descendants of the social hygiene movement (e.g., Planned Parenthood, Society for the Scientific Study of Sex) wage an ongoing battle with conservative religious and quasi-political groups (e.g., Eagle Forum, Citizens for Decency), they all have an instrumentalist approach to sexuality education. Their litmus test for an effective sexuality education program is its "effect" on the extent of adolescent heterosexual activity, STDs, and pregnancies. Both sorts of groups agree that sexual abstinence among adolescents is desirable, though they disagree on the effectiveness of sexuality education programs in reducing teenage sexual activity, the relevance of this message to adolescents, and its practicality in the era of AIDS. For *both* sorts of groups, reduction in the degree of adolescent heterosexual coital activity is the benchmark for judging the success of sexuality education.

For example, while serving as secretary of education, William Bennett (1987) delivered an address entitled "Truth in Sex: Why Johnny Can't Abstain." After citing statistically the consequences of youthful sexual intercourse (pregnancy, abortion, unwed teenagers—*all of which focus on the female*), he noted that "these numbers are an irrefutable indictment of sex education's overall effectiveness in *reducing teenage sexual activity* and pregnancies" (p. 143; emphasis added). More recently, the Republican Policy Committee, in its report on the effectiveness of teen pregnancy programs, chastised the "architects of federal family planning policy," who

> have said that if children are taught how to avoid pregnancy and are given the means to do so, then teen pregnancy rates will plummet. . . . Federal family programs have compiled an unenviable record over two decades. It is a record of higher teen pregnancy rates, more abortions and an unprecedented number of nonmarital births. (Armstrong, 1990, p. 18).

In a recent article entitled "Helping Teenagers Postpone Sexual Involvement," which appeared in *Family Life Perspectives*, a journal published by the Planned Parenthood Federation, the authors, acknowledging the overall ineffectiveness of conventional programs in reducing teenage sexual activity, report:

> Nearly three-quarters of the [low-income, minority] students in the program group had not had sexual intercourse before participating in the program. . . . Those who had the program did delay sexual involvement. By the end of eighth grade, students who had not participated in the program were as much as five times more likely to have begun having sex than were those who had had the program. Program students were also more likely to

continue to *postpone sexual involvement.* (Howard & McCabe, 1990, p. 25; emphasis added)

In short, the dispensing of sexual knowledge as a prophylactic for the unwelcomed consequences of freewheeling sexual behavior is the cornerstone of modern sexuality education. While members of the Republican Policy Committee and Citizens for Decency advocate abstinence through the *Sex Respect* curriculum and campaign to "just say no," their counterparts in organizations such as Planned Parenthood promote contraception in an effort to eradicate teenage pregnancy. Both groups view sexuality as historically fixed and focus on teenage sexual behavior and its consequences. An informed understanding of sexuality as socially constructed and historically changing—detailed in this book, particularly in Chapters 2, 7, and 8—is lacking in almost all of contemporary sexual discourse and scholarship and is noticeably absent in the sexuality education curriculum provided to adolescents.

This narrow conceptualization of sexuality and concomitant instrumentalist approach to sexuality education squarely places both sorts of groups described above under the same ideological umbrella. Though they may disagree on the desirability of integrating sexuality into the curriculum, their near exclusive focus on teenage pregnancy and sexually transmitted diseases reflects a common ideology. As Joseph Diorio (1985) argues:

> If heterosexual copulation is not the natural essence of human sexual practice and if the maintenance of the belief that such copulation is essential to sex is part of the political institutions of patriarchy, then sex educators are serving, wittingly or otherwise, as agents of the political, sexual socialization of adolescents. By failing to consider sexual activity as anything but copulation, sex education literature and programs reinforce not only the tendency to think of sex in those limited terms, but the survival of arguably oppressive political practices and structures as well. (p. 253)

This dominant sexual ideology is readily apparent in states' curriculum materials, which not only are woefully out of date, particularly in the area of AIDS, but ignore the historical and cultural aspects of sexuality (de Mauro, 1990). Many convey the conventional view of sexuality as a natural human drive to be held in abeyance through self-control, self-management, and postponement of sexual gratification. In the process, these curricula and those who use them socialize adolescents into a narrow and simplistic understanding of sexuality.

Power and Ideology in Sexuality and the Curriculum

Scholars have cogently demonstrated an integral relationship between control of the body and control of the body politic. Wilhelm Reich

(1971) discussed the connection between conventional sexual morality and relations of domination and subordination; Herbert Marcuse (1966) articulated the relationship between advanced capitalism and sexuality; Michel Foucault (1980) traced the rise of the disciplines of medicine, education, and psychology and the regulation of human activities, particularly sexuality; and Shulamith Firestone (1970) critically explored the primacy of vaginal orgasm and the lack of alternative visions for reproductive and sexual arrangements.

Elaborating upon the ideas of such scholars, Dennis Carlson discusses the ideological bases for contemporary discourse on sexuality education in Chapter 2. Though there have been changes in perspectives on human sexuality and the place of sexuality in the curriculum during the past century, he emphasizes that the two dominant perspectives—traditionalism and progressivism—are ideologies that "share much in common." For example, like the traditionalists, progressives "incorporated many traditional values, although they were less condemning and more therapeutic in their approach to the 'problem' of sexuality."

Sexuality, then, is more a construct of ideology and culture than it is a collection of information about biology and the body; power and control are central to our modern understanding of sexuality and ourselves as sexual beings—a point well articulated in *Science and Gender* (Bleier, 1984):

> Sex (being symbolic and identical with love and intimacy, at least for women in our Western cultures) is by its very physical nature the most seductive, private, intrusive, direct, and possessing way to exert power and control. For this reason and because it lends itself so well to the combination of intimacy, psychological seduction, and physical strength, sex is potentially the most effective and abusive way to control women psychologically, physically, or through degradation and humiliation, and to maintain individual women's subjection to a particular man and collective women's social and political subjection. (p. 181)

How we define and express our sexuality has significant political implications. At the judicial level these political implications are clearly evident in recent Supreme Court rulings in *Bowers v. Hardwick* (1986), reaffirming the illegality of homosexual sodomy, and *Webster v. Reproductive Health Services* (1989), passing control of reproductive rights from the woman to the state. In Chapter 3, James Whitson meticulously documents court decisions as he "analyzes the ideology behind First Amendment interpretations that would permit the censorship of sexuality from the curriculum." Although a review of case law and state statutes suggests that student participation must be voluntary and subject to parental consent (Faye, 1988), Whitson characterizes the desire to restrict sexual knowledge from students or to allow students access to knowledge only with parental consent as a demand for a "prophylactic curriculum." At the micro level this results in "reinforcing the notion popular among so many students that they cannot expect to learn anything real in school, since what they are presented with in the classroom has no relationship to life in the real world"; at the macro level these school-based "desexualized notions of human understanding and existence" contribute to an impotent body politic.

There is, then, an integral relationship between the learning of human reproduction and the reproduction of social relations. Understandings of gendered and sexual arrangements, teenage pregnancy, and child sexual abuse further illustrate this relationship.

Gendered and Sexual Arrangements. Catharine MacKinnon (1982) describes sexuality as "the linchpin of gender inequality" (p. 533), and Ruth Bleier (1984) calls it "the kingpin in the patriarchal formations that serve to oppress women" (p. 164). Until recently, the relationship between gender and sexuality has been largely unexplored by sexuality educators and curriculum scholars. For example, in our contemporary culture, sex (as opposed to age, social status, or religious belief) is the principal delimiter in everyday language. "Where is *he* going?" "What is *Mary* doing today?" are two simple examples of gender-specific language. This gender-based language reflects sexual divisions and our conceptions of male-female relationships. For example, names for males generally use active sexual constructions (e.g., Paul fucked Mary, not Mary fucked Paul); female names fit comfortably in the passive voice (e.g., Mary was fucked by Paul). In everyday discourse "Mary fucked Paul" is used only when describing a nonsexual event that places Paul in a dilemma (e.g., Mary reporting Paul for date rape) (Baker, 1975).

Susan Shurberg Klein is a major spokesperson for linking gender equity with sexuality education. Klein (1987) writes in the *Peabody Journal of Education*:

> There is substantial evidence that sex equity and sex education experts have gone their separate ways and generally either ignored or distanced themselves from each other. Most sex educators in the United States have not explicitly taught sex equitable sexual attitudes, knowledge, and behavior. Thus, they often reinforced the "double standard" or inaccurate stereotypes about females and males. Similarly, advocates of sex equity in education have generally avoided dealing with sexuality. (p.1)

Chapter 4 and other chapters in this collection show how inaccurate stereotypes are taught and reinforced. One example is the double standard that results in your gender determining the type and extent of sexual knowledge taught to you. Herz and Reis's study (1987) shows that black, inner-city male youths are more knowledgeable about their own physical development than are their female peers. There is also a double standard in the differing roles assumed by parents with their sons and daughters when discussing sexuality. The most common pattern is an active mother and an absent father (Fox, Colombo, Clevenger, & Ferguson, 1986). Through interviews with black and white mothers and fathers, one group of researchers conclude:

> As a group the fathers seemed most comfortable with the role of monitor, rule enforcer, or disciplinarian. They saw themselves and their wives saw them as the "fall back position," the back-up person, the "bottom line," the one to whom teens ultimately must answer for their behavior. This role assignment of authority figure to fathers is the counterpart of the assignment of the listener and intermediary roles to mothers. Each role assignment is based upon traditional presumptions about gender-linked capabilities and inabilities. (Fox, Colombo, Clevenger & Ferguson, 1988, p. 364)

Elsewhere, Klein (1988) has suggested specific strategies for enabling students to "cope with sexuality in a non-sexist way" (p. 73), including the use of sexual attention and attraction to reduce barriers to gender equity and facilitate cross-gender friendships. While Klein notes the convergence of these two fields of interest and the scholars and practitioners who work within them, she does *not* suggest that issues of sexuality may be subsumed into those of gender. Sexuality and gender are, as Vance and Snitow (1984) rightly assert, separate but interrelated categories:

> Just as earlier feminist theory separated gender and class, so to separate gender and sex is to reveal clearly the specific features of each system. Despite the many interrelationships of sexuality and gender, sexuality is not a residual category, a subcategory of gender; nor are theories of gender fully adequate to account for sexuality. The task is to describe and analyze how cultural connections are made between female bodies and what comes to be understood as "woman" or "female sexuality." (p. 130)

An example of this interrelationship is the manner in which popular culture depicts the female sexual experience. Meryle Altman (1984), examining popular sexual literature such as *Everything You Always Wanted to Know About Sex* and *The Pleasure Bond*, explores how such literature reflects conventional discourse about sexuality with a cultural ideology that focuses on heterosexual intercourse and biological reproduction. She concludes:

> The way a woman experiences her sexuality, the ways we represent our sexuality to ourselves and enact that representation, are almost impossible

to separate from the representations our culture makes available to us. Our awareness of this has made it possible to talk historically about changes in sexuality, based on changes in what sexual behaviors and forms are in the cultural repertory, which are valued, which are silenced, and what women's power relationship to such representation is. (p. 115)

Sexology, health, and sexuality education textbooks, according to some scholars, also reflect a distorted view of the female sexual experience (Ehrenreich, Hess, & Jacobs, 1986; Goettsch, 1987; Myerson, 1986; 1987; Pollis, 1986; Whatley, 1985). For example,

> History teaches us . . . that female sexuality has been subject to varying degrees of power and social control, from legal and cultural proscriptions to enforced pregnancy to genital mutilation. . . . Although the textbook authors do discuss sexual violence and some provide good analyses of its social antecedents, they generally fail to incorporate these insights throughout the text. So we are left with the impression, in one section, that women are socialized for passivity and men for aggressiveness, but, by the next chapter, they are equally participating sexual partners. This contradiction raises the larger issue: can sexuality in this society be free from power relations? (Goettsch, 1987, p. 327)

In Chapter 5, Eleanor Linn and her coauthors explore the power aspect of sexual harassment and its relationship to gender, and the authors of Chapter 4 illustrate the differing messages about sexuality conveyed to boys and girls through discussion of their sexual scripting during childhood. Mara Sapon-Shevin recalls a childhood in which "girls weren't supposed to get aroused; we were supposed to repress not only our own sexual inclinations, but also those of the boys. And, most difficult of all, we were supposed to accomplish all of this with a minimum of sexual knowledge or explicitness." The type of sexual knowledge conveyed to young women and the divorce between sexual knowledge and sexual feelings is well illustrated by Jackson (1978) in her analysis of the typical imagery of the meeting of the egg and sperm

> This type of imagery hardly relates to the sexual feelings and experiences of adolescents and moreover, presents female sexual and reproductive functioning as an entirely passive experience. The egg can never be heroic—it just waits around for the sperm. . . . As long as sex education is defined as it is, its content is unlikely to change radically. As conventionally taught it has little to do with *sexuality* but is confined purely to *sex*. This distinction is not merely a play on words, for sexuality involves a great deal more than biological sex, it is concerned with feelings, experiences, values and above all, relationships. . . . The tendency to equate sex education with reproductive biology thus leads automatically to a form of sexism whereby information regarding the female sexual response is omitted. Yet this form of sex

education is, ironically, considered more relevant to girls in keeping with the definition of them as future wives and mothers. (pp. 347–348)

The sexism that permeates most sexuality education classes also presents problems for the adolescent male. In Chapter 4, Jesse Goodman examines the male experience in sexuality education. Describing his difficulty in establishing meaningful relationships with females or males during adolescence, he writes, "I spent most of my adolescence in a perpetual state of loneliness when it came to my relationships with girls. Unfortunately, this same scripting made it necessary for me to conceal these feelings of loneliness from my male friends, and as I look back on it, even from myself." As these authors detail, adolescent sexual scripting continues to influence their adult lives.

Teenage Pregnancy. In her classic essay "Sexuality, Schooling, and Adolescent Females: The Missing Discourse of Desire," Michelle Fine (1988) argues that emphasizing the fearful consequences of adolescent pregnancy perpetuates the ideology of the female as a victim of male sexuality. She writes:

> To avoid being victimized, females learn to defend themselves against disease, pregnancy, and "being used." The discourse of victimization supports sex education, including AIDS education, with parental consent. Suggested classroom activities emphasize "saying no," practicing abstinence, enumerating the social and emotional risks of sexual intimacy, and listing the possible diseases associated with sexual intimacy. The language, as well as the questions asked and not asked, represents females as the actual and potential victims of male desire. . . . The naming of desire, pleasure, or sexual entitlement, particularly for females, barely exists in the formal agenda of public schooling on sexuality. When spoken, it its tagged with reminders of "consequences"—emotional, physical, moral, reproductive, and/or financial. (pp. 32–33)

Based upon more than 400 in-depth interviews with female adolescents over a ten-year period, Thompson (1990) advocates an "erotic education" that exemplifies this "naming of desire, pleasure, or sexual entitlement":

> An erotic education would be narrative as well as expository and provide a psychological context for understanding sexual experience. It would include lessons in how to explore the body: how to masturbate; how to come; how to respect another's desire; how to bring another—of either gender—to orgasm. (p. 358)

While the "discourse of desire" has been absent throughout the history of sexuality education, the elevation of teenage pregnancy to the status of a national crisis is a recent phenomenon (Vinovskis, 1981). In exploring the construction of the "problem" of teenage pregnancy and childbirth, Riessman & Nathanson (1986) argue that while there has been an overall *decrease* in the proportion of adolescent births to total births in the 1980s, the emergence of teenage pregnancy as a serious national problem coincided with the greater visibility of white, middle-class pregnant adolescents and the coalition of New Right politicians and preachers. Given the conservative tenor of the 1980s, the problem was defined as individual and moral. This conservative coalition ignored the social context of grinding poverty (in which the medical risks of teenage pregnancy increase), the cultural complexities of adolescence (the certainty of a reduced black male population beyond the teenage years or the need to achieve maturity and acceptance through parenthood), and personal despair (creating life in a world absent of love or as a promise for unfulfilled dreams); adolescents were to "just say no" (David, 1984; Mosher, 1989). The teenage pregnancy burden fell to the individual, principally the female; the social responsibility for eradicating poverty, ignorance, and despair fell to no one, as the men dominating the national agenda squandered national resources on big-boy toys like Star Wars, and junk bonds.

Some leaders of mainstream sexuality education now acknowledge the importance of this social context. Peter Scales (1989), for example, writes:

> The wrong agenda is having just more sexuality education, or earlier, or with better trained teachers. The right agenda . . . places sexuality education into a more realistic perspective. Such an agenda must be based on (a) a broad head start for all children; (b) action to lessen poverty and welfare dependence through policies that empower people; (c) greater attention to the life skills needs of the 70 percent of children who will not get a college degree; and (d) expanded opportunities for young people to become better linked with their communities through service and voluntarism. (p. 175)

The mistake, articulated by Diane Lee and Louise Berman in Chapter 14 of this volume, has been to conceptualize teenage pregnancy as a "well-structured" problem—a problem having only one correct solution.

The dilemma of teen motherhood also reflects a form of social control that challenges the patriarchal order—a grave concern to conservative sexuality researchers: "Some part of public concern over teenage pregnancy undoubtedly centers on illegitimate birth and childrearing . . . which states that no child should be brought into the world without a sociological father to act as guardian, protector, and link with the community" (Shornack, 1986, p. 307). Unwed mothers or nonvirgin single women are not the problem; rather, they are symptomatic of the crumbling of a patriarchal order in which sexuality and gender are the linch-pins of the body politic.[3]

Child Sexual Abuse. The tragedy of child abuse is a phenomenon familiar to too many adults and children. The likelihood of a female being sexually abused before she reaches her 18th birthday is one in four, according to one study (Seattle Institute for Child Advocacy, 1985), while others have reported rates of child abuse ranging from 15% to 38% (Finkelhor, 1986). By some estimates, more than 500,000 boys are sexually abused each year (Hunter, 1989). Most abuse cases will go unreported, though they will remain vivid in the memories of the abused as they grow into adults—sometimes to abuse their own children.

As troubling as the sexual abuse of children is, one must pause to consider the troubling results of a spate of recent child-abuse cases that have resulted in acquittal or mistrial verdicts. Cases such as the Mc-Martin preschool imbroglio demonstrate that despite questionable evidence and evidence-gathering techniques, vocal child advocates—including people in the helping professions, the media, and parents—can create a political environment in which publicly elected officials feel compelled to spend enormous sums of money prosecuting and retrying cases that lack credibility (Best, 1990; Gardner, 1991; Kendrick, 1988).

The impact of these trials extend beyond the courtroom. A *New York Times* article describes one adverse consequence:

> At a time when there is pressure on men to be more caring and demonstrative to children, more and more men and organizations are worrying that casual physical contact with children may create the impression of sexual misconduct. . . . "I call it the presumption of perversion," said Mark Poklner, director of a children's center in Oak Park, Ill. "There's so much emphasis on child abuse that almost any thinking man alone with a child is conscious that someone might think he is doing it for some perverse purpose. (Nordheimer, 1990, p. 1A)

Another consequence of the national spotlight on child sexual abuse is the proliferation of units in the school curriculum designed to teach elementary-age children sexual safety. In order to prevent child sexual abuse, these units often stress avoidance of strangers and the concept of "bad touches" in the "private parts." However, the child's interpretation of these concepts may be something very different, as Whatley and Trudell (1989) point out:

> When child abuse prevention education is taught from a position that views sex as dangerous, children learn fear of sex. . . . The message conveyed is that these parts are in themselves dangerous and dirty, since they cannot even be named. What does this tell a child who has enjoyed touching her

clitoris or his penis? If the text is that touch in these unmentionable areas is "bad touch," the subtext is anti-sexuality and anti-pleasure. (p. 179)

Concerns about child sexual abuse also reflect unwarranted beliefs about childhood, the sexual lives of children, and the role of the state in regulating children's consensual sexual behavior.

The concept of childhood, as noted in Aries's classic work *Centuries of Childhood* (1962) and supported by other scholarship (Beales, 1985; Klein, 1990; Suransky, 1982), is quite contemporary. By 1700, the adult perception of children as miniature adults changed to that of sexually innocent creatures. As the world moved from a preindustrial to an industrial economy in the late eighteenth century, middle-class children and their mothers were placed in "nonproductive" roles in the home and at school. In his historical description of how modern concepts of childhood and adolescence affected medical, religious, and educational beliefs about sexuality, Neuman (1975) relates this extended economic dependency of the child and adolescent to the simultaneous decline in the age of menarche and the onset of puberty. Based upon his review of scholarship in the field, he concludes:

> From the early nineteenth century onwards, then, and perhaps earlier in the aristocracy and upper bourgeoisie, the age of puberty declined, and the gap between biological childhood and social adulthood widened. The concept of adolescence, an unsettled (and for parents, unsettling) period of *Sturm und Drang*, came to characterize this gap. To be sure, adolescence was not unknown before the nineteenth century, but only then, thanks to the declining puberty age and ever-longer periods of education and training, did it become a part of the life cycle of thousands of middle-class youths. The period of adolescence only really ended when a youth completed his schooling, established himself in a job, married, and founded a new household. (p. 7)

The absence of an historical understanding of the changing conception of childhood coupled with an ever-lowering age of puberty and an ever-increasing age before adulthood characterizes much of the work and writing of sexuality educators (as well as policymakers). Their ahistorical view of childhood and adolescence may very well exacerbate the very "problem" of sexual illiteracy that they seek to combat, as policymakers and parents refuse to discuss (or to sanction classroom discussion of) sexuality in an open, honest, and frank manner with "children."

The consequence of sexual illiteracy is sexually mature adolescents with intellectually immature sexual understandings. In their extensive study of the sexual thinking of hundreds of children between the ages of 5 and 15 in three English-speaking societies, Ronald and Juliette Goldman (1982) reported a substantial time lag both in children's level of thinking and problem-solving in general, and in their capacity to think rationally about sexuality in particular. This retardation of children's sexual thinking may account for the childlike understanding of sexuality among sexually active teenagers, which transforms the sexuality education classroom into a remediation program of sexual terminology—providing explanations that children should have learned at a much earlier age.

Further, sexual feelings, thoughts, and behaviors exist before birth and throughout childhood (Jackson, 1982; Kinsey, Pomeroy, & Martin, 1948). Although a child's conception of sexuality differs in several important ways from that of an adult, the child's sexual needs and interests are difficult to deny despite the ideologies of childhood innocence and vulnerability reified by sexual abuse experts and reinforced in the media (Kitzinger, 1988; Plummer, 1990). Nevertheless, the concept of the child as a sexual being and the recognition of childhood sex play as an integral component of growing up is alien to many adults—a point illustrated by Kate Millett (1984):

> Sex itself is presented as a crime to children. It is how adults control children, how they forbid them sexuality. . . . Adults absolutely proscribe and forbid, and police to be sure there is no sexual activity among children. Despite the degree of sexual activity that actually goes on among children, I think adults have been all too effective, not only in poisoning sexuality but also in preventing children from understanding or experiencing it. (pp. 218–219)

One of the most controversial aspects of sexuality is adult/child sexual activity. The issue that has generated the most publicity in recent years has been relations between men and boys (Best, 1990; Brongersma, 1990; Sandfort, 1987; Thorstad, 1990). This issue, perhaps more than any other, unites such disparate groups as feminists, pro-family legislators, gay activists, and a sensationalist media in a chorus of condemnation. However, by focusing on the adult "sex offender," we tend to ignore the role of the state in controlling consensual sexual activity and in denying sexual choice among youth. Not surprisingly, few people comment on how sexual taboos about age (intergenerational sex) and family relations (incest) reproduce existing patriarchal relations.

Feminist Gayle Rubin (1981) has described adult/child sexual relations, transvestism, and sadomasochism as points on the "sexual fringe." She cautions, though,

> We must not reject all sexual contact between adults and young people as inherently oppressive. . . . The sexual fringe is a scary place. Its inhabitants are despised. Its activities are considered criminal. Those who do not live there are advised that it is a dangerous place to visit, a realm of violence and

psychopathy. But the fringe is also a repository for all the varieties of sexual expression which have been rejected by society. While some of that experience should stay in the limbo to which it has been consigned, much of it is worth reclaiming. There is a lot of wisdom, and a lot to learn, out on the fringe. (pp. 114–115)

The failure to acknowledge children as sexual beings and to question the state's right to deny sexual expression on the premise of "protecting children" is bothersome. Kate Millett states in *Sexual Politics:*

A sexual revolution begins with the emancipation of women, who are the chief victims of patriarchy, and also with the ending of homosexual oppression. Part of the patriarchal family structure involves the control of the sexual life of children; indeed, the control of children totally. Children have virtually no rights guaranteed by law in our society. . . . Certainly, one of children's essential rights is to express themselves sexually, probably primarily with each other but with adults as well. (Quoted in Blasius, 1981, pp. 80–81)

CONCLUDING REMARKS

Like our understanding of the school curriculum, we approach sexuality from a technorational worldview. Although viewed as an instrument for sexual control, sexuality education is in fact an instrument for social control. But as many of the authors in this edited volume argue, sexuality education can be as liberating as it is now debilitating.

We can marry critical thinking and heartfelt discussions to the sexuality curriculum by encouraging students to examine the origins of their sexual beliefs, feelings, and values:

What does it mean to be "male" and "female"?
Why are certain sexual practices preferred in our culture?
Why do I feel uncomfortable talking to my parents about sexuality?

In the process, we must not divorce personal insights from social analysis: "I feel more comfortable with my sexual desires" must be accompanied by "I understand how groups manipulate my sexual desires for their own ends." We must engage our students and teachers in critical conversations that illuminate the personal and social contradictions of living in a libidinally repressive society that has for too long silenced the discourse of desire (Fine, 1988; McDade, 1987; Sears, in press). In advocating the "critical teaching of sex and pregnancy," Laurie McDade (1987) asserts that teachers and students must embark on an immediate engagement in the act of knowing and interrogating reality as it occurs in the daily life of people and communities. Questions regarding teacher and student understandings of their world must be voiced, and both need to engage in creating a discourse of examination before explanation may be approached. (p. 77)

But sexual silence dominates schools of education and "Since teachers and administrators typically have little or no formal training in this hidden curriculum, they are often baffled about what to do when they confront sex and sexism in their classroom and schools" (Sadker, Sadker, & Shakeshaft, 1989, p. 214).

Sexuality education in schools of education should be not only a terrain for personal and social enquiry but also a place to raise fundamental questions among competing sexual ideologies. As Earls and her co-authors document in Chapter 15, such dialogue is lacking in contemporary discourse on sexuality and the curriculum because of consensus held by sexuality education forces. These forces contemplate instrumentalist questions alone—How effective? How often? Conspicuously absent is critical conversation revolving around how we conceptualize sexual knowledge, what kind of sexual knowledge is of most worth, and who should have access to what types of sexual knowledge. The contributors to *Sexuality and the Curriculum* engage in this fundamental discussion.

NOTES

1. For a recent essay asserting the necessity of "rigorous sexual science" evidenced in organizations such as SSSS, see Abramson, 1990. Pollis (1988) assesses the lack of impact of feminism on sexual science and documents the neo-positivist epistemology evidenced in the *Journal of Sex Research*, the journal of SSSS, whose membership is dominated by scholars from psychology, psychiatry, and medicine.

2. For a provocative and recent analysis of the debates within the feminist community of scholars on the relationship between gender and sexuality, see Valverde, 1989.

3. The "connection between a neo-conservative ideology of sexual repression and a coercive economy directed at the 'epidemic of teenage pregnancy' " (McDade, 1987, p. 64) has been amply documented elsewhere (David, 1984; Riessman & Nathanson, 1986).

REFERENCES

Abramson, P. (1990). Sexual science: Emerging discipline or oxymoron? *Journal of Sex Research, 27*(2), 147–165.

Alexander, C., Ensminger, M., Kim, Y., Smith, J., Johnson, K., & Dolan, L. (1989). Early sexual activity among adolescents in small towns and rural areas: Race and gender patterns. *Family Planning Perspectives, 21*(6), 261–266.

Altman, M. (1984). Everything they always wanted you to know: The ideology of popular sex literature. In C. Vance (Ed.), *Pleasure and danger: Exploring female sexuality* (pp. 115–130). Boston: Routledge & Kegan Paul.

Aries, P. (1962). *Centuries of childhood.* New York: Random House.

Armstrong, W. (1990, January 22). *Teen pregnancy: Have federal programs worked?* Washington, DC: U.S. Republican Policy Committee.

Baker, R. (1975). "Pricks" and "chicks": A plea for "persons." In R. Baker & F. Elliston (Eds.), *Philosophy and sex* (pp. 45–64). Buffalo, NY: Prometheus.

Beales, R. (1985). The child in seventeenth-century America. In J. Hawes & N. Hiner (Eds.), *American childhood: A research guide and historical handbook* (pp. 15–56). Westport, CT: Greenwood.

Bennett, W. (1987). Truth in sex: Why Johnny can't abstain. *Education, 108*(2), 142–147.

Best, J. (1990). *Threatened children: Rhetoric and concern about child victims.* Chicago: University of Chicago Press.

Blasius, M. (1981). Sexual revolution and the liberation of children. In D. Tsang (Ed.), *The age taboo: Gay male sexuality, power and consent* (pp. 80–83). Boston: Alyson.

Bleier, R. (1984). *Science and gender: A critique of biology and its theories on women.* New York: Pergamon.

Bowers v. Hardwick, 478 U.S. 186, 106 S.Ct. 2841, 921 L.Ed.2d 140 (1986).

Brongersma, E. (1990). *Loving boys: Vol. 2.* Elmhurst, New York: Academic.

Campbell, T., & Campbell, D. (1986). Adolescent interest in human sexuality: The questions kids ask. *Journal of Sex Education and Therapy, 12*(2), 47–50.

Children's Defense Fund (1987). *Adolescent pregnancy: An anatomy of a social problem in search of comprehensive solutions.* Washington: Author.

Cuban, L. (1986). Sex and school reform. *Phi Delta Kappan, 68,* 319–321.

Cvetkovich, G., Lieberman, K., & Miller, W. (1978). Sex role development and teenage contraceptive use. *Adolescence, 13,* 231–236.

David, M. (1984). Teaching and preaching sexual morality: The New Right's anti-feminism in Britain and the U.S.A. *Journal of Education, 166*(1), 63–76.

Davis, S. M., & Harris, M. B. (1982). Sexual knowledge, sexual interest, and sources of sexual information of rural and urban adolescents from three cultures. *Adolescence, 17*(66), 471–492.

Dawson, D. (1986). The effects of sexual education on adolescent behavior. *Family Planning Perspective, 18*(4), 162–170.

de Anda, R., Becerra, R., & Fielder, E. (1988). Sexuality, pregnancy, and motherhood among Mexican-American adolescents. *Journal of Adolescent Research, 3*(3–4), 403–411.

de Mauro, D. (1990). Sexuality education in 1990: A review of state sexuality and AIDS education curricula. *SIECUS Report, 18*(2), 1–9.

Diorio, J. (1985). Contraception, copulation domination, and the theoretical barrenness of sex education literature. *Educational Theory, 35*(3), 239–254.

Ehrenreich, B., Hess, E., & Jacobs, G. (1986, July/August). Unbuckling the Bible belt: The Christian Right discovers sex. *Mother Jones*, pp. 46–51, 78, 80, 82, 85.

Fausto-Sterling, A. (1985). *Myths of gender: Biological theories about women and men.* New York: Basic Books.

Faye, C. (1988). Implications of the First Amendment on sex education in the public school system in the United States (Doctoral dissertation, Pepperdine University). *Dissertation Abstracts International, 49,* 2467A.

Fine, M. (1988). Sexuality, schooling and adolescent females: The missing discourse of desire. *Harvard Educational Review, 58*(1), 29–53.

Finkelhor, D. (1986). *A sourcebook on childhood sexual abuse.* Beverly Hills: Sage.

Firestone, S. (1970). *Dialectics of sex.* New York: Morrow.

Forrest, J., & Silverman, J. (1989). What public school teachers teach about preventing pregnancy, AIDS and sexually transmitted diseases. *Family Planning Perspectives, 21*(2), 65–72.

Foucault, M. (1980). *The history of sexuality: Vol. 1. An introduction* (R. Hurley, Trans.). New York: Random House.

Fox, G., Colombo, M., Clevenger, W., & Ferguson, C. (1986). The family context of adolescent sexuality and sex roles. In G. Leight & G. Peterson (Eds.), *Adolescents in families.* (pp. 179–204). Cincinnati: South Western.

Fox, G., Colombo, M., Clevenger, W., & Ferguson, C. (1988). Parental division of labor in adolescent sexual socialization. *Journal of Contemporary Ethnography, 17*(3), 349–371.

Furstenberg, F. (1987). Race differences in the timing of adolescent intercourse. *American Sociological Review, 52*(4), 511–518.

Gardner, R. (1991). *Sex abuse hysteria.* Cresskill, NJ: Creative Therapeutics.

Gingiss, P., & Hamilton, R. (1989). Teacher perspectives after implementing a human sexuality education program. *Journal of School Health, 59*(10), 427–431.

Goettsch, S. (1987). Textbook sexual inadequacy: A review of sexuality texts. *Teaching Sociology, 15*(3), 324–338.

Goldman, R., & Goldman, J. (1982). *Children's sexual thinking.* London: Routledge & Kegan Paul.

Haffner, D. (1990). *Sex education 2000: A call to action.* New York: Sex Information and Education Council of the U.S.

Herz, E., & Reis, J. (1987). Family life education for younger inner-city teens: Identifying needs. *Journal of Youth and Adolescence, 16*(4), 361–377.

Howard, M., & McCabe, J. (1990). Helping teenagers postpone sexual involvement. *Family Planning Perspectives, 22*(1), 21–26.

Imber, M. (1984). First World War, sex education and the American Social Hygiene Association's campaign against venereal disease. *Journal of Educational Administration and History, 16*(1), 47–56.

Irvine, J. (1990). *Disorders of desire: Sex and gender in modern American sexology.* Philadelphia: Temple University Press.

Jackson, S. (1978). How to make babies: Sexism in sex education. *Women's Studies International Quarterly, 1*(4), 341–352.

Jackson, S. (1982). *Childhood and sexuality.* Oxford: Blackwell.

Juhasz, A. M., Kaufman, B., & Meyer, H. (1986). Adolescent attitudes and beliefs about sexual behavior. *Child and Adolescent Social Work Journal, 3*(3), 177–193.

Kahn, J. (1990, September 7). Sex education: US gets an F. *Boston Globe*, p. 37.

Kendrick, M. (1988). *Anatomy of a nightmare: The failure of society in dealing with child sexual abuse.* Toronto: Macmillan.

Kenney, A., Guardado, S., & Brown, L. (1989). Sex education and AIDS education in the schools: What states and large school districts are doing. *Family Planning Perspectives, 21*(2), 56–64.

Kinsey, A., Pomeroy, W., & Martin, C. (1948). *Sexual behavior in the human male.* Philadelphia: W. B. Saunders.

Kirby, D. (1989). Research of effectiveness of sex education programs. *Theory Into Practice, 28*(3), 165–171.

Kitzinger, J. (1988). Defending innocence: Ideologies of childhood. *Feminist Review, 28,* 77–87.

Klein, H. (1990). Adolescence, youth and young adulthood: Rethinking current conceptualizations of life stage. *Youth and Society, 21*(4), 446–471.

Klein, S. S. (1987). The issue: Sex equity and sexuality in education. *Peabody Journal of Education, 64*(4), 1–13.

Klein, S. S. (1988). Sex education and gender equity. *Educational Leadership, 45*(6), 69–75.

Leo, J. (1987). Should schools offer sex education? *Reader's Digest, 130,* 138–142.

MacKinnon, C. (1982). Feminism, Marxism, method, and the state: An agenda for theory. *Signs, 7*(3), 515–544.

Marcuse, H. (1966). *Eros and civilization: A philosophical inquiry into Freud.* Boston: Beacon.

Marsiglio, W., & Mott, F. (1986). The impact of sex education on sexual activity, contraceptive use and premarital pregnancy among American teenagers. *Family Planning Perspectives, 18*(4), 151.

McDade, L. (1987). Sex, pregnancy, and schooling: Obstacles to a critical teaching of the body. *Journal of Education, 169*(3), 58–79.

Millett, K. (1984). Beyond politics? Children and sexuality. In C. Vance (Ed.), *Pleasure and danger: Exploring female sexuality* (pp. 217–224). Boston: Routledge & Kegan Paul.

Mosher, D. (1989). Threat to sexual freedom: Moralistic intolerance instills a spiral of silence. *Journal of Sex Research, 26*(4), 492–509.

Myerson, M. (1986). The politics of sexual knowledge: Feminism and sexology textbooks. *Frontiers, 9*(1), 66–71.

Myerson, M. (1987). Sex equity and sexuality in college level sex education courses. *Peabody Journal of Education, 64*(4), 71–87.

Neuman, R. P. (1975). Masturbation, madness, and the modern concepts of childhood and adolescence. *Journal of Social History, 8*(3), 1–27.

Nordheimer, J. (1990, August 5). Caring for children, men find new assumptions and rules. *New York Times*, p. 1A.

Orr, M. (1982). Sex education and contraceptive education in U.S. public high schools. *Family Planning Perspectives, 14*(6), 304–313.

Pinar, W. (1988). *Contemporary curriculum discourses.* Scottsdale, AZ: Gorsuch Scarisbrick.

Plummer, K. (1990). Understanding childhood sexualities. *Journal of Homosexuality, 20* (1/2), 231–249.

Pollis, C. (1986). Sensitive drawings of sexual activity in human sexuality textbooks: An analysis on communication and bias. *Journal of Homosexuality, 13*(1), 59–73.

Pollis, C. (1988). An assessment of the impact of feminism on sexual science. *Journal of Sex Research, 25*(1), 85–105.

Reich, W. (1971). *The inversion of compulsory sexual morality.* New York: Farrar, Straus, & Giroux. (Original work published 1931)

Riessman, C. K., & Nathanson, C. (1986). The management of reproduction: Social construction of risk and responsibility. In L. Aiken, & D. Mechanic (Eds.). *Applications of social science to clinical medicine and health policy* (pp. 251–281). New Brunswick, NJ: Rutgers University Press.

Rubin, G. (1981). Sexual politics, the new right and the sexual fringe. In D. Tsang (Ed.), *The age taboo: Gay male sexuality, power, and consent* (pp. 108–115). Boston: Alyson.

Sadker, M., Sadker, D., & Shakeshaft, C. (1989). Sex, sexism, and the preparation of educators. *Peabody Journal of Education, 64*(4), 213–224.

Sandfort, T. (1987). *Boys on their sexual contacts with men.* Elmhurst, NY: Academic.

Scales, P. (1989). Overcoming future barriers to sexuality education. *Theory Into Practice, 28*(3), 172–176.

Scott-Jones, D., & Turney, S. (1988). Sex education, contraceptive and reproductive knowledge, and contraceptive use among black adolescent females. *Journal of Adolescent Research, 3*(2), 171–187.

Sears, J. (in press). Responding to the sexual diversity of faculty and students: Sexual praxis and the critically reflective administrator. In C. Capper (Ed.), *Social context of education.* New York: SUNY Press.

Seattle Institute for Child Advocacy. (1985). *Talking about touching: A personal safety curriculum.* Seattle, WA: Author.

Shornack, L. (1986). Teenage pregnancy: A problem of sexual decision-making or of social organization? *International Journal of Sociology of the Family, 16*(2), 307–326.

Solomon, R. (1975). Sex and perversion. In R. Baker & F. Elliston (Eds.), *Philosophy and sex* (pp. 268–302). Buffalo, NY: Prometheus.

Sonenstein, F., & Pittman, K. (1984). The availability of sex education in large city school districts. *Family Planning Perspectives, 16*(1), 19–25.

Strong, B. (1972). The ideas of the early sex education movement in America, 1890–1920. *History of Education Quarterly, 12*(2), 129–161.

Suransky, V. (1982). *The erosion of childhood.* Chicago: University of Chicago Press.

Thompson, S. (1990). Putting a big thing into a little hole: Teenage girls' accounts of sexual initiation. *Journal of Sex Research, 27*(3), 341–361.

Thorstad, D. (1990). Man/boy love and the American gay movement. *Journal of Homosexuality, 20* (1/2), 251–274.

Valverde, M. (1989). Beyond gender dangers and private pleasures: Theory and ethics in the sex debates. *Feminist Studies, 15*(2), 237–254.

Vance, C., & Snitow, A. (1984). Thinking sex: Notes for a radical theory of sexuality. In C. Vance (Ed.), *Pleasure and danger: Exploring female sexuality* (pp. 121–142). Boston: Routledge & Kegan Paul.

Vinovskis, M. (1981). An "epidemic" of adolescent pregnancy? Some historical considerations. *Journal of Family History, 6,* 205–230.

Webster v. Reproductive Health Services, 109 S.Ct. 3040 (1989).

Whatley, M. (1985). Male and female hormones: Misinterpretations of biology in school health and sex education. In V. Sapiro (Ed.), *Women, biology, and public policy.* (pp. 67–89). Beverly Hills, CA: Sage.

Whatley, M. H. (1987). Biological determinism and gender issues in sexuality education. *Journal of Sex Education and Therapy, 13*(2), 26–29.

Whatley, M. H. (1988). Photographic images of blacks in sexuality texts. *Curriculum Inquiry, 18*(2), 137–155.

Whatley, M. H., & Trudell B. (1989). Sexual abuse prevention and sexuality education: Interconnecting issues. *Theory Into Practice, 28*(3), 177–182.

Zabin, L., Hirsch, M., Smith, E., & Hardy, J. (1984). Adolescent sexual attitudes and behavior: Are they consistent? *Family Planning Perspectives, 16*(4), 181–185.

Zabin, L., Hirsch, M., Smith, E., Street, R., & Hardy, J. (1986b). Evaluation of a pregnancy prevention program for urban teenagers. *Family Planning Perspectives, 18*(3), 119–126.

CHAPTER 2

Ideological Conflict and Change in the Sexuality Curriculum

DENNIS L. CARLSON

In this essay I describe and critique four ideologies that have influenced, in varying degrees, the way we think about human sexuality within a social context, and by extension what we teach about sexuality in public schools. These include:

1. A *traditionalist* ideology of sexual sin and sickness that was dominant in the first several decades of the 20th century
2. A *progressive* ideology of sexual "adjustment" and secular state management of sexual "problems"
3. A *radical Freudian* ideology of nonrepressive sexuality and post-capitalist society
4. A *libertarian* ideology of sexual diversity and individual sexual rights

I mean these ideologies to be viewed as representative of the taken-for-granted perspectives or belief systems that characterize various identifiable and relatively coherent positions in the cultural discourse on sexuality. I explore what these ideologies have in common as much as I examine their differences. While each of these ideologies emerged within a particular historical period, each has continued to influence the discourse in sexuality education to a greater or lesser degree. Although the traditional and progressive ideologies in particular share much in common, the history of sexuality education in this century is the story of an ongoing struggle between these two dominant or "mainstream" ideologies.

What follows is both an ideological and a discursive analysis of human sexuality. By *discourse* I mean what gets "talked about" within a culture and the talking itself. All beliefs and values find expression in concrete acts of discourse between individuals and groups, and we may even go so far as to say that beliefs and values do not exist prior to their discursive constitution. In this regard the work of Michel Foucault (1980) is particularly important since he explicitly places the study of sexuality within the context of a history of cultural discourse in his long, unfinished work *The History of Sexuality*. More specifically, he provides us with an analytic framework for deconstructing various discourses on sexuality in terms of the power relations they constitute: an "analytics" of the "specific domains formed by relations of power" (p. 82). Of course, while discourse enters into the constitution of social reality, it also takes for granted much of the existing, prestructured social world and represents certain social interests over others. This is where the notion of *ideology* can contribute to our understanding of cultural discourse on human sexuality. Ideology is a relatively coherent set of taken-for-granted values and beliefs that presents the interests of one class or group as those of the society as a whole. The concept of ideology, as it has been developed primarily in the neo-Marxist tradition, implies an "interested" analysis of discourse. Dominant groups are understood as maintaining their dominance at least partially because they are successful in disseminating ideas that legitimate their positions of domination (Apple, 1979). I do not wish, however, to present an analysis of sexuality purely in terms of class relations and dynamics (something that is typically implied in ideological analysis in the neo-Marxist tradition). Instead, my intent is to develop an interested analysis of cultural discourse in terms of *class, gender,* and *sexual preference.* These various axes of power are related, although not in a deterministic or unidirectional manner, and each has a somewhat unique history of autonomous development.

There is a vast literature on human sexuality and sexuality education. Rather than attempt an overview of this literature, I have chosen to limit my comments to an analysis of a relatively few books and authors who represent well particular ideological perspectives or who have been particularly influential in defining the issues. No doubt the most influential figure in the 20th-century Western discourse on sexuality was Sigmund Freud. Each of the four ideological positions has sponsored its own commentary on, revision, and rereading of Freud, and each has found in him justification for a particular approach to sexuality education. In the discussion of radical Freudianism, I focus upon the works of Wilhelm Reich (1945, 1971) and Herbert Marcuse (1966); in characterizing the libertarian ideology I focus on the works of Alfred Kinsey (Kinsey, Pomeroy, & Martin, 1948; Kinsey, Pomeroy, Martin, & Gebhard, 1953) and William Masters and Virginia Johnson (1966, 1970). I conclude with comments on how the study of human sexuality may be reconstituted as a subfield of cultural studies or liberal arts, thereby integrating it within the broad study of historically-developing cultural discourses.

THE TRADITIONAL IDEOLOGY

In the late 19th and early 20th centuries the perspective on sexuality that civic, religious, and educational leaders most uniformly endorsed was what Foucault (1980) has called "Victorian puritanism" (p. 22) and which I will refer to as the traditional ideology. The core values and precepts of this ideology were traditional in the sense that they upheld a moralistic conception of sexuality and sin that has deep roots in Judeo-Christian culture, although it was also a modern ideology to the extent that it incorporated scientific and economic perspectives in support of sexual puritanism.

The traditional ideology was consistent with traditional Judeo-Christian doctrine in several ways. First, it endorsed asceticism, the self-disciplined renunciation of bodily pleasures, which in turn is based on the dichotomization of body and mind, spirit and flesh. While the mind is viewed as important in maintaining the spiritual side of the individual for eternal life, the body is believed to corrupt and tempt the spirit away from its true path (Petras, 1978). Second, traditional Judeo-Christian religious doctrine affirms sexual activity only within the confines of marriage for the purpose of bearing children; and from the restriction against nonprocreative sexuality is derived a long list of prohibitions against "adultery," "sodomy," and homosexuality (Delamater, 1989). Finally, religious traditionalism is associated with support for an interrelated network of patriarchal authority structures in various institutions, including the family, the church, and the state. Religious and civic leaders in the Victorian era argued, much as religious traditionalists do today, that the family was being torn apart by "modern" influences that threatened the very foundations of civilization and authority. The situation could be reversed by returning to an idealized patriarchal family grounded on authority and clearly defined roles in which women were to be good mothers, homemakers, and wives, and in all of these roles thoroughly subordinated.

However, by the early 20th century, these traditional values were also incorporated, at least partially, into the new sciences of Darwinism and human psychology; so that early sexuality educators often legitimated moralistic statements with "scientific" theory or data. Freud's theory of society was particularly important in this regard, since it encapsulated so many traditionalist themes. It was traditionalist, first of all, in that it was primarily an *essentialist* theory, that is, one that views the repression and sublimation of sexuality as necessary to "civilization" itself. To Freud, modern industrial civilization was the crowning achievement of human development, made possible because humankind had pulled itself up by its own bootstraps (to borrow the popular metaphor of the age) from the barbarism, chaos, and savagery of the

natural or "primitive" world and accepted the "duty" of responsible labor and the need for legitimate authority. Furthermore, the development of each individual, even in modern civilization, *recapitulated* or re-
traced the development of the species from savagery to civilization—a
belief Freud shared with other important theorists of his day, including
(in education) Granville Stanley Hall and John Dewey (Cremin, 1961).
Education, then, was presented as a process of "civilizing little savages,"
much as European colonialism was understood as part of a benign process of "civilizing" the "primate" peoples of Africa, Asia, and America.

Freud's recapitulation theory was grounded upon the division of
the life force into two major principles: the *pleasure principle* and the *reality principle*. Of the former, which is the organizing principle of the
young child and "primitive" humankind, Freud (1930/1961b) noted: "It
aims, on the one hand, at an absence of pain and unpleasure, and, on
the other, at the experiencing of strong feelings of pleasure" (p. 124). All
animalistic behavior in the "natural" world was thus explainable as an
effort to attain immediate gratification of instinctual desires and/or to
avoid unpleasure. In more specifically sexual terms, the pleasure principle was uninhibited by social constraints, which resulted in "polymorphous perversity," an amorphous form of "immature" sexuality in which
the individual finds sexual interest in a number of forms and with partners of either or both genders. According to Freud (1920/1961a), the
pleasure principle can never fully achieve its desire, and long-term happiness necessitates a good deal of hard work, responsibility, and self-
discipline. Thus, he believed that the pleasure principle was gradually
replaced in the developing individual, through the processes of informal
socialization and formal education, by the reality principle. The reality
principle "does not abandon the intention of ultimately obtaining pleasure, but it nevertheless demands and carries into effect the postponement of satisfaction, the abandonment of a number of possibilities of
gaining satisfaction and the temporary toleration of unpleasure as a step
on the long indirect road to pleasure" (p. 4). In utilitarian terms, the
reality principle represents enlightened and long-term self-interest. The
"well-adjusted" adult learns how to channel sexuality into socially acceptable outlets (sublimation) and to limit sexual expression to procreation. "Just as a cautious business-man avoids tying up all his capital in
one concern," Freud (1930/1961b) argued, so the well-adjusted individual learns to avoid investing too heavily in the pleasure principle (p. 33).
Freud thus legitimated a world of instinctual renunciation and compulsory labor as not only an unavoidable necessity but also as a wise personal investment of psychic capital (Cohen, 1982).

In this regard, Freud took for granted the influential "semen theory
of power" that so captivated Victorians. According to this theory, semen
was a major source of nourishment for the mind and body if it were

allowed to be reabsorbed by the blood rather than expended or "wasted" in sexual indulgence. Friedrich Nietzsche (1954), in seeking to formulate a philosophy of power, had observed that "the reabsorption of semen by the blood is the strongest nourishment and, perhaps more than any other factor, it prompts the stimulus of power, the unrest of all forces toward the overcoming of resistance" (p. 75). The influential sexuality educator John Cowan (1874) contended that reabsorbed semen was transformed in the brain into "grand conceptions of the true, the beautiful, the useful, or into fresh emotions of joy and impulses of kindness" (p. 92). Since only men produced semen, this theory legitimized patriarchal power relations at the same time that it legitimized the repression of overt sexuality. And since semen was treated as a commodity of value that needed to be saved and invested wisely rather than squandered or wasted, the semen theory of power took for granted and reinforced the economic rationality of the capitalist worldview. As a strong will enabled an individual to ward off the temptations of the flesh, it also enabled the individual to succeed in business (Strong, 1972).

In support of the semen theory of power, early sexuality educators sought to refute the commonsense belief in "sexual necessity" for adolescent males. Adolescent girls were viewed as less of a "problem" since they presumably had few sexual feelings (Imber, 1982). They were to learn the importance of "duty" as opposed to personal happiness. Of the need to accept one's "lot in life" and "suffer in silence," Freud (1930/ 1961b) wrote: "When we justly find fault with the present state of our civilization for so inadequately fulfilling our demands for a plan of life that shall make us happy, and for allowing the existence of so much suffering which could probably be avoided . . . we may also familiarize ourselves with the idea that there are difficulties attaching to the nature of civilization which will not yield to any attempt at reform" (p. 70). For women this proved to be a notion that legitimated continued oppression.

Aside from Freudian theory, early sexuality educators drew upon a scientific-medical theory that linked sin with sickness. Because Victorians associated bodily cleanliness with virtue and moral purity it was presumed that one could "inoculate" oneself against various diseases and nervous conditions through a strict regimen of bodily hygiene. More specifically, sexual hygiene involved avoiding intimate (or even casual) contact with those who were sexually "unclean" and "diseased." This was to be the best prophylactic or preventative measure against contracting sexually transmitted and other degenerative diseases—a message clearly communicated in the title of the nation's first society, organized in 1905, to promote sexuality education in the schools, The American Society of Sanitary and Moral Prophylaxis. The emphasis upon sexual hygiene is also revealed in a report from the U.S. Surgeon General and the U.S. Bureau of Education (1922) that suggested that high school sexuality education for girls should have as its objectives to make girls more careful about "marrying a man who is free from . . . diseases, to make them more careful as to their choice of friends, and to take precautions in public toilets" (p. 62). A lack of sexual hygiene (including having sex with prostitutes or military men who might be infected with venereal diseases, having sexual relations with "feeble-minded" persons, or even having sex to "excess") was associated with physical and mental degeneracy. Disease, consequently, was depicted as the "wages of sin," much as AIDS has been depicted by traditionalists in contemporary American society. As Cowan (1874) observed, "the heaven-ordained law to increase and multiply and replenish the earth is being . . . greatly perverted, avoided, broken, and by ways and means that not only prevent the carrying out of the spirit of the command, but, *with a just judgement, bring the perpetrators thereof to a life of bodily sickness [and] mental suffering*" (p. 21; emphasis added). Early sexuality educators argued that most bodily ailments, including "nearly all the inflammatory and chronic diseases that afflict mankind, and especially womankind" were the result of sexual sin and poor sexual hygiene. Among women, "female hysteria," moodiness, and "nervousness" were said to result from a failure in sexual role adjustment. Young people, it was argued, needed education on sexual hygiene because the least educated, rather than being protected and innocent, "are the ones who, through wrong and perverted natures, have committed sexual sins" (p. 22).

The traditionalist ideology is, of course, still with us and its influence is considerable among certain segments of the population. It no longer represents the official or approved ideology of professional educators, but its influence is strong among a relatively poor, uneducated, rural population. In the current AIDS crisis, as I noted earlier, traditionalists have reasserted the association between sin and sickness. Elements of the state, under the Reagan administration, also pursued a traditionalist ideology. For example, a U.S. Department of Health and Human Services–funded program to promote sexual abstinence among teenagers, called "Sex Respect," emphasized a "just say no" approach to sexuality education with slogans such as, "Pet your dog, not your date" and "Control your urgin', be a virgin (Flax, 1990). In 1988 a bill was introduced in the New Jersey legislature, and nearly passed, that would have required that all "family life" courses in the state's public schools teach "the scientific evidence that abstinence from sexual activity is the only completely reliable means of preventing the sexual transmission of acquired immune deficiency syndrome and other sexually transmitted diseases and of avoiding pregnancy until the individual is ready as an adult to establish a mutually faithful relationship in the context of marriage" (Sullivan, 1988, p. 4). Of course, there is no evidence to suggest that abstinence is (or for that matter ever was) a realistic option for adolescents, or that sexually transmitted diseases can only be controlled through complete abstinence. In the age of AIDS, adolescents are far more likely to be receptive to information on "safe sex," than no sex; and by continuing to urge them to "just say no" to sex rather than informing them of safe-sex practices, traditionalists may actually contribute to the spread of sexually transmitted diseases. Traditionalists also continue to promote a *sexuality as victimization* curriculum for adolescent girls through portrayal of male sexuality as violent and coercive. Suggested classroom activities emphasize "practicing abstinence, enumerating the social and emotional risks of sexual intimacy, and listing the possible diseases associated with sexual intimacy" (Fine, 1988, p. 32). While adolescent girls obviously need to learn how to avoid becoming victims within a patriarchal culture, a strict emphasis upon sexuality as victimization fails to lay the groundwork for any positive or affirming conception of female sexuality. It also fails to uncover the range of victimization of women at work and home and diverts attention away from the structures that oppress women more generally (Fine, 1988). Finally, contemporary traditionalists have supported the censorship of sexuality and sexual desire from the curriculum. This means, most significantly, that they have sought (with some limited success) to ban books from school libraries and the school curriculum that include sexually explicit passages or challenge conventional sexual roles, as James Anthony Whitson documents in Chapter 3 of this book. This effort of censoring sexuality must be understood as part of a broader concern by traditionalists with the repression of sexuality and a return to traditional sexual role and power relations. Censorship and sexual repression are thus aspects of a common ideological project.

PROGRESSIVE IDEOLOGY

In the 1920s, a new progressive ideology began to gain wide influence among educators, becoming the new orthodoxy within the profession by the 1930s. Progressives were proudly secular rather than religious in orientation, claiming to represent "modern," rational, scientific approaches to understanding and dealing with social problems. In fact, progressives incorporated many traditional values, although they were less condemning and more therapeutic in their approach to the "problem" of sexuality. Progressives also adopted a social utilitarianism that was more pragmatic than that of the traditionalists, especially in their treatment of premarital sex, contraceptives, and abortion. That is, questions of whether to use contraceptives or have an abortion were phrased in terms of "what works," given a realistic assessment of the situation, in the fight against teenage pregnancies and sexually transmitted diseases. Finally, and related to the emphasis upon social utilitarianism, progressives were enamored of the idea that the modern state could help solve social problems through rational planning and policy making, an idea they applied to the problems of sexually transmitted diseases, unwanted pregnancies, population control, and the improvement of the genetic stock of the population (racial hygiene or eugenics). One can understand, then, why American sexuality educators generally looked with great interest to the "social experiments" being conducted by the state in Soviet Russia and Nazi Germany in the 1930s, while tending not to see the potential problems inherent in such totalitarian or statist approaches to defining and "solving" social problems. These antiindividualistic and antidemocratic tendencies in progressivism, more than anything else, probably contributed to its decline in American education after World War II (Cremin, 1961).

Traditionalists had invoked Freud's theory of sublimation in support of their views, but Freudian theory and the psychoanalytic movement that developed out of it were ultimately more compatible with progressivism than traditionalism. This is understandable if we view progressivism and Freudian psychology as emanating from a common cultural source and as elements of a common discourse. In general terms, progressive educators emphasized a child-centered, developmental approach to learning, consistent with the Freudian theory of child development. Furthermore, both progressivism and Freudian psychology emphasized a holistic conception of individual growth and development: Social, emotional, psychological, and physical growth were viewed as inseparably linked, so that one had to educate the "whole child." This provided a powerful rationale for mandating sexuality education and "family life" courses in the nation's public schools. Freud also viewed the development of the child as "open" rather than biologically or genetically determined (for the most part), and thus prone to maladjustment if not carefully guided by knowledgeable parents and professional educators. Finally, Freudian psychology provided progressives with a "modern" sexual ethic: one grounded not on repression (at least exclusively) but rather upon sublimation and limited expression, and one more consistent with secular than sacred values. In other words, while the traditionalists read Freud in a way that emphasized the importance of a good deal of repression and sublimation of sexuality, progressives emphasized Freud's commitment to sexual moderation rather than abstinence. In fact, Freud (1930/1961b) had maintained that among the upper-middle-class patients he treated, overrepression and a highly developed superego or sense of guilt were more often the source of various traumas, anxieties, and psychic blockages than underrepression. In some individuals, this repression was so complete that a productive engagement with life was replaced by "permanent internal unhappiness" (p. 83). Freud was thus led to conclude that "temptations to instinctual satisfaction . . . are merely increased by constant frustration, whereas an occasional satisfaction of them causes them to diminish, at least for the time being" (p. 81).

In these ways, Freud gave some legitimacy to a theory of "sexual necessity" even though the emphasis was clearly on sexual sublimation. Similarly, progressive sexuality educators generally advocated an almost complete sublimation of sexuality as the ideal, but recognized some variability in "normal" sexual adjustment. Lester Kirkendall (1940) advocated "partial sublimation" for the average adolescent boy, a form of adjustment in which "the physical manifestations of sex are usually confined to occasional erections and involuntary seminal emissions" (p. 30). However, Kirkendall reported that one seemingly "well-adjusted" young man had "never stopped masturbation but now believes it does him no harm as a form of adjustment. . . . His social relationships with both sexes are . . . quite satisfactory" (p. 30). Masturbation, then, while never encouraged by progressive educators, was never actively discouraged either so long as it was practiced in moderation. On the other hand "petting" was discouraged, since it could lead, against initial intentions, to intercourse and a possible unwanted pregnancy. According to Kirkendall, "The experience of others shows that if you don't want to go the whole way, you had better not start" (p. 99). The appeal here is not to moral codes against premarital intercourse, but to the enlightened self-interest of the adolescent male and to the utilitarian social objective of avoiding unwanted pregnancies.

While progressives discouraged sexual experimentation among adolescents, their pragmatic social utilitarianism also led them to be increasingly supportive of contraceptives and even abortion as weapons in the "war" against teenage pregnancy. They based their argument on several propositions. First, Malthus' study of populations suggested that war, famine, and pestilence exert negative population control in the absence of positive checks on population, including birth control. Virginia Richmond (1934), an influential sexuality educator in the 1930s, located both abortion and contraceptives within the domain of positive checks on population with deep roots in human culture, as revealed by the new science of anthropology. She noted: "Many tribes knew no better method [of birth control] than infanticide. . . . There came a time, however, when women learned how to produce abortion. . . . Exceedingly primitive peoples have knowledge of *abortifacients*, agents that produce abortion, of one kind or another. However, contraceptive methods or means of preventing conception are found also in many widely separated primitive tribes" (p. 30). Finding both abortions and contraceptives in primitive societies gave credence to the argument that they were "normal" adaptations and not, as religious critics had argued, immoral or "unnatural." In fact, consistent with the perspective of structural-functional anthropology, it was possible to conclude that persistent practices such as these must serve an important social function.

Progressives also argued, more pragmatically, that individuals would find ways of having abortions and using contraceptives regardless of how much church leaders condemned these practices, that if contraceptives were more readily available there would be less need for abortions, and that by refusing to sanction these practices or even provide young people with information on them, educators lost the respect and trust of adolescents. Progressive educators also pointed to the direct social costs of enforced ignorance. One result of making abortions illegal and illicit, they argued, was that many American women died unnecessarily each year from complications after attempting to give themselves abortions or after receiving an abortion from an unlicensed doctor. Richmond (1934) reported that in the early 1930s "an appalling number [of deaths] occur each year under circumstances that raise the suspicion of abortion, procured illegally or self-induced. . . . The death rate from abortion appears to be rising rapidly, not only in this country but all over the world, except in Russia where abortion has been legalized" (p. 272). Similarly, she noted, when contraceptives were not widely available and people lacked scientific information on contraceptives, they could be "taken advantage of" by charlatans and could "obtain articles or chemicals often harmful to health and sometimes dangerous" (p. 274). The answer, for the progressives, was a more enlightened approach to sexual problems in society, and more sexuality education in the public schools by specially trained and licensed professionals.

In sharp opposition to traditionalists, Richmond (1934) also argued that "social workers and students of society . . . are becoming convinced that in very many cases it is better for both mother and child if the girl does not marry, especially at so early an age" (p. 258). Single mothers were to live at home with their parents until a suitable husband could be found. Later, by the 1950s, and especially in the inner city, such single mothers were to become wards of the welfare state, under the watchful eye of the social worker. Just as getting married at an early age was actively discouraged, even in the case of pregnancy, so the dissolution of overly conflictual marriages was acknowledged as an option. Once more, the early progressives looked to Soviet Russia for leadership and as "a vast social laboratory where all sorts of experiments are being carried out" to better manage human sexuality (p. 266).

Belief in social utilitarianism and support for state intervention to solve pressing social problems also led some progressive educators to support the then-influential racial "hygiene" or eugenics movement in America. Eugenics, the science of racial improvement through selective breeding, was based on the assumption that the genetically weak and unfit placed a particularly heavy financial burden on society and contributed "weak" or "degenerate" genes to the racial gene pool. According to Richmond (1934), "No one denies the staggering cost to the State of our institutions for the feeble-minded, the insane, and the criminals," which included court and legal proceeding costs, charitable donations, and the cost of clinical and hospital treatment and supervision, all of which were "supported by the responsible members of society for the benefit of the irresponsible" (p. 277). By 1932, 27 states had enacted eugenics laws requiring that the state certify all marriages to ensure that only genetically "fit" individuals married, and granting the state the right to sterilize individuals identified as idiots, imbeciles, epileptics, feeble-minded, insane, and in some cases "moral degenerates" (homosexuals) and "sexual criminals" (child molesters and rapists). Over 10,000 sterilizations were eventually performed. In reporting on this "progress," Richmond argued that it represented just a "drop in the bucket, and that a much more extensive eugenics program will be required." In this regard, she cited the eugenics program just getting underway at that time in Germany, where 400,000 were to be sterilized, and noted that "other nations will watch this program with great interest" (p. 277). This statement reads as sadly ironic and tragically misguided in light of what followed in Germany, and it suggests, once more, that the central weakness of progressivism was its tendency to support, almost unquestioningly, monumental state initiatives to overcome persistent "social problems" that stand in the way of the New Society.

By the early 1950s progressivism and "life-adjustment" education fell under increasing attack, particularly for its collectivist, authoritarian tendencies. In the era of the Cold War, as Americans celebrated a return to individual competitiveness, professional educators rarely identified themselves as progressives. Nevertheless, the progressive ideology has continued to be very influential in sexuality or "family life" education, a discipline almost tailor-made for progressive approaches. It has also influenced state policy designed to promote "family planning" among the urban poor and in the Third World through an increased reliance upon contraceptives and abortion. Among the chief advocates of this perspective since the 1960s have been Planned Parenthood and (internationally) the U.S. Agency for International Development (AID). The latter is perhaps the largest distributor of condoms and other birth control devices in the world and has funded projects to establish abortion clinics in a number of Third World countries since the 1950s. While "family planning" for the urban poor and the Third World may be beneficial to the recipients, and the social burden of providing welfare for the children of the poor is undeniably great, this progressive perspective is also compatible with an implicitly racist and elitist view of society associated with a fear that the poor and nonwhite are outreproducing the white, middle class. In this regard, "family planning" represents an extension of the eugenics movement. Interestingly, while conservatives might be expected to support more "family planning" for the poor, both Planned Parenthood and AID became targets of attack by religious fundamentalists during the 1980s, and President Reagan approved a policy whereby family planning agencies that sought federal support would have to stipulate in advance that the money would not be used to perform or advocate abortions, or even advise women on the procedure. This instance of conflict between neoprogressive and traditionalist perspectives suggests just how far apart the two groups have become on many issues, although each has as an objective the strengthening of the middle-class family.

That split was also apparent in reaction to a National Research Council report entitled *Risking the Future: Adolescent Sexuality, Pregnancy and Child Bearing* (1986), which represented an endorsement of neoprogressive pragmatism and utilitarianism in addressing the rising problem of teenage pregnancy in the inner city. The report concluded that the birth control pill was the "safest and most effective" contraceptive for adolescent girls and recommended "aggressive public education to dispel myths about health risks for young women" (Werner, 1986, p. 1). It also recommended that condom machines be placed in areas where adolescent boys congregate, such as high school restrooms. Finally, it advocated that school-based health clinics be established in high schools to distribute birth control devices and information on birth control to students. The social utilitarianism of the report is evident in its emphasis upon the severely limited career opportunities of teenage parents, and the economic burden on society of maintaining these families, which the report placed at $16.6 billion in federal outlays for Aid to Dependent Children, Medicaid, and food stamps in 1985 (National Research Council, 1986; Werner, 1986). The National Right to Life Committee immediately attacked the report for being "a major pro-abortion document," and the secretary of education suggested that providing birth control information in schools "undermines the efforts of others who are trying to send a different message to young people" (Fiske, 1986, p. B3). That message was the traditional one of abstinence until marriage, a message neoprogressives claimed was unrealistic and thus dangerous. At this point, it is difficult to say which of these two ideologies will gain in influence over the next decade and which one will lose ground. On one hand, the end of the Reagan era and a general decline in the influence of religious fundamentalism suggests that neoprogressivism is likely to enjoy a resurgence in the 1990s. On the other hand, if the AIDS epidemic remains unchecked a reactionary attitude may gain influence that equates sexual "sin" with sickness and sees salvation as possible only through a return to asceticism, antihomosexuality, and the traditional family. In either case, it seems likely that the discourse on sexuality education will continue to involve a conflict between the ideologies of traditionalism and progressivism, at least for the foreseeable future.

RADICAL FREUDIAN IDEOLOGY

For all their differences, both of the ideologies I have examined to this point largely accept the current distribution of class, gender, and sexual preference power in society and focus attention upon various "problems" that threaten the stability of the current system. Differences between progressives and traditionalists have to do with questions as to how much repression is necessary to maintain the current order, and what are the most effective ways of managing deviations from the established sexual norm. But there has also been another discourse on sexuality in 20th-century Western culture that is decidedly postconventional and even libertine. This has been a marginalized discourse, as one might expect, yet it has exercised considerable influence over academic thinking on human sexuality and has influenced the public school sexuality curriculum to at least some degree over the past two decades or so. This postconventional discourse on sexuality may be divided into two quite different ideological perspectives, which I will call *radical Freudianism* and *sexual libertarianism*. Since I have already presented an overview of Freud's perspective in discussing traditionalist and progressive ideologies, I begin by describing the positions of two radical Freudians: Wilhelm Reich, who founded the "sexual politics" movement in Weimar Republic Germany, and Herbert Marcuse, whose *Eros and Civilization* (1966) influenced the counterculture and sexual liberation movements of the 1960s and 1970s.

In his practice as a psychoanalyst in treating both working-class and middle-class patients, Reich (1931/1971) was led to conclude, consistent with Freud, that many individuals were "infected with sexual and neurotic disturbances" related to an overly rigid adherence to conventional morality (p. xviii). Reich concluded that the working-class patients he treated were just as inhibited, or more so, than the middle-class patients Freud analyzed. As a Marxist, however, Reich proposed a new answer to Freud's famous question, "What interest has society in sexual repression?" His answer was that "morality is a social product that rises and then passes away, and in the class state it is in the service of the ruling class" (p. xvi). Reich argued that the ruling class maintains its control of the working class at least partially through sexual repression. This occurs, he believed, in two interrelated ways. First, control is maintained by channeling or sublimating sexual energy into the political realm, where it supports relations of political domination and subordination, a type of national sadomasochism. Fascism appeals to and molds a particular "character structure" within a population that is based on repressed sexuality and manifested in relations of domination and subordination in various institutional spheres. Second, by recreating in the traditional nuclear family the basic relations of class society, relations of domination and subordination are learned in the home before they become politicized. Here Reich quoted Friedrich Engels's *The Origin of the Family*, which maintained that "in the individual family . . . we have a miniature picture of the same conflicts and contradictions in which society, split into classes since the beginnings of civilization, has been moving, unable to solve or overcome them" (p. 146). Reich (1931/1971) concluded that the "natural morality" of the primitive matriarchal clans, in which people had "sexual freedom based on gratification" was infinitely superior to the repressive patriarchy of industrial capitalism (pp. 146–147). Compulsory monogamy and patriarchal rule had risen out of and encouraged the concentration of wealth in the hands of a few rich men and was consistent with the development of an authoritarian rather than a self-governing or democratic character structure. To achieve socialism, this character structure had to change; sexuality had to become less repressed and more egalitarian (and in Reich's view the two went together).

The implications of this radical politicization of sexual repression by Reich were worked out in the controversial "Sex-Pol" movement, which brought sexual education and a new sexual ideology to the working class of Germany in the 1920s and early 1930s (Cohen, 1982). Reich sought to encourage among the German working class many of the ideals of the revolutionary sexuality education then officially supported in Soviet Russia, including an acceptance of adolescent sexuality, nonmonogamous relationships, and bearing children out of wedlock. After a visit to Russia in the late 1920s, for example, he observed that "the question whether one wanted to become a sexual partner was being asked more and more openly and unhesitatingly. . . . An acquaintance was in the eighth month of pregnancy, but nobody had asked who the child's father was. A family offered to put up a visitor but didn't have enough room, so the sixteen-year-old daughter said openly to her parents: 'I'll go sleep with X [her boyfriend]'" (pp. xxiii–xxiv). In Soviet schools adolescents were informed openly about procreation, birth, contraception, and venereal disease. Abortions were available and encouraged, and prostitution was largely eliminated. Women were depicted as equals of men in the household and the economy, traditional patriarchal practices were criticized, and permissive or self-regulating patterns of child rearing were encouraged (Cohen, 1982). The official Soviet position on homosexuality was also "modern" and rather tolerant, at least in the beginning under Lenin. All of this official ideology of sexuality in the Soviet Union found its way into the Sex-Pol movement in Germany, although Reich went beyond the official Communist party line in calling for a revolutionary form of working-class desublimation of sexuality, with an emphasis upon "genital gratification" rather than reproduction, and the Communist party of Germany ultimately disassociated itself from Reich's views and withdrew its support of the Sex-Pol movement. Reich also became increasingly disenchanted with the Soviets as, under the influence of Stalinism, they became more traditional and repressive in their views on sexuality. For example, in 1934 the official Soviet party line was changed so that homosexuality was viewed as a "sign of a degenerate culture of the perverse bourgeoisie" and a "social crime." The widespread persecution of homosexuals began in January 1934, with mass arrests in the major cities of Soviet Russia. Homosexuals joined other "counterrevolutionary" groups in the rapidly expanding gulags of the Stalinist era, and many died there (Reich, 1945).

Reich provides the basis for one particular form of radical sexual politics. But Reich still places sexuality at the service of the revolution and the socialist state, and to this extent he was a radical progressive. The "good" worker and party member is to be forged by encouraging a rejection of bourgeois sexual mores regarding monogamy and other forms of sexual "ownership" and by encouraging gender equality in sexual relations and family life. Reich's vision of "liberated" sexuality does not extend beyond nonmonogamous, heterosexual, genital intercourse among equal partners. While Reich did not believe in condemning or persecuting homosexuals, he did believe that homosexuality would no longer be "necessary" once individuals had free and open access to heterosexual intercourse; it would then presumably disappear, along with other "perversions." Reich finally broke with the official Communist party line, but his perspective is still one of sexual uniformity and "politically correct" sexuality. In America, the notion of a politically correct sexuality has also had its appeal among some on the political Left, even if what gets taken for politically correct sexuality has changed with time. In some ways, this perspective represents an attempt to purify the body politic of sexual diversity, and make sexuality serve an idealized social order of conforming, well-adjusted individuals, much like the traditional and progressive ideologies.

If Reich represents a particular strand of doctrinaire thinking among the Old Left, then Marcuse represents a quite different strand, more attuned to the American counterculture and "New Left" of the 1960s and early 1970s than to Soviet-style socialism. In *Eros and Civilization* (1966), Marcuse took up Freud's questions regarding civilization and its discontents once more, suggesting that Freud actually laid the basis for a society in which the pleasure principle would not need to be repressed. In very basic terms, he argued that while a good deal of repression and sublimation was necessary to build "civilization" to its current advanced level, it was wrong to suppose that civilization would always require subordination of the pleasure principle to the reality principle, or that a dichotomization of these two principles was necessary. Instead, "the very achievements of repressive civilization seem to create the preconditions for the gradual abolition of repression" (p. 5). Such a change in society need not imply a relapse into barbarism, as Freud feared, since "occurring at the height of civilization, as a consequence not of defeat but of victory in the struggle for existence, and supported by a free society, such liberation might have very different results. It would still be a reversal of the process of civilization, a subversion of culture—but *after* culture had done its work and created the mankind and the world that could be free" (p. 198). What Marcuse is suggesting here is a restatement of the Marxist notion that alienated labor is not the inevitable lot of humankind, that once the technological means of production and methods of distribution of goods in a society reach a certain point of development (as Marcuse believed they had by the mid-20th century), humankind as a whole had the capacity to meet its basic material needs without imposing on individuals the necessity of a life of alienated labor and repression. For the first time, according to Marcuse, humankind was in a position to reap the fruits of thousands of years of labor. Computers and automated production processes could replace much of the drugery of alienated, routinized labor and allow for more free time for leisure and creative pursuits. The body, no longer used as an instrument of alienated labor, would be resexualized, accompanied by "a reactivation of all erotogenic zones and, consequently, in a resurgence of pregenital polymorphous sexuality and in a decline of genital supremacy. The body in its entirety would become an object of cathexis, a thing to be enjoyed—an instrument of pleasure" (p. 201). There are echoes here of the *Kama Sutra* intertwined with Freudian analysis in support of a return to a more "infantile" (as Freud would say) and generalized sexuality that is not primarily genital intercourse or orgasm oriented—"the primacy of the genital function is broken" (p. 205). Thus, while Reich viewed genital sexuality as the goal in rebellion against bourgeois inhibitions, Marcuse recognized genital sexuality as repressive as well, since it narrowed and constrained sexual expression. Instead of viewing a reactivation of prehistoric and childhood sexual desires as a regression (as Freud had), Marcuse argued that "it may well be the opposite" since it would free up long-repressed potential and desire. Even sadomasochistic sexuality, he argued, is part of our polymorphous perversity, our instinctual being, and when expressed in a free and consensual manner it cannot be equated with the activities of SS troops (pp. 202–203). Along with a general reactivation of instinctual sexuality, Marcuse believed that in a nonrepressive society there would be "an enlargement of the meaning of sexuality itself" involving a resurgence in the creativity of work and all spheres of human activity. Work itself would become "libidinal and erotic" since it would be expressive and creative (p. 208). In Marxist terms, the freeing of the pleasure principle is thus associated with a return to nonalienated labor. This is, in fact, a sublimation theory of sorts, but one that no longer distinguishes between work and play, between the reality principle and the pleasure principle.

As I noted earlier, Marcuse's model of a liberated sexuality is consistent with the values of the counter-cultural movement of the 1960s, which challenged the thinking of previous generations on sexuality and the "good life." Salvation was to come not through hard work and self-discipline but through a recapturing of pleasure and love (in all its forms). The traditional family and hierarchical institutional structures at all levels that supported the repressive society were resisted as people experimented with alternative institutional structures. While Marcuse believed that the liberation of Eros did not threaten civilization as such, the counter-cultural movement clearly did threaten hierarchical institutional structures in advanced capitalist America, and its more extreme manifestations had been rather forcefully suppressed by the mid 1970s. In its more mainstream form, the counterculture's emphasis upon the pursuit of pleasure proved to be containable and even exploitable within the consumer society. Still, the counterculture presented an important critique of contemporary Western culture, and the call for moving beyond its values (and destructive tendencies) is likely to have continuing relevance in the decades ahead. Currently, its influence over the sexuality curriculum is minimal, and this probably has to do with the fact that critical theoretical perspectives extend the scope of sexuality education far beyond issues of biological functioning and psychological "adjustment." Once sexuality is understood to be implicated in the constitution of power relations, and as related to work, creativity, and the pursuit of happiness, a number of fundamental sociocultural and political issues are raised that are threatening to many teachers, administrators, state education officials, and elements in the community.

LIBERTARIAN IDEOLOGY

The final ideology I want to examine is also postconventional. That is, it rejects a narrow view that understands sexuality primarily in terms of vice and virtue or "normality" and "perversion," the hallmarks of traditional and progressive ideologies. Yet it is not in any self-conscious or deliberate manner a radical political ideology that links sexual power relations to the power relations and dynamics of patriarchal, advanced capitalist society. Its radicalness lies, rather, in a "freeing" of sexuality from social utilitarianism or political purpose and in a championing of individual sexual rights. In choosing to label this ideology libertarian, I imply several things. First, libertarian implies a *libertine* perspective that proudly celebrates sexuality and sexual diversity in defiance of established mores. More important, it also implies *political libertarianism*. Although adherents of this sexual ideology rarely identify their views as political, they in fact take for granted a libertarian perspective. According to this perspective, each individual is the ultimate judge of his or her own behavior, and what is "right" for one person may be wrong for another. The only ethical codes accepted by strict libertarians are those of *reciprocity* (I must grant you the same freedom of choice you grant me) and *consensuality* (individuals must enter into relations as consenting adults who agree on the terms of their relationship). Economically this implies *laissez faire* capitalism and a minimalist state—the ideal of classical economic theory; sexually it implies letting consenting adults (rather than the church, the state, or the psychiatric establishment) decide what is good for them. Alfred Kinsey (Kinsey et al., 1953), for example, maintained that society should properly "attempt to control sexual relations which are secured through the use of force or undue intimidation," but should otherwise interfere as little as possible in the affairs of individuals (p. 476). No attempt is made to prescribe a proper mode of sexual adjustment, and to this extent the libertarian ideology is more "neutral" than others because it does not favor or value one form of sexuality over another. In fact, it values diversity rather than conformity to established norms.

Kinsey was a statistician and taxonomist of sexuality rather than a theoretician of sexual politics. Yet his treatment of sexuality is likely to shock many conventional readers, even today. As Paul Robinson (1976) points out, Kinsey "is this century's foremost sexual demystifier. . . . [Not] only did Kinsey lack Freud's sense of the demonic element in human sexuality, he was also as untainted by romanticism as any major sexual theorist. . . . [His research] effected a kind of democratization of human sexual affairs. It brought the most tabooed activities under the same conceptual roof as marital relations and in the process rendered them innocuous" (p. 118). The two single most influential volumes to come out of Kinsey's Institute for Sex Research at Indiana University are *Sexual Behavior in the Human Male* (1948) and *Sexual Behavior in the Human Female* (1953). Together, these studies provide the best statistical evidence available, even four decades later, on the sexual activities of a broad cross-section of Americans—a tribute to the mass of data Kinsey was able to collect and the sophisticated statistical methods used to ensure that a representative sample was obtained.

Perhaps the most striking and consistent picture that emerges from these studies is of a wide range of "normal" sexual adjustment. First, there was a wide variability in normal sexual drive and output among individuals. Kinsey observed, for example, that one male in his study could recall only one orgasm in 30 years, while another male recorded as many as 30 orgasms in one week. Second, and more significant, there was wide variability in sexual response or behavior. Kinsey documented six forms of sexual response among men and women (masturbation, nocturnal emissions or sexual dreams, heterosexual petting, heterosexual intercourse, homosexual relations, and bestiality.) All of these alternative responses were treated more or less equally, although not all were equally prevalent in the population. What made all sexual responses equal to Kinsey was that each resulted, or could result, in a common physiological response: sexual "output" or orgasm. Kinsey did not, in this regard, distinguish one orgasm from another; all were treated as equal units of sexual outlet. For that matter, male and female orgasms could not be clearly distinguished, he argued, since "all orgasms appear to be physiologically similar quantities, whether they are derived from masturbation, heterosexual, homosexual, or other sorts of activities" (1953, p. 511).

Probably the most common form of sexual outlet among both men and women, according to Kinsey, was masturbation. Although females seemed to indulge in masturbation less than males, Kinsey (1953) reported that of every possible type of sexual activity, "masturbation . . . is the one in which the female most frequently reaches orgasm" (p. 132). Heterosexual intercourse was thus dethroned as the most erotic or even preferred form of sexual behavior. Kinsey indicated that masturbation was pervasive, harmless, and perhaps even therapeutic and rejected the psychoanalytic view that it indicated psychic immaturity. According to Kinsey, "We may assert that we have recognized exceedingly few cases, if indeed there have been any outside of a few psychotics, in which either physical or mental damage has resulted from masturbatory activity" (p. 167). In this one sentence, Kinsey demolished the rationale sexuality educators had used for decades in arguing against masturbation as an "unhealthy habit" and implicitly challenged the whole notion of sublimation, the cornerstone of both traditional and progressive ideologies.

Many viewed Kinsey as a sexual egalitarian, and in some important ways he was. For example, he argued that sexual response was similar in both men and women, thus countering the prevalent notion that women did not experience sexual feeling as much as men did. Furthermore, in viewing the clitoris rather than the vagina as the focus of female sexual arousal and in arguing that the clitoris was most fully stimulated in masturbation, Kinsey encouraged a view of women as more than the passive receptacles of the male sexual organ. In spite of this, Kinsey was not yet a feminist and took for granted a male-centered perspective on human sexuality. For example, he concluded that "In most mammals the behavior of the female in a heterosexual performance usually involves the acceptance of the male which is trying to make intromission. The female at such a moment is less aggressive than the male, even passive in her acceptance of the male's approaches, and subordinate in position to him. . . . There is no sexual relation until the female has been sufficiently subdued to allow the male to effect coitus" (1948, p. 613). Such a perspective shows traces of the social Darwinian thinking of the early 20th century by reinforcing patriarchal gender relations and legitimating the use of force in making the female submit. Kinsey's male-centered perspective is also evident in his contention that while women have orgasms, they have them less frequently than do men, and they are less important in overall female sexual response. In supporting this notion, he argues that "outside of the human species, orgasm is infrequent and possibly absent among females of most species of mammals" (1953, p. 135)—a highly dubious proposition based on little scientific data. Furthermore, the reduction of sexual relations to the achievement of sexual "outlet" takes for granted a particularly male view of sexuality, with attention focused on the most efficient and direct means of achieving orgasm.

Kinsey's male-centrism is also seen in his glorification of adolescent males as all-around sexual athletes, based on the fact that their sexual desire and orgasmic "output" are greatest and because they are least repressed. In focusing attention upon adolescent male sexuality, Kinsey (1948) distinguishes between sexuality "strong" and "weak" males. Those who reach puberty earliest, he says, also have the highest sex drive in adolescence, and they continue to outperform other males throughout their active sex lives. Kinsey clearly regrds them as superior both physically and socially to boys who reach puberty later. He remarks, for example, that "these early-adolescent males are more often the more alert, energetic, vivacious, spontaneous, physically active, socially extrovert, and/or aggressive individuals in the population," while late-blooming boys have a diminished sexual output and are more typically "slow, quiet, mild in manner, [and] without force" (p. 325). Kinsey thus affirms the conventional patriarchal wisdom in American society that "masculinity" is unequally distributed, that some men have more than others, and that those who have the most are naturally superior.

While Kinsey represents a particularly male-centered libertarianism, Masters and Johnson's research may be viewed as expressive of a more balanced or even feminist libertarianism, in keeping with the changing times. They are best known for *Human Sexual Response* (1966) and *Human Sexual Inadequacy* (1970), two studies designed, either directly or indirectly, to help married couples lead happier sex lives with fewer sexual "dysfunctions" or "disorders" (Lehrman, 1970; Robinson 1976, Chapter 3). Both of these books reflected and contributed to increased role equalization within the middle-class, college-educated group that Masters and Johnson studied. In a number of ways, women were even depicted as sexually superior to men. They can, for example, achieve multiple orgasms, stay sexually aroused longer, and seem more inclined to enjoy a variety of amorphous response patterns in comparison to men, who are more genital and orgasm oriented.

While Masters and Johnson's concern with sexual adjustment harks back to the progressive, psychoanalytic tradition, they understood "proper" adjustment (at least within marriage) in a very libertine and libertarian way. In the modern marriage, they argued, success is to be measured at least partially by whether or not both partners' sexual desires are met. Marriage is like a sexual contract between consenting heterosexual adults, and like all contracts it must be to the advantage of both parties. With many couples, especially the most dysfunctional ones, one or both partners are not getting their sexual needs met—most typically the woman. Masters and Johnson treated sexual dysfunctions as a component of the overall relationship: If a husband is impotent or a wife unresponsive, the other partner is very much involved both in the cause of the problem and in its treatment. The goal of therapy, consequently, is to open up sexual communication channels between partners so that they can make their needs better known and to provide couples with factual information on how to increase and maintain sexual arousal. Each partner is treated as an equal, and as such is made responsible for ensuring that his or her sexual needs are met, along with the sexual needs of his or her partner, through open verbal communication of desires and through the use of "body language" (by guiding the hands of the partner, and so forth). Rather than striving to achieve orgasms, both partners are encouraged to explore sensory pleasures. In all of these ways, partners in stable, long-term relationships are encouraged to desublimate in order to increase their sexual utility function, get more out of their relationships, and ensure that their relationships hold together and grow. Sexual relations and problems, following a libertarian logic, are of vital concern to the involved parties but not to the larger society or state.

The ideology of sexual libertarianism began to influence the sexuality curriculum in some limited ways by the 1960s and has become the dominant discourse in many college-level texts designed for use in undergraduate human sexuality courses. At the college level, educators feel freer to speak of sexual desire and fulfillment in positive terms and to emphasize the "open" negotiation of sexual roles and relations. For example, in one popular college text an entire chapter is devoted to the topic of "negotiating relationships." The authors claim that "developing a sexual relationship and keeping it alive and healthy usually involves continuing sensitive negotiation. . . . To get together sexually with another person, we need to understand not only our own ideas about what sex means but theirs, too" (Nass & Fisher, 1988, p. 112). Another college text makes the case for sexual diversity rather than homogeneity in concluding that "the 'traditional' pattern of American family and marriage and the 'traditional' American sexual value system are mythic concepts with no reality because we can see a wide variety of lifestyles and sexual values documented in any serious history of American culture" (Francoeur, 1982, p. 42). This form of sexual libertarianism has not yet established itself in the public school curriculum. Public education has been, and continues to be, closely linked to the promotion of conventional "family values" and sexual roles; libertarianism radically breaks with this tradition. Furthermore, a libertarian curriculum, with its emphasis upon the sexual "rights" of consenting adults, is viewed as inappropriate for adolescents who have no such rights. In recent years, however, support for adolescent sexual rights has grown among some scholars, and the debate on this issue is likely to become more heated in the years ahead (Rodman, Lewis, & Griffith, 1984).

CONCLUSION

I have provided a basis for a discursive, ideological analysis of the sexuality curriculum by examining four alternative, if also overlapping, ideologies that have influenced thinking about sexuality education in 20th-century America. Although traditionalism seems the most outmoded, it is perhaps also the most resilient since its roots go so deep within the culture. In some ways, the traditionalist ideology represents a response to justified concern about nihilistic tendencies in "modern" advanced capitalist society, and an attempt to recapture a set of values beyond the narrowly instrumental and individualistic. Thus, we should not dismiss traditionalism merely as a form of narrow-mindedness. It is misguided, however, because it idealizes and romanticizes a past that was, for many if not most people, highly oppressive.

Progressivism may be the most potentially dangerous of the ideologies, although it seems quite benign in many forms. It is the ideology of the national state, "Big Brother," and social engineering. The rise of the centralized bureaucratic state is one of the major developments of the 20th century, and progressivism legitimated the consolidation of power in the hands of the new bureaucratic managerial elites. Although national policy with regard to sexuality and the body politic is needed, progressives have always emphasized conformity to rather uniform norms of sexual and social conduct and incorporated antidemocratic tendencies.

The most viable, critical alternative to the traditional and progressive ideologies may lie in an integration of radical Freudianism and libertarianism, rather than one or the other. The emphasis upon individual sexual rights, including the right to control what happens to one's body, is important in the women's and gay and lesbian movements; and the protection of sexual rights, including the rights of sexual minorities, should be a central focus in any alternative to traditionalism and progressivism. But a strict focus upon individual rights is not enough and may even deflect attention away from the need to struggle on broader cultural fronts. What libertarianism lacks is theory or discourse that links power relations organized and constituted around sexuality with a more general and inclusive theory of power relations in the culture. This is where radical Freudian and other critical theoretical orientations can prove useful, for they help us to recognize the social interests served by existent power relations and to question the "naturalness" of the given social world. They also provide a basis for rethinking human sexuality in nonalienating, nonoppressive, and (hence) liberating forms.

In order to approach the study of human sexuality in these complex ways, sexuality education itself needs to be reconceptualized. First, let me suggest what I do *not* mean by sexuality education. I do not mean a curriculum that focuses primarily upon the biological aspects of human sexuality and reproduction. While instruction in the physiology of human reproduction is important, a biology course seems the most appropriate place to receive such instruction. Nor should sexuality education be defined as the study of sexual hygiene, that is, sexually transmitted diseases, contraceptive methods, and so forth. This information is important for young people to know, and it should be presented in health and physical education classes, but it should not be the heart of a sexuality curriculum. Nor should sexuality education be primarily normative or prescriptive, as traditionalists and progressives have conceived it. The role of public education should not be to indoctrinate or support a shaping of the individual to fit a uniform social mold. Finally, sexuality education should not assume a therapeutic role, either in the sense of having students talk about problems and concerns with their sexual relations or teaching students sexual skills and techniques (following the Masters and Johnson model). While therapy may be useful in some situations, it should be provided by school or family counselors and has no proper role in the curriculum.

In opposition to the dominant definition of sexuality education as the study of sexual physiology, hygiene, "adjustment," or techniques, I would suggest that it be defined as a subfield of *cultural studies, liberal arts,* or *history*. I use the first two terms interchangeably here, although "liberal arts" tends to imply a traditionalist perspective on the "great books," while "cultural studies" implies a deconstructive analysis of contemporary culture, including mass culture. We learn much about the social meaning assigned to human sexuality through both approaches, although cultural studies seems more directly applicable to the study of sexual meaning in contemporary society. History I take to be the study of culture over time and thus not fully separable from cultural studies. In the study of sexuality, a historical perspective is essential in helping students recognize that contemporary values and beliefs about sexuality are not the same for all time and all people. Rather, sexual power relations have a dynamic, unresolved quality, have changed substantially over time, and are now in the process of changing. So conceived, sexuality education becomes critical and analytical and thus both personally and socially empowering. This, I believe, is the only way of restoring academic respectability and pedagogic integrity to a discipline that has been relegated to "family life education" and "life adjustment education" for far too long.

REFERENCES

Apple, M. (1979). *Ideology and curriculum.* Boston: Routledge & Kegan Paul.

Cohen, I. (1982). *Ideology and unconsciousness: Reich, Freud, and Marx.* New York: New York University Press.

Cowan, J. (1874). *The science of a new life.* New York: Source Book.

Cremin, L. (1961). *The transformation of the school.* New York: Random House.

Delamater, J. (1989). The social control of human sexuality. In K. McKinney & S. Sprecher (Eds.), *Human sexuality: The societal and interpersonal context* (pp. 30–62). Norwood, NJ: Ablex.

Fine, M. (1988). Sexuality, schooling, and adolescent females: The missing discourse of desire. *Harvard Educational Review, 58* (1), 29–53.

Fiske, E. (1986, October 31). Birth advice in schools condemned by Bennett. *New York Times,* p. B3.

Flax, E. (1990, March 14). Sex-education urging chastity sparks controversy in South Carolina. *Education Week,* p. 8.

Foucault, M. (1980). *The history of sexuality: Vol. 1. An Introduction* (R. Hurley, Trans.). New York: Random House.

Francoeur, R. (1982). *Becoming a sexual person.* New York: Wiley.

Freud, S. (1961a). *Beyond the pleasure principle* (J. Strachey, Trans. & Ed.). New York: W. W. Norton. (Original work published 1920)

Freud, S. (1961b). *Civilization and its discontents* (J. Strachey, Trans. & Ed.). New York: W. W. Norton. (Original work published 1930)

Imber, M. (1982). Toward a theory of curriculum reform: An analysis of the first campaign for sex education. *Curriculum Inquiry, 12* (4), 339–362.

Kinsey, A., Pomeroy, W., & Martin, C. (1948). *Sexual behavior in the human male.* Philadelphia: W. B. Saunders.

Kinsey, A., Pomeroy, W., Martin, C., & Gebhard, P. (1953). *Sexual behavior in the human female*. Philadelphia: W. B. Saunders.

Kirkendall, L. (1940). *Sex adjustments of young men*. New York: Harper & Row.

Lehrman, N. (1970). *Masters and Johnson explained*. Chicago: Playboy.

Marcuse, H. (1966). *Eros and civilization: A philosophical inquiry into Freud*. Boston: Beacon.

Masters, W., & Johnson, V. (1966). *Human sexual response*. Boston: Little, Brown.

Masters, W., & Johnson, V. (1970). *Human sexual inadequacy*. Boston: Little, Brown.

Nass, G., & Fisher, M. (1988). *Sexuality Today*. Boston: Jones and Bartlett.

National Research Council. (1986). *Risking the future: Adolescent sexuality, pregnancy and childbearing*. Washington, DC: Author.

Nietzsche, F. (1954). Notes (1880–81). In Walter Kaufmann (Ed.), *The portable Nietzsche* (p. 75). New York: Viking.

Petras, J. (1978). *The social meaning of human sexuality*. Boston: Allyn & Bacon.

Reich, W. (1945). *The sexual revolution: Toward a self-governing character structure*. New York: Orgone Institute.

Reich, W. (1971). *The invasion of compulsory sex-morality*. New York: Farrar, Straus & Giroux. (Original work published 1931)

Richmond, V. (1934). *An introduction to sex education*. New York: Farrar & Rinehart.

Robinson, P. (1976). *The modernization of sex: Havelock Ellis, Alfred Kinsey, William Masters and Virginia Johnson*. New York: Harper & Row.

Rodman, H., Lewis, S., & Griffith, S. (1984). *The sexual rights of adolescents*. New York: Columbia University Press.

Strong, B. (1972, summer). Ideas of the early sex education movement in America, 1890–1920. *History of Education Quarterly*, pp. 129–161.

Sullivan, J. (1988, November 20). Teaching of sexual abstinence urged. *New York Times*, New Jersey section, p. 4.

U.S. Surgeon General and U.S. Bureau of Education. (1922). *High schools and sex education*. Washington, DC: U.S. Government Printing Office.

Werner, L. (1986, December 10). U.S. council urges birth control to combat teen-age pregnancies. *New York times*, pp. A1ff.

CHAPTER 3

Sexuality and Censorship in the Curriculum

Beyond Formalistic Legal Analysis

JAMES ANTHONY WHITSON

In Chapter 2, Dennis Carlson argues for a conception of sexuality education as a subfield within history, the liberal arts, or cultural studies. This chapter analyzes the ideology behind First Amendment interpretations that would permit the censorship of sexuality from the curriculum. My response to that ideology leads me to take another step in the direction toward which Carlson has pointed us: Instead of seeing sexuality as an analytically distinct subfield, I suggest that it is necessary to understand cultural studies and the liberal arts in general as inquiries into a reality that exists within inextricably intersecting spatial, temporal, and sexual dimensions of human existence, in such a way that liberal education could no more survive the elimination of the sexual dimension than it could survive elimination of the historical dimension.

LEGAL CASES ON SEXUALITY AND SCHOOL CENSORSHIP

Politically motivated censorship efforts have been directed at the public school curriculum since the Reconstruction era following the Civil War. Before the 1960s, however, censors attacked only a few works of fiction, and for reasons other than their treatment of sexuality (Jenkinson, 1986; Burress, 1989). Since then, the frequency of curriculum censorship incidents has mushroomed; they are more often instigated by religious interests; and they have become more preoccupied with sex-related themes and language. This is not, as some might suggest, simply a response to any recent introduction of modern literature containing sexual material. That explanation is belied, for example, by the fairly typical case of *Virgil v. School Board of Columbia County, Florida* (1989). In *Virgil*, the textbook anthology used in an 11th- and 12th-grade humanities course was attacked because it included *The Miller's Tale* by Geoffrey Chaucer and *Lysistrata* by Aristophanes. Both of those works have been standard items in the adolescent curriculum for centuries, long before the new antisex censors began their campaigns against modern works like J. D. Salinger's *The Catcher in the Rye*. The parents challenging the textbook in the *Virgil* case were a local minister and his wife. A specially appointed advisory committee recommended that the textbook should continue to be used, but that *Lysistrata* and *The Miller's Tale* not be assigned as required reading in the course. Against this recommendation from its own review committee, the school board voted to discontinue any future use of the book in its curriculum. Reasons given included "the sexuality in the two selections," "a belief that the subject matter of the selections was immoral, insofar as the selections involved graphic, humorous treatment of sexual intercourse and dealt with sexual intercourse out of wedlock," and "a belief that the sexuality of the selections was violative of the socially and philosophically conservative mores, principles and values of most of the Columbia County populace" (677 F. Supp. at 1549).

Recent attacks on the curriculum have featured arguments that non-religious treatment of sexuality and other subjects in the schools amounts to inculcation of an alternative religion of "secular humanism," in violation of the First Amendment prohibition against any state "establishment" of religion (see especially *Smith v. Bd. of School Commissioners of Mobile County*, 1987). This argument was first propounded in attacks against sex education programs in the 1960s, and is best understood in relation to the Supreme Court cases in which school prayer, school Bible-reading, and a state law against teaching evolution had all been recently declared unconstitutional as violations of the establishment clause in the First Amendment. In *Cornwell v. State Bd. of Ed.* (1969), for example, the plaintiffs complained not only that sex education infringed on the "free exercise" of their religion but also that "the teaching of sex in the Baltimore County Schools will in fact establish religious concepts" (at 342). The judge had little trouble dismissing the establishment clause claim in *Cornwell* as simply unsupported by the precedents. Such cases show, however, that the mobilization of religious interests against sex education in the schools must be understood partly as a response to the success of legal challenges to the influence that religion had traditionally enjoyed in public schools in many districts throughout the United States.

The courts have generally continued to support state and local school authorities in cases dealing with sex education programs. In *Smith v. Ricci* (1982), for example, the Supreme Court of New Jersey upheld a regulation by the State Board of Education requiring local districts to provide a family-life education program, including sex education, in the curricula of all elementary and secondary schools. The court dismissed the same free exercise and establishment clause arguments that had failed in other states a decade earlier, partly on the basis that the state regulation required procedures for exempting students whose parents objected to any part of the program on religious grounds. No such exemption was provided for by the Philadelphia program implementing the Pennsylvania Board's decision to include sex education in the school curriculum; but in *Aubrey v. School District of Philadelphia* (1981), the state court ruled in favor of the district when it was sued for damages by a student whose graduation was delayed by her failure to obtain a passing grade in a health education class, which required an examination on sex education material that her parents did not approve.

Mandatory health and sex education requirements have become more common with the rising concern about AIDS in the late 1980s. In *Ware v. Valley Stream H.S. Dist.* (1989), a New York State appeals court upheld a regulation promulgated by the state commissioner of education that required all elementary and secondary students to receive education on AIDS and on alcohol and drug abuse. The court explained that

> in cases involving religious objections to school curricula, the courts have repeatedly placed the State's educational interest above the exercise of unbridled religious freedom. . . . Moreover, the object of the instant State educational interest is the protection of the public health, which is itself a compelling State interest. . . . and the prevention of AIDS transmission has itself been defined as a substantial and compelling State interest. (545 N.Y.S. 2d at 320)

The court is not actually ruling here that sex education ought to be taught, or required for all students. The court is ruling, rather, that the commissioner does have the power to require it. In other words, the Constitution does not interfere with the power of state or local authorities to act as they see fit, which means that the Constitution also permits state authorities to decide that sex education will not be included in the curriculum. In *Mercer v. Michigan State Board of Education* (1974), the federal court dismissed claims by a teacher and a physician who argued that a state law prohibiting instruction on birth control in the public schools was unconstitutional because it violated First Amendment rights of teachers and students. As all these cases indicate, the inclusion of sex education in the elementary and secondary school curriculum will generally be treated as something to be politically determined as a matter of legislative policy, and not as a constitutional matter on which courts would overrule decisions by the state or local legislative and administrative bodies.

In *DiBona v. Matthews* (1990), a California appellate court ruled that college administrators violated the First Amendment when they canceled a drama class because of plans to stage a play that the administrators feared would provoke opposition from religious leaders, leading to a disturbance in the local community. Although this case seems to represent the traditional application of the First Amendment in protecting intellectual freedom against interference form political or administrative officials, recent constitutional developments suggest that such applications can no longer be expected with much confidence, especially at the precollegiate elementary and secondary levels. In *DiBona*, the court ruled that cancellation of the class could not be justified by vulgar language in the play; but the conclusion that the cancellation was unconstitutional rested largely on the court's finding that the college administrators did not have a reasonable basis for predicting the community disturbance that they cited as the reason for their action. In this way, the court's reasoning in *DiBona* illustrates the kind of analysis that has been used since *Tinker v. Des Moines* (1969) in ruling against school officials on First Amendment grounds. In *Tinker*, the U.S. Supreme Court ruled that it was unconstitutional for school officials to prohibit students from wearing black armbands in protest against the war in Vietnam. The Court explained that this prohibition was not justified by a merely *unsubstantiated fear* of disruptive controversy, and that limitations on such expressive activity by the students could be justified only if officials had a *substantial basis* for expecting that disruption of the school's educational activity would otherwise result.

From 1969 until the *Hazelwood* decision in 1988 (discussed below), many courts decided First Amendment education cases on the basis of a generalized principle, derived from *Tinker*, that evidence of a substantial likelihood of harm must be available before officials could interfere with communication in the schools. Until 1988, many courts used this test from *Tinker* as the standard for assessing whether First Amendment rights had been violated in a wide variety of education cases, including cases involving school library books, textbooks, and other curriculum materials (see, for example, *Parducci v. Rutland*, 1970; *Right to Read Defense Committee v. Chelsea*, 1978; and *Dean v. Timpson I.S.D.*, 1979). In the years between *Tinker* and the 1988 *Hazelwood* case, however, most courts did *not* apply the *Tinker* standard as a limitation on the authority of school officials to control textbooks and other curriculum materials. In *Zykan v. Warsaw* (1980), for example, the court ruled that there was nothing in the Constitution to deprive a local school board of the power to remove books both from courses and from the school library on the basis of the school board members' "social, political and moral tastes" (at 1306). The center of this Warsaw, Indiana, dispute (in which not only books but also courses were eliminated, and two teachers lost their jobs) was a course on women in literature (see Arons, 1983/1986, for details of this very bitter conflict). A comparable case was *Fisher v. Fairbanks* (1985), where the court upheld the school board's authority to fire a tenured teacher partly for using an unapproved novel in a unit on gay rights, which he had included in a social studies course on American minorities. Observing that there was no reason to doubt the teacher's assertion that the book was an appropriate resource for teaching about social discrimination against homosexuals, the court explained that "the question . . . is not whether the use of a particular book in a course is appropriate but whether the teacher or the administrator is to decide appropriateness in cases of conflict" (at 216).

Since 1988, the U.S. Supreme Court decision in *Hazelwood v. Kuhlmeier* seems to have established the general rule that school officials do have almost unlimited discretionary authority in controlling courses and materials in the curriculum. Two other cases are particularly noteworthy as leading up to *Hazelwood*. First, in *Island Trees v. Pico* (1982), the Court divided sharply over whether any First Amendment rights of high school students might have been violated by the removal of eleven books from their school library. The fragmented voting and opinions by the Justices in *Pico* are too complex to explain here (see Whitson, 1991, for a more detailed analysis of this case, and of the transition from *Tinker* to *Hazelwood*). At this point, it is enough to note that Burger, Rehnquist, Powell, and O'Connor pointed toward the *Hazelwood* decision by voting to affirm a summary judgment against the students in *Pico*, on the grounds that removal of the books by school officials would be constitutional regardless of whatever facts the students might be able to prove in a trial. This movement by the Court was confirmed in *Bethel v. Fraser* (1986), when the Supreme Court upheld disciplinary action against a student for using sexually suggestive double entendre in a speech urging the election of another student to an office in the student government.

Finally, in *Hazelwood v. Kuhlmeier* (1988), the Supreme Court upheld the authority of a high school principal to censor the contents of the student newspaper. In that case, the principal removed pages containing one article on the experiences of three pregnant students, and another on the impact of divorce on students at the school. The Court made use of *Fraser* as a precedent for declaring that the student newspaper, like Fraser's speech in the student government campaign, was part of the school-sponsored curriculum, and that it was therefore not governed by the *Tinker* standard. Instead, the Court said that cases like this one involving student newspapers, school plays, and other school-sponsored activities should be governed by the general rule that the First Amendment does not impose such limitations on the discretionary authority of school officials in their control over the curriculum.

This is the rule followed by the lower court in *Virgil* (discussed above), in which the trial judge explained that, although she did not agree with the school board's decision to ban a humanities text because it included *Lysistrata* and *The Miller's Tale*, she felt that the Supreme Court ruling in *Hazelwood* (just one week earlier) compelled her to conclude that the First Amendment does not prohibit the board from making that decision. *Hazelwood* is now the leading precedent that state and federal courts will generally feel bound to observe in ruling on cases in which the free speech clause of the First Amendment is invoked to challenge censorship of the curriculum by school officials.

EXPOSITION AND CRITIQUE OF FORMALISTIC LEGAL ANALYSIS

The Supreme Court Justices who voted in favor of the school officials in *Pico, Fraser,* and *Hazelwood* would insist that they were not voting in favor of censorship. Like the lower court judge in *Virgil*, they might even disagree with the censorship action itself. Instead of supporting *censorship*, they would insist that what they are supporting is the *authority* of school officials to run their schools as they see fit, without judicial interference, even if this must include authority for censorship activity with which the judges personally might disagree.

Those who support this rationale argue that it is a matter of limiting judges to their proper role, one of deferring to the legislative and administrative officials unless their actions are prohibited by the text of the Constitution itself. With respect to sexuality and the curriculum, it would be argued that no provision of the Constitution deprives school officials of the authority to decide either to include sex education, or to censor textbooks, courses, student newspapers and school plays, or even to ban sex-related topics from being included in health education courses. Because the Constitution itself does not expressly deal with such questions, it is argued that they are questions for democratically accountable officials to decide, and that unelected judges should not be allowed, instead, to interpose their own decisions, based on their own personal ideologies instead of the express provisions of the Constitution. In First Amendment education cases such as *Fraser* and *Hazelwood*, moreover, the majority opinions emphasize that judicial deference to school officials is essential, so that the educators can be free to exercise the discretionary authority that they need in order to perform the educational mission of the schools.

Legal Ideology and the Curriculum

We are now able to see the profoundly ideological discourse of sexuality and education being imposed through this rationale, even though it purports to repudiate any such ideological imposition by the courts. Throughout *Fraser* and *Hazelwood*, the majority opinions portray the general principle as one of leaving these decisions to the *educators*, so that they are free to use their best judgment in performing the "basic educational mission" of the schools (*Fraser*, at 685). As a rationale for ruling in favor of the school board and school administrators, however, this seems wildly out of line with the true circumstances in the vast majority of censorship cases that will be governed by these precedents. In most school censorship cases that reach the appellate courts, it is the teachers, school librarians, drama coaches, and newspaper advisors who are being countermanded by the politicians and the school administrators. A high percentage of these cases are in fact brought to court by teachers who have been fired because of texts that they chose to use in class (see, e.g., *Zykan*, 1980, and *Fisher*, 1985, discussed above). Who, then, are the "educators" in these cases?

Recognition of school board members and administrators as the educators—even against classroom teachers—follows logically from this Court majority's own ideological theory of education. In *Fraser* and *Hazelwood*, and before that in *Pico*, these justices have stressed repeatedly that the purpose of public education is to inculcate politically selected information, beliefs, and values. This ideology was articulated earlier in *Ambach v. Norwick* (1979), in which the Court upheld a New York statute barring aliens from becoming certified as teachers. The Court majority reasoned that teachers are like police officers in performing a critical governmental function, so that it is proper for the government to exclude aliens from teaching as a measure to ensure that the students will not be exposed to unauthorized influences in the classroom. This rationale logically supports the politically determined dismissal of a teacher for including feminist materials in a course on women in literature (*Zykan*, 1980) or including materials on gay rights in a course on minorities in America (*Fisher*, 1985). It might also logically support excluding feminists or gays from even being employed as teachers (cf. Walden & Culverhouse, 1989).

In *Pico*, the opinions by Brennan and Blackmun echoed a different view of the purposes of public education, which had been expressed in opinions by Supreme Court justices since the 1940s. This view also affirms the legitimacy of efforts to promote politically preferred values and beliefs in the schools, but only through noncoercive means such as "persuasion and example," and not through the exclusion of alternative beliefs and values, or other attempts to manipulate students in the "sphere of intellect and spirit" protected by the First Amendment (see Whitson, 1991). In his *Pico* dissent, however, Justice Rehnquist (with the agreement of Burger, Powell, and O'Connor) declared that when the government is acting in its role as educator, it is not subject to the same First Amendment limitations as it is when acting in its role as sovereign (*Island Trees v. Pico*, 1982, at 910). Again, this follows logically form Rehnquist's own understanding of the nature of education, revealed in a definition that he puts forward (without justification, apparently on the assumption that this is merely a restatement of common knowledge) as the premise of his argument: "Education consists of the selective presentation and explanation of ideas" (at 914). If this were true, then it would follow that the primary question for curriculum development is Who has the authority to choose which ideas the children should be taught? This is the approach taken in *Mercer*, the 1974 case (discussed above) in which the plaintiffs were challenging a Michigan law against teaching about birth control. The *Mercer* court ruled in favor of the legislature's action, explaining that it is "the authorities" who "must choose which portions of the world's knowledge will be included in the curriculum's programs and courses, and which portions will be left for grasping from other sources, such as the family, peers, or other institutions" (at 586).

The fallacy in this notion of the curriculum, seen as a meal served up especially for children with selectively prescribed "portions" of knowledge, can be recognized quite clearly in relation to questions concerning sexuality in the curriculum. The problem can be seen, for example, in *Pico*, where the school board members justified removal of some of the books, in part, on the grounds that the works were "anti-American." Brennan notes that when they were asked for an example of "anti-Americanism" in the banned books, two board members referred to Alice Childress's novel *A Hero Ain't Nothin' But a Sandwich* (1973/1982), because it "notes at one point that George Washington was a slave-holder" (*Island Trees v. Pico*, 1982, at 873, fn. 25). Although we can certainly argue, as Brennan does, that the students should be recognized as having First Amendment rights to receive such information, this argument itself does not reveal the problem with regarding such issues as questions of simply choosing "portions" from a vast world of discrete bits of information of that kind. The fact that Washington owned slaves is incidental to the more complex and ironic passage in question, which deals with role and identity conflicts in the life of Nigeria Greene (the character who is speaking in that passage), an African-American teacher in a contemporary urban school. A reader who thinks that *information about Washington* is the subject of this passage needs the kind of reading lessons for which this book might well be used. The passage would not be complete, however, without the teacher/narrator's comment that "Washington owned a slave woman whose cookin was so fine that he freed her while he was still livin. She musta really known how to barbecue!" (Childress, 1973/1982, p. 43). To understand that comment, the student needs to be reading at a level of textual comprehension far more complex than mere statements of propositional fact. At this level, the complexities of language and of human life and consciousness cannot be separated without the most tremendously destructive violence, such as the violence of ripping the sexual and historical dimensions from this story of American and African-American identity formation.

Childress (1989) has herself spoken on the way that censorship that purportedly aims at excluding only sexual language and references has the effect of excluding the language, lives, and voices of racial and cultural minorities. Indeed, it does seem difficult if not impossible to imagine how the experience of African-Americans in this country could be portrayed without the language and sexuality of Childress's own works, or the works of Maya Angelou, James Baldwin, Langston Hughes, Alice Walker, or Richard Wright—to name just a few highly acclaimed writers and poets whose representations of the African-American experience have been attacked by censors for the sexuality in their themes and language.

Ironically, the nonexplicit sexual references in the passage about Washington appear to have escaped the censors' notice. The censors were objecting to that passage for its "anti-Americanism" but did not mention its references to sexuality, even though such references were specifically objected to when they appeared in more explicit form throughout the books on the censors' list. Questions about the significance of the specific forms of expression in these works alert us to another fundamental problem in the formalistic legal analysis employed by Rehnquist and the other justices voting to uphold censorship actions by the local school authorities. In *Pico*, Justice Brennan's argument against the constitutionality of censorship was based on his observation that the "Constitution does not permit the official suppression of *ideas*" (*Island Trees v. Pico*, 1982, at 871, his emphasis). Rehnquist answered that although he "can cheerfully concede" this basic principle (at 907), it has no application in a case like *Pico*, because the officials were only banning the particular books, and were not precluding classroom discussion of the themes addressed in the books.

This reasoning was developed in an earlier case dealing with one of the books on the *Pico* list, *Down These Mean Streets*, by Piri Thomas (1967/ 1974). When that novel was challenged in *Presidents Council v. Community School Board* (1972), the federal judge noted that presumably "the educational value of this work, aside from whatever literary merit it may have, is to acquaint the predominantly white, middle-class junior high school students of Queens County with the bitter realities facing their contemporaries in Spanish Harlem" (at 291). The judge then reasoned that it was not unconstitutional for the board to ban the book for its sexual language and content, because "the teacher is still free to discuss the Barrio and its problems in the classroom" (at 292), and hence "the discussion of the book or the problems which it encompasses or the ideas it espouses have not been prohibited by the Board's action in removing the book" (at 293).

This was the rationale applied by Rehnquist 10 years later, when he argued that removal of this book and the other books in *Pico* did not involve any unconstitutional suppression of the ideas contained in them. From this, we see how Rehnquist and his followers on the Court cannot actually decide these cases simply by deferring to the local school officials; rather, they are free to take that step only after they have first imposed their own ideological definition of "ideas," and of what they would recognize as an unconstitutional "suppression of ideas." Within their formalistic legal ideology, we see that "ideas" are defined as something separate from particular expressions, so that expressions can be banned without suppressing the ideas themselves. Sexually allusive language, it seems, counts as nothing more than an expressive embellishment; and even sexual content itself is regarded as something extrinsic to the serious thematic ideas in a book like *Down These Mean Streets*.

This disparaging view of the significance of sexuality and the specific language used in Piri Thomas's book is undoubtedly not shared by the many teachers whose assessments of its pedagogical value have led them to adopt the book for classroom use. It is certainly not shared by Thomas, who thought the language important enough to include a glossary of the Spanish Harlem idiom. Ideas about barrio life expressed in other idioms would not be the same ideas as those expressed by the characters in Thomas's novel, just as some other statement of the facts about George Washington would not express the same idea as Nigeria Greene's comment, in the Childress book, about the "fine cookin'" of George Washington's slave.

When this argument is made with reference to specific groups, it runs the risk of reinforcing myths and stereotypes of an exaggerated sexuality in those populations. Stereotypes that today are projected onto people of color were projected onto Italian-Americans and other immigrants when they were newly arrived. Indeed, such ethnic and racial stereotypes can even persist in supposedly enlightened textbooks on human sexuality (Whatley, 1988). We must all, teachers and students, learn to appreciate that sexuality is an inextricable dimension of life for all people in all cultures. We must be prepared to understand clearly, for example, that when Childress has one of her characters tell us the story about Washington and his cook, this is as much a story about George Washington and white America as it is a story about the slave woman and black America. Censorship of sexual language and themes may put the white majority at less risk that their voices and culture will be excluded utterly, but perhaps only because the majority is better situated to insert apple pie (or cherry tree) self-representations distorted by an ideological repression of sexuality, which in turn intensifies the projection of sexuality onto other groups.

The record of censorship is replete with concrete examples. Censors sometimes nominate their own substitutions. In *Minarcini v. Strongsville* (1976), for example, when the school board banned *Catch 22*, by Joseph Heller, and two novels by Kurt Vonnegut, one school board member recommended that biographies of Herbert Hoover, Douglas MacArthur, and Captain Eddie Rickenbacker be used instead. The connection between sexuality and warfare in the works by Heller and Vonnegut is not just a theme of their invention, but a broadly recognized concern in the consciousness of modern literary and political culture. This was thematized more broadly in *Slaughterhouse-Five* (one of the books banned in *Pico*), in which Vonnegut used sexuality as one dimension for exploring relationships between the atrocities he witnessed in the Second World War (including the bombing of Dresden) and the life of white middle-class America in the late 1960s and early 1970s, the time of America's military exploits in Vietnam.

Such relationships between sexuality and warfare, in the languages of local and global conflicts, and of personal life histories and generational politics, were also explored by the renowned psychiatrist Robert Jay Lifton (1969) in an *Atlantic Monthly* article on the significance of anti-war and other youth protest movements of the time. In *Keefe v. Geanakos* (1969), when the head of a high school English department used Lifton's article in his senior English class, the school committee started action to discharge him because the article included a discussion of the social, psychological, and historical significance of the way protesters were using the term *motherfucker*. The court ruled in favor of the teacher (a result that could not be expected today, following *Hazelwood*), explaining that if high school seniors need to be protected from the shock of exposure to such words in current use, then "we would fear for their future" (at 361). Since then, Lifton has co-authored a book (Lifton & Markusen, 1990) that includes discussion of the sexual dimension in what the authors describe a the "genocidal mentality" found in both the Nazi Holocaust and in the threat of nuclear annihilation.

Of course, Lifton or Vonnegut may be all wrong in their interpretations, but the point is to recognize how their work reflects the nature of sexuality as an inextricable dimension of the indivisible reality that we must teach about throughout the school curriculum. Such examples indicate the larger cost of allowing sexuality to be censored from the curriculum, for they illustrate how exclusion of the sexual dimension would preclude honest or realistic treatment of subjects that are retained in the curriculum.

The curricular significance of sexuality can be seen more clearly by comparison with a point of consensus that emerged from the "secular humanism" case, in which both sides agreed that U.S. history would be distorted by the exclusion of religion, which (like sexuality in my argument here) is an integral dimension of historical reality. In *Smith v. Mobile*

(1987), one of the complaints against the high school history texts is that they systematically excluded references to religion and its importance in the history of the United States. Advocates on both sides agreed that this would be an unacceptable deficiency in textbooks on American history, since repression of religious references would leave only an ideologically distorted version of the country's history. The two sides differed on the degree to which the books at issue actually suffered from this defect, but everyone agreed that stories about the Pilgrims, or about Martin Luther King's role in the civil rights movement, would simply be false and unacceptable if they were told without explaining the religious background, motivations, visions, and ideals of the people who have given us this history.

Theoretical Perspectives

A curriculum that is true to the reality that it purports to teach about cannot begin with the systematic repression of any of the essential dimensions that are fundamental to that manifold reality, including the religious, sexual, linguistic, economic, or any other dimensions that may be essential to the subject being taught. It is not as if there are detachable sexual parts that can be separated from the remaining corpus of the subject being taught. Any aspect of the subject, rather, may need to be considered as its existence is determined in relation to a number of dimensions all at once. Evangelical religion, for example, can no more be understood as existing outside of the sexual dimension than can sexuality be understood outside of the religious and spiritual dimensions of human life. The phenomenologist Merleau-Ponty (1945/1962) has explained how sexuality must be incorporated, along with spatiality and temporality, as a fundamental dimension of our human existence:

> Existence . . . cannot be anything—spatial, sexual, temporal—without being so in its entirety, without taking up and carrying forward its "attributes" and making them into so many dimensions of its being, with the result that an analysis of any one of them that is at all searching really touches upon subjectivity itself. . . . all problems are concentric. . . . If we succeed in understanding the subject, it will not be in its pure form, but by seeking it at the intersection of its dimensions. (pp. 410–11)

The understanding that is called for here can be supported from a variety of theoretical perspectives. The development of Michel Foucault's theoretical perspective is exemplary. As holder of the chair in History of Systems of Thought at the Collège de France, Foucault began with sweeping "archeological" investigations of the human sciences (1966) and of epistemic formations on a global scale (1969). These studies led him, however, to the conclusion that the disciplines of knowledge cannot be understood without comprehending their relation to the history of sexuality (1976–1984). In his chapter in this volume, Carlson cites Foucault's work to show how discourses *on* sexuality must be understood within the history of broader cultural discourses. We are now prepared to take a further step, in recognizing that the discourses of literature, history, and other school subjects cannot be taught and learned authentically if cut off from the context of the broader discourses within which they are embedded, discourses that are irreducibly sexual as well as literary, historical, religious, economic, and so forth.

Feminist scholars have of course been at the forefront of theoretical work showing the inadequacy of desexualized notions of human understanding and existence. For example, Robin Schott (1988) demonstrates the disabling ascetic bias in traditional theories of cognition; and Sandra Harding (1986) provides a critical feminist analysis of the natural and social science disciplines. Valerie Walkerdine (1988) demonstrates how a feminist perspective reveals the sexual dimension of mathematics teaching, in which the girls (as well as the lower-class boys) are more likely to be instructed in a mathematical discourse of immediate and transitory wish-fulfillment, associated with the "Imaginary order" (as described by the French psychoanalytic theorist Jacques Lacan). Meanwhile, the boys (especially those from the more privileged classes) are instructed in a more abstract, context-independent mathematical discourse, associated with the Symbolic order, in which the satisfaction of fulfilling transient wishes is supplanted by pursuit of a more enduring "mastery of reason," by which desire itself is to be conquered, even at the cost of alienation from self and others in the world of concrete, sensual reality.

Despite the enormous relevance and importance of these and other theoretical perspectives, they do not speak for themselves in response to questions from those who are embroiled in the thick of conflicts over censorship in education. The pioneering work of curriculum theorists (e.g., van Manen, 1990; Grumet, 1988; Pagano, 1990) drawing from phenomenology, psychoanalysis, feminism, and other theoretical perspectives is invaluable for purposes of demonstrating the need to understand education in a holistic way, including sexual and other constitutive dimensions of the curriculum and school experience, even though none of these works is concerned with narrowly defined issues of sexuality as such. Their concrete, experientially grounded accounts of educational processes provide a basis for substantial theoretical contributions to the traditions from which their work is derived. They also provide models for the translation of those theoretical perspectives into the kind of detailed and specific accounts of pedagogy that can be recognized and used by school practitioners in the dialogical practice of helping the public, and other professionals in both law and education, to understand how education really works, and why it could not be expected to survive a systematic censorship of sexuality (or any other fundamentally constitutive dimension of discourse and understanding) from the curriculum.

This is a free country, as they say, and we are free to say whatever we want to about theories of the First Amendment or of constitutional interpretation As educators, however, we are likely to be heard merely as opinionated laypersons by the judges and lawyers arguing these cases—until, that is, we begin to articulate the fundamental understandings of curriculum that would confute their formalistic analyses of education. The lawyers and judges are themselves the laypersons, after all, when it comes to understanding matters of curriculum and instruction, for which the contributions of educators are now needed in providing theoretical reflection on long years of practical experience in the schools.

Safe Texts: The Prophylactic Curriculum

We have briefly noted an array of perspectives that clarify the theoretical and practical significance of basic insights shared by teachers through direct experience, such as the understanding that authentic texts will naturally reflect the reality of human life in all its integrated unity. To look at Thomas's *Down These Mean Streets* (1974) as an example, we might note that the glossary of 135 items contains eight sexual references (e.g., *"chinga:* intercourse" and*"puta:* whore"—or ten, if *culo* and *fundillo* (ass, rear end) are counted as sexual terms); but it also contains no less than seven terms referring to religion. The novel as a whole is actually an autobiographical story of religious redemption, culminating in a chapter titled "I swears to God and the Virgin"; and Thomas followed this book with another titled *Savior, Savior, Hold My Hand.* Censors who would ban the book because it includes sexual references, but who might welcome more attention to religious themes, run the risk of excluding all but the most inauthentic, sanitized, implausible, and ineffective texts from use in the curriculum—thus reinforcing the notion popular among so many students that they cannot expect to learn anything real in school, since what they are presented with in the classroom has no relationship to life in the real world.

Yet, this is a risk that censors seem willing to take. For many, it appears that their ideal curriculum would not be a source of learning, but a barrier device to obstruct learning. Apparently, they lack the faith in their own beliefs and values that would support them in promoting education, with confidence in the ability of their beliefs and values to be adopted willingly by informed and educated students. Instead of promoting education, these censors demand a prophylactic curriculum to protect students from exposure to alternative ideas, as in *Mozert v.*

Hawkins County Board of Education (1987), where the district court judge noted plaintiffs' expressed fear that children exposed to the Holt reading series "might adopt the views of a feminist, a humanist, a pacifist, an anti-Christian, a vegetarian, or an advocate of 'one-world government'" (647 F. Supp. at 1199).

The demand for a prophylactic curriculum may be characterized by an insistence that authentic texts from the real world should be avoided, and that students should be given only texts that have been artificially developed especially for classroom use, as in *Brubaker v. Board of Education* (1974), where the court upheld the firing of three teachers in 1970 for distributing a brochure on the 1969 rock music festival at Woodstock. The court expressed particular concern over the sexuality expressed in lines such as this: "Woodstock felt like a swell of energy, wave of elation that fills the heart *and flows on over the lover beside you*" (at 975, emphasis added by the court). One point in the school board's statement of reasons for firing the teachers, noted with approval by the court, was that the brochure had not been specially prepared "as a tool for school instruction" (at 979).

In my own teaching of pre-service teacher education classes, I have heard stories of foreign-language teachers being challenged for using popular European magazines such as *Der Stern* or *Paris Match* because of uncovered breasts appearing in some of the photographs. The willingness to exclude authentic French or German sources even from a French or German language class is epitomized by the statute upheld in *Ambach* (1979), which would prevent a French or German citizen from being certified to teach their own native language, for fear of the alien influences that they might introduce. The demand for a prophylactic curriculum has also been expressed in calls to rid classrooms and school libraries of works by any writer who is or may have been homosexual, including Emily Dickinson, Willa Cather, Tennessee Williams, Oscar Wilde, T. E. Lawrence, Jean Genet, Gertrude Stein, Virginia Woolf, Walt Whitman, André Gide, Jean Cocteau, Gore Vidal, John Milton, Hans Christian Anderson, Marcel Proust, Horatio Alger Jr., Truman Capote, and Rod McKuen (Jenkinson, 1979/1982, p. 85).

DEALING WITH CENSORSHIP

Several sources are available providing information and potential contacts for teachers who may be confronted with a censorship challenge. The National Council of Teachers of English (Davis, 1979), Phi Delta Kappa (Jenkinson, 1986), and People for the American Way (Hulsizer, 1989) have all published materials that provide information on censorship incidents and trends, reports of results in legal cases, strategies for avoiding conflicts and for succeeding when the conflicts cannot be avoided, descriptions of the censorship groups and their strategies, and the names and addresses of contacts who might be able to provide further information and assistance. The organizations publishing these reports can be expected to produce updated resources from time to time.

Dutile (1986) provides a thorough critical analysis of statutory and case law with implications for several aspects of sexuality and the curriculum. The single most extensive compilation and analysis of school censorship incidents is Burress (1989). The most comprehensive periodical report is the *Newsletter on Intellectual Freedom* put out six times a year by the Office for Intellectual Freedom of the American Library Association. This office is an essential contact any time the school library is involved in a censorship dispute. (Addresses for this and other agencies are provided in the annotated resources section at the end of this book.) People for the American Way also publishes a report each August (e.g., 1990) compiling and analyzing incidents over the past academic year. For teachers who do not know who else to call for help, this organization would be a good initial contact. They will often be able to refer teachers to the most appropriate source of help for their particular problem, and in some cases (including the *Mozert* and *Smith v. Mobile* cases discussed in this chapter) they have even taken on a major role in providing legal representation, sometimes in cooperation with other organizations such as the American Civil Liberties Union. The best source of help will often be professional organizations such as the National Education Association or the American Federation of Teachers and their state and local affiliates. Teachers in particular fields such as social studies, English, biology, and health education should also check their national organizations to find out what help may be available.

Even before rounding up allies and preparing for war, however, teachers would often be well advised to see how much support they can get from their own local schools and communities. In many cases teachers faced with censorship demands have been decisively supported by the parents and community. Censors should not be permitted to portray themselves as representing the cause of parental rights against the teachers; the majority of parents, once they do become involved, generally support the curriculum that responsible teachers have developed for their children. Censors should also not be permitted to portray the issue as a conflict between religious parents and antireligious (or "secular humanist") educators. In *Mozert*, for example, a very conservative Southern Baptist community supported the curriculum against a fringe group that portrayed itself as taking God's side against the infidels.

Likewise, teachers should avoid whenever possible allowing challenges to develop into conflicts between teachers and administrators. Very often the administrators begin by supporting teachers and librarians in the advice they give to their superiors (e.g., a principal's advice to the superintendent, or the latter's advice to the school board). Once a decision to oppose a teacher or librarian has been made at a higher level, however, the administrator in most cases carries out that decision without further argument. It may therefore be especially important to cultivate respect, understanding, and good communication on curriculum matters before the administrator is put into the position of having to respond to a censorship challenge.

In general, the best provision against efforts to censor sexuality from the curriculum is an understanding, in advance of any challenge, of why sexuality must not be excluded. Although there are obvious points to be made against elimination of specific sexual information in particular (e.g., information on preventing sexually transmitted diseases), my analysis suggests another line of argument. Instead of seeing such issues in terms of ideologies concerning sex in particular, I have suggested that there are more fundamental ideologies involved: ideologies of curriculum, of education, and of cognition in their broadest aspects. One consequence of this conclusion is to reveal that far more is at stake in efforts to censor sexuality from the curriculum than the concerns of those involved directly, for example, in teaching sex education. Rather, the integrity of the entire curriculum, and of the mission of the schools in general, is at stake. If the administration, parents, and community can be brought to understand how these broader interests are implicated in the censorship of sexuality, then the beleaguered literature or sex education teacher should no longer lack support in the face of such challenges to the curriculum.

REFERENCES

Ambach v. Norwick, 441 U.S. 68 (1979).

Arons, S. (1986). *Compelling belief: The culture of American schooling.* Amherst: University of Massachusetts Press. (Original work published 1983)

Aubrey v. School District of Philadelphia, 63 Pa. Cmwlth. 330, 437 A.2d 1306 (1981).

Bethel School District v. Fraser, 478 U.S. 675 (1986).

Brubaker v. Board of Education, School District 149, Cook County, Ill., 502 F.2d 973 (7th Cir. 1974).

Burress, L. (1989). *Battle of the books: Literary censorship in the public schools, 1950–1985.* Metuchen, NJ: Scarecrow.

Childress, A. (1982). *A hero ain't nothin' but a sandwich.* New York: Avon/Flare. (Original work published 1973)

Childress, A. (1989). Black authors, banned books. *Newsletter on Intellectual Freedom, 38*(6), 212, 241–43.

Cornwell v. State Board of Education, 314 F. Supp. 340 (Md. 1969).

Davis, J. E. (Ed.). (1979). *Dealing with censorship.* Urbana, IL: National Council of Teachers of English.

Dean v. Timpson Independent School District, 486 F. Supp. 302 (E.D. Tex. 1979).

DiBona v. Matthews, 220 CalApp. 3d 1329, 269 Cal. Rptr. 882 (Cal.App. 4 Dist. 1990).

Dutile, F. N. (1986). *Sex, schools, and the law: A study of the legal implications of sexual matters relating to the public school curriculum (with a separate chapter on sex education), the public school library, the personal lives of teachers and students, and the student press.* Springfield, IL: Charles C. Thomas.

Fisher v. Fairbanks North Star Borough School District, 704 P.2d 213 (Alaska 1985).

Foucault, M. (1966). *Les mots et les choses: Une archéologie des sciences humaine.* Paris: Gallimard.

Foucault, M. (1969). *L'archéologie du savoir.* Paris: Gallimard.

Foucault, M. (1976–1984). *Histoire de la sexualité* (Vols. 1–3). Paris: Gallimard.

[Fraser] See Bethel v. Fraser.

Grumet, M. R. (1988). *Bitter milk: Women and teaching.* Amherst: University of Massachusetts Press.

Harding, S. (1986). *The science question in feminism.* Ithaca: Cornell University Press.

Hazelwood School District v. Kuhlmeier, 484 U.S. 260 (1988).

Hulsizer, D. (1989). *Protecting the freedom to learn: A citizen's guide.* Washington: People for the American Way.

Island Trees . . . School District v. Pico, 457 U.S. 853 (1982).

Jenkinson, E. B. (1982). *Censors in the classroom.* New York: Avon. (Original work published by Southern Illinois University Press, 1979)

Jenkinson, E. B. (1986). *The schoolbook protest movement: 40 questions and answers.* Bloomington, IN: Phi Delta Kappa Educational Foundation.

Keefe v. Geanakos, 418 F.2d 359 (1st Cir. 1969).

Lifton, R. J. (1969, September). The young and the old: Notes on a new history, part I. *Atlantic Monthly,* pp. 47–54.

Lifton, R. J., & Markusen, E. (1990). *The genocidal mentality: Nazi Holocaust and nuclear threat.* New York: Basic Books.

Mercer v. Michigan State Board of Education, 379 F. Supp. 580 (E.D. Mich. 1974), aff'd mem. 419 U.S. 1081 (1974).

Merleau-Ponty, M. (1962). *Phenomenology of perception.* London: Routledge & Kegan Paul. (Original work published 1945)

Minarcini v. Strongsville City School District, 541 F.2d 577 (6th Cir. 1976).

Mozert v. Hawkins County Board of Education, 827 F.2d 1058 (6th Cir. 1987), reversing 647 F. Supp. 1194 (1986), cert. denied, 484 U.S. 1066, 108 S.Ct. 1029 (1988).

Pagano, J. (1990). *Exiles and communities: Teaching in the patriarchal wilderness.* Albany: SUNY Press.

Parducci v. Rutland, 316 F. Supp. 352 (M.D. Ala. 1970).

People for the American Way (1990). *Attacks on the freedom to learn, 1989–1990 report.* Washington: Author.

[Pico] See Island trees . . . School District v. Pico.

Presidents Council, District 25 v. Community School Board No. 25, 457 F.2d 289 (2nd Cir. 1972).

Right to Read Defense Committee v. School Committee of Chelsea, 454 F.Supp. 703 (D. Mass. 1978).

Schott, R. M. (1988). *Cognition and eros: A critique of the Kantian paradigm.* Boston: Beacon.

Smith et al. v. Board of School Commissioners of Mobile County, 827 F.2d 684 (11th Cir. 1987).

Smith v. Ricci, 89 N.J. 514, 446 A.2d 501 (1982), appeal denied, 459 U.S. 962.

Thomas, P. (1974). *Down these mean streets.* New York: Vintage. (Original work published 1967)

Tinker v. Des Moines . . . School District, 393 U.S. 503 (1969).

van Manen, M. (1990). *Researching lived experience: Human science for an action sensitive pedagogy.* Albany: SUNY Press.

Virgil v. School Board of Columbia County, Florida, 862 F.2d 1517 (11th Cir. 1989), affirming 677 F. Supp. 1547 (1988).

Walden, J. C., & Culverhouse, R. (1989, October 12). Homosexuality and public education. *Education Law Reporter, 55*(1), 7–31.

Walkerdine, V. (1988). *The mastery of reason: Cognitive development and the production of rationality.* London and New York: Routledge.

Ware v. Valley Stream High School District, 545 N.Y.S. 2d 316 (1989).

Whatley, M. H. (1988). Photographic images of Blacks in sexuality texts. *Curriculum Inquiry, 18*(2), 137–55.

Whitson, J. A. (1991). *Constitution and curriculum: Hermeneutical semiotics of cases and controversies in education, law, and social science.* London and Philadelphia: Falmer.

Zykan v. Warsaw, 631 F.2d 1300 (7th Cir. 1980).

Whose Sexuality Is It Anyway?

MARIAMNE H. WHATLEY

Even in the late afternoon drowsiness of my 3-hour health education class in a teacher education program, any mention of sexuality education sparks an immediate response. However, the interest is not in such potentially provocative issues as safer sex but in safer teaching; one of the first questions from the class is usually whether they will get "in trouble" for teaching this material. When I ask for a definition of "in trouble," the stated fears range from irate calls from parents to being fired from their jobs. It is clear that both the teachers in training and the experienced teachers in my classes have picked up a strong message that it is dangerous to teach about sexuality and that every care must be taken to avoid attracting notice or stirring up controversy.

FEAR OF SEX EDUCATION

All the data I cite to the class about public support, especially from parents, for sexuality education in the schools does nothing to assuage these fears, as it is clear to the students that one disgruntled person in their local community is sufficient to do damage. As James Sears points out in Chapter 1, much of sexuality education is designed and presented to avoid community conflict. Adapting readily to this approach, teachers in training quickly assume a defensive teaching position in discussing sexuality education. It is not that they have lost their idealism, but rather that they have put it aside temporarily for this specific topic.

Instead of focusing on strategies to teach sexuality in the best ways to facilitate communication with students on this complex and sensitive topic, the class effort ends up directed toward developing strategies to avoid conflict and controversy. These teachers in training constantly generate worst-case scenarios, suggestions, and creative solutions ("I heard that if the students ask you questions, then it's o.k. to answer, but you can't bring it up directly yourself" or "What if we just leave condoms in an unlocked drawer but never actually *give* a student one?"). Comprehensive curriculum development, lesson plans, and learning activities seem driven not by theories of education but by the fear of attack.

Much of this fear seems to be the result of the conservative shift in the debates around sexuality education due to the constant attacks from the New Right. Just as this pressure has shifted debates on economic, social, and other educational issues, the New Right and religious fundamentalist groups have created a climate in which the most moderate approaches to sexuality education can seem radical (Trudell & Whatley, in press). Any discussion of values, choices, or decision making (beyond the decision to say no) is identified as suspect. For example, the curriculum *Values and Choices* (Search Institute, 1986) recently came under strong attack in one Wisconsin community as being too liberal and permissive. As some progressive parents rushed to defend it, they discovered it was in fact a fairly conservative curriculum. Bonnie Trudell and I evaluated both *Values and Choices* and the favored curriculum of the New Right, *Sex Respect* (Mast, 1986), in terms of sex equity issues (Trudell & Whatley, in press). Even though these two are frequently set up in opposition to each other and are characterized as having huge differences, they actually share many messages and themes. The broad message in both is that abstinence, especially for young women, is the only choice, and this message is delivered by emphasizing the negative consequences for teenagers of having intercourse. The attacks on *Values and Choices* have been largely precipitated by the inclusion of a small amount of contraceptive information and an *optional* video sequence on homosexuality.

As with many other issues, the Right controls the terms of the debate. Rather than arguing for the teaching of the more "controversial" issues, such as sexual pleasure, gay and lesbian issues, abortion, contraception, and values in sexual decision making, sexuality educators find themselves trying to make their teaching look even more innocuous and based on abstinence. This is certainly understandable; it is hard for me to keep discussing abortion as an option when students walk out of class in protest or deny even the basic facts about health risks of abortion compared to pregnancy. In Chapter 3 James Whitson addresses some crucial debates about control of the curriculum through various forms of censorship, but this censorship will be unnecessary if sexuality educators self-censor in response to objections they might face.

This self-censorship and other attempts to appease those who attack sexuality education can undermine any progressive work that has been accomplished in this area. In the same way that it has become difficult to distinguish Democrats from Republicans in the United States and Labour from the Tories in Great Britain, we may no longer be able to distinguish the so-called progressive approaches to sexuality education from the conservative ones. As Sears pointed out in Chapter 1, from 1980 to 1990 the number of states that require sexuality education increased from 3 to 22. However, that is hardly a victory if the mandates do not contain provisions for sexuality education that encourages or, at least, permits the presentation of material that is often eliminated as too controversial. In addition, perhaps, the act of *mandating* sexuality education also puts strict limits on the content and approach. If a specific subject is required throughout the state, it must not offend any vocal constituents of the legislators who vote on these issues. It is easy to imagine that the various compromises in a state legislature might result in a bill requiring sexuality education, but loaded down with the provisions that it would be completely based on abstinence, with no mention of contraception, abortion, homosexuality (except if presented in terms of problems or dangers), or sexual pleasure. There are certainly many situations, short of this extreme, in which educators might suggest that *no* sexuality education may be better than what is available.

WHAT DOES SEXUALITY EDUCATION HAVE TO DO WITH REAL LIFE?

If the parameters of sexuality education are even partially determined by the fear of controversy, then educators are probably ignoring what should be a major determinant of sexuality curricula—the reality of their students' lives. James Whitson discusses in Chapter 3 the "notion popular among so many students that they cannot expect to learn anything real in school, since what they are presented with in the classroom has no relationship to life in the real world." In Bonnie Trudell's (1990) ethnographic study of sexuality education, one of the most telling comments from a student was that the course content on sexuality was "just the stuff you had to know. I don't know if we'll ever use it" (p. 88). If educators address the reality of their students' lives, there will be controversy. Students are sexually active in every way possible, with themselves and with others, feel sexual desires, are sexually exploited, become pregnant, cause pregnancy, have abortions, have babies, catch diseases, explore their own sexuality, explore and exploit others' sexualities, are sexually violent, wrestle with issues of power and control. What does a lecture on the dangers of premarital intercourse say to them?

The recommendations that Dennis Carlson makes at the end of Chapter 2 are very important in terms of working from the real concerns of students. He suggests that sexuality education be seen in the context of cultural studies, liberal arts, and history, stating that "so conceived, sexuality education becomes critical and analytical and thus both personally and socially empowering." If the textbook content is any guide, much of the sexuality education at the college level does address historical issues and gives some cross-cultural perspective. This approach, however, has not filtered down to the high schools. In order to introduce sexuality in a broader cultural perspective, educators need to be more aware of their students' sexual knowledge and concerns, using these to help them formulate the approaches they may take to a number of issues.

Recently, I saw on television an example of the interest students will show when sexuality issues are recognized as part of the reality of their lives. On a local news program, there was coverage of a forum at a high school on the issue of parental consent for abortion. The forum was co-sponsored by student anti-abortion and pro-choice groups. It is clear that the issue of parental consent is directly relevant to their lives but that they are often not considered players in the debate. In her comments, an antiabortion legislator referred to "abortion mills" and was immediately challenged by an angry woman high school student who insisted that she should refer to these as abortion clinics. The condescending reply of the legislator that the student was "spunky" for calling her on her language was not well received by the student body. Another woman student made a forceful speech, arguing that nobody else should be making decisions about her body and that, since she was the one who "laid down and did what [she] did," the decision about the consequences was also hers. Watching this, I wondered if there were people who really thought that if you did not discuss these issues in the schools, the students would never find out about abortion. It was also a strong reminder of the ways in which the voices of students are unheard in the debates that most directly affect them. The student audience looked deeply involved and attentive; the ones who spoke had strong feelings that reflected an analysis of issues around power and control over their bodies and their sexuality. These students were ready for a sexuality education that would center on these issues and that would give them a chance to develop their views in a setting that helped them see issues of sexuality in a full social, cultural, and political context.

Many educators have argued for bringing discussions and analysis of popular culture to the classroom in order to bridge the gap between school knowledge and lived knowledge. Formal sexuality education in the schools provides only a fraction of the sexuality knowledge students acquire. For example, in analyzing the construction of men's sexuality in school sex education and in adolescent films, I found that what appeared to be issues of concern to young men were left out of much of the formal sexuality curriculum (Whatley, 1988). While progressive educators seemed sensitive to allaying anxieties about inappropriate erections, wet dreams, and penis size, they ignored the issues of power and control—exemplified in such recurring themes as sexuality as conquest and women as trophies—examined the films adolescents saw as "authentic." By paying closer attention to what adolescents are responding to in music videos and films, educators may be more effective in identifying their concerns around sexuality and in initiating a critique of the construction of gender and sexuality in our culture.

Obviously, bringing popular culture into the classroom is going to stir up controversy, especially at a time when there are battles over direct censorship of the arts, including photographic exhibits and rap concerts, and censorship through lack of funding of a wide range of art forms, including poetry and theater. When there are debates about what should be allowed for general public consumption, even for adults, it is clear that what might be considered appropriate in the schools is even more limited.

However, it is important to recognize that popular films and music videos can play a role in shaping sexuality discourses circulating among adolescents. For example, Madonna's video "Justify My Love" became the focus of a great deal of media attention when it was banned from MTV. One of the fascinating aspects of the controversy was that all the reports in the media and all personal recountings might have been about different videos. It seemed to work as a video Rorschach in which people saw their fantasies or their worst fears. (Were there two women kissing? Were there men dressed as woman? Or were they women dressed as men?) In a video that is apparently about sexual fantasies and about celebrating the diversity (the all-purpose liberal phrase) of human sexual experience and desires, this range of responses is probably very appropriate.

I am *not* recommending the viewing of "Justify My Love" in the classroom. I am, however, recommending that, because themes around sexuality are so pervasive and even dominant in the media popular with adolescents, these issues can be appropriately and usefully raised in the classroom. When there is an obviously popular film or music video, educators can take advantage of the opportunity to raise important sexuality issues. For example, by banning "Justify My Love," MTV has assured a great deal of knowledge about the video among adults and adolescents; therefore, a relatively informed discussion would be possible. Sexual fantasies are usually considered appropriate for analysis in terms of adult sexuality, but not in terms of adolescents. Discussion of the issues of sexual fantasy raised in this video may be a good way to lead into the concept that fantasies are a way of safely exploring while maintaining control, and that they do not necessarily represent what we want in reality.

By paying attention to what adolescents are listening to and watching, educators not only acquire information about interests and concerns, but also have a means of entering discussion. For example, I have used the popular films of John Hughes, such as *The Breakfast Club*, to work with students on critiquing rigid gender roles and the double standards of sexual behavior. As another example, returning to Madonna, she has portrayed herself in her videos and in interviews as a woman in control of her own sexuality, and she has a devoted following of young women who respond to "this sort of empowering fantasy" (Fiske, 1989, p. 113). It would not be difficult to initiate discussion about what it means to control one's own sexuality by approaching the topic through an analysis and critique of Madonna's image. Some of the most important issues in terms of how we live as sexual beings in the world can be approached and analyzed through fairly accessible popular culture examples.

CONCLUSION

Just as "Justify My Love" serves as an inkblot test, so does sexuality education. Many critics see in it not what is actually there but what they fear, and supporters, instead of arguing for a thoughtful, comprehensive curriculum, try to avoid including anything that might trigger one of those fears. Many educators discuss values clarification (one of those phrases that usually evokes negative reactions from the New Right) to help students learn to make informed decisions. Perhaps as sexuality educators, we need to do more values clarification for ourselves in terms of our teaching. We need to develop our view of sexuality education from a position in which we have clearly identified what we want it to be in its ideal form, not what we can "get away with" before the watchdogs of the Right bite us.

Recently, in a reversal of the conservative trend, two parents brought a suit against a school board to stop the use of a curriculum that they felt violated sex-equity legislation and, to the surprise of many, won. In a school board election, a candidate was soundly defeated *because* of his homophobic stand against teaching "tolerance" for diverse sexual preferences. It is possible that if educators act from a position of strength in which they can support what they do, more community members, parents, and voters like the ones above will be visible. Progressive sexuality educators cannot cede the whole territory of sexuality education to the Right. There must be a concerted effort to identify what we value in sexuality education, to establish what students and their parents (not just a vocal few) want from it, and to make decisions about inclusion of material in sexuality education based on what will make it truly useful in our students' lives.

REFERENCES

Fiske, J. (1989). *Reading the popular.* Boston: Unwin Hyman.
Mast, C. K. (1986). *Sex respect: The option of true sexual freedom.* Golf, IL: Project Respect.

Search Institute. (1986). *Human sexuality: Values and choices*. Minneapolis, MN: Author.

Trudell, B. (1990). Selection, presentation, and student interpretation of an educational film on teenage pregnancy: A critical ethnographic investigation. In E. Ellsworth & M. H. Whatley (Eds.), *The ideology of images in educational media: Hidden curriculums in the classroom* (pp. 74–106). New York: Teachers College Press.

Trudell, B., & Whatley, M. H. (in press). Sex equity principles for evaluating sexuality education materials. In S. Klein (Ed.), *Sex equity and sexuality in education*. Albany, NY: SUNY Press.

Whatley, M. H. (1988). Raging hormones and powerful cars: The construction of men's sexuality in school sex education and popular adolescent films. *Journal of Education, 170*(3), 100–121.

Part II

GENDER AND SEXUALITY

Gender—the personal conviction about being male or female—and sexuality—the desire to express one's emotional or erotic feelings toward another human being in a physical manner—are two interrelated though distinctive concepts. In this society, the social significance of being male and female and the sexual expectations, responsibilities, and privileges held by men and women are interwoven in a patriarchal and heterosexist web of power and desire, childhood and adolescent scripts, and culture and ideology. The authors in this section discuss one or more of these dimensions as they explore social, political, and curricular implications of our too often taken-for-granted conceptions of gender and sexuality.

In Chapter 4, Mara Sapon-Shevin and Jesse Goodman bring together male and female perspectives to examine the way in which conceptualizations of "womanhood" and "manhood" (sexual scripting) and the relations between men and women are shaped by the sexuality education students receive (or fail to receive). Through a combination of autobiographical reflection and analysis, and the use of critical social and feminist theories, the authors discuss the development of sexual scripts that reify gendered relationships dividing adolescents into two separate but unequal sexual worlds: the adolescent male world of sexual power and prowess that devalues sensitivity and introspection, the adolescent female world of sexual passivity and shame that stymies sexual curiosity and inhibits sexual knowledge. Recalling their childhood pasts in which "sex was something that men wanted, women had to be careful about, and nobody could talk about," these authors explore ways in which schools can work to provide experiences and teaching that allows (and encourages) men and women to see each other as allies in the struggle for sexual and gender equity.

A manifestation of how males and females view themselves and the "opposite sex" as sexual beings is sexual harrassment—the focus of Chapter 5. Often ignored and generally unreported, this distressingly pervasive and destructive presence in our schools further reinforces conventional sexual scripts. Eleanor Linn, Nan Stein, Jackie Young, and Saundra Davis illuminate how all students—as victims, perpetrators or bystanders—are affected by the presence of sexual harassment in the school's hidden curriculum. Following an overview of the legal and philosophical approaches to understanding sexual harassment, the authors describe the power-relations aspects of sexual harassment as it applies to K–12 schools. The chapter concludes with a review of existing programs and resources for compliant management and prevention programs in schools.

At a very early age children are socialized into sexual roles—being a "real boy" or a "real girl." This current organization of sexuality for children, particularly the sexual repression and social constraints commonplace in many elementary schools, has a political dimension. While none of the authors in this book would contest the interrelationships of gender and sexuality vis-à-vis the political culture, there would likely be considerable disagreement regarding specific curriculum and pedagogy. The debates that took place in the 1930s regarding educational indoctrination and liberation between progressive educators and social reconstructionists is illustrative (Bowers, 1969). Chapter 6, by Christine LaCerva, is a welcome addition to this edited collection; it raises this critical issue while describing the pedagogy of the Barbara Taylor School, which is based on social therapy, a controversial approach advanced by Fred Newman and his associates. Although social therapy is criticized by some as indoctrinating (Berlet, 1987a, 1987b; Flynn, 1988; Kelley, 1987), LaCerva provides a different assessment of this particular therapeutic approach, the school, and its pedagogy.

In Chapter 7, I draw upon anthropological, historical, and sociological studies to elaborate on the linkages between gender and sexuality. This chapter explores the problematic concept of gender and sexual identities by illuminating the impact of culture and ideology. Appropriating feminist theory, I argue that "the social construction of gender and sexuality (i.e., the transference of biological divisions of maleness and femaleness into social categories), the delegation of human roles and traits according to conceptions of femininity and masculinity, and the proscription of same-sex activities rationalize a particular way of organizing society—patriarchy." Thus, challenging gendered and sexual scripts has profound political implications that explain, in part, the resistance to a wide range of reforms ranging from rejecting biologically based sexuality education curricula to recognizing same-sex relationships within and outside of the school. I conclude, however, that these well-intentioned reforms reify gender and sexuality and I admonish educators to adopt a critically based sexuality curriculum that encourages critical thinking, embraces sexual diversity, and challenges categorical thinking.

Mary Margaret Fonow and Debian Marty explore the pedagogical implications of this constructionist view of sexuality by evaluating their efforts in teaching about sexual identity in higher education. Data for this article were gathered from hundreds of general education students enrolled in an Introduction to Women's Studies course. The authors analyzed open-ended student evaluation forms, conducted interviews, and made classroom observations. Chapter 8 details pedagogical strategies such as panels, oral histories, role playing, and films that can challenge students' categorical thinking. At the same time, the authors discuss student and institutional resistance as well as ethical considerations.

Susan Shurberg Klein, a staff member of the U.S. Office of Education, has written extensively in the area of gender equity. As a private citizen, Klein addresses three questions in her commentary to Part II: "Why should we care about gender and sexuality when we try to improve the school curriculum? What are the key ways that gender and sexuality interact? What can you do to improve the treatment of sexuality in the formal and informal curricula to benefit females and males?"

REFERENCES

Berlet, C. (1987a). *Clouds blur the rainbow: The other side of the New Alliance Party.* Cambridge, MA: Political Research Associates.

Berlet, C. (1987b). Fiction and the New Alliance Party. *Radical America, 21*(5), 7–16.

Bowers, C. (1969). *The progressive educator and the Depression: The radical years.* New York: Random House.

Flynn, S. (1988, February 26–March 3). Thunder on the left: The cultish ways of the New Alliance Party. *The Boston Phoenix,* pp. 1, 8.

Kelley, K. (1987, December 23). New Alliance: Therapy cult or political party? *Guardian,* p. 3.

CHAPTER 4

Learning to Be the Opposite Sex

Sexuality Education and Sexual Scripting in Early Adolescence

MARA SAPON-SHEVIN AND JESSE GOODMAN

It is widely recognized that as children age into early adolescence, they become increasingly active in the formation of their sexual identities. Early adolescents' understandings of concepts such as eroticism, desire, arousal, intimacy, and responsibility are influenced by socially learned activities and symbols. Several sociologists (e.g., Gagnon & Simon, 1973; Thorne & Luria, 1986) suggest that these learned meanings become "sexual scripts" that children use to a large extent in the formation of their sexual identities. These scripts define for early adolescents who does what with whom, what activities are appropriate when, and what it (sexual feelings, attitudes, behaviors) "all means." As Miller and Simon (1981) note, these scripts are closely related to adult, societal views of gender and sexuality.

One of the most disturbing messages of this sexual scripting is that human sexuality is specialized by gender; that is, boys need not be knowledgeable nor too concerned about girls' sexuality, and vice versa. Although boys and girls exist in close physical proximity, in our society they live in culturally separate worlds (Best, 1983; Eder & Hallinan, 1978; Lockheed, 1985). Schofield (1982/1989) observes that gender segregation is stronger than racial segregation in elementary and middle school and suggests that due to the potential for "romantic" implications, cross-gendered heterosexual friendships become increasingly difficult to maintain as boys and girls enter middle school. Shrum (1988) indicates that the cultural and psychological distance that exists between boys and girls is greater during late elementary and middle school years than either before or after. Thorne and Luria (1986) note that this "living in different worlds" is particularly strong when it comes to heterosexual sexual scripting. In short, adolescent boys and girls know little or nothing about each others' sexual scripting." The messages that early adolescents receive from living in two different worlds is that when it comes to sexuality, members of the opposite gender are relative "aliens." As a result, there is often mistrust, fear, and vulnerability associated with interactions between male and female early adolescents.

In this chapter we argue that the conventional sexual scripting that young adolescents receive in our society needs to be directly challenged in our schools. We call upon educators to help young adolescents learn how they can become allies rather aliens to each other. Toward this goal, we first explore, through autobiographical analysis, ways in which the scripting affects the lives of real people. Next, we analyze conventional sexual education materials, and then give a brief illustration of the type of curricular effort we feel is needed. Finally, we argue that sexuality education must be linked to broader social and political struggles for justice.

AUTOBIOGRAPHICAL REFLECTIONS: OUR OWN STORIES

It is important to emphasize that the analysis that follows is rooted in the lives of white, able-bodied, middle-class, second-generation Jewish, heterosexual individuals who were born in the late 1940s and early 1950s and raised in urban and suburban communities. The adolescent sexual scripting of people of color, homosexuals, and differently abled individuals, while sharing some similarities with our experiences, will naturally differ in significant ways.

Jesse's Story: "So You Got to Second Base"

I thought it would be relatively easy to write an autobiographical reflection of the sexual scripting I constructed as a young adolescent. However, once I began, I soon discovered how difficult it would be. What should I say? How much of my own sexual struggles should I reveal? Is it safe to come out from behind my academic jargon, which can be used so easily as a mask? This strain to express myself soon illuminated for me one of the most powerful scripts I internalized as a boy: When it comes to sexuality, it is better to keep silent and not disclose my feelings or ideas, especially as part of a public forum.

During the early 1960s, when I was in middle school, boys were not exposed to any information on sexuality. I remember, as Mara will describe, watching the girls in sixth grade leave the room for a special "sex movie." The message we got—similar to the one Mara was given—was that we were not even supposed to ask the girls about this movie. Officially speaking, information regarding sex was accessible only to girls, and it was taboo to discuss this information with them. I could only fantasize what they might have been shown—naked women perhaps! I did not receive any formal sexuality education until graduate school, when I took a course on human sexuality as part of my master's degree.

In sixth grade my sexual scripting began to crystallize. It was then that I first thought about what it means to "do sex." One afternoon, I learned from a friend that sexual activity between two people could be expressed and understood using baseball terminology. Becoming a sexual being meant to participate in a new "game." Like other games we played, it had rules (one had to go to first base before proceeding to second), and the goals were to become "good at" playing the game and, of course, to "win." Girls became the "playing field" and winning meant getting as "far as possible." The acceptable "distance" (stated in terms of first base through home run) progressed as we aged. Given my white, suburban background, kissing or "first base" was the norm for middle schoolers beginning this new game, but occasionally we heard stories about someone "petting" and thus "getting to second base." While I was not a "player" through much of my middle school years, images of this new type of baseball filled me with desire and trepidation.

Much of my scripting was connected to feelings of arousal and repression. Like most boys in our society, I encountered many opportunities to become sexually aroused. We could easily obtain pictures of nude women, advertising used sexual innuendo to sell products, and motion picture producers were initiating semi–sexually explicit scenes (glimpses of nudity, bedroom scenes) into films. Perhaps most important, however, was the popularity of *Playboy* magazine. Up until this time, men's magazines focused on hobbies (e.g., carpentry, auto mechanics) or outdoor life (e.g., sports, hunting, camping). The image of a "real man" was someone who was married, had kids, and liked to build furniture, play baseball, or hunt deer. With the advent of *Playboy* this image changed dramatically. As I started my middle school years, the image of a real man became that of a playboy, someone who didn't need to get married to have sex, and who felt that having lots of girls (especially "bunnies") was preferable to having just one. This new "real man" was cool, confident, and debonair. While overt and covert messages to be sexual abounded in our society, I also received messages that it was somehow wrong to be sexually aroused. I was told that "good girls" (especially those in middle school) don't "do it." So just as I was experiencing heterosexual desires for the first time, I was also internalizing the need to repress these feelings either because the girls that were most attractive to me seemed inaccessible or because these sexual desires were "wrong."

Of course, the most powerful aspect of arousal scripting concerned the need to be heterosexual. While my friends and I pretended to "make out" with each other in someone's attic after school (we each took turns being the girl), we were careful to assert out heterosexuality in all other domains of our lives. "Fag," "queer," or "homo" were common epithets we yelled at someone who was not exhibiting sufficiently "manly" behavior in a given situation. Homophobia was at the core of any scripting I internalized related to sexual arousal and desire.

Another aspect of my sexual scripting had to do with power and competition. "Getting a girl" meant that one was in competition with other boys who might "get" her. My friends and I looked at each other as adversaries rather than as confidants. Among the students in our middle school, there was a clearly visible but unspoken of hierarchy of popularity. My self-image was badly bruised due to my exclusion from the most "popular" group in our school. I took what comfort I could in knowing that at least I was not on the bottom of this hierarchy.

Competition and power also played an important role in the game itself. Among my male friends it was important to be seen as a "big hitter" who could run fast around the bases. While I knew it was wrong to impose my will on other people (i.e., girls), there was tremendous peer pressure to exert one's power on the playing field. These contradictory messages were constantly playing against each other throughout my adolescence. I remember the first time I wanted to kiss a girl romantically. I wanted to reach out to her, but I was afraid that she would resist. I remember thinking that if I exerted my power and imposed my will on her, I would feel guilty. However, I also thought about what my male friends would think if I didn't live up to their expectations of me. Would they think me less than a man if I reported to them that I hadn't even tried to kiss her? It is now easy to see why my self-worth was seriously undermined by the sexual scripting I internalized during my middle-school years.

When reflecting upon my sexual scripting during these formative years, the feelings that stand out most strongly are those of isolation and loneliness. That is, the sexual scripting I was encouraged to adopt actively cut me off from developing meaningful relationships with either female or male friends. My sexual scripting called upon me to be the one who initiated contact with girls, which meant risking rejection. The more I was attracted to a particular girl, the more I felt intimidated by the thought of making this initial contact. Given my tenuous self-image, the possibility of rejection was too risky for me. As a result, I spent most of my adolescence in a state of loneliness when it came to girls. Unfortunately, this same scripting made it necessary for me to conceal these feelings of loneliness from my male friends, and as I look back on it, even from myself.

Images of power, prestige, and coolness seemed to make sense then, given what was transmitted through our popular culture; but these images provided no guidance when it came to developing intimate relationships with either girls or my male friends. When reexamining this period of my life, it was the ability to be intimate and to nurture (and be nurtured) that I most feared and about which I most needed to learn. However, the code of silence that permeated my sexual scripting kept me locked within my own isolation.

Mara's Story: "Don't Tell the Boys About the Movie We Saw"

The most prominent descriptors of my sexuality education, both formal and informal, were curiosity and fear. I received little information about my own sexuality and physiology, none at all about boys' bodies and sexuality, and had no opportunities for conversation or interaction. What little formal information came as part of the school curriculum was given in isolation from boys, so not only did I know little about them, I also had no idea what they had been told about me.

Formal sexuality education was limited to the movie we saw in the sixth grade. I remember the brightly colored graphics of a young woman "growing" breasts and the cartoon depiction of the egg descending from the ovary into the uterus and then disappearing somehow. Only the girls saw the movie—and we were each given a pamphlet explaining menstruation that we were told to take home and discuss with our mothers. It was a confusing time—this "thing" was going to happen to us, and we were petrified that it would, equally petrified that it wouldn't, but mostly horrified that the boys might find out! Although it was never made explicit, the clear message was: This information is for you only. Don't tell the boys about the movie; don't tell the boys about periods; and certainly never tell a boy that you are having yours! When we wanted to be excused from showering in gym, we said we had our "friend" (or our friend from Philadelphia), never that we had our periods. Sexual things were not to be discussed, not even in gym class with only girls present. Sexual things were certainly not to be discussed in the presence of what we came to perceive as "the enemy"—members of the "opposite sex," who were different from us, dangerous to us, and definitely not in solidarity with us.

One memory stands out very clearly. It was several months after we had seen the movie, and we had a substitute teacher during science. She asked a male student to read aloud, and he did badly. After he ran through the end of yet another sentence without pausing, the substitute teacher shouted, "What's the matter with you? Don't you know what a period is?" I remember that the whole class became absolutely consumed with near-hysterical laughter—the girls were afraid that the boys did know, a little smug about the fact that they might not, but most of all, scared they would ask or that the teacher would continue her inquisition.

Everyone was curious, anxious to assess his or her own knowledge, and vitally interested in what other people knew about sex. But there was no easy way to ask. I remember classmates passing around copies of the Ann Landers Sex Quiz, a ten-item survey of sexual experience that yielded a score from something like "pure as the driven snow" to "fast and likely to end up in trouble." As the test traveled, people boasted about their scores; you didn't want to be at the low end of the scale, since that made you stupid and inexperienced, but neither did you want to be at the high end, since that would make you a "slut." I remember struggling with two items from the test: "Have you ever given or received a hickey?" and "Have you ever kissed a boy/girl in your pajamas?" I didn't know what a hickey was, and when I asked, I remember the hoots and hollers of scorn and disbelief about my naïveté and stupidity ("Well, if you don't know what it is, it's obvious you haven't done it!"). I also remember that I couldn't figure out the significance of kissing in your pajamas, since to me, pajamas were associated with bedtime and stories, and I couldn't see how they were sexual or erotic or dangerous in any way. I was embarrassed by my low score and lack of sophistication and experience; I tried to act cool and sophisticated and imply that I knew a lot more than I was divulging, always afraid I would be found out.

It was out of the question to talk about sex with boys; and, sadly, homophobia got in the way of intimate exchanges between girls, including sharing fears and concerns about sexuality. I had a very close female friend all through high school, and we often spent the night together, sleeping in a big double bed. She wrote me lengthy love poems, and I remember being both flattered and deeply uncomfortable. Certainly I loved her, but not like that. I wanted to be close to her—we were intimate in so many ways—but extensive physical closeness was both very appealing and very frightening. Since neither of us had very much contact with boys (we weren't popular), we especially didn't want to be seen as linked together sexually.

I scoured our house for books, but found very few. I remember pouring over the Kinsey report (Kinsey, Pomeroy, & Martin, 1948) but finding the reading difficult, clinical, and not helpful in answering the questions I had. I remember practicing the three big words—erection, ejaculation, and orgasm—over and over again, anxious to master their meanings and the sequence in which they occurred. I didn't want to look or act stupid and uninformed.

My brother had a book, *Sex and the Single Man*, by Albert Ellis (1963), which I devoured looking for information. Most of what I remember was a lengthy discussion of the ways for men to trick women into kissing them—for example, opening the car and then positioning yourself so that they ended up kissing you. It was clear from my reading that sex was something that men wanted, women had to be careful about, and nobody could talk about.

The information from my mother was even more oblique and confusing. Although she was warm and loving and clearly interested in my welfare, her own background made it very difficult for her to talk about sex directly. Her advice to me included: "Always put a newspaper down on a boy's lap before you sit on it" (Why? How will a newspaper keep my skirt from getting dirty?); "Never put yourself in a compromising position (I had no idea what that meant, or what was wrong with compromising, usually considered a virtue); and "Don't start any fires you're not prepared to put out." This last piece of information was particularly useless, since I had no information at all about such fires, how one started them, or about how one put them out. More powerful, however, was the underlying assumption that sex was something boys wanted and girls didn't, and that it was the girl's responsibility to keep anything "bad" from happening. What if I, a girl, wanted to start a fire? That must make me really wicked or strange.

Like Jesse, I was isolated and lonely; eager to know but afraid to find out; full of curiosity but bereft of resources. But our stories hold prominent differences in that arousal and repression were played out in very different ways. Girls weren't supposed to get aroused; we were supposed to repress not only our own sexual inclinations, but also those of the boys. And most difficult of all, we were supposed to accomplish all of this with a minimum of sexual knowledge or explicitness. The power differential between boys and girls was also already clear: boys did the asking, girls the waiting; boys did the leading, girls the following; boys wanted sex, girls were supposed to resist. Yet I was told that I was somehow powerful, since I could get boys "worked up" so that they were out of control. I was both dependent and powerless, ignorant yet unwittingly powerful, and I was in charge of keeping things under control—a heavy burden to bear in ignorance.

Mara's Story Continues: Learning to Be an Ally

My attempts at becoming an ally to men and at helping men to become my allies have become more intense and focused as I understand more of the nature of women and men's isolation and oppression. Some of the prominent barriers to men and women being allies with relation to sexuality issues became clear to me several years ago when I was scheduled for a hysterectomy. Worried and upset about the forthcoming surgery, I turned to my friends and colleagues for support. Most women were comfortable hearing about the physical problems that prompted the surgery, related my story to their own, and were anxious to be supportive. Garnering the support of my male friends and colleagues, whom I was anxious to have as part of my support system, was more difficult. Two specific barriers had to be overcome. The first was that one "doesn't talk about this stuff with men," the logical extension of not telling the boys about the movie or our periods. One was supposed to say only that one would be missing work because of "health problems," or perhaps because of a "woman's thing," not to be specified; I was not to offer further detail and men were not supposed to ask. A second barrier to be overcome was many men's startling ignorance about women's bodies and physiology. I was stunned by the fact that many men with whom I spoke, all of whom were sexually active and many of whom were married, had no idea where the uterus was located, what was involved in a hysterectomy, or what effect such surgery would have on subsequent physiological processes like menstruation, potential pregnancy, or on sexuality. I found myself reaching for a pad and pencil and drawing pictures: this is the vagina, this is the uterus, this is the cervix, here are the ovaries, here's what they'll do. While such discussions were occasionally embarrassing, the predominant response from the men with whom I interacted was sincere gratitude that these mysteries had finally been revealed, and that they could now be "insiders" and supporters rather than excluded bystanders.

If the most prominent barriers to men and women becoming each other's allies are ignorance and lack of connectedness, then solutions must lie in education and information sharing, and in getting closely connected to people of the "opposite sex." I must figure out ways to learn about men, their bodies, and their sexuality. Only some of this learning can be done through reading and academic study; the most significant part can only happen in situations in which I am able to hear men's voices on these issues or in relationships with men that enable them to share their experiences, difficulties, and issues with me. While much of what men must do in order to become my ally is their work and can't or shouldn't be seen as my responsibility, there are also things I can do in order to facilitate that process, including creating safe spaces and relationships with men in which I can speak in my own voice, share my experiences, and tell them explicitly what I need from them as my allies. I must find ways to include men in women's discourse, to allow them to participate in women's knowledge and ways of knowing.

This last goal is extremely difficult; longstanding patterns of isolation and segregation coupled with deeply felt fear and vulnerability make it difficult to trust men with information about our bodies and our sexuality. We are afraid that if we tell them who we really are, what our bodies are really like, what we feel, what we want, where we hurt, and what we are afraid of, then somehow we will become more vulnerable, more at risk of exploitation and manipulation. Our embarrassment in talking about these issues with men is simply the surface manifestation of our very real fears of sexist oppression and violence toward our bodies. Becoming allies is difficult and frightening work, but not knowing and not talking have not brought women safety and security, nor men liberation from oppressive roles.

Jesse Responds: Building Allied Relationships

As Mara has done, I now wish to discuss my attempts to establish relationships with women as allies. As she noted, education is important. Obviously, one thing I can do is commit myself to learning more about women's sexuality and lives while being more open and expressive of my own with them. Instead of discussing specific attempts to form these allied relationships, I want to discuss some of the dilemmas that I face in my efforts to do so.

There are many self-serving reasons why I might want to develop allied relationships with women and dramatically alter our current sexual scripting. Under patriarchy I feel that I have suffered from high levels of stress, have had a difficult time developing meaningful personal relationships, and have suffered from self-alienation. While my own possibilities have been distorted by patriarchy, I must recognize that I have garnered significant power and privilege as a result. Perhaps the most important issue I have faced in developing allied relationships with women is learning to confront this privilege. It is relatively easy to recognize the oppression that I or others experience at the hands of "those in power," yet much more difficult to become aware of the way in which my own power, as a man in our society, may oppress others. Listening, observing, and sensitively responding to others' lives have not been part of my sexual scripting, and it is the lack of these very characteristics that often end up oppressing the women and girls with whom I come into contact. Sometimes, for example, I unconsciously interrupt women and discount what they have said simply because they are women and not men. Recognizing my complicity in the oppression of women has given rise to several other dilemmas that I face in efforts to develop the kind of relationships Mara and I suggest here.

For me to establish allied relationships suggests that the personal is political; it implies that I will speak out against sexism in our society and in my personal life. While it is relatively easy to understand intellectually the way in which one's own sexual scripting has been oppressive to oneself and others, actually countering this socialization and redirecting my actions in day-to-day relationships has been extremely difficult. The gap between my intellectual understanding and my continued manifestation of sexist behaviors and attitudes has made me confront the issue of hypocrisy. In order to avoid being seen as a hypocrite, I have considered muting my own voice in the belief that I should "get my act together" before I can expect changes from others. However, waiting until I achieve perfection seems irresponsible. Charges of hypocrisy, whether originating from myself or others, would inevitably lead to a stifling brand of self-censorship. If perfection became a prerequisite for legitimate advocacy then we would all soon be perpetual mutes. I am compelled to speak out against sexism in our society, and this very commitment has forced me to risk being seen as a hypocrite. Working through these feelings within myself and among the people with whom I associate is central to building genuine allied relationships.

Interpersonal communication is another dilemma to be faced. As Mara noted, communication is key to developing allied relationships. However, being open and honest with my feelings and thoughts has at times resulted in the silencing of women. I have at times consciously decided to remain quiet in situations in which women are participating, especially if gender issues are being discussed. However, I then ask myself if this "holding back" is not just a subtle form of paternalism; is my silence an indication that women are not capable of dealing with my input? On the other hand, interjecting my ideas into all situations can be seen as a subtle form of bullying; once again, a man feels it is necessary to comment on everything being discussed, even when the subject is "women." Working through the complex tension between paternalism and intervention is central to building allied relationships.

Finally, as Mara mentioned, the issue of trust must be confronted in establishing these relationships. Several women I know have voiced concern about the role that I, as a man, can play in advancing the overall goal of gender equity. They are reasonably skeptical toward someone who would voluntarily work to undermine his own privileged status. Put bluntly, they question whether I can be trusted. This lack of trust has been exacerbated by the "men's liberation movement." Focused on the psychological oppression men have felt as a result of our society's pervasive masculine socialization, the men's liberation literature has ignored the source of this oppression (i.e., patriarchy) and at times presents its arguments with a self-serving, antifeminist tone: "You women think you have it bad; well, we men have it worse." Although this literature has provided me and other men with insight into the ways in which our sexual scripting undermines our desires to be fully human, women might rightfully ask how committed to women's equality men can be when their involvement, focusing narrowly on their own liberation from the strictures of sex-role stereotyping, lacks a concomitant, dialectical understanding of women's oppression. In building allied relationships, perhaps the most important and yet most difficult barrier to overcome lies in the level of trust that must be established between men and women.

REDIRECTING THE SEXUAL SCRIPTS OF EARLY ADOLESCENTS

Although the vast majority of adults in our society now favor the inclusion of sexuality education lessons into the middle school curriculum and 70% of these lessons are taught to mixed-gendered groups of children (Kenney & Orr, 1984), most sexuality education curricula reinforce the traditional sexual scripts previously illustrated.

Several researchers (e.g., Trudell, 1988; Myerson, 1986; Whatley, 1985, 1987, 1988) have noted that in an effort to avoid public controversy, most sexuality education coursework reflects a "scientific" orientation in which biological facts and social statistics dominate what is taught. Almost completely absent from conventional sexuality education is the study of the social and psychological content within which young adolescents become sexual beings. Discussions of value laden topics such as criteria for determining acceptable types of sexual activities; feelings of sexual arousal, desires, and pleasure; dynamics of power in sexual relationships; and reproductive control (among others) are almost totally ignored in middle and high school sexuality education classes. This "value neutral" posture on the part of teachers and curriculum materials surreptitiously presents a biological determinist perspective to explain sexual identity formation and relationships. Whatley's (1987, 1988) curricular research illustrates the way in which this biological determinist perspective covertly reinforces the conventional sexual scripting found in our society. For example, she (1988) states that

> The recurring theme in [sexuality education] texts and curricular materials is that there is a powerful, innate, hormonally determined sex drive in men, with very little indication that there might be some equivalent in women. The message is that women, having little trouble overcoming their weak libidos, are responsible for saying "no" to men, who ideally should learn "proper control" but are often too strongly hormonally driven to be able to stop on their own. The responsibility for men's sexuality clearly falls on the woman, as she must be careful never to "lead him on," to always resist his advances, and if unsuccessful, to ensure that contraception is used. Many teenage men and women readily support this view of women's responsibility for men's sexual behavior: if he is sexually aggressive, it is her fault for dressing, walking, speaking, or acting in a way that triggered his uncontrollable drive. (p. 104)

Given the types of messages that children receive in our schools and society, we argue that sexuality education needs to overtly address and redirect the sexual scripts of early adolescents.

What Progress Have We Made? New Books, Old Message

This year at school, Mara's ten-year-old daughter was shown a movie on adolescent body changes and menstruation. Although boys and girls did see the same film together, the students were then separated for a discussion and given separate booklets to take home. The two booklets, *Changing: A Booklet for Girls* and *Changing: A Booklet for Boys*

(Procter and Gamble, 1983b, 1983a), illustrate some of the ways in which women's knowledge and men's knowledge is still partial, separated, and controlled and imparted in ways that thwart ally-building.

The booklet for girls begins with the words of a hypothetical 10-year old who is wondering about menstruation—what it is and when it will happen to her—and finally overcomes her resistance and approaches her mother. Her mother, looking "relieved," sits down with her daughter and gives her the booklet.

The booklet focuses on menstruation and includes an explanation of the hormonal cycle, with pictures of the "genital area," including uterus, ovaries, vagina, fallopian tubes, uretha, and anus (with no mention of the clitoris). It tells you what to do if your period starts at school, what cramps are, and how to plot your menstrual cycle on the calendar. Also included are sections entitled "Shaping Up" (including proper nutrition and exercise) and "Looking Your Best" (pimples and how to avoid them). Of particular interest are two other sections, "About Boys" and "Choosing Menstrual Protection." "About Boys" is three pages long and begins with an anecdote about Joanie, who notices changes in her older brother Andrew: He's growing a lot, stumbles over the furniture, hardly ever says hello, lies in bed staring at the ceiling, and showers a lot. When Joanie gets angry at her brother for using up all the hot water, her mother tells her that he's "growing up pretty fast" and that she should "bear with him," and then gives Joanie a little booklet to explain about the changes in boys. Already the patterns of separation and alienation have begun. One wonders why Joanie's mother can't talk to her about Andrew's changes, or why Joanie and Andrew don't appear able to talk about these things themselves.

This section explains that boys are also experiencing "growing up" changes, and that these include rapid growth, underarm and genital area hair, increased oil production in skin and scalp, perspiration odor, and rapidly shifting moods caused by changing hormone levels. There is a diagram of the male reproductive system, with the penis, testicles, and scrotum labeled, but there is no mention of erections, wet dreams, masturbation, or intercourse.

The section on choosing menstrual protection is lengthy, not surprising since this booklet is published by a manufacturer of "feminine products." It includes a brief history of the "progress" of menstrual protection, followed by a lengthy explanation of the various kinds of products, including panty liners, Mini Pads, Slender for Teens Pads, Thin Maxi Pads, Maxi Pads, Plus Pads, and tampons. The booklet stresses the need for constant "protection"—of your clothes from blood, and yourself from discovery and embarrassment; wear a pad all the time and no one will ever know, especially, one hopes, the boys.

The booklet never mentions positive emotions of any kind related to sexuality, only "rapidly shifting moods caused by changing hormone levels." Neither masturbation nor intercourse are ever discussed, beyond the passively stated, "While it's in the fallopian tube, the egg cell can be fertilized by a sperm cell from a male" (p. 6).

The booklet for boys is a close parallel. It begins with an older brother (not the father) giving a booklet to a younger, inquisitive brother who is wondering about his body; the older brother is mocking and scornful of the younger boy and never really talks to him but simply tosses him a booklet. The booklet then goes on to explain about physiological changes and the male reproductive system and how it works. Various male body parts are identified and described, and the mechanics of an erection are explained, including the fact that "after a boy has reached puberty, he may have erections without warning and for no apparent reason. This is perfectly normal. These erections usually go away in a few minutes" (p. 5). No mention is made of masturbation, or of the fact that having an erection or ejaculating might feel good and that one might want to get an erection (rather than being grateful that it disappears within minutes). The booklet contains no mention of intercourse.

In the booklet for boys, most of the section entitled "About Girls" is devoted to an explanation of "the menstrual cycle." It begins with an anecdote about how Ben notices that his cousin Joanie, to whom he has always been close, seems different. Something happens when they are off on vacation together: Ben notices that Joanie is in the bathroom a lot and worries that she is "sick or something." When he inquires, he is told by Joanie that "it's none of his business," dismissed by his aunt who says that perhaps his mother should explain it to him, and told by his mother that "it's a complicated thing to explain," and that she doesn't "quite know where to start." She gives him a brochure to read.

These booklets show that only limited information is provided to young people, and that different information is given to boys and girls. Their clear message, as evidenced by the dialogue about people of the other gender, is that one can find out about body changes and sexuality only indirectly. We can see the development of the conspiracy of silence; certain things just can't be discussed, not even between a mother and a daughter or a younger and older brother. Isolation becomes the pattern, silence the vehicle.

Ursina's Sexuality Class: A Middle School Course for Redirecting Sexual Scripts

Ursina teaches science and art at Harmony Middle School (grades 7 and 8) in Bloomington, Indiana. Harmony is committed to the creation of an education that is rooted within a progressive, democratic ethos. While its independent status separates it from public schools in many ways, the students come from a broad range of social, economic, racial, and ethnic origins (see Goodman, in press). Ursina did not teach her human sexuality course from a "value-neutral" position. To the contrary, she was openly ideological and taught the course from an overt, anti-sexist perspective. Although biological information regarding adolescent development and reproduction was carefully examined, the significance of this class stemmed from its social and psychological themes. These included giving her students a voice, helping them to appreciate their bodies, exploring the dynamics of human sexual relationships, and identifying the problems of teenage sexual conduct and potential pregnancy. Due to space limitations, we will illustrate only one of these themes as an example of the way in which this course countered the conventional sexual scripting typically found in our schools and society.

As previously mentioned, perhaps the most devastating message young adolescents receive in our society is that boys and girls are on "opposite" sides of humanity. Honest communication between adolescent boys and girls is extremely rare as they move into middle school, and this lack of communication between genders seems to continue for many individuals well into adulthood. Like most young adolescents in our society, the middle school students at Harmony were relatively shy about discussing sexual feelings and behaviors in mixed-gendered groups, especially in the presence of adults. However, Ursina was strongly committed to helping her students overcome their mutual distrust by learning how to communicate verbally with each other about sexual topics. While not forcing any individual to speak, Ursina created an atmosphere that encouraged these young people to share their ideas, questions, and concerns regarding human sexuality. For example, during the first class session the students discussed the "ground rules" needed to facilitate their communication. Four rules emerged from this discussion:

1. Anything that is said by any student during class is confidential.
2. There is no such thing as a "stupid" question (the students recognized that everyone came to this class with a different knowledge base, and that there was a need to respect each other no matter what information or misinformation one might have. In particular, they agreed that no one should laugh at anyone else for asking a "dumb" question.
3. No one should purposely ask a "stupid" question in order to make fun of what was being discussed.
4. Students had the right to ask personal questions to other students, but the students being asked also had the right not to answer.

In addition, Ursina established a question box in the room, where students could write questions anonymously and have them answered in a public forum.

Students also had an opportunity to influence the content of this course by generating a list of potential topics and then selecting those in which they were most interested. While not every student-generated topic was addressed, having students generate this list gave them the message that a wide range of topics could be examined in this class and that their interests would be taken into consideration in determining its content. Ground rules, a question box, and student-generated topics all created a foundation upon which the students could communicate with each other about subjects that were formerly taboo.

In addition, the course was structured to help break through the gendered silence previously mentioned. All materials for the course (e.g., films, guest speakers, books) were available for and used by both the boys and girls. For example, two pamphlets authored by Planned Parenthood, *The Problem With Puberty* (1981) and *So You Don't Want to Be a Sex Object* (1984), were originally written for boys and girls respectively. However, Ursina had each student read both pamphlets. After they studied these materials, she had the boys play the role of fathers who explain the physiological and emotional aspects of adolescent development to the girls in the class, who played the role of 10-year-old daughters. Then she had the girls, playing the role of mothers, explain the same information to their "sons." Ursina believed that boys should learn as much as possible about girls' sexuality, and vice versa.

Finally, the communication between the boys and girls in this class was enhanced by Ursina's educational values and talents. Although she was "openly ideological" and taught this course from an antisexist perspective, she was deeply committed to giving points of view that were different from her own a "fair hearing" in her classroom (Kelly, 1986). Rather than holding herself at a distance and treating knowledge as an object for student consumption, over the course of the year Ursina developed close, personal relationships with these students. She viewed education as a mutually constructive experience in which the teacher and students learn and teach together. Although she maintained a certain degree of authority, she was, as Dewey (1938) suggested, the leader from inside this community rather than external to it. Ursina was knowledgeable and dynamic, and she used her talents and knowledge to help her students become more empowered and socially responsible. She genuinely cared about the welfare of every student in her class, and it was obvious that each student knew it! By establishing the atmosphere, ground rules, course structure, and activities that she did, Ursina helped students find their own voice and confronted directly our society's covert prohibition against having boys and girls learn and communicate together about human sexuality.

CONCLUSION

This chapter has analyzed some of the ways in which gender roles and relations are shaped by the formal and informal sexuality education received by young adolescents. Through an examination of the experiences of a man and a woman, we can begin to see the heavy toll taken by limited information, an atmosphere of isolation and distrust, and the lack of explicit attention to developing mutual understanding and communication. We recognize, however, that these are not only educational issues, but also cultural and political ones. Decisions about what to teach, what not to teach, and how to teach are grounded not only in pragmatic constraints but are also framed by more global ideologies and values about men, women, society, and social justice and by the allocation of power and resources. Thus, debates about sexuality education will inevitably be influenced by the beliefs and values of those in decision-making positions, and will be grounded in a host of political agendas that may or may not be articulated. Members of conservative political groups who conceptualize sexuality education as "chastity class" (Watzman, 1990) are quite clear in promoting value-laden sexuality education and in declaring that "knowledge alone is not enough— clear directions must be given to help youth know not only how to decide but what to decide" (p. 93).

Thus, if our vision of sexuality education is based on some assumptions about social justice, changing the oppressive society, and reallocating power and resources, then our sexuality education programs will need to be equally forthright in explicitly situating information about sexuality within much broader contexts. We will have to become far clearer ourselves (so that we can make clear to our students) about the relation between what knowledge is imparted and how, and our subsequent abilities to reshape social and political structures so that they are equitable and just. It is a difficult task, yet we have no choice but to be diligent and thoughtful; the stakes are very high.

REFERENCES

Best, R. (1983). *We all have scars: What boys and girls learn in elementary schools.* Bloomington: Indiana University Press.

Dewey, J. (1938). *Experience and education.* New York: Macmillan.

Eder, D., & Hallinan, M. (1978). Sex differences in children's friendships. *American Sociological Review, 43*(2), 237–250.

Ellis, A. (1963). *Sex and the single man.* New York: Stuart.

Gagnon, J., & Simon, W. (1973). *Sexual conduct.* Chicago: Aldine.

Goodman, J. (in press). *Elementary schooling for critical democracy.* Albany: SUNY Press.

Kelly, T. (1986). Discussing controversial issues: Four perspectives on the teacher's role. *Theory and Research in Social Education, 14*(2), 113–138.

Kenney, A., & Orr, M. (1984). Sex education: An overview of current programs, policies, and research. *Phi Delta Kappan, 65,* 491–496.

Kinsey, A., Pomeroy, W., & Martin, C. (1948). *Sexual behavior in the human male.* Philadelphia: W. B. Saunders.

Lockheed, M. (1985). Sex equity in classroom organization and climate. In S. Klein (Ed.), *Handbook for achieving sex equity through education* (pp. 189–217). Baltimore: Johns Hopkins University Press.

Miller, P., & Simon, W. (1981). The development of sexuality in adolescence. In J. Adelson (Ed.), *Handbook of adolescent psychology* (pp. 383–407). New York: Wiley.

Myerson, M. (1986). The politics of sexual knowledge: Feminism and sexology textbooks. *Frontiers, 9*(1), 66–71.

Planned Parenthood. (1981). *The problem with puberty.* Lakewood, CO: RAJ Publications.

Planned Parenthood. (1984). *So you don't want to be a sex object.* Lakewood, CO: RAJ Publications.

Procter and Gamble Company. (1983a). *Changing: A booklet for boys.* Cincinnati, OH: Author.

Procter and Gamble Company. (1983b). *Changing: A booklet for girls.* Cincinnati, OH: Author.

Schofield, J. (1989). *Black and white in school: Trust, tension, or tolerance?* New York: Teachers College Press. (Original work published 1982)

Shrum, W. (1988). Friendship in school: Gender and racial homophily. *Sociology of Education, 61*(4), 227–239.

Thorne, B., & Luria, Z. (1986). Sexuality and gender in children's daily worlds. *Social Problems, 33*(3), 176–190.

Trudell, B. (1988). *Constructing the sexuality curriculum-in-use: An ethnographic study of a ninth-grade sex education class.* Unpublished doctoral dissertation, University of Wisconsin, Madison.

Watzman, N. (1990, July/August). When sex and ed becomes chastity class. *Utne Reader,* pp. 92–97.

Whatley, M. (1985). Male and female hormones: Misinterpretations of biology in school health and sex education. In V. Sapiro (Ed.), *Women, biology, and public policy* (pp. 67–89). Beverly Hills: Sage.

Whatley, M. (1987). Biological determinism and gender issues in sexuality education: Interconnected dilemmas and dreams. *Journal of Sex Education and Therapy, 13*(2), 26–29.

Whatley, M. (1988). Raging hormones and powerful cars: The construction of men's sexuality in school sex education and popular adolescent films. *Journal of Education, 170*(3), 100–121.

CHAPTER 5

Bitter Lessons for All

Sexual Harassment in Schools

ELEANOR LINN, NAN D. STEIN, AND JACKIE YOUNG, WITH SAUNDRA DAVIS

Sexual harassment is about power and sexuality—two issues deeply entwined in our society and in our schools. We therefore see the necessity of discussing sexual harassment and its power aspects when addressing the broader issue of sexuality in the curriculum.

The bitter lessons of sexual harassment profoundly influence how young women and men perceive themselves and each other. Whether experienced directly or through observation or hearsay, the presence of sexual harassment in schools shapes young people's conceptualization of male and female roles, of power and powerlessness, of freedom and democracy. Sexual harassment diminishes students' ability to develop personal power and potential. Its presence alienates many students from pursuing the lofty goals of the stated curriculum. And perhaps most destructively, young women's social, emotional, and sexual development is contaminated when they are as familiar with the shame and anger of sexual harassment as with the sweet pleasures of sexual desire.

In this chapter, we describe the power aspects of sexual harassment as they apply specifically to schools. We outline the philosophical and legal approaches to understanding sexual harassment, present operational definitions, and report on estimates of the pervasiveness of sexual harassment in schools. Lastly, we briefly review the major components of existing complaint management and prevention programs in schools, and provide suggestions for their successful implementation.

POWER ASPECTS OF SEXUAL HARASSMENT IN SCHOOLS

Sexual harassment is essentially about the abuse of power in relationships. School-place interactions between administrators and faculty, teachers and students, older students and younger students are expected to be mutually respectful and reflective of traditional relationship dynamics, which in our society are associated with authority, age, and status. But the occurrence of sexual harassment in the schools exploits and confuses these relationships, often revealing gender and sexual orientation as the unacknowledged, yet more powerful markers, of status. In a school situation, behaviors such as teasing, joking, or flirting in a sexual manner—which may be considered appropriate in social situations—become highly inappropriate. In an educational institution, sexually loaded behaviors become a violation of trust and an enactment of the power hierarchy.

While gender is the most defining aspect of sexual harassment, all forms of status, such as race, ethnicity, language group, physical or sensory disabilities, socioeconomic and job role status, size, and age, frequently interact in occurrences of sexual harassment to heighten the perceived vulnerability of some individuals. For example, an Asian male teacher wrestles with and tickles female students, also Asian. While the behavior appears playful, some students feel powerless and know that they are not able to tickle their teacher aggressively in the same manner. The students feign delight but complain to their parents about feeling uncomfortable. When a female teacher is sexually harassed by a male custodian of the same race, it is the greater power of gender over job status that is the basis for the teacher's fear of physical retaliation if she reports him. When black female students are asked overly personal questions about their boyfriends by a white male teacher, it is gender, race, age, and job role status that interact to pollute their environment. When students with limited English proficiency laugh uncomfortably at the sexually explicit remarks hurled at them by their English-speaking classmates, it is the fear of further ethnic harassment that keeps them from reporting the incident. And when high school males harass each other with homophobic epithets, it is heterosexism and gender that overlap and serve as underlying forces for the power differential that defines hostile peer relationships.

Our society reinforces distinct gender roles and a double standard for expressing sexuality. Gender roles carry with them strict rules, norms, and standards of behavior, the most salient being everyone's continuous assertion of the supremacy of masculinity. Gregory Herek (1987) writes, "To be a man in contemporary American society is to be homophobic—that is, to be hostile toward homosexual persons in general and gay men in particular" (p. 68). To ensure this form of "masculinity," a male is required to deny or suppress any characteristic that appears to be "feminine"; these include any task, skill, activity, occupation, gesture, color of clothing, choice of words, tonal inflection, topics of conversation, or display of emotions that might be labeled as "feminine." Verbal harassment in the form of homophobic name-calling is common in schools. The label "sissy" is as potent today for its intention to humiliate as in past generations. Its female parallel, "tomboy," may suggest to some people that a female has acquired the power of masculinity, a taboo power that they find threatening. We have even spoken to young men who believe that lesbians love women because they have not sexually experienced what "real men" are like. Their hostile actions toward lesbians may go beyond verbal harassment to physical assault and rape to "prove their point."

The traditional division of labor in the home, school, and workplace along with the social pressures to continually assert our gender roles has led to separate cultures for females and males, with different experiences, habits, assumptions, and beliefs. To believe that males are aggressive and females, passive; males are rough and females, soft; males are rational and females, emotional; males are strong and females, weak is to perpetuate an overarching culture in which the predominant belief is that males are more powerful than females. Feminist scholar Elizabeth Janeway (1981) explains that "power and weakness are thus factored into masculine and feminine gender images quite explicitly. Virile men are decisive and forceful . . . feminine women are passive" (p. 8).

Such an unfortunate attitude about gender and power further seeds many aspects of people's behavior in schools. One example is female students' resistance to entering nontraditional classes, programs, and occupations (e.g., mathematics, science, and technology). When trailblazing females do enter these classes, they are often harassed for having greater opportunities to "move up" and act unfemale; male students often resent the competition for their "rightly deserved" space and feel pushed down to positions of less power. Males may feel an undesired role reversal of girls over boys. Sexual harassment is thus used as a convenient mechanism for keeping women down "in their place" and blocking their chances for economic opportunity and self-sufficiency.

Another way to view sexual harassment is in terms of its omnipresence in our language and communication habits. Essentially, power is the perceived potential for influence in a relationship; and influence, the result of power in action, cannot occur without communication. Thus power, culture, and communication are closely related. Michael Parenti (1978) notes that viewing power as a systemic force requires examining the influence of culture on our ideas. "Cultural beliefs do not just 'happen,' they are mediated through a social structure and are, to a large degree, the products of those groups which control the material resources of a society, those who control the institutional and communication systems and who enjoy special access to the symbolic environment and to mass constituencies" (p. 43). Parenti argues that because of cultural influences, we must go beyond the interpersonal when seeking definitions of power. In our culture, violence against women as a group and the prevalence of sexual harassment in the workplace and in our schools reflect the power structure of our society, a society preoccupied with sex and sexual domination. Because sexual discrimination through male gender dominance is evident in our language habits, power relations as expressed in our language and communication patterns need examining, discussing, and acknowledging.

While sexuality education in the schools is often limited to academic discussions of physical anatomy, as discussed in Chapters 1, 7, 9, and 10 in this book, our ordinary discussions about women, sexual intercourse, sexuality, and love are filled with hidden messages. Students use the language of sexual intercourse daily, filled with references to women as sexual objects. For example, Julia Stanley (Eakins, 1978) found about 220 sexual terms for females and only 20 for males (p. 5).

To further demonstrate how women are seen as sexual objects in our language, philosopher Robert Baker (1984) analyzed the sentence "A had sexual intercourse with B," selecting commonly used synonyms for "had intercourse with." Predictably, he found "Jane was laid (or fucked, screwed, banged) by Dick" a common sentence construction that is easily understood. The reverse, "Dick was laid by Jane," sounds strange and unfamiliar, thus indicating how our language assumes that men are active and women are passive (p. 249). It is not just philosophers who understand the one-sidedness of sexual relationships as displayed in our language. High school students also recognize and freely use the sentence structure that Baker identified as common, while they rarely or never use the construction he calls unfamiliar.

But most significant, Baker notes, is the linguistic demonstration that the female role in intercourse is that of a person being taken advantage of, or harmed. Baker writes,

> One of the strongest possible ways of telling someone that you wish to harm him is to tell him to assume the female sexual role relative to you. Again, to say to someone, "go fuck yourself" is to order him to harm himself, while to call someone a "mother fucker" is not so much a play on his Oedipal fears as to accuse him of being so low that he would inflict the greatest imaginable harm (fucking) upon that person who is most dear to him (his mother). (p. 256)

Powerlessness is a reality learned by females and minorities both in school and in the world at large through repeated experiences of not being heard. It is further reinforced through the sexist and racist traditions that negate the credibility of females and minorities when they do speak out to challenge the reality of the powerful.

Stereotypic beliefs about different cultural groups cannot be used to excuse the behavior of perpetrators or victims of sexual harassment. For example, while it is a stereotype that certain cultures are more aggressive or passive than others, cultural beliefs do influence what people find to be offensive and how they react to offensive behavior. For some women, cultural beliefs have taught them that in order to survive, you don't make trouble; don't speak up if you are harrassed. Indeed, for some women cultural beliefs have taught them that the act of speaking up is more shameful than the act of harassment. For other women, cultural beliefs have included a strong tradition of speaking up and affirming the powerfulness of women. The dominant culture's belief in the supremacy of masculinity has, however, often punished those who are culturally different, especially when differences pose a threat to the power status quo. Many women have thus been faced with the intolerable choice of denying their cultural beliefs or conforming to what is considered a deviant reality. These dilemmas are apparent in teenagers' discussions about sexual harassment. Speak up and you'll be destroyed in one way; remain silent and you'll be destroyed in another.

ETYMOLOGY AND THEORY DEVELOPMENT

Although the term *sexual harassment* is a relatively new one in our vocabularies, the concept is quite old. References to sexual harassment, though not labeled as such, abound in novels, plays, diaries, folktales, and other archives of human experience. The verb *to harass* was used in old English, meaning literally "to set a dog on someone." The viciousness and power aspect of harassment is, thus, inherent in its etymology.

The term *sexual harassment* grew out of women discussing their experiences in consciousness-raising groups and rape prevention efforts in the 1970s. The identification of parallels in women's experiences, the process of labeling those parallel experiences, and the ability to see the personal as political all contributed to a wave of social and psychological empowerment of women that profoundly influenced American society. The term was then codified in the Equal Employment Opportunities Commission's 1980 definition.[1]

Current theoretical work on sexual harassment focuses on the experience of the victim, or potential victim, and the school or other institution's ability to support her reality. The presence or absence of sexual harassment depends on the victim's perception of "unwelcome" sexual behavior. Complaint management programs focus on supporting and empowering the victim, so that she will be heard and the situation will be resolved to her benefit. Prevention programs focus on the empowerment of women by changing the culture and structure of the institution. This process of constructing theory, language, and model programs from shared personal experience follows an existential phenomenological approach to problem-solving, one that is familiar to many feminists but that is quite alien to most school administrators, who value a more positivist and mechanistic view of management and problem-solving. It is this approach that has allowed us to move from the sharing of personal stories, to the development of theory about the power aspect of sexual harassment, and on to the implementation of successful prevention programs.

LEGAL APPROACHES TO SEXUAL HARASSMENT IN SCHOOLS

Our work with schools has demonstrated that a legal approach is crucial in changing the gender power relations and the presence of sexual harassment in schools. Recourse to the law is essentially a method wherein the less powerful borrow power from a higher authority in order to create change. The law pits social norms that render women powerless against legal concepts of equal protection and due process. Moreover, the use of law creates an unprecedented coalition between administrators, whose interest is to reduce the organization's liability, and feminists, who seek to eliminate sexual harassment.

Sexual harassment is illegal in schools. It is a form of sex discrimination prohibited by the Fourteenth Amendment, Title IX of the Educational Amendments of 1972, Title VII of the Civil Rights Act (1964, amended 1972), and state criminal and civil statutes. Some forms of sexual harassment may also be actionable as child abuse, sexual assault, rape, pornography, criminal or civil libel, slander or defamation of character. Both students and employees are legally protected against sexual harassment, regardless of whether the perpetrator is an employee, a student, or an individual who is part of an organization with which the school has a contractual agreement. Victims, as well as educators or community members acting on the victim's behalf, may file sexual harassment complaints.

Despite the numerous applicable statutes and the prevalence of sexual harassment in schools, relatively few complaints are filed, still fewer cases are heard, and even fewer are found actionable. The reasons for this massive nonenforcement of sexual harassment regulations are complex and imbedded within our social and legal structures. To begin, victims may not recognize that they are being harassed if they have no words for describing their experience. Instead they may think that they are having a personal problem and, given society's frequent response, may blame themselves for having caused the harassment. Other victims may recognize the harassment but fear reporting it because they are likely to be accused of having caused the harassment themselves. Traditionally, women in our culture have been held responsible for men's sexual behavior. Victims may also fear that reporting an incident will make them more vulnerable to further harassment or subject to reprisals in terms of poor grades, evaluations, demotions, or reassignments. Moreover, those victims who do report sexual harassment may be advised as a result of ignorance, or threatened as a result of malevolence, to drop charges. Countersuits, intimidation, and adverse publicity frequently do plague a victim who reports sexual harassment.

Several cases of sexual harassment in schools have involved the firing of staff or the awarding of damages to the victim. Although the criteria for judging these cases are highly inconsistent, punishment occurs frequently enough for schools to pay attention to such charges. In 11 of 12 recent cases of student-related sexual harassment, the perpetrator was a school employee: three building level administrators, four teachers, one counselor, one bus driver, and two unspecified employees. In six cases, high school girls were the victims, with multiple victims in two of these cases; the other victims were a junior high school girl, an elementary school boy, a female school psychologist, and a woman teacher. Two cases involved inappropriate remarks and leers; five involved alleged sexual molestation with a broad range of charges; three involved alleged rape; and two involved the failure of school authorities to report suspected sexual abuse in the school. Only one of the three alleged rape cases resulted in a prison sentence (10 years). Of the five molestation cases, one led to a misdemeanor conviction with a suspended sentence of 300 hours of community service and $150 fine; one involved a $150,000 out of court settlement; one upheld the dismissal of the perpetrator; and one allowed the perpetrator to resign; and the outcome of the last was unclear. The two cases that involved inappropriate remarks resulted in the dismissal of the perpetrator. Vergon (1989) found a similar pattern in Title VII employment-related case law regarding sexually and racially "hostile environments" in which degree of offensiveness, coercion, repetitiveness, pervasiveness, and the availability of recourse were criteria weighed by the court, but were not applied consistently.

Recently, however, a new avenue for the adjudication of sexual harassment and child abuse of minors by school district personnel was created in the 1989 precedent-setting case of *Stoneking v. Bradford* (87–3637), heard before the U.S. Court of Appeals for the Third Circuit. In this case, the court held that public school officials had violated a student's Fourteenth Amendment right to "liberty" when they failed to protect her from sexual abuse by school employees. This decision paved the way for the former high school student to sue the school district and individual school officials for negligent supervision of the band director, who had sexually assaulted the girl in the course of his official responsibilities.

The significance of this case cannot be underestimated. It opens the door for others to use the equal protection clause of the Fourteenth Amendment in sexual harassment cases in schools, and it means that aggrieved individuals need not distinguish between sexual harassment and sexual abuse when making a complaint. The most important aspect of this case, however, is that it shifts the liability from the perpetrator to the school district and its officers. "It is real obvious," said Steve Russell, attorney for the Pennsylvania School Board Association, "that when school districts get allegations, they can no longer ignore them or just hope that it goes away" ("School Administrators Can Be Sued," 1989, p. 20).

OPERATIONAL DEFINITIONS OF SEXUAL HARASSMENT

A focus on the law and the remedies it offers does not give us the interpersonal dynamics that every incident of sexual harassment encompasses, for the law trains our attention only on the victim/subject and the accused/perpetrator of the harassment.[2] More often than not, especially when the sexual harassment is between peers in a school setting, there are also bystanders and colluders who support the supremacy of male power in the school culture. Some bystanders may be "innocent" witnesses who do not encourage the harasser yet do not intervene on behalf of the victim/subject. Other bystanders may be more actively involved in the incident, either because of their personal relationship with the participants or because of their physical proximity to the incident. They may play rolls that range from denying that anything of consequence is happening to ones that escalate the harassment.

Collusion occurs *after* the incident, as the subject/victim begins to tell her story to her friends and to the school authorities. Assuming she can get beyond the silencing our culture encourages her to do, her recounting of the events is often met with skepticism. The culture of her peers will more likely support gossip and ostracism than lend her respect and praise for speaking out against her harasser(s). Concurrently, the school authorities may punish her by humiliating her and blaming her for the incident, and may even dismiss her accusations. Such actions on the part of the school officials do more than protect harassers and maintain the climate that fosters and tolerates harassment and discrimination; they build cynicism about education and create a loss of confidence in school policy effectiveness that destroys trust toward the very people who are supposed to protect students. Ultimately such actions turn school into an unsafe place. These consequences are felt not only by the victim/subject, but also by the bystanders, both "innocent" witnesses and colluders, who have now, too, tasted the bitter lessons of sexual harassment.

When the specter or hint of a sexually tinged relationship between a minor and an adult in a school setting emerges, confusion or cover-up seem to be the typical response. More is at stake here, because the sexual harassment has entered a new domain, that of child abuse and criminal felonious behavior. Within the past decade, our society has realized the magnitude and significance of the problem of child sexual abuse. Finkkelhor reports that by age 18, 1 out of every 5 girls, and 1 out of every 10 boys, will have experienced some form of sexual abuse (cited in Massachusetts Department of Public Health, 1984). Although this abuse is most likely to occur within the family and with decreasing frequency as the age of the child and his or her independence increases, elementary and secondary schools are not immune from this problem (Stein & Kaser, 1989).

Despite the lack of documented occurrences in public schools, incidents of sexual abuse and sexual harassment do occur, and the offenders are frequently clustered in a few particular capacities within the school community. Such roles as coach, driver education teacher, and extracurricular adviser often require individual contact with students, often in private settings, and often in a capacity that can build trust and intimacy. Although these same adults may serve in a dual capacity as classroom teachers, examples suggest a less frequent occurrence of physical sexual harassment from these individuals when they are in their classroom roles as opposed to their adjunctive roles. These incidents of physical sexual harassment are often reported to sex-equity specialists at the local, state, and national levels. In most cases, however, calls to the Title IX/Sex Equity Coordinators are jurisdictionally futile because if the child who is the subject of this inappropriate sexual attention is a minor (in most states under the age of 18), then alleged incidents must be reported as charges of alleged criminal misconduct to the state agency that has authority for child welfare and child protection.

More often than not, reported

> transgressions between adult teachers and their students are not acts of "child abuse" because no touching, which is the prerequisite for child abuse under most state laws, has occurred. Rather, there have been sexist and inappropriate behaviors and/or language, either in public or in private, and in the search to quickly and vigilantly label these inappropriate behaviors, the term "child abuse" has been applied. In the ensuing investigation, the allegations of child abuse are usually dropped, and the more accurate and broad charge of "sex discrimination" is lost. This rush to judgment, albeit from the best of intentions, has left the real culprit, "sex discrimination," free to wander. (Bogart & Stein, 1989, p. 158)

In those cases in which touching has taken place, "mandated reporters"[3] must follow the use of state statutes on child abuse through an already overburdened and volatile judicial system, a path that may offer little or no satisfactory redress except in the most horrific instances of sexual abuse. We are faced with a cruel dilemma: "By mobilizing considerable effort and attention through legal and social channels to the most serious incidents of child abuse, we fail to provide sanctions against what [have] become the more commonplace occurrences of sex discrimination and sexual harassment" (Stein & Kaser, 1989, p. 5).

PERVASIVENESS OF SEXUAL HARASSMENT IN SCHOOLS

Sexual harassment occurs in the mundane, daily matters of school life: in the corridors and stairwells; in the cafeteria, chemistry lab, and carpentry shop; in the gym and parking lot; on school buses, in the driver's ed car, and on practice fields. Yet despite its frequency, sexual harassment is rarely reported, tallied, investigated, or systematically documented because it is simply not in the power structure's interest to do so. Occasionally sexual harassment is reported to guidance counselors, administrators, or teachers, who, whether or not they resolve the situation, may pass along the allegations to agencies charged with resolving complaints of sex discrimination. More often than not, nothing is done with this information, and the problem and conditions fester, spawning an atmosphere that at the very least permits and tolerates sexual harassment, and more likely interferes with the right to an equal educational opportunity and equal protection under the law.

Feminist educators and equity specialists at the local, state, and national levels, particularly in the state education agencies of California, Massachusetts, Hawaii, and Minnesota, have been collecting information on the incidence of sexual harassment in schools since the late 1970s. In 1978, incidents of peer sexual harassment among students in secondary schools were reported to the Massachusetts Department of Education. Data collected in subsequent years showed patterns and profiles of sexual harassment indicating that young women were indeed harassed by their peers. In general, these behaviors, though illegal under Title IX as a form of sex discrimination, have nonetheless been overlooked, tolerated, or condoned by school officials. Their effects on the whole school climate, as well as on the subject/victim, have been minimized or dismissed.

In 1980–81, the first study on peer-to-peer sexual harassment in high schools was administered by Nan Stein of the Massachusetts Department of Education with assistance from the Alliance Against Sexual Coercion. It included a survey and in-depth interviews. The research revealed the following:

- Young women are much more likely to be victims of sexual harassment, especially in the more severe forms of unwanted physical attention, than their male counterparts.

- Sexual harassment is a problem for many students in high school, in both vocational high schools and in comprehensive schools. It is not the case that sexual harassment occurs only when young women are in the minority, as they often are in vocational schools or in courses that have been previously considered sex role nontraditional. Sexual harassment is a typical part of the fabric of daily life in schools where young women comprise 50% of the school population.
- Student-to-student sexual harassment is more prevalent than teacher-to-student sexual harassment.
- Peer-to-peer sexual harassment ranged from verbal and written comments to physical assault and attempted rape.
- Sexual harassment on the job is not unfamiliar to high school students, whether the job is part of the school curriculum, as in a "co-op" job supervised by school personnel, or acquired independently of the school.

Sexual harassment has an adverse effect on teaching and learning both in the classroom and outside of it. Students who have experienced sexual harassment report an array of consequences, with direct and indirect effects. Some experiences left an immediate impact while others lingered in a latent state, surfacing at a later date. Among the immediate effects were feelings of embarrassment, fear or retaliation, anger, powerlessness, loss of self-confidence, and cynicism about education and teachers. Students also identified physical symptoms, including insomnia and listlessness, and reported a reduced ability to perform schoolwork, excessive absenteeism, or tardiness. They also indicated that sexual harassment led them to transfer from a particular course or course of study and, in some cases, to withdraw from school. It goes without saying that the presence of any one of these conditions constitutes a denial of equal educational opportunity.

More subtle experiences of harassment produced less tangible consequences. Students who felt betrayed, discredited, or compromised by peers, and unsupported by school staff, seemed less trusting of people in general and less enthusiastic about pursuing their education. Victims/subjects of sexual harassment as well as the bystanders and witnesses to incidents of sexual harassment expressed a loss of confidence in the effectiveness of school policies. In fact, positive feelings and beliefs about justice and caring may be in jeopardy if such a "poisoned environment" is allowed to persist. Such a loss of community, let alone the loss of hope for a just and caring community, may have a greater impact upon young women than upon young men, whether or not these young women are victims of sexual harassment (Gilligan, 1985).

We can also judge the pervasive concern with educating the school community about the problem of sexual harassment, if not actual instances of harassment, by looking at the number of requests for the use or purchase of materials pertaining to the prevention and elimination of sexual harassment. With data on the purchase of four resources in particular, we can extrapolate with confidence that sexual harassment is acknowledged to exist and perceived as a problem in secondary schools.

The Massachusetts Department of Education first came out with a curriculum guide entitled *Who's Hurt and Who's Liable: Sexual Harassment in Massachusetts Schools* in 1979; 500 copies were printed and made available to school districts at no cost (Stein, 1979/1986). No distribution records were kept, but copies went predominantly to school district personnel within Massachusetts. Five hundred copies were printed in September 1981 and again in June 1982, when the curriculum was updated and revised. This time they were distributed to sex-equity coordinators in all of the states and sent, at no cost, to the desegregation assistance centers (DACs) and to a variety of women's advocacy groups. It was also accepted into ERIC (#ED 215 254), made available at a variety of conferences, and publicized in journals and newsletters that circulate in the academic/feminist communities. The Massachusetts Department of Education completed final revision of the curriculum in 1986, printing 500 copies each year until 1989 and granting several requests to reprint *Who's Hurt and Who's Liable*.

In 1982, the Massachusetts Department of Education also produced—first as a slide show, then as a filmstrip, and finally as a videotape—*No Laughing Matter: High School Students and Sexual Harassment*. This media production initially cost $200 and sold close to 20 copies in its original format. After its conversion to a synchronized tape/filmstrip, the price was lowered to $45. In this format, and in its latest incarnation as a videotape, which sells for $20, 118 copies have been sold. The breakdown of the sales indicates that 56 copies went to school districts, 22 copies to state departments of education, 19 copies to universities, and 18 copies to other agencies and organizations.

Another set of tape/filmstrips was developed in 1985 by the Sex Equity Office of the California Department of Education. These two filmstrips, *It's Not Funny if It Hurts* and *Think About It . . . It Won't Go Away*, sell as a set for $20. Data supplied by the California Department of Education show 197 sales from 1985 through 1989, the majority to unified districts (K–12 systems) in California, and secondarily to agencies outside of California. These filmstrips have also been loaned by the California Department of Education to 272 school districts and other community-based organizations.

Pervasiveness of the concern with sexual harassment is perhaps most powerfully presented through data on the sales of a booklet produced by the Programs for Educational Opportunity (formerly called the Center for Sex Equity in Schools) at the University of Michigan. This booklet, *Tune in to Your Rights*, was created in 1985, and as of December 1989, about 44,000 copies had been disseminated. The initial 6,000 copies were mailed free of charge to school district personnel in the Great Lakes region, to sex-equity personnel in state departments of education, and to selected national educational and women's issues leaders. The remaining 38,000 copies have been sold at a nominal price to a total of 141 organizations in all 50 states including secondary and middle schools, postsecondary institutions, unions, teacher centers, libraries, youth organizations, state departments of education, and desegregation assistance centers around the country.

Data are less definitive about how schools use this booklet, but 57% of the schools who have purchased multiple copies have reported back on how they are using it. High school use was reported more than twice as frequently as middle school use; middle school use was reported somewhat more frequently than vocational school use. Typical school use appears to be in one class or in a special workshop. Perhaps these data indicate that sexual harassment is most commonly addressed as a response to a critical incident in one building, although some schools do appear to be making it a regular part of the curriculum. Suffice it to say that the popular appeal and sales of this booklet strongly suggest that sexual harassment is recognized as a problem that requires intervention (Linn, 1989).

ADVICE ABOUT CURRENT STRATEGIES TO USE IN SCHOOLS

Most important in the development of effective prevention and complaint management programs are strategies to break the silence and the hidden blame that surrounds sexual harassment. Whether an organization chooses to create awareness through a survey, a media campaign, a speak-out, or the development of a policy depends largely on the formality of the organization, the types of arguments that will sway it, its level of denial, and the placement of key activists who are seeking change.

The first steps need to focus on getting people to talk, to feel concern and outrage about the offensiveness of a recent incident or about the pervasiveness of sexual harassment in the organization. People need to feel a sense of wrongdoing. They also need help in making connections between the harassing behaviors, the ensuing harm, and societal outcomes. The use of a provocative poster, such as the one developed by the Hawaii Department of Education (1984), which is included in the

Annotated Resources at the end of the book, can be a catalyst for informal discussion.

A crucial next step is to implement a sexual harassment policy and complaint management system. Without these, the organization has no way to collect data about and respond to incidents that are reported, leaving victims who do come forward vulnerable to further organizational victimization. This unfortunate situation is most likely to happen if feminist activists from within the school and the community try to enact change without forming a coalition with school legal authorities. Often the creation of such a policy can take years, especially if the authorities are unwilling to admit that harassment is taking place. Authorities fear (and rightly so) that a policy will increase the number of complaints, yet fail to recognize that their lack of policy will increase their own liability in the eyes of the court.

Every sexual harassment policy should plainly state that sexual harassment is unacceptable, will not be tolerated, and will lead to disciplinary action. The policy should clearly define sexual harassment; its notification process; procedures for how to file, hear, investigate, decide, and appeal complaints; sanctions for unwanted behavior; a monitoring plan; and an educational plan for involving the entire school community. Sample policies may be found in *Who's Hurt and Who's Liable* (Stein, 1986) and the *Title IX Line* (1983) issue on sexual harassment.

The school district must then identify and train a multicultural, gender representative team of compliant managers in each building. Overlays of racism and ethnocentrism are best diminished if a diverse group of complaint managers is available to students. In terms of power relations, a multicultural, gender representative group is necessary for forming a coalition of activists committed to eliminating all forms of harassment. The organization will want to centralize the complaint management function to make it less expensive and less time-consuming. Administrators may also place a higher priority on consistency over quality of resolution. They may want to limit the number and role of people who receive confidential information, either to contain confidential information about suspected perpetrators or to limit the authority of lower status employees, such as counselors and teachers.

Complaint managers should have a thorough understanding of the power dynamics of sexual harassment, school policy, and legal guidelines. They should know which cases can be resolved informally, which need to be reported formally, and which may require legal attention. Complaint managers should be people who are especially well trusted by students and staff who are at greatest risk for victimization: all women, women of color, women in nontraditional roles, minorities in nontraditional roles, disabled people, lesbians, gay men, and bisexual people. Complaint managers should also be skilled in human relations, in cross-cultural communication, and in specific techniques such as the third-person letter-writing technique.[4] They should be culturally sensitive to the needs of students from diverse cultural backgrounds and should be able to talk to students about sexual harassment in the language that students prefer. The Massachusetts curriculum guide *Who's Hurt and Who's Liable* (Stein, 1986) can be used as the core material for complaint manager training.

The school that takes its antiharassment campaign seriously will also infuse this issue throughout the curriculum. In social studies classes, sexual harassment will be discussed historically and culturally as a workforce issue and as a matter of law. In English and literature classes, students will read books in which sexual harassment arises as a literary theme or psychological issue.[5] In career planning classes, human relations, counseling, and nontraditional student support groups, sexual harassment will be discussed as an impediment to human development. Discussion of date rape and domestic violence will be part of the curriculum. The student handbook, school rules, and safety orientation sessions for laboratory and industrial arts classes will thoroughly cover the school's policy and the harm that sexual harassment does to everyone in the school community.

Finally, a school that truly wants to make a difference in combatting sexual harassment will appoint a diverse and committed group of people responsible for continually managing, improving, and modifying the school's response to this issue. This group will keep public attention focused on the issue, collect information about the school's progress, and advocate for further prevention initiatives.

In essence, our major goal is to change the culture of schools. We need to focus on the creation of substantive change, rather than on the reduction of district liability. We need to press for interventions that are as long range and institutionalized as possible as we build measures, programs, resources, and events that bring sexual harassment into the mainstream of education. We need to build effective coalitions with other groups who are also victims of harassment and continually model positive cross-gender relationships everywhere in our lives.

The effects of sexual harassment plague women's lives and their reality and cause incalculable damage to the health and quality of our society. The character of our schools and our world is severely compromised by sexual harassment, as is our hope, and the hope of countless students, for a just future. When women's reality becomes part of our culture's shared reality, when both women and men learn from each other with genuine trust and mutual respect, then we can hope that the bitter lessons of sexual harassment will become but a memory, and that school will become a place in which everyone can partake of sweet liberty and justice for all.

NOTES

1. "Unwelcome sexual advances, requests for sexual favors, and other verbal or physical conduct of a sexual nature constitute sexual harassment when: a) submission to such conduct is made either explicitly or implicitly a term or condition of an individual's employment; b) submission to or rejection of such conduct by an individual is used as the basis for employment decisions affecting such individual; c) such conduct has the purpose or effect of substantially interfering with an individual's work performance or creating an intimidating, hostile, or offensive working environment." (Federal Register, November 10, 1980, p. 746676)

2. We prefer to use the word *subject*, to indicate that anyone can be the subject or recipient of unwanted attention rather than use the word *victim*, which is a legal notion, often accompanied by paralyzing psychosocial consequences. We shall continue to use both words, victim and subject, in tandem.

3. According to Massachusetts regulations, a "mandated reporter" means "any physician, medical intern, . . . public or private school teacher, educational administrator, guidance or family counselor, day care worker, probation officer, social worker, foster parent, firefighter or police officer, who, in his/her professional capacity shall have reasonable cause to believe that a child is suffering from a reportable condition. The term also includes any person in charge of a medical or other public or private institution, school or facility, or his/her designee who has been notified by a member of his/her staff of a reportable condition. In such case the staff member is not required to report, but the person in charge is. No mandated reporter shall be liable in any civil or criminal action by reason of submitting a report. No other person making a report shall be liable in any civil or criminal action by reason of submitting a report if it was made in good faith." (Massachusetts General Laws, 110 CMR 4.00)

4. This technique, which was developed by Mary Rowe, special assistant to the president at the Massachusetts Institute of Technology, is described in University of Michigan (1985), pp. 16–18, and in Stein (1986), pp. 58–61.

5. For example, Charlotte Brontë, *Villette*; Edna Ferber, *Roast Beef Medium*; Fay Weldon, *The Life and Loves of a She-Devil*; Alice Walker, *The Color Purple*; Sylvia Plath, *The Bell Jar*; William Shakespeare, *The Taming of the Shrew*.

REFERENCES

Baker, R. (1984). Conceptions of sex—pricks and chicks: A plea for persons. In R. Baker & F. Elliston (Eds.), *Philosophy and Sex* (pp. 249–267). New York: Prometheus.

Bogart, K., & Stein, N. (1989). Breaking the silence: Sexual harassment in education, sex equity and sexuality in education. *Peabody Journal of Education*, 64(4), 146–163.

California Department of Education, Sex Equity Office. (1985). *It's not funny if it hurts* and *Think about it . . . it won't go away*. Sacramento: Author.

Eakins, B. W., & Eakins, R. (1978). *Sex differences in human communication*. Boston: Houghton Mifflin.

Gilligan, C. (1985). *In a different voice.* Cambridge: Harvard University Press.

Hawaii Department of Education, Project Esteem. (1984). *Sexual harassment: It's uncool.* Honolulu: Author.

Herek, G. M. (1987). On heterosexual masculinity: Some physical consequences of the social construction of gender and sexuality. In M. Kimmel (Ed.), *Changing men: New Directions on men and masculinity* (pp. 68–82). Newbury Park, CA: Sage.

Hughes, J. O., & Sandler, B. R. (1988). *Peer harassment: Hassles for women on campus.* Washington, DC: Association of American Colleges, Project on the Status and Education of Women.

Janeway, E. (1981). *Powers of the weak.* New York: Morrow.

Kiscaden, L. (1988). *It's not fun/it's illegal. The identification and prevention of sexual harassment of teenagers. A curriculum.* St. Paul: Minnesota Department of Education.

Klein, F. (1988). *Working woman sexual harassment survey.* (Available from *Working Woman,* Box MM, 342 Madison Ave., New York, NY 10173)

Linn, E. (1989). *Internal reports on materials dissemination.* Unpublished reports, University of Michigan, Programs for Educational Opportunity, Ann Arbor.

Massachusetts Department of Education. (1989). *Internal reports on materials dissemination, 1979–1989.* Unpublished reports, Massachusetts Department of Education, Quincy.

Massachusetts Department of Education, Bureau of Educational Resources and Television. (1982). *No laughing matter: High school students and sexual harassment.* Quincy: Author.

Massachusetts Department of Public Health, Resource Center for the Prevention of Family Violence and Sexual Assault. (1984). *Preventing family violence: A Curriculum for Adolescents.* Boston: Author.

Northwest Women's Law Center. (1984). *Sexual harassment in the schools* (Multi-Cultural Resource Series). Olympia, WA: Department of Public Instruction, Office for Equity Education.

Parenti, M. (1978). *Power and the powerless.* New York: St. Martin's.

Sandroff, R. (1988, December). Sexual harassment in the Fortune 500. *Working Woman,* pp. 69–73.

School administrators can be sued for overlooking sexual harassment by staff. (1989, September 28). *School Law News, 17,* 20.

Sexual harassment in the federal workplace: An update. (1988). Washington, DC: Merit System Protection Board.

Sexual harassment is no laughing matter [Special issue]. (1983). *Title IX Line,* 4(1). (Available from Center for Sex Equity in Schools, Programs for Educational Opportunity, University of Michigan)

Stein, N. (1981). *Sexual harassment of high school students: Preliminary research results.* Quincy: Massachusetts Department of Education.

Stein, N. (Ed.). (1986). *Who's hurt and who's liable: Sexual harassment in Massachusetts schools.* Quincy: Massachusetts Department of Education, Civil Rights/Chapter 622 Project. (Original work published 1979)

Stein, N., & Kaser, J. (1989). *On the line: Prevention of sexual harassment and sexual abuse of students in schools.* Unpublished manuscript.

Stoneking v. Bradford. U.S. Third Circuit Court of Appeals, 87–3636, 882 F. 2d 720, 58 U.S.L.W. 2135, 55 Ed. Law Rep. 429.

Strauss, S. (1988, March). Sexual harassment in the school: Legal implications for principals. *National Association of Secondary School Principals Bulletin*, pp. 93–97.

University of Michigan, Programs for Educational Opportunity. (1985). *Tune in to your rights: A guide for teenagers about turning off sexual harassment*. Ann Arbor: Author.

CHAPTER 6

Talking About Talking About Sex

The Organization of Possibilities

CHRISTINE LaCERVA

Tameka[1] is 6 years old, African-American, poor, a first-grade student. Tameka and her classmates talk, laugh, fight, and, on the best of days, work together with their teacher, whose goals are to build a democratic and nonabusive classroom environment. They attend the Barbara Taylor School in Harlem, an independent, multiracial elementary school that is developing a radically humanistic pedagogy, one based on the premise that children are producers and changers, not consumers and, for the most part, passive recipients, determined *by* but not determiners *of* their environment.

Today, as usual, the teacher begins the morning group by asking, "How's the class doing?" Many students want to talk about their relationships with each other. One boy relates an incident that took place in the after-school program: Bobby, a boy in the middle grades, kissed Tameka very hard on the mouth when the teacher was not looking. Tameka had been upset but was not able to talk about what happened or how she felt. As the boy speaks, the other boys laugh among themselves; the girls are quiet. Another child says, "He raped her." Nervous, but unhesitant, the teacher asks if Tameka had wanted to be kissed. "No" is the response.

The teacher decides to try to help the group create an environment in which it is possible to talk openly and honestly about this incident and what it means to the children. She tries not to presume to know how they understand what happened nor how Tameka or any of the other children feel. Rather, she takes this opportunity to *build the group*, to assist the children in the collective activity of *building the kind of environment* where they can speak of these sexual issues. She begins by discovering how well the *existing environment* is suited to explore these matters.

She asks the students what they think about what took place; what is the history of what happened; what are their reactions to talking about kissing? Tameka, although an acknowledged leader of the class, remains silent and withdrawn. She is not willing, at this time (in the existing environment), to talk about the incident or her feelings about it.

Some students say they think what happened is "a bad thing" and that "boys do this kind of thing to girls." It is the teacher's view that what happened was not an issue of morality, a matter of inherently good or bad behavior, but was a social issue—sex roles and sexuality are socially produced and organized. Because of this viewpoint, she works for the 20 minutes of this morning's group to *socialize* "Tameka's problem" so that it eventually becomes not an abstract social problem but *the class's problem.* She invites the students to talk about sexuality: What do they think it is? How does it look in the classroom? On the street? On TV? She helps them to create a nonrepressive environment where they can talk about these issues openly and nonjudgmentally.

There is a lot of laughing and fooling around; the children appear nervous. The teacher herself feels the pull to admonish the boys for having done something bad. And she can see that attitude in how the children are acting. She shares some of her own conflicts and nervousness with them: that she finds it difficult to talk about sex and sexuality but thinks it would be very helpful for everyone to do so; that she needs help from them in order to lead the discussion and facilitate the creation of the new environment. "Do you want to do this?" "How should we start?" The children are 6 and 7 years old. They are African-American, Caribbean, African, Puerto Rican, Dominican, and Jewish.

One girl says to the teacher that it's hard for her to talk too. Others join in and the discussion continues. The boys say they thought they could do whatever they wanted to the girls as long as no one was around. The girls say they feel like they have to put up with this kind of sex play in order for the boys to like them. The teacher asks them why and urges them to say more, to respond to each other, unthreateningly challenging their understandings of themselves, going deeper into their partially formed belief systems, definitions, assumptions, values, and conflicts.

Some of the girls ask Tameka how she felt. Then they answer for her by saying how they think she felt. The teacher continues to question the students: Did Tameka want to be kissed? Did she like getting the attention? Tameka, herself, is still unable to participate in the discussion. The other students express their conflicts. On the one hand, Tameka didn't want to be kissed *in that way;* on the other hand, she did like the attention and often played up to the boys. The teacher tells them she herself has had this experience of simultaneously liking and not liking something that is happening and that while we are all taught that conflicts are bad things to have, people are conflicted all the time! It's not *bad*—it's *normal.* Tameka nods her head and begins to talk about what happened.

This chapter and the pedagogical practice that it describes posit that the current organization of gender, sexuality, learning, and development—which many take to be socially, sexually, and intellectually repressive—can be qualitatively reorganized in ways that free young children to learn, develop, be giving to others, and provide leadership to adults in how to be nonabusive and decent.

This is, of course, a large claim. In the view of the founders of the Barbara Taylor School, it is what education *has* to be about in the last decade of the 20th century, when high underdevelopment, poverty, destruction, and abuse characterize the lives of so many of our children. The following pages describe neither a completed model nor a validated theory; rather, they are an attempt to present a methodology currently being practiced. This "practice of method" (Holzman & Newman, 1979), following Vygotsky's (1978, 1987) seminal work on development and learning, *is*, in my opinion, best characterized as *the organization of possibility*—so that children and adults can be free to choose to live in ways that support human growth.

I begin with a discussion of gender, sex role socialization, sexuality, and sexual development that relate to schooling. The findings and limitations I describe point, in my view, to the need for an approach like the one practiced at the Barbara Taylor School. Next, I summarize the methodology of social therapy, the foundation of the pedagogical approach of the school. I focus on how sexuality is understood and dealt with not as a curriculum content area but as a component of the child's total development. Anecdotes, such as the one at the beginning of the chapter, are presented to illustrate some of what goes on at the Barbara Taylor School.

SEX ROLES AND SOCIALIZATION

It is now generally accepted that children are *socialized* into sex roles, into particular ways of being, seeing, and doing. From Maccoby and Jacklin's (1974) comprehensive review of (mostly experimental, empirical) research on gender differences, to Gilligan's explorations into both the repression and expression of girls' and women's "different voice" (1982; Gilligan, Lyons, & Hanmer, 1990), to the analyses by critical and feminist psychologists, sociologists, philosophers, and educators, such as Jaggar and Rothenberg (1978) and Walkerdine (1987; Walkerdine & Lucey, 1989), we have learned how girls come to relate to themselves and be related to by others as passive, emotional, and nurturing, while boys are related to as active, aggressive, rational, and unemotional. Many researchers self-consciously critique the science that has produced these "findings," specifying the extent to which the epistemological and ontological framework through which we view human development is thoroughly male dominated (Chodorow, 1978; Harding, 1984; Holzman & Rosen, 1984; Jaggar & Rothenberg, 1978; Weisstein, 1971). I find that the best of these critiques address the male-dominated methodology and ideology as inseparable from the race and class biases also woven into the fabric of the accepted scientific method (Fulani, 1988; Henriques, Hollway, Urwin, Venn, & Walkerdine, 1984). The reasons for the proliferation of gender studies are complex, but it seems to me that this growing awareness owes much to the political activism of the '60s; the liberation struggles of African-Americans, Latinos, Native Americans, women, and lesbians and gays created an environment in which intellectuals could begin to link their progressive politics with their scientific and professional practice.

From all of these studies and my personal experiences as an educator, I have concluded that by the time they are 3 or 4 years old, children are remarkably knowledgeable (if not conscious of what they know) about what it means to be a "real girl" and a "real boy." The toys they play with, the clothes they wear, the way they talk and communicate, the friends they choose, and how they express their emotions both reveal and determine *who they are*. For example, boys are not free to cry or be tender; the most acceptable boy-to-boy physicality is aggressive, not affectionate. Boys learn to touch girls when no one is looking, to take advantage of those who are younger and probably won't tell, and to boast about it among their peers. They learn to be unemotional, ungiving, and "strong"—attributes of "real men." Girls, on the other hand, learn the social activities that will help them become "real women"—to be good, obedient, helpful, and not too smart; to be cooperative and not make trouble; to be coquettish and to act cute to get what they want; to walk and talk in ways that will obtain the approval of the boys in their class and the men in their families.

In my opinion, the impact of this socialization on intellectual, sexual, and social development is profound. The openness, energy, and inquisitiveness of young children—their straight talk, uncategorical ways of seeing, and relative "comfort with conflict" (Holzman & Strickland, 1989)—are closed down as the sexual and social roles available to them *become* their means of expressing themselves. In short, what it means to develop into mature, functional women and men is to become more and more sexually and intellectually repressed! I believe that this situation—coupled with the epidemic of sexist and antigay attitudes and violence in our society, including in our schools; the alarmingly high *pushout* rates (called dropout rates by government statisticians) among children of color and poor children; and the growing strength and credibility of right-wing ideology and leaders—calls for a pedagogy that confronts the intersection of gender, sexuality, and learning.

DECONSTRUCTING GENDER, SEXUALITY, AND LEARNING

Two leading developmental researchers, Carol Gilligan and Valerie Walkerdine, have conducted studies whose findings I find suggestive of such a pedagogy.

In her pioneering study of moral development, Gilligan (1982) challenged both the male-dominated methodology and the finding of male moral superiority that had to that point been scientifically unquestioned by psychologists and educators alike. She claimed that women and men have two different moralities, implying that they live in two separate but overlapping realities created by sociocultural conditions. Women are socialized to an "ethic of caring" and men to an "ethic of reason." This finding had evaded researchers before Gilligan in part because of "the diffidence prevalent among women, their reluctance to speak publicly in their voice, given the constraints imposed on them by their lack of power and the politics of relations between the sexes" (p. 70).

Recently, Gilligan and her colleagues have deepened their analysis by focusing on female adolescent development (Gilligan et al., 1990). Previous work by Gilligan found a sequence of adolescent girls' development that was not rooted in childhood.

> Instead, it seemed a response to a crisis, and the crisis seemed to be adolescence. Adolescence poses problems of connection for girls coming of age in Western culture, and girls are tempted or encouraged to solve these problems by excluding themselves or excluding others—that is, by being a good woman, or by being selfish. (Gilligan et al., 1990, pp. 9–10)

How adolescent girls experience and respond to this crisis is described by Gilligan and her colleagues through the voices of a group of adolescent girls and the researchers' neo-Freudian interpretative mechanisms of *crisis* and *connection*. At this age, girls notice women's silence and powerlessness; it is a time when they "are in danger of losing their connection with others and also a time when girls, gaining voice and knowledge, are in danger of knowing the unseen and speaking the unspoken and thus losing connection with what is commonly taken to be 'reality.' (Gilligan et al., 1990, p. 24)

While Gilligan does not address the impact of such socialization on learning and intellectual development, my experience leads me to believe that connections are easily made. I can see them, for example, in Tameka's initial silence and in her and her classmates' responses in the morning group.

As one of Great Britain's leading theorists and researchers into gender and class issues, Walkerdine (1984; 1987) is concerned with specifying how subjectivity, identity, and sexuality are socially and historically constituted. In her view, sex role socialization is not a simple process of girls and boys fitting into certain roles; rather it is produced by the complex relationship between beliefs, discourse, and actions. She and her colleagues have documented how our ideas and discourse about gender, sexuality, and intelligence are intimately intertwined with what women "are"—passive, well behaved, unable to reason, and so forth—and the impact of what women "are" on girls' intellectual development. For example, Walkerdine's studies on mathematics (Girls and Mathematics Unit, 1989) examine the relationship between girls' mathematics performance, how teachers talk about the differences between boys and girls, and how teachers relate to boys and girls. Teachers report that girls are in fact quite good at math, but the teachers attribute this high performance to "hard work," not to intelligence. On the other hand, teachers attribute boys' high performance in mathematics to intelligence.

Utilizing a psychoanalytic framework to show the relationship between cultural norms and the psychological production of feminine desire, Walkerdine (1987) examines how preparation for female adolescent sexuality is mediated by girls' comic books. The comics' story lines are revealing of the kind of personality theories and discourse about girls and boys that are typical of school, with "good" girls and "bad" girls possessing mutually exclusive personalities. She states:

> It is the production of girls as characters within stories, as objects within particular discourses, that generates and sanctions certain sorts of intellectuality and certain forms of feminity. Educational practices are a locus at which the production of intellectuality and the production of femininity intersect. (p. 117)

THE ROLE OF SOCIAL THERAPY IN THE FORMATION OF THE BARBARA TAYLOR SCHOOL

Walkerdine and Gilligan, it seems to me, make connections between gender, sexuality, and learning and development, in beginning to delineate how the production of femininity and masculinity produces both the way women and men "do thinking" and how we think about how women and men "do thinking." However, in my view, their methodology, which I characterize as one of description or deconstruction, can go only so far in creating a pedagogy that fosters development. What is needed is a *constructive* methodology, that is, a methodology that creates a new organization and relationship between gender, sexuality, and development.

It is in this way that the approach practiced at the Barbara Taylor School departs from the critical tradition. Deconstruction occurs through the activity of constructing something new. It is an *activist critique,* or an anticritique in Marx's sense—revolutionary practice, not critique, is what is critical (Newman, 1983; Holzman & Newman, 1979). Marx repeatedly polemicized against "mental criticism" as he put forth his conception of history:

> All forms and products of consciousness cannot be dissolved by mental criticism, by resolution into "self-consciousness" or transformation into "apparitions," "spectres," "fancies," etc. but only by the practical overthrow of the actual social relations which gave rise to this idealistic humbug; . . . not criticism but revolution is the driving force of history, also of religion, of philosophy and all other types of theory. (Marx & Engels, 1970, pp. 58–59)

And in the *Theses on Feuerbach* Marx stated: "The coincidence of the changing of circumstances and of human activity or self-changing can be conceived and rationally understood only as *revolutionary practice"* (p. 121).

Marx's methodological approach as it has been developed over the past 20 years by Fred Newman (1983, 1988a, 1988b, Holzman & Newman, 1979; Holzman & Polk, 1988) into the clinical and educational psychology called social therapy is the basis of the pedagogy practiced at the Barbara Taylor School. I will present a brief summary of social therapy before returning to the classrooms of the Barbara Taylor School.

Social therapy is a noninterpretive, *organizing* activity (Holzman & Newman, 1979; Newman, 1988a) based on the premise that human development is socially produced and organized and that it can be reorganized (Marx & Engels, 1970; Vygotsky, 1978, 1987). According to this premise, contemporary society is characterized by the *misorganization* of human relations and development in that the very process of human development that has evolved historically hides the fact of its sociality! Our sociality is repressed; the contradictory nature of development is that to be socialized is to be privatized; development *is* privatization. Thus, we are *socialized* to understand ourselves and others as quasi-passive and privatized perceivers/conceivers/participants, our emotions as *inside* ourselves, our smartness as "natural," our shame as unexpressible. These understandings of self are real! This distorted developmental process—being, seeing, and doing *privately, separately, dualistically* in an environment that is, in fact, social, connected, and whole—halts development. Social therapy is a response to this specific world-historic social condition: given that the world is whole and that human beings are its social producers, and yet the dominant socialization process is one in which we relate to the world as dualistically divided (alienated) from individual products (i.e., ourselves), how do we reorganize it so that we can relate to the world as it is, i.e., historically? How do we reinitiate development? How do we close the gap between our privatized sense of socialness and our capacity to produce and the means for expressing/realizing these characteristics of our humanity?

The answer social therapy provides is a specific—but widely applicable—practice, viz., that of *creating the very environments* that make this reinitiation of development possible. "Production is what reinitiates development" (Newman, 1988b, p. 191). This building process of necessity involves the breaking out (deconstruction) of the institutional constraints that have stopped development. For example, the collective activity of building environments where children can give expression to their pain, fears, joys, and conflicts of being socialized to become "real women" and "real men" is simultaneously the breaking out of these rigid and stultifying roles. Producing an environment where everyone in a class can learn and develop is simultaneously breaking out of the competitive, privatized, authoritarian, racist, sexist, and overly cognitive organization of learning that is characteristic of contemporary schools.

It should be apparent, even with this brief summary of social therapy, that such a critical practice is in direct confrontation with the dominant psychology and ideology. Social therapy has a different politic and does not hide it. The particular values of social therapy and their expression in practice make social therapy controversial.[2]

The pedagogical practice of the Barbara Taylor School is deeply political in that it is designed to change an educational institution that makes it very difficult for all children, but especially poor children and children of color, to develop and learn, be creative and productive, and express their humanity and decency. Such pedagogy organizes possibilities for children, their families, teachers, and the entire community to develop new tools and options that are in their own self-community interest.

This application of social therapy does not occur in a vacuum, but involves the school and its builders in relationships with political, cultural, and legal institutions—not only those that work to preserve the status quo but also those that, like the Barbara Taylor School, are sufficiently independent to work for radical social change. These connections—social therapy's politics—are yet another source of its controversiality, and, in my view, of its success. A pedagogy that organizes possibilities for people to develop new tools and options that are in their own self-community interest necessarily involves reorganizing the relationship between gender, sexuality, and learning, for their current relationship grows out of and perpetuates barriers to development: racism, sexism, classism, homophobia; abusive behavior; and the separation of emotionality from learning (Holzman & Strickland, 1989).

CONSTRUCTING A NEW PROGRESSIVE SEXUALITY

The reorganization process in the classroom must also be an expanding, inclusionary activity that builds new kinds of relationships with parents, teachers, and students. Helping children collectively produce their own development cannot be done without the participation of their parents. How do parents think about their children's intellectual and sexual development? What do they want their children to be learning about sexuality? How do they think their children should be taught?

At the Barbara Taylor School a parents meeting was held early in the year to discuss these issues and provide an opportunity for parents to participate in an open dialogue on sexuality at the school. Teachers, support staff, and a group of parents who were particularly interested in working on the development of a sexuality curriculum attended the meeting. As educational director, I opened the discussion by sharing the ongoing work of Tameka's class. The staff of the school had agreed that it was very important to include parents and create a context for all of us—parents, teachers, and staff—to shape how and what we were all doing with the children regarding these issues. The children seemed to want to work on these issues; how did the parents and staff feel about it? What kind of conflicts were being raised for all of us as we opened up the controversial topics of sexuality and sex with children?

The parents, who were black, Latino, white, gay, and straight, listened. The teachers and I spoke about the methodology of social therapy and our goals of wanting to build the conditions for children to talk openly with us about their ideas, belief systems, and values. Sexuality had never before been discussed in this grouping of parents and staff, where relationships between people were very new. Everyone present sought to create the conditions needed to break out of the social roles of parent and teacher, for if we remained in them, it would be difficult to talk openly about children and sexuality, much less provide leadership to the children on how to do so.

Tameka's mother spoke first. She was concerned that her daughter had not told her about the incident of being kissed in the after-school program. Was there something wrong that Tameka couldn't talk to her? She could see that Tameka was often passive and that the boys could walk all over her. She wanted to know if there was something that could be done to help the girls be more powerful. Other mothers said they too wanted their daughters to be able to speak up for themselves. Conflict arose during this discussion. A young black father said he disagreed with how Tameka's teacher had handled the incident. Wasn't the teacher really just shutting down the natural curiosity of boys at this age? He didn't want his son to feel it was wrong to explore his sexuality. A black woman, noticeably disturbed by his remarks, said she thought it was extremely important that boys learn at an early age that they can't do whatever they want, sexually speaking or otherwise. To do so is sexist and hurtful to the girls.

The question on the table was how could we—as a collective of parents, students, and teachers—promote a progressive, nonabusive sexuality for children. Rafaella, a Latina whose daughter is 3, put her head in her hands laughing. She said she had just realized that if we wanted to help the kids break out of these social roles and have a more progressive sexuality, then the parents would have to do so as well! She said she wasn't very good at this either. She had many conflicts about who she was as a woman and judgments about other women. Another issue was what we are saying, at home and at school, to our kids about being gay. An older parent said this all was really hard to talk about. He half-jokingly said that it seemed the kids were far better at it than we were.

At this point, the group took stock: parents and teachers would have to be role models in order to support the children working on these issues. Could we, the Barbara Taylor School Collective, do it? What would we need to build in order to support each other as role models? Tameka's father said the parents needed to know more about social therapy. Rafaella suggested that the parents would need to learn more about each other's histories, as they barely knew each other. The parents decided to write their histories so they could learn about each other and use their diverse racial and cultural traditions to create a multicultural reader for their children. This would help establish the conditions for more intimate and powerful relationships with each other. They would follow the children's lead by creating the conditions they, as parents, needed.

To continue the dialogue of the parents' meeting, the staff and I began to deepen our understanding of our own personal experiences and conflicts related to sexuality, gender, and learning. At the Barbara Taylor School, this self-reflexive activity is seen as critical to challenging the sexist and heterosexual agenda in society and incorporating critical sex education into the curriculum (see also Chapters 4 and 7 in this volume). The staff discussed how we understood ourselves as women and what the impact of sexism on our lives has been. We also shared our understandings and experiences of homosexuality. Prompted by the upper-grade students, ages 11 through 15, asking whether their teacher, Julie, was gay—she is—we decided Julie needed to teach us what she knew about sexuality and what it meant to her to be a lesbian, for, without this, we would not be able to provide leadership to the students. For Julie, being gay wasn't just about sex, but about deciding to do relationships differently. It had been part of growing up questioning how things were: Why did girls have to walk and talk a certain way? Why did boys and girls have to act the way they did with each other? Why were so many relationships between men and women so abusive? For her, being gay, she said, was a political decision on how to live her life.

In the subsequent discussion Julie had with her class about being gay, she and the students spoke both of their conflicts about *talking about* being gay and conflicts about being gay. A few days after this discussion, Julie's class requested that she teach them a class on sex and sexuality. Although we did not question the students as to why they were asking, it is my understanding that the young boys and girls had built the conditions they needed to open up difficult and often embarrassing issues. The students generated a list of questions: How come it's hard to feel good about your body? How do you deal with friends who are putting themselves in dangerous sexual situations? How come people are gay? What do you do when your boyfriend is really cute but he treats you bad? The students worked hard to figure out how they could talk about these issues in a way that was respectful and supportive of everyone in the class, including Julie.

At the end of the school year, the students in Julie's class asked if they could present Julie with an award for excellence in teaching at the last parents' meeting of the year. Much to the surprise of the staff, the boys asked if they could give the award. In a room full of parents and teachers, the upper-grade boys shouted, "We love you, Julie!" The teachers and parents were astounded. They had never before seen boys that age make such a public display of their emotionality. They had clearly stepped out of their roles as "real men." Through the activity of examining traditional roles, sexism, and homophobia and building new ways of being intimate and sexual, the boys had learned to struggle to be tender, emotional, and giving.

Parents, teachers, and students at the Barbara Taylor School continue to talk about sex, sexuality, and learning. We continue the activity of building nonrepressive, nonabusive environments, which, in our view, is the methodology we practice—the organization of possibilities for children and adults to be free to choose ways to live that support their growth as human beings.

NOTES

1. All names used throughout this chapter are fictitious.
2. In correspondence during the development of this chapter, James Sears asked that I address the "controversy surrounding social therapy"—specifically, according to Sears, "social therapy's alleged cultism, opportunism, totalitarian style, and its leading of 'vulnerable' clients into a particular political agenda" (personal communication, November 9, 1990). Sears cites Chip Berlet, a staff researcher at the Cambridge, Massachusetts–based Political Research Associates, as one source of these allegations. While not wishing to divert attention

from the topic of this chapter, I welcome Sears's invitation to address the controversy directly.

First, it is important to note that Berlet's allegations concerning social therapy occur in the context of a political critique. Berlet's research was carried out at the request of Political Research Associates. The pro-socialist/left-of-center New Alliance Party is the fourth largest party in the United States, and two New Alliance Party leaders, Lenora B. Fulani and Fred Newman, are also social therapists. In my opinion, Berlet's analysis of social therapy appears to be an attempt to discredit Fulani, Newman, and the New Alliance Party. I do not believe that he examined any of the articles or books published over the past 12 years on social therapy (Holzman & Polk, 1988; Holzman & Newman, 1979; Holzman & Strickland, 1989) or conducted any interviews with clients or therapists in social therapy practices (or with parents, staff, or children at the Barbara Taylor School).

Nonetheless, I find Berlet's accusations important to address because, to the extent that they capture the controversiality surrounding social therapy, they reveal serious substantive and methodological disagreements that exist within the progressive psychology movement.

Berlet's (1987) critique of social therapy centers around three main points. First, he says that the claim that there is "a methodological link between the psychological and the political . . . [is] a justification for indoctrinating members [presumably he is referring here to the New Alliance Party] through so-called 'therapy'" (p. 7). As readers of this volume are aware, and as referenced by other authors, there is a long and respected tradition of exploring and developing the relationship between psychology and politics—led perhaps most notably by Wilhelm Reich (1970), and dealt with implicitly, if not explicitly, by Freud (1960) himself in his analysis of social organization and civil society. Indeed, critiques of conventional psychology and the politics it engenders, and attempts to develop truly humanistic psychological theory and practice have been the centerpiece of international efforts such as those of the Frankfurt School (Habermas, 1970; Jay, 1973; Marcuse, 1964) and other critical theorists (Broughton, 1987), activity theorists (e.g., Leont'ev, 1978; Vygotsky, 1987; Wertsch, 1985), and phenomenological psychologists (e.g., Giorgi, 1970; Freire, 1972; Fanon, 1967). Within the United States, the most vocal of the critics were the radical, feminist, black, and lesbian and gay psychology movements of the 1960s (see Brown, 1987)—all based on a critique of the medical model that directly addressed the failure of traditional psychology and psychiatry to connect the personal with the political. Social therapy is part of this tradition and has continued to develop over the last 20 years.

Second, Berlet (1987) says, "For a patient to know the therapist is involved in a particular political movement is to consciously or unconsciously steer the patient, who is in a dependent and fragile relationship with the therapist, toward that political movement" (p. 9). Again, Berlet's charge of indoctrination misses the whole point of social therapy, which has been discussed at length in writings by Fulani (1988), Newman (1983, 1988a, 1988b) and other theoreticians and practitioners of social therapy (Holzman & Polk, 1988; Holzman & Rosen, 1984; Holzman & Strickland, 1989). Social therapy is not an alternative form of indoctrination, political or otherwise. Rather, social therapy is anti-indoctrination, not merely in its content, but in its very form (Holzman & Newman, 1979; Holzman & Polk, 1988). For while social therapy has incorporated many of the substantive critiques of radical, feminist, black, and lesbian and gay psychology, it goes beyond those critiques to raise a methodological challenge (Holzman & Newman, 1979). This methodological challenge is evident in the account of the Barbara Taylor School staff's efforts to organize an environment that allows children to talk openly about sex, an environment that requires breaking down the authoritarian role of the teacher.

Berlet's accusation (1987, pp. 8–9) that conscious or unconscious "steering" is operative in a social therapeutic relationship wherein the therapist is active in, for example, the New Alliance Party—and with it the notion of hiding one's political beliefs to prevent undue influence over a patient—assumes as a given that the therapist must be an authoritarian figure. The methodological challenge of social therapy is to organize environments that enable people to break down societally determined social roles, including the role of the authoritarian knower.

Third, Berlet (1987) says that "for several years psychologists and groups concerned about cults have questioned the ethics of the process used by the Institutes for Social Therapy" (p. 10). These opinions should certainly be weighed against the published work of writers supporting social therapy: Holzman, 1987; Holzman & Newman, 1979; Holzman & Polk, 1988; Holzman & Strickland, 1989; Biesta & Miedema, 1989; diAngelis, 1986. In addition, social therapists have been speakers and workshop leaders for the past 10 years at organizations such as the American Psychological Association (APA), the American Educational Research Association (AERA), the National Association of Social Workers (NASW), the American Orthopsychiatric Association, the Association for Women in Psychology (AWP), the Interamerican Society of Psychology, and many others. (Well over 200 such presentations have been made; I can list only a few of them here: APA—Holzman, 1986, 1987, 1988; Fulani, 1986; Pearl, 1988; AERA—Holzman, LaCerva, Strickland, 1988; American Orthopsychiatric Association—Holzman, LaCerva, Newman, 1984; Taylor, 1990; AWP—Daren, Holzman, Strickland, 1989; NASW—Pearl, Polk, 1988; Interamerican Society of Psychology—Fulani, Rivera, Holzman, Newman, 1987.)

Berlet's writings have, fortunately, done little by way of retarding the development of social therapy or the Barbara Taylor School. In certain circumstances, however, such reporting can serve to prevent members of the academic and research community from being exposed to the discoveries of the social therapeutic approach. Indeed, it almost prevented the publication of this chapter.

REFERENCES

Berlet, C. (1987). *Clouds blur the rainbow: The other side of the New Alliance Party.* (Political Research Associates Topical Report). Cambridge, MA: Political Research Associates.

Biesta, G., & Miedema, S. (1989). Vygotskij in Harlem: de Barbara Taylor School. *Jeugd en samenleving, 9,* 1–4.

Broughton, J. M. (Ed.). (1987). *Critical theories of psychological development.* New York: Plenum.

Brown, P. (Ed.). (1987). *Radical psychology.* New York: Harper & Row.

Chodorow, N. (1978). *The reproduction of mothering: Psychoanalysis and the sociology of gender.* Berkeley: University of California Press.

diAngelis, T. (1986, November). Community psychology from the bottom up. *APA Monitor,* pp. 21–25.

Fanon, F. (1967). *Black skin, white masks.* New York: Grove.

Freire, P. (1972). *Pedagogy of the oppressed.* New York: Herder & Herder.

Freud, S. (1960). *Civilization and its discontents.* New York: Bantam.

Fulani, L. (Ed.). (1988). *The psychopathology of everyday racism and sexism.* New York: Harrington Park.

Gilligan, C. (1982). *In a different voice: Psychological theory and women's development.* Cambridge, MA: Harvard University Press.

Gilligan, C., Lyons, N., & Hanmer, T. (1990). *Making connections: The relational worlds of adolescent girls at the Emma Willard School.* Cambridge, MA: Harvard University Press.

Giorgi, A. (1970). *Psychology as human science.* New York: Harper & Row.

Girls and Mathematics Unit. (1989). *Counting girls out.* London: Virago.

Habermas, J. (1970). *Toward a rational society.* Boston: Beacon.

Harding, S. (1984). Is gender a variable in conceptions of rationality? A survey of issues. In C. Gould (Ed.), *Beyond domination: New perspectives on women and philosophy* (pp. 43–63). Totowa, NJ: Rowman & Allanheld.

Henriques, J., Hollway, W., Urwin, C., Venn, C., & Walkerdine, V. (1984). *Changing the subject: Psychology, social regulation and subjectivity.* London: Methuen.

Holzman, L. (1987). People need power: An introduction to the Institute for Social Therapy & Research. *The Humanistic Psychologist, 15,* 105–113.

Holzman, L., & Newman, F. (1979). *The practice of method: An introduction to the foundations of social therapy.* New York: Institute for Social Therapy and Research.

Holzman, L., & Polk, H. (Eds.). (1988). *History is the cure: A social therapy reader.* New York: Castillo.

Holzman, L., & Rosen, F. (1984). Left-wing sexism: A masculine disorder. *Practice, 2,* 113–128.

Holzman, L., & Strickland, G. (1989). Developing poor and minority children as leaders with the Barbara Taylor School Educational Model. *Journal of Negro Education, 58,* 383–395.

Jaggar, A., & Rothenberg, P. (1978). *Feminist frameworks.* New York: McGraw-Hill.

Jay, M. (Ed.). (1973). *The dialectical imagination: A history of the Frankfurt School and the Institute of Social Research.* Boston: Little, Brown.

Leont'ev, A. N. (1978). *Activity, Consciousness and personality.* Englewood Cliffs, NJ: Prentice-Hall.

Maccoby, E., & Jacklin, C. (1974). *The psychology of sex differences.* Stanford, CA: Stanford University Press.

Marcuse, H. (1964). *One dimensional man.* Boston: Beacon.

Marx, K., & Engels, F. (1970). *The German ideology* (C. J. Arthur, Ed.). New York: International.

Newman, F. (1983). Practical-critical activities. *Practice, 1,* 53–101.

Newman, F. (1988). Crisis normalization and depression: A new approach to a growing epidemic. In L. Holzman & H. Polk (Eds.), *History is the cure: A social therapy reader* (pp. 202–219). New York: Castillo.

Newman, F. (1988). How do we reinitiate development in social therapy? In L. Holzman & H. Polk (Eds.), *History is the cure: A social therapy reader* (pp. 181–193). New York: Castillo.

Reich, W. (1970). *The mass psychology of fascism.* New York: Farrar, Straus & Giroux.

Vygotsky, L. (1978). *Mind in society.* Cambridge, MA: Harvard University Press.

Vygotsky, L. (1987). *The collected works of L. S. Vygotsky* (vol. 1). New York: Plenum.

Walkerdine, V. (1984). Developmental psychology and the child-centred pedagogy: The insertion of Piaget into early education. In J. Henriques, W. Holloway, C. Urwin, C. Venn, & V. Walkerdine (Eds.), *Changing the subject: Psychology, social regulation and subjectivity* (pp. 153–202). London: Methuen.

Walkerdine, V. (1987). No laughing matter: Girls' comics and the preparation for adolescent sexuality. In J. Broughton (Ed.), *Critical theories of psychological development* (pp. 87–125). New York: Plenum.

Walkerdine, V., & Lucey, H. (1989). *Democracy in the kitchen.* London: Virago.

Weisstein, N. (1971). Psychology constructs the female. In V. Gornick & B. Moran (Eds.), *Woman in sexist society* (pp. 207–223). New York: Basic.

Wertsch, J. (1985). *Vygotsky and the social formation of mind.* Cambridge, MA: Harvard University Press.

CHAPTER 7

The Impact of Culture and Ideology on the Construction of Gender and Sexual Identities

Developing a Critically Based Sexuality Curriculum

JAMES T. SEARS

Homosexuality is one of the most controversial areas in sexuality education (Forrest & Silverman, 1989). Some states and school districts have banned the discussion of this topic within the formal curriculum. For example, South Carolina legislators barred discussion of homosexuality in the curriculum except in the context of discussing AIDS, and the principal of a Wisconsin public school banned the publication of an issue of a student newspaper that included anonymous interviews with lesbian and gay students. Homosexuality and homosexual students are therefore useful points from which to explore the limits and possibilities of sexuality education for the American adolescent of the 1990s.

As I will illustrate in this chapter, the fear of homosexuality and the reluctance to include this topic in the school curriculum are due, in part, to the social threat that same-sex relations pose to a male-dominated culture. Blurring gender roles and challenging sexual norms rock the very foundation of a society rooted in male privilege and misogynistic attitudes. The fear of a boy acting as a girl and the disgust at a male submitting to the passionate caress of another man are reactions that reflect the challenge to male privilege; the social indifference to a girl engaging in boy-like behavior and a man's pleasure in watching two women engage in sexual intimacies reflect the undercurrent of misogyny hidden by the ideology of heterosexuality.

The first part of this chapter explores the concepts of gender to illuminate issues of social control, ideology, and culture. In the second part

This chapter represents a significantly revised excerpt from *Growing up Gay in the South: Race, Gender, and Journeys of the Spirit*, by James T. Sears (New York: Haworth Press). Copyright © 1991 by Gay and Lesbian Advocacy Research Project, Inc.

of this chapter, I discuss the curricular implications of these ideas by noting the limitations of conventional sexuality education programs and outlining a critically based sexuality curriculum that teaches for sexual diversity and challenges categorical thinking.

CONSTRUCTING GENDER

At a very early age, children in the United States learn gender appropriate behaviors through the assignment of household tasks and childhood toys, adult expectations for their dress and demeanor, and so forth (e.g., White & Brinkerhoff, 1981). Despite this early, prolonged, and extensive socialization process, some children, like Everetta and Isaiah,[1] fail to comply with gender-role norms. Whether refusing to jump rope or play football, there are consequences suffered by these gender nonconformists (Sears, 1989; Sears, 1991).

"The boys like to pick on me for some reason. I wouldn't let them. I would fight back. Most of the other girls, you know, they were just too femme," said Everetta. During recess, Everetta generally would be found roughhousing with the boys while her female classmates jumped rope, played on the swings, or talked quietly on the school steps. Seldom would a school day go by in which Everetta, wearing heavy-rimmed black glasses bandaged together with tape, did not return home without soiled or torn clothes. Her parents, though, didn't seem too concerned with Everetta's tomboyish behavior. "It was like, 'You'll outgrow it,' so I wasn't really given a hard time about being a tomboy at that age." As Everetta entered womanhood, her parents and teachers, like Ms. Peagler, became less understanding. "Ms. Peagler would say, 'That's not right, Everetta. You don't need to be . . . walking like a boy, talking like a boy, and acting like one.' . . . Then she sat me down and told me how a young woman should and should not act and what a young lady should and should not wear."

"I did not fit into the patterns that I was supposed to," explained Isaiah. He did not want to play football; he preferred to play with girls and was labeled "sissy" in elementary school. "That was something that they [the other children] could recognize. I was a whole lot less guarded about how I acted back then." By the time Isaiah entered middle school, however: "I was acting the way other people expected me to act. I just had to learn how to act other people's way."

Conventional studies of gender socialization fail to explain the issue of gender identity and its relationship, if any, to sexual identity. Michele Barrett (1980) observes: "Few of these studies systematically engage with the question of sexual practice, or erotic behaviour, and how this does or does not relate to socially acquired gender identity. This absence

. . . reflects the marginality of sexuality in the conventional socialization approach" (p. 63).

As Chapter 4 in this book details, boys and girls have distinctive gendered, sexual scripts, and as they mature into adolescence, there is increased pressure to read from them. Undergirding parental concern and peer harassment over cross-gender behavior among boys is its association with homosexuality, while, for girls, the underlying concern over this behavior is their physical appeal to males.[2] For both, sexual concerns underlie considerations of gender nonconformity—concerns rooted in a belief system that reifies gender and sexuality. This belief system, as documented in Part I of this book, is integrally connected with cultural values, ideology, and social control.

Barrett (1980) goes on to point out the importance of the distinction between gender and sexuality and the relationship of these concepts to the social structure. For example, though substantial scholarship has been devoted to sissiness, "defeminization," and homosexuality, little research has been done on tomboyism, "demasculinization," and lesbianism. This reflects not only the comparatively little stigmatization associated with childhood tomboy behavior but also the centrality of the male in our society. "Defeminization" innocuously suggests that a boy's adoption of "female" traits, not adult misogny, is the problem; the outward repudiation of male dress and demeanor is a visible rejection of male power and prestige.

The Impact of Culture

Being born male or female, exhibiting masculinity or femininity, and desiring men or women are three human components that can be arranged in several distinct combinations reflected in terms such as *hermaphrodite, transvestite, bisexual, sissy boy, transsexual,* and *homosexual.* While biological sex is established at conception,[3] gender identity (personal conviction about being male or female) is thought to develop between 18 months and 4 years; the internalization of cultural expectations for gender roles is believed to be established between 3 and 7 years of age (Gramick, 1984; Van Wyk & Geist, 1984; Vance & Green, 1984).

Anthropologists report a wide variety of human gender arrangements (e.g., Davenport, 1965; Mead, 1935). Their findings portray a rich tapestry of male behavior and suggest that this great elasticity in gender roles and traits is culturally ordered, not divinely ordained. In New Guinea, for example, the interests of men in the Tchambuli tribe include art, gossip, and shopping, while women adopt what we might consider masculine roles. On the Trobriand Islands, both husband and wife nurture and care for their children. In northern Madagascar, Yegale men assume their wive's surnames, perform domestic duties, and obediently comply with female demands. These and other studies are discussed in Ann Oakley's (1972) influential work. She concludes:

> Quite often one finds these examples of masculinity and femininity in other societies dismissed as eccentric, deviant, peculiar, and irrelevant to the mainstream of human development. This is an absurdly ethnocentric view. . . . The chief importance of biological sex in determining social roles is in providing a universal and obvious division around which other distinctions can be organised. In deciding which activities are to fall on each side of the boundary, the important factor is culture. (pp. 58, 156)

Even within cultures known for relatively rigid codes of male and female behavior, there are acceptable forms of cross-gender behavior for males (Talamini, 1982). Womanless weddings are routinely held in churches within rural communities of the South as fund-raising events. In Japan we find the centuries-honored Kabuki tradition in which men assume theatrical roles as women. In Africa, Masai boys wear women's clothing for several months following circumcision. In Holland, on the island of Marken, boys are dressed as girls until they reach the age of 7. In the United States, even the society pages consider Halloween and Mardi Gras appropriate occasions for such cross-dressing.

While the concept of maleness varies from culture to culture, no society has ignored the temptation to extend physical differences between "males" and "females" into its language, social structure, or ideology. This "sexing of the world," notes British anthropologist Allen Abramson (1984), occurs when "objects and roles tend to become imaginatively annexed to either the male or the female in a way that, conjunctually, may appear to be 'natural' and 'eternal'" (p. 196). As these objects and roles become reified, those who deviate from them are often ostracized. But to claim that such behavior is "unnatural" is to ignore the spectrum of human diversity and to divide the world simplistically and artificially into gendered halves.

Even in those societies in which gender-role divisions are similar to our own, the cultural responses to cross-gender behavior differs markedly. For example, Kenneth Clark (1956), in his classic study *The Nude*, noted that mockery of male "queens" at gymnasia can be found depicted on Greek vases; and Kent Gerard and Gert Hekma's *The Pursuit of Sodomy: Male Homosexuality in Renaissance and Enlightenment Europe* (1989) is filled with accounts of effeminacy used as evidence in sexual prosecutions of the period. In contrast, within 19th-century American Indian cultures, males who did not conform to masculine behavior or dress often assumed special ceremonial roles as healers, shamans, and seers.

Parents of a PaPago Indian son, for example, who suspected that he might be different would "build a small bush enclosure. Inside the enclosure they place a man's bow and arrows, and also a woman's basket. At the appointed time, the boy is brought to the enclosure as the adults watch from the outside" (Williams, 1986, p. 24). After the boy enters the enclosure it is set afire. If the boy takes the basket in hand as he flees, he is recognized by the tribe as a *berdache*—a position of respect and economic status within his community.

Despite the fact that it occurs routinely in other species, across time, and among other contemporary cultures, female gender-role reversal is less documented and, possibly, less prevalent than male gender-role reversal (Goldstein, 1982). For example, the female *berdache* was a relatively rare phenomenon in Native American culture. Anthropologist Harriet Whitehead (1981) posits an explanation:

> The phenomena of adult reproductive processes added to and underscored an image of femininity that could weaken and be counterbalanced by masculine occupations only if the physiological processes themselves were held to be eliminable. Throughout most of North America, they were not so held, at least not for that period of a woman's life when she was realistically capable of taking up the hunter-warrior way of life. Becoming a member of the opposite sex was, therefore, predominantly a male game. (p. 93)

The Impact of Ideology

Society provides the collective cultural history, social scripts, and language that form the foundation for these gendered identities. Further, the personal meanings of our regional, social class, racial, gender, and sexual identities are inextricably woven into a culture in which being upper class or working class, black or white, male or female, homosexual or heterosexual have social significance. While the intersections of social class, race, gender, and sexuality vary for each person, their existence and importance within our culture are social facts with negative social consequences for those who do not share membership in the dominant groups.

Scholars from a variety of academic disciplines have argued that categorizing human beings according to their role in the biological process is central in the reproduction of their culture. Sociologist Kenneth Plummer (1981), feminist Mary Daly (1973), anthropologist Claude Levi-Strauss (1969), and social theorist Michel Foucault (1978) have all explored the ideological aspect of the construction of gender and sexuality. These and other scholars convincingly argue that "appropriate and inappropriate" gender behaviors are culturally based and that sexual biographies are integrally related to issues of ideology and social control. As Farganis (1986) states:

> What it means to be a woman, or gendered, is neither fixed nor indeterminably variable, but that interaction between how one defines oneself and the

historical circumstances which encase the act of selfhood. The rooting of a "feminine character" in time and place allows us to see it as political, as subject to the social arrangement of the particular society. (p. 80)

In the United States, the social construction of gender and sexuality (i.e., the transference of biological divisions of maleness and femaleness into social categories), the delegation of human roles and traits according to conceptions of femininity and masculinity, and the proscription of certain sexual activities rationalize a particular way of organizing society— patriarchy.

Patriarchy is a system of social arrangements in which the female is economically, politically, and psychologically dependent upon the male (Lerner, 1986). This dependency extends from her roles in the private sphere (housewife, mother) to her status in the public arena (worker, consumer). It is reflected in her comparatively weak control over her economic and reproductive destiny (Zaretzky, 1976) and, as Chapter 5 illustrated, may be manifested in sexual harassment—a reflection of this lack of power. Through patriarchy the body politic is ideologically reproduced by distinguishing "male" and "female"; and by creating division of opportunities and rewards, traits and interests, privileges and responsibilities in favor of men (Chodorow, 1978).

This social arrangement, while reflected in the products conceived and marketed in big city boardrooms, is rooted in small town bedrooms and classrooms. Legislators may prop up forms of patriarchy (e.g., divorce law, marital rape), but it is legitimized by hundreds of thousands of ideological cops who define the significance of gender and delimit meanings of sexuality.

Challenging Culture and Ideology

From this perspective, children like Everetta who continue to flaunt their deviant gender behaviors challenge more than social sensibilities; they challenge the foundation of our social system. The ability to define and delimit appropriate gender behaviors and expressions of sexuality is nothing less than the power to shape society; those who threaten to defy these roles thus challenge the hegemony of patriarchy. Self-identified lesbians, bisexuals, and gay men who challenge gender roles are the cultural bandits of the New Age.

The emergence of this New Age of public and private relationships signals the crumbling of a worldview spanning 2 millennia of everyday social discourse. The fear of a social Armageddon lies at the root of misogynist attitudes, sodomy statutes, and heterosexist curricula. A 13-year-old tomboy or a 17-year-old drag queen does more than threaten persons with insecure gender identities; they threaten the social order.

For this reason, understanding and reducing homophobia among educators cannot be addressed at the individual level of bigotry or psychopathology; educators' homophobic attitudes and feelings must be understood within a societal context in which ideological beliefs and cultural values prop up existing relations of power and control within society.

Becoming a homosexual, despite contrary claims of the Radical Right, poses no social threat; *being* sexual by discarding and challenging gender and sexual norms challenges the very foundations of our society. For example, if lesbians and gay men merely reverse sex roles and bifurcate relationships into roles such as "butch/femme" or "dominant/submissive," then the opportunity to publicly challenge sexual and gender categories is lost.

Choosing same-sex partners does little to end heterosexist society. The greatest dangers are privatizing homosexual relationships, characterizing lesbians and gay men as basically the same as heterosexual women and men, reducing homosexuality to only a small part of what constitutes a human being, and asserting that homosexuality poses no threat to either heterosexuality or the larger social and political structures. Kitzinger (1987) declares:

> Our "inner selves"—the way we think and feel and how we define ourselves—are connected in an active and reciprocal way with the larger social and political structures and processes in the context of which they are constructed. It is for this reason that, as many radical and revolutionary movements of oppressed peoples have argued, "the personal is the political." (p. 62)

Sexuality education is more than sexual hydraulics and sexual hygiene or the cant of the "just say no" *Sex Respect* curriculum. But it is also more than accepting one's sexuality and exercising prudence in sexual activity. By virtue of the genuine interest of adolescents in sexuality, sexuality education can pose questions and provide knowledge that challenge students' everyday concepts of gender and sexuality. More important, sexuality education can help bridge the gap between the personal and political by exploring the ideological bases for gender and sexual identities. Finally, sexuality education can convey the multiple forms of sexual expression and the plasticity of sexual identity to adolescents and, in the process, explore questions about power and ideology in society.

A CRITICALLY BASED SEXUALITY CURRICULUM

Sex, as many a high school student will freely admit, is an integral part of school life. Though some are reluctant to formally integrate this topic into school subjects, covert sexual instruction comprises a large part of the hidden curriculum: the exchange of lustful looks in the hallway or romantic notes in the classroom; half-glances in the locker-room shower or erotic day dreams in study hall; the homoerotic camaraderie of sports teams; and the sexual energy pulsating in even the most boring of classes. From every vantage point, there are couples: couples holding hands as they enter school; couples dissolving into an endless wet kiss between school bells; couples exchanging rings with ephemeral vows of devotion and love.

The culture of the school mirrors the larger society; schools socialize boys and girls into their presumed heterosexual destiny. On any given day in any particular high school these feelings span the sexual continuum, yet only those feelings at the heterosexual end are publicly acknowledged and peer approved. Unfortunately, when sexuality education is formally discussed in health or biology class, heterosexual mechanics is most often presented (leave it to schools to make even the most interesting subject emotionally dry, moralistically rigid, and intellectually sterile).

Developing critical-thinking skills is a stated priority in many school districts, yet few school districts extend these skills across the curriculum. Sexuality education is a case in point. Sexual values are taught, not explored; sexual danger is stressed while sexual pleasure is minimized; and heterosexual intercourse is placed at the apex of the pyramid of sexual desire. Never asked, never encouraged, never addressed are questions such as:

> How does *being* male or female define one's sexual options?
> How do sexual options and values vary across time and culture?
> Why is masturbation considered less desirable than sexual intercourse?
> Who is "gay"? Who is "straight"? How is it that such arbitrary distinctions exist?

There is a great need for a healthy, frank, and honest depiction of the fluidity of sexual behavior and the arbitrariness of sexual identities. Yet, too many educators are partners in a conspiracy of sexual silence in which sexual knowledge is what is salvaged after the scissors-and-paste philosophy of some religious zealots or homosexual activists is applied. This is not the time to accede to the interests of self-created minorities. The fluidity of human sexual response and the capacity of people to create and recreate their sexual identities are integral components of a critical sexuality curriculum.

Teaching for Sexual Diversity

One way to begin developing a critically based sexuality curriculum is to challenge the heterosexual agenda in school and society, first by asking educators to examine their personal feelings about sexuality and thoughts about education.[4] This involves asking personal questions, such as:

How do I feel when talking about sexuality?
During my childhood, how was the subject of homosexuality treated?
Did I have any friends who later identified themselves as bisexual, gay, or lesbian?
How comfortable am I in expressing feelings toward members of my own gender?

This also involves addressing political questions, such as:

In a democratic society, what should schools teach?
Can schools instill knowledge about the world without encouraging self-knowledge?
Are democratic attitudes, values of tolerance and respect for diversity, and the development of critical thinking fostered in the school curriculum?
Within an effective learning environment, what relationships should exist between educators and students?

Public schools in a democratic society are a marketplace for ideas. "Access to ideas," as Justice Brennan wrote, "prepares students for active and effective participation in the pluralistic, often contentious society in which they will soon be adult members" (quoted in Dutile, 1986, p. 37). But spreading ominously across America is a virulent plague of sexual ignorance and fear. Too many schoolchildren remain ignorant of the diversity of human sexuality, and too many teachers and students fear discussing sexuality beyond whispered conversations, cruel jokes, or sexual innuendo (Sears, in press). This plague, so toxic to compassion and common sense, is spread by purveyors of a supposedly moral agenda. But I find the concern of these religious True Believers hardly moral. They do not want to eradicate ignorance and fear; rather they want schools to propagate their skewed concept of morality and sexual orthodoxy. Because they accept the axiom that sexual knowledge may lead to sexual activity, no Tree of Knowledge is welcomed in the Eden of the True Believer.

The educator has an important role in a democratic society: to en-

courage intellectual flexibility, to foster analytical thought, and to expand tolerance. Sadly, many public schools incubate a narrow set of
moral and religious beliefs: A page from a *teacher's* textbook on health
science is ordered removed by the board of education for its discussion
of birth control; books with references to homosexuality are removed
from the shelves of a high school library; teachers are threatened with
dismissal and criminal liability for discussing homosexuality. Schools,
held hostage to Bible-thumping fundamentalists and right-wing ideo-
logues, are painful places for students who experience same-sex erotic
feelings to learn, and they are breeding grounds of intolerance and social bigotry for those repressing these feelings. A healthy understanding
of the panorama of human sexual experience must be integrated into our
schools as well as our society. Frank discussions and accurate information can replace schoolyard banter and sexual myths. Traditionally, a
watered-down version of this task has been ghettoized in the school's
sexuality education curriculum.

As documented elsewhere in this book, the quality of sexuality education curricula is poor across the nation. This curriculum primarily consists of sexual hydraulics and social relations skills. Homosexuality is the
topic least mentioned by respondents and bisexuality is not even an option open for debate. Even in those states where there are no penalties
for deviating from the heterosexual agenda, many school districts forbid
discussion of such controversial topics, or teachers, like Mrs. Warren in
Chapter 10, take it upon themselves to avoid them.

The public hysteria associated with AIDS; the anti-human-rights
legislation such as Britain's infamous Section 28 prohibiting local gov-
ernments, schools, and other public agencies from "promoting homosexuality or its acceptability"; the adverse court ruling such as the *Bowers
v. Hardwick* (1986) decision reaffirming state homosexuality sodomy
laws; and the unabated initiatives of the Religious Right to discredit and
discontinue the few supportive counseling programs, such as Project 10
in Los Angeles, for homosexual-identified students—all call for concerted effort by education and allied professions to counteract the heterosexual agenda of most sexuality education efforts. Specific strategies
and materials that foster an awareness of homosexuality and homosexual persons already have been proposed (e.g., DeVito, 1981; Powell,
1987; Sears, 1983; Wilson, 1984). Educators have been admonished by
scholars and activists alike to sit down and talk with bisexual, lesbian,
and gay adults to learn firsthand about the special problems they faced
in school; the importance of lesbian and gay educators as role models for
homosexual students has been stressed, as has the need for public
school systems to follow the lead of communities such as Berkeley and
Cambridge in adopting anti-slur policies and nonharassment guidelines
(e.g., Chism, Cano, & Pruitt, 1989; Hetrick & Martin, 1987; Martin &

Hetrick, 1988; Ross-Reynolds & Hardy, 1985; Sears, 1987; Slater, 1988). In some schools, antihomophobia workshops with students and educators have been advocated and conducted (e.g., Dillon, 1986; Schneider & Tremble, 1986).[5] Professional educators as well as lesbian and gay activists ask, at the very least, for the construction of a nonjudgmental atmosphere in which homosexual-identified students can come to terms with their sexuality (e.g., Benvenuti, 1986; Sears, 1988), the acquisition by school libraries of biographical books where students can discover the homosexuality of some famous people, and the integration of references to homosexual men and women as well as the topic of homosexuality into the high school curriculum (Hipple, Yarbrough, & Kaplan, 1984; Jenkins, 1990; Sears, 1983).

The claim of scholars and activists that the homosexual experience has been expurgated from the high school curriculum has merit. In English, for example, students can read Whitman's a "Song of Myself" in *Leaves of Grass* or McCuller's *The Ballad of the Sad Cafe* without gleaning a hint of these authors' physical love for persons of their own sex; in the classics, they can translate the drama of Sophocles and the philosophy of Socrates without ever exploring ancient Greek homosexual practices; in history, they can study the military genius of Alexander the Great without ever learning the importance of male lovers for him and other members of his army; in mathematics, students can marvel at the genius of computer founder Alan Turing yet remain ignorant of his sexual struggles; in physical education, students can exchange "fag" jokes while admiring sports stars such as Martina Navratilova and David Kopay; music and drama students play from the works of Bessie Smith or Oscar Wilde without knowing to whom some of their art was dedicated.

Given recent resolutions by professional associations such as the National Educational Association (1988) and the Association for Supervision and Curriculum Development (1990) on the necessity for schools to meet the needs of homosexual students, some teachers have begun to write about the academic difficulties confronting such students.

> During an autobiography unit a student who has lesbian parents fails to turn in an entry about how his family is unique, claiming that he can't think of anything to write about. . . . At the middle school and high school level where I teach, the peer group reigns supreme. . . . For students attempting to hide their identity, the writing classroom is both scary and frustrating. (Smith, 1989, pp. 2–4).

But the writing classroom, as Brunner aptly demonstrates in Chapter 11, can be a promising place for adolescents to explore sexuality. Teachers are now exploring ways to provide gay, lesbian, and bisexual students a voice on paper and seeking ways for others to acknowledge sexual diversity (Hart, 1989; Hewett, 1989), and the Dallas-based National Gay Alliance for Young Adults now sponsors a nationwide writing contest, with cash awards, for 10th- through 12th-grade students on the theme "What is it like being gay or lesbian in America today?"

Challenging Categorical Thinking

While some may argue that these advocates want to replace the heterosexual curriculum with a homosexual one, it is more fair to say that they seek to redress the imbalance currently found within the schools. Unquestionably, such imbalance exists. For example, in reviews of representations of homosexuality in high school and college health texts, researchers have found few references to the subject, and many of those references are blatantly homophobic (McDonald, 1981; Newton, 1982; Whitlock & DiLapi, 1983). And those few texts that treat homosexuality in at least a neutral manner tend to ghettoize it by discussing the topic in a condensed section or by switching from a personalized "you" voice to a detached "they." "This treatment," note health care specialists Katherine Whitlock and Elena DiLapi (1983), "implies that homosexuality is less significant than or inferior to heterosexuality—an auxiliary form of sexuality, if you will, and somehow just not 'the real thing' " (p. 20).

Redressing the heterosexual imbalance by adopting the strategies cited above, however, will not challenge the heterosexual agenda. Rather, it reifies sexuality, splitting it into unequal heterosexual and homosexual categories. This strategy reaffirms a sexual caste structure in which the vast majority are (genetically fortunate?) heterosexual persons and a minority (the infamous 10%?) are homosexually oriented. Same-sex fantasies or behaviors by the majority can simply be written off as childhood exploits or evidence of middle-age crises; heteroerotic feelings and experiences by the minority can simply be rationalized as existential escapes from biological destiny or political duty. Women and men who affirm their bisexuality become the untouchables in this system of sexual castes.

Incorporating the homosexual experience into the school curriculum, hiring homosexual-identified educators, and adopting anti-slur policies will not adequately address the sexuality needs and interest of our children. Discussing the homoerotic poetry of Sappho or Dickinson is not the same as exploring the homoerotic imagery that all of us experience. Highlighting the achievements of Alexander the Great or David Kopay while failing to discuss the homoerotic component of men in combat—whether on the battleground or the gridiron—does not illuminate how many of our social institutions are built over a river of subterranean same-sex feelings. Integrating one or two openly lesbian or gay educators into a teaching staff of 50 does little to dispel the belief that only a minority engage in homosexual behavior or share intimate same-sex feelings.

A central objective of a critical sexuality curriculum is to challenge students' (and educators') categorical thinking. For example, a critical examination of sex roles, as advocated in Chapter 4, could elucidate questions such as: "Where do these roles come from?" "How are we socialized to them?" "How are they enforced?" "How do 'masculinity' and 'femininity' fit with maleness and femaleness?" (MacDonald, 1974, p. 179). In the process, students may come to understand both the social construction and the absurdity of such either/or concepts.

Categorical thinking can also be challenged by integrating discussions of sexuality throughout the curriculum. Conventional sexuality education, taught as a separate unit or integrated into biology or health science, communicates that sexuality can be appropriately separated from the mainstream of school life. Just as healthy sexuality can be expressed in a variety of ways and cannot be segregated to one aspect of a person's life, so, too, must it be discussed freely and openly in a wide range of courses, from literature to social sciences to the natural and applied sciences. In Chapter 2 Carlson's suggestion of developing an undergraduate course in cultural studies rooted in a thorough exploration of sexuality is one strategy appropriate in higher education. There are other higher education examples that I will briefly review.

In the next chapter, Fonow and Marty describe how they challenge conventional thinking about sexual identity from a feminist perspective in a basic women's studies survey undergraduate course at Ohio State. Using role-playing exercises, oral histories, simulations, coming-out stories, films, and lesbian and heterosexual panels, they "help students confront and challenge the naturalness of human arrangements" as they ask, "How do we ground a sexual politics that deconstructs sexual identity?"

Richard Mohr (1989) teaches philosophy at the University of Illinois, Urbana. Advocating a philosophical basis for gay men's studies, he argues that the women's studies model and its emphasis on theory is essential for confronting homosexual stereotypes as "norm-laden ideology." Assigning social history and the natural sciences to a "subordinate role," he believes that ethics and moral education ought to be the intellectual foundation for the study and teaching of homosexuality. He writes, "Gay studies is the study of gays as a minority—the normative study of the social circumstances and treatment of gays. . . . As a moral project which criticizes and prescribes social forms . . . [gay studies] need[s] to be critically and philosophically informed" (p. 130).

Kay Williamson and Jacqueline Williams (1990), teaching at the University of Massachusetts, prepare undergraduate students to teach physical education. A course on equity awareness encourages college juniors to reflect on problems of sexism, racism, motor elitism, and homophobia. By encouraging students to critically examine personal experiences and school observations through the use of biographical activities, noncompetitive games, films, and discussions, these teachers couple the personal and social worlds. "The undergraduates reflected on many questions: 'As teachers, would they collude in prejudice and ridicule homosexual persons?' 'How would they feel and act if one of their own children were gay?' 'What is their position on employment of gay and lesbian teachers?' " (p. 121).

Anthony D'Augelli teaches an undergraduate course on human development at the Pennsylvania State University. Operating from a human development model whose propositions reflect a constructionist orientation (e.g., affectional interests are a lifelong developmental process; human sexual behavior is malleable; an individual's development is unique). D'Augelli (1991) applies a Freirian teaching model to assist students in making connections between their personal sexual histories and the dialectical impact of culture, history, and ideology. As his students explore their personal feelings and beliefs about aging, families, and friendship, he draws upon the social and behavioral sciences to bridge their feelings and beliefs with a critical understanding of culture, history, and society.

Although these authors teach in different intellectual disciplines, all agree on the necessity of a critically based sexuality curriculum.

CONCLUSION

For the first time in recent history, the media and the schools are publicly discussing the long taboo topic of sexuality. The renewed emphasis on sexuality education, fueled by the AIDS crisis and the efforts of the former U.S. surgeon general, has legitimized the discussion of topics, such as condoms and homosexuality, in some school districts that only a few years ago would have self-righteously ignored them. From public service announcements promoting abstinence and safer sex to evening news reports on issues affecting lesbian and gay communities, the veil of sexual silence is lifting. While this issue now is at the public forefront, we must work for a healthy, frank, and honest depiction of the fluidity of sexual behavior and a critical examination of the arbitrariness of gender and sexual identities.

NOTES

1. All names are pseudonyms. Interviews were conducted between July 1986 and February 1988. For a discussion of the methodology employed, see Sears, 1991, pp. 431–464.

2. For example, Green and Money (1966) noted the interrelationships between effeminacy, role-taking, and stage-acting among a small sample of effeminate males during childhood. However, on both logical and empirical grounds the etiological linkage of homosexuality to social sex roles is questionable (Ross, 1983).

3. There are case studies of individuals whose genetic and anatomic characteristics do not match at birth. These children, raised male or female according to their physical characteristics, fail to develop gender-appropriate secondary sex characteristics during puberty and thus face a conflict between their gender and biological identities (e.g., Money, Devore, & Norman, 1986).

4. Other sources of ideas for educational strategies in working with homosexual students or addressing homosexuality within the school curriculum include: Jenkins, 1990; Morey, 1984; Sears, 1983.

5. Researchers also have reported on the positive impact that seminars, lectures, guest speakers, films, debate, and dialogue have had on reducing prejudice against lesbians and gay men (e.g., MacLaury, 1982; Rudolph, 1988). Those courses that demanded active involvement by students, such as role-playing, appeared the most promising in effecting and sustaining attitudinal change (Watter, 1987).

REFERENCES

Abramson, A. (1984). *Sarah: A sexual biography.* Albany, SUNY Press.

Association for Supervision and Curriculum Development. (1990, July). *ASCD adopts resolution on student orientation* [press release].

Barrett, M. (1980). *Women's oppression today: Problems in Marxist feminist analysis.* London: Verson.

Benvenuti, A. (1986). *Assessing and addressing the special challenge of gay and lesbian students for high school counseling programs.* Paper presented at the annual meeting of the California Educational Research Association. ERIC Reproduction No. ED 279 958)

Bowers v. Hardwick, 478 U.S. 186, 106 S.Ct. 2841, 92L.Ed.2d 140 (1986).

Chism, N., Cano, J., & Pruitt, A. (1989). Teaching in a diverse environment: Knowledge and skills needed by TAs. In J. Nyquist, R. Abbot, & D. Wulff (Eds.), *Teaching assistant training in the 1990s* (pp. 23–36). San Francisco: Jossey-Bass.

Chodorow, N. (1978). *The reproduction of mothering: Psychoanalysis and the sociology of gender.* Berkeley: University of California Press.

Clark, K. (1956). *The nude: A study of ideal art.* Princeton, NJ: Princeton University Press.

Daly, M. (1973). *Beyond God the father: Toward a philosophy of women's liberation.* Boston: Beacon.

D'Augelli, A. (1991). Teaching lesbian and gay development: A pedagogy of the oppressed. In W. Tierney (Ed.), *Culture and ideology in higher education: Advancing a critical agenda* (pp. 213–233). New York: Praeger.

Davenport, W. (1965). Sexual patterns and their regulation in a society of the Southwest Pacific. In F. Beach (Ed.), *Sex and behavior* (pp. 164–207). New York: Wiley.

DeVito, J. (1981). Educational responsibilities to gay male and lesbian students. In J. Chesbro (Ed.), *Gayspeak: Gay male and lesbian communication* (pp. 197–207). New York: Pilgrim.

Dillon, C. (1986). Preparing college health professionals to deliver gay-affirmative services. *Journal of American College Health, 35*(1), 36–40.

Dutile, F. (1986). *Sex, schools and the law.* Springfield, IL: Thomas.

Farganis, S. (1986). *Social reconstruction of the feminine character.* Totowa, NJ: Rowman & Littlefield.

Forrest, J., & Silverman, J. (1989). What public school teachers teach about preventing pregnancy, AIDS and sexually transmitted diseases. *Family Planning Perspectives, 21*(2), 65–72.

Foucault, M. (1978). *The history of sexuality: Vol. 1. An introduction.* New York: Pantheon.

Gerard, K., & Hekma, G. (1989). *The pursuit of sodomy: Male homosexuality in Renaissance and Enlightenment Europe.* New York: Harrington Park.

Goldstein, M. (1982). Some tolerant attitudes toward female homosexuality throughout history. *Journal of Psychohistory, 9*(4), 437–460.

Gramick, J. (1984). Developing a lesbian identity. In T. Darty & S. Potter (Eds.), *Women-identified women* (pp. 31–44). Palo Alto, CA: Mayfield.

Green, R., & Money, J. (1966). Stage-acting, role-taking, and effeminate impersonation during boyhood. *Archives of General Psychiatry, 15*(11), 535–538.

Hart, E. (1989). *Literacy and the empowerment of lesbian and gay students.* Paper presented at the annual meeting of the Conference on College Composition and Communication. (ERIC Reproduction No. ED 304 662)

Hetrick, E., & Martin, A. D. (1987). Developmental issues and their resolution for gay and lesbian adolescents. *Journal of Homosexuality, 14*(1/2), 25–43.

Hewett, G. (1989). A rhetoric of androgyny: The composition, teaching and ethics of gender (Doctoral dissertation, State University of New York at Albany, 1989). *Dissertation Abstracts International, 50,* 2476A.

Hipple, T., Yarbrough, J., & Kaplan, J. (1984). Twenty adolescent novels (and more) that counselors should know about. *School Counselor, 32*(2), 142–148.

Jenkins, C. (1990, September 1). Being gay: Gay/lesbian characters and concerns in young adult books. *Booklist,* pp. 39–41.

Kitzinger, C. (1987). *The social construction of lesbianism.* London: Sage.

Lerner, G. (1986). *The creation of patriarchy.* New York: Oxford University Press.

Levi-Strauss, C. (1969). *The elementary structures of kinship.* Boston: Beacon.

MacDonald, A. (1974). The importance of sex-role to gay liberation. *Homosexual Counseling Journal, 1*(4), 169–180.

MacLaury, S. (1982). *A comparison of three methods of teaching about human sexuality to determine their effectiveness in positively modifying attitudes about homosexuality.* Unpublished doctoral dissertation, New York University, New York.

Martin, A. D., & Hetrick, E. (1988). The stigmatization of gay and lesbian adolescents. *Journal of Homosexuality, 15*(1–2), 163–185.

McDonald, G. (1981). Misrepresentation, liberalism, and heterosexual bias in introductory psychology textbooks. *Journal of Homosexuality, 6*(3), 45–59.

Mead, M. (1935). *Sex and temperament in three primitive societies.* New York: Morrow.

Mohr, R. (1989). Gay studies as moral vision. *Educational Theory, 39*(2), 121–132.

Money, J., Devore, H., & Norman, B. (1986). Gender identity and gender transposition: Longitudinal study of 32 male hermaphrodites assigned as girls. *Journal of Sex and Marital Therapy, 12*(3), 165–181.

Morey, R. (1984). *Demystifying homosexuality: A teaching guide about lesbians and gay men.* New York: Irvington.

National Educational Association. (1988, July). *NEA urges special attention to gay/lesbian students* [press release].

Newton, D. (1982). A note on the treatment of homosexuality in sex education classes in the secondary school. *Journal of Homosexuality, 8*(1), 97–99.

Oakley, A. (1972). *Sex, gender and society.* New York: Harper & Row.

Plummer, K. (1981). *The making of the modern homosexual.* London: Hutchinson.

Powell, R. (1987). Homosexual behavior and the school counselor. *School Counselor, 34*(3), 202–208.

Ross, M. (1983). Homosexuality and social sex roles: A re-evaluation. *Journal of Homosexuality. 9*(1), 1–6.

Ross-Reynolds, G., & Hardy, B. (1985). Crisis counseling for disparate adolescent sexual dilemmas: Pregnancy and homosexuality. *School Psychology Review, 14*(3), 300–312.

Rudolph, J. (1988). The effects of a multimodal seminar on mental practitioners' attitudes toward homosexuality, authoritarianism, and counseling effectiveness (Doctoral dissertation, Lehigh University, 1988). *Dissertation Abstracts International, 49,* 2873B.

Schneider, M., & Tremble, B. (1986). Training service providers to work with gay or lesbian adolescents: A workshop. *Journal of Counseling and Development, 65*(2), 98–99.

Sears, J. (1983). Sexuality: Taking off the masks. *Changing Schools, 11,* 12–13.

Sears, J. (1987). Peering into the well of loneliness: The responsibility of educators to gay and lesbian youth. In A. Molnar (Ed.), *Social issues and education: Challenge and responsibility* (pp. 79–100). Alexandria, VA: Association for Supervision & Curriculum Development.

Sears, J. (1988). Growing up gay: Is anyone there to listen? *American School Counselor Association Newsletter, 26,* 8–9.

Sears, J. (1989). The impact of gender and race on growing up lesbian and gay in the South. *NWSA Journal, 1*(3), 422–457.

Sears, J. (1991). *Growing up gay in the South: Race, gender, and journeys of the spirit.* New York: Haworth.

Sears, J. (in press). Educators, homosexuality, and homosexual students: Are personal feelings related to professional beliefs? *Journal of Homosexuality.*

Slater, B. (1988). Essential issues in working with lesbian and gay male youths. *Professional Psychology: Research and Practice, 19*(2), 226–235.

Smith, L. (1989). *Writers who are gay and lesbian adolescents: The impact of social context.* Paper presented at the annual meeting of the Conference on College Composition and Communication. (ERIC Document No. ED 304 695).

Talamini, J. (1982). *Boys will be girls: The hidden world of the heterosexual male transvestite.* Landham, MD: University Press of America.

Vance, B., & Green, V. (1984). Lesbian identities. *Psychology of Women Quarterly,* *8*(3), 293–307.

Van Wyke, P., & Geist, C. (1984). Psychosocial development of heterosexual, bisexual, and homosexual behavior. *Archives of Sexual Behavior, 13*(6), 505–544.

Watter, D. (1987). Teaching about homosexuality: A review of the literature. *Journal of Sex Education and Therapy, 13*(2), 63–66.

White, L., & Brinkerhoff, D. (1981). The sexual division of labor: Evidence from childhood. *Social Forces, 60*(1), 170–181.

Whitehead, H. (1981). The bow and the burden strap: A new look at institutionalized homosexuality in native North Americans. In S. Ortner, & H. Whitehead (Eds.), *Sexual meanings: The cultural construction of gender and sexuality* (pp. 80–115). Cambridge, MA: Cambridge University Press.

Whitlock, K., & DiLapi, E. (1983). "Friendly fire": Homophobia in sex education literature. *Interracial Books for Children Bulletin, 14*(3/4), 20–23.

Williams, W. (1986). *The spirit and the flesh.* Boston: Beacon.

Williamson, K., & Williams, J. (1990). Promoting equity awareness in the preparation of physical education students. *Teaching Education, 3*(1), 117–123.

Wilson, D. (1984). The open library. *English Journal, 43*(7), 60–63.

Zaretzky, E. (1976). *Capitalism, the family and personal life.* New York: Harper.

CHAPTER 8

Teaching College Students About Sexual Identity from Feminist Perspectives

MARY MARGARET FONOW AND DEBIAN MARTY

> Never before have I examined so much the question of why I am
> the way I am. (Ohio State University Student)

Feminist activists and scholars have long acknowledged the significance of sexuality to our understanding of women's lives and experiences. The major contributions of feminist analysis include

1. The political nature of sex, which serves as a source of both liberation and oppression
2. The compulsory nature of heterosexuality and the viability of homosexuality and bisexuality
3. The delineation of the sex/gender system and the roles of homophobia in sustaining this system and homosexuality in challenging it
4. The variability in sexual orientation on both an individual and social/historical level
5. The influences of social and cultural differences such as race, gender, social class, and sexual orientation in shaping sexual experience and meaning
6. The significance of culture and social institutions, especially language, media, religion, art, literature, science, and medicine, in constructing sexual identity, desire, and expression
7. The role of the state in regulating sexual expression and behavior

Many of these theoretical insights, particularly those rooted in the constructionist perspective, are already more fully elaborated on in Chapter 7 by Sears. Our intentions in this essay are to draw out the teaching implications of constructionist approaches developed by feminists; to evaluate our efforts in implementing these approaches in women's studies classes; and, borrowing insights from postmodern feminism, to offer suggestions for changes in how we teach about sexual identity.

Our discussion is based on our own teaching experience, interviews with other instructors, and written student responses to lesbian panels. We limit our concerns primarily to how the topic of sexual identity is taught to general education students enrolled in a basic survey course on women offered by the Center for Women's Studies at Ohio State University, a large research-oriented university of 58,000 students. The course itself is a general, interdisciplinary overview of women's lives and experiences and covers such topics as work, health, sexuality and reproduction, family, religion, media, education, race, class, poverty, violence against women, politics, and the women's movement. The course has no prerequisites, fulfills both a general education and social diversity requirement, and enrolls about 1,700 students a year, a fourth of whom are men.

COURSE GOALS

We are aware of the limitations in constructionist arguments (Epstein, 1987; Vance, 1989) and of the existence of essentialist tendencies in some important feminist writing on sexuality (Daly, 1978, 1984; Grahn, 1984). Nonetheless, we deliberately chose constructionist approaches for this particular audience because such approaches encourage students to be more self-reflective about their own sexuality and more aware of other forms of difference that often divide us. We emphasize in the course that both gender and sexual identity are socially constructed; that each is subject to variation across culture, race, and class; and that, while norm violations are difficult and often painful, such violations are not impossible and in fact are often necessary to achieve mental health. Students read first-person accounts and interviews with individuals who have challenged gender norms and/or the heterosexual imperative. Growing-up narratives and coming-out stories, a staple of lesbian and gay culture, help students to understand socialization pressures as well as the joy of self-discovery. (Selected examples of this genre are Baetz, 1980; Barret, 1989; Beck, 1989; Cruikshank, 1980; Devor, 1989; Penelope & Valentine, 1990; Penelope & Wolfe, 1989; Sears, 1989.)

Our final goal is to begin to have students shift their focus of analysis from homophobia to heterosexism through the process of deconstructing heterosexuality. We ask students to reexamine the notion of "choice" in light of basic social institutions and human arrangements, organized around the heterosexual imperative, that hide lesbian alternatives. We get students to identify and analyze the pressures they have encountered from parents, teachers, clergy, peers, and popular culture to adopt a heterosexual identity.

ACTIVITIES AND READINGS

We accomplish these goals in various ways. One often difficult exercise utilized by a few of the Center's instructors is the hypothetical "coming out" letter to parents. In the course of writing the letter (or a justification for why they cannot, for those students who protest the assignment), students identify the internal and external obstacles to claiming a gay or lesbian identity.

Students notice the embeddedness of heterosexuality as a cultural norm when they analyze the institution and ideology of romantic love, particularly as it is expressed in popular culture, that is, in greeting cards, song lyrics, romance novels, and movies.

Role-playing exercises and simulations also help students confront and challenge the naturalness of human arrangements. For example, we have a set of role-playing exercises built around general work/family dilemmas. The exercises include a skit requiring students to reenact an office Christmas party to which a lesbian accountant brings her Jewish partner. Other role-plays have included lesbian mothers at a PTA meeting and a lesbian arranging health care for her partner.

Students are introduced to historical shifts in cultural definitions of sexuality and intimacy through the work of Carol Smith-Rosenberg (1975), who argues that deep affection and often sensual love between women friends were common and widely accepted in the homosocial worlds of middle-class women in the 19th century. Our students are shocked to learn that romantic friendships were permissible during this time period and that it was not until the turn of the century that such relationships came to be seen as suspect.

This historical approach lends itself to our examination of the economic and social changes in the 20th century that made it possible for women and men not only to choose a gay identity but also to begin to build communities and construct a politic around such an identity. Interestingly enough, these are the same social forces that gave young people greater freedom and autonomy. Here we might have students read D'Emilio's "Capitalism and Gay Identity" (1984) and/or show the film *Before Stonewall*. Next, we turn to the writing of working-class lesbians (Beck, 1989; Zandy, 1990) and to lesbians of color (Anzaldua, 1987, 1990; Asian Women United, 1989; Brant, 1984; Gunn, 1984; Moraga, 1983; Smith, 1983) to show the constraints placed on these newfound freedoms by racism, sexism, and class oppression.

Throughout the course students are asked to examine women's lives and experiences along the lines of differences other than gender, such as sexuality, social class, race and ethnicity, age, and physical ability. We always ask them to clarify which women's experiences they are analyzing. We apply this same principle to the study of lesbians, for it is important to address not only commonalities and differences between lesbians and heterosexuals but also to look at commonalities and differences among lesbians.

Often it is the experience of women with multiple "marginalized" and/or "politicized" identities that help our students understand multiple systems of oppression and what is to be gained by the elimination of oppression based on these differences. Many instructors assign Audre Lorde's (1984) classic article "Age, Race, Class, and Sex: Women Redefining Difference," or selected short stories from *The Things That Divide Us*, by Conlon, da Silva, and Wilson (1986), or poetry from *This Bridge Called My Back: Writings by Radical Women of Color*, edited by Moraga and Anzaldua (1981).

By placing sexuality in its political and historical context, feminists and others have urged educators to move beyond the mere description and categorization of sexual identity. Bringing marginalized groups to the center allows oppressed people to speak on their own terms while challenging the political arrangements that oppress them. To further this end, women's studies instructors have instituted the practice of using lesbian panels.

LESBIAN PANELS

Late in the term, usually around the seventh or eighth week, instructors invite a panel of guest speakers to discuss their lesbianism with the students. Typically, speakers share biographical information about their coming out or coming to consciousness as lesbians. Most of the students' questions focus on intrapersonal and interpersonal relationships: How do lesbians relate with their families of origin, lovers, friends, co-workers, employers? How do lesbians negotiate the terrain of disapproval? When and how did they know about their lesbianism?

The opportunity to speak allows panel participants to name and define their lives in accordance with their experience (for related discussion, see Cruikshank, 1982; Maran, 1990; Parmeter & Reti, 1988). Given the personal nature of their narratives, panelists cannot and do not claim to speak for all lesbian experiences and generally speakers issue a disclaimer stating they speak only for themselves.

While this standard caveat may release lesbian speakers from intellectual accountability as token representatives of all lesbians, it does not release most speakers from the social and emotional costs inherent in the responsibility of conveying corrective information to a potentially begrudging and sometimes hostile audience. Communicating about the lives of lesbians presents a central challenge, since one of the most prevalent misconceptions held by students insists that lesbians are solely defined by their sexual orientation. We ask them, as members of a social group whose membership is determined by sexual criteria, to speak about their experiences in ways that transcend audience stereotypes based on sexual categorization. Meredith Maran (1990), a speaker from the Pacific Center for Sexual Minorities in Berkeley, California, addresses this concern from the panelist's point of view:

> It strikes me then that people we speak to during these engagements—the students and workers and inmates and teachers—know . . . [little] of our lives. That by opening up only the sexual aspect of ourselves for discussion, we are inviting them to see us as one-dimensional sexual beings, and simultaneously demanding that they relinquish that stereotype. (p. 70)

While lesbians are struggling to be defined by more than the gender of their sex partners, it is, nonetheless, their sexual attraction to women that is at the core of both societal and student opposition. This paradox can constrain the presentation of honest information about lesbian sexuality.

Student Reactions

Students must struggle to see past their stereotypes—stereotypes that feel comfortable and that serve important psychological and social functions for them (Herek, 1984). Throughout the term we ask students to reexamine their most cherished values and assumptions about human nature, gender, and the nature of relations between the sexes. When we succeed, they no longer see gender as a fixed and stable category. Can we say the same for heterosexuality? Though we have carefully woven information about the experiences and contributions of lesbians throughout the course, our best efforts to deconstruct heterosexuality are tested most severely by the face-to-face confrontation with lesbians.

As many contributors to this anthology document, most college students bring little or no formal education about sexual orientation to college level discussions of gay and lesbian themes. At both the primary and secondary levels, the topic of homosexuality is either ignored or defined as a social, moral, or health problem.

In addition to a lack of knowledge, students also bring to the college classroom their own sexual histories, experiences, and insecurities, all of which have been shaped by their gender, age, race, class, and sexual orientation and which interact in complex ways with our efforts to teach about sexuality and sexual orientation. Side by side, in the same class-room, are lesbian, bisexual, and gay students of various racial and ethnic backgrounds, children and other relatives of gays and lesbians; hetero-sexual students from a variety of racial and ethnic backgrounds; incest and rape survivors; students who are not yet sexually active; and stu-dents with a good deal of sexual experience.

This diversity in the classroom is both a challenge and a resource. While we are careful not to equate other systems of oppression to hom-ophobia or heterosexism or conflate the experiences of other marginal-ized groups with those of gays and lesbians, minority students often draw the parallels between racism and homophobia. For example, a black student, outraged when one panelist talked about employment discrimination against gay people, dramatically told the class:

> I'm sick of this. What gives people the right to impose their petty prejudices on others? Do you think as a black person I care what you think about me or say about me behind my back? But if you try and take away my livelihood, my education, my job, then you are going to have a fight on your hands.

A white woman who had dated a black man made the following connec-tion:

> The fact that lesbians sometimes have to hide their partners is simi-lar to interracial dating. I was in an interracial relationship for nearly six years, and had to hide that from my family. They never even met him, and wouldn't! I guess that "coming out" is impor-tant to your happiness in relationships. It hurts to hide the one you love.

Lesbian and gay students have mixed reactions to the lesbian panels and our other efforts to teach about their experiences. These reactions range from pride and self-validation, to fear of exposure and embarrass-ment about overgeneralizations, to anger when other students reveal their homophobia. One woman wrote, "I feel very supported in being a lesbian . . . a sense of camaraderie and positive re-enforcement." An-other lesbian, concerned about overgeneralizations, wrote, "I feel it is very important to state in the beginning (like one of the women did) that it was her own opinion. She was not representing the opinions of all lesbians, just her own." A third student, concerned about group image, commented, "The one thing I liked about the panelists was they didn't make comments to the students that might offend them."

Those who identify themselves as family members and friends of gay men and lesbians may also find validation in the gay-affirming classroom. One student volunteered the following:

> I've never judged a person based on sexual preference. My fiancé's father is a homosexual and he has been living with his partner ever since his divorce, 12 years ago. Homosexual couples can also raise children in an open-minded and moralistic way.

Among heterosexual students, only a small number of written reactions to the lesbian panel could be clearly labeled hostile. These remarks included, "Makes me feel sick" . . . "Uncomfortable and disgusted" . . . "Sinful" . . . "Gross."

However, most students, while awkward and sometimes ambivalent, indicate some degree of acceptance or understanding of the experiences, feelings, or rights of the lesbian panelists. The majority of students report they felt more comfortable with gays and lesbians, or with homosexuality, after the panel. Typical responses were: "Gay people aren't as scary to me anymore"; "I feel more open minded because of being confronted face to face with homosexuals"; "The stereotypes I had were really shattered . . . I feel more of an understanding."

Ethical considerations demand careful attention to the creation of a safe environment in which all participants can discuss sensitive topics. Gay students and instructors will be exposed to the homophobic reactions of nongay students who need to have enough freedom to reveal their prejudices and lack of knowledge in order to have them challenged. In order for real learning to occur, confrontations with students about their homophobia must be dealt with directly and in a way that does not shame or humiliate the offending student and that at the same time repairs the damage done to the self-respect of gay, lesbian, and bisexual students.

It is also important not to reproduce in the classroom the racism, class privilege, sexism, and heterosexism found in society. To foster a positive environment in which students can acquire an understanding of diversity, including sexual diversity, some instructors distribute a set of guidelines developed by Lynn Weber Cannon (1990) that lays the ground rules for classroom discussions of social and cultural diversity. Early in the course we talk about the power of words to coerce and silence as well as to liberate, and we insist that students use language that honors diversity. We also find it useful to disclose our own struggles with racism, sexism, heterosexism, and class bias. (For other discussions of homophobia in the classroom see Berg, Kowaleski, LeGuin, Weinauer, & Wolfe, 1989; Bleich, 1989; Crumpacker & Vander Haegen, 1987.)

Implications

It is evident from our experience that in an effort to transcend descriptive categorization, lesbianism must first be reclaimed from dominant stereotyping and presented as a fully "normal" human experience. Within the process of naming and defining their own lives, speakers repair and validate an experiential, as opposed to an ideological, lesbian identity. As students hear the speakers talk about their aspirations, needs, desires, and practical day-to-day living, many respond by recognizing how "normal" lesbians are. One student wrote, "Homosexuals have the same human desires as heterosexuals, only towards the same sex. They want love, respect, knowledge, etc. In fact, they're probably a lot more human and honest than most heterosexuals I know." Other students have written, "It [the panel] makes a lesbian more human, like myself, instead of being someone weird"; and "The panel made me realize even more that there is no difference between heterosexuals and homosexuals, both lead the same types of lives, both have feelings and both put their pants on the same way."

Beyond humanizing the topic, panelists identify homophobia as the culprit responsible for distorting lesbian lives in the first place. When speakers reveal homophobia as the ideological barrier keeping lesbian and gay people from the common roundtable of humanity, they make it simultaneously evident that there is nothing inherently deviant or inhuman in being a lesbian. As a result, many students come to understand that homophobic beliefs and practices, not lesbians themselves, are responsible for stigma. One student wrote, "It is not a problem that lesbians are lesbians, it is the problem of prejudice on the part of others." Another reported, "The panel made me feel pity for people who are homophobic because everyone is different and should be accepted by others for who they are and not their sexual orientation."

Students sometimes make painful connections about their own homophobia, as did the student who wrote, "On the first day of class I opened my big mouth and said I am very prejudiced against homosexuals. I feel now I am more open." Another student reported, "It made me feel bad about how I've made gay/lesbian jokes in the past, but the panel made me see for myself that they are real people with real feelings."

This process of relocating responsibility for homophobic attitudes often occurs in discussions of lesbian parenting. Students frequently cite society's prejudice to argue against gay parenting and exhibit concern about the anxiety gays' children must inevitably suffer because of their parents' nonconformity. Helping students to recognize homophobia as the problem, and not lesbian mothers, validates lesbian experience and choices, parallels the parenting responsibilities of lesbians with those of other parents from oppressed groups, and legitimates the feelings and concerns of the children of gays and lesbians, some of whom are in the class.

Once audience members recognize the normalcy of lesbian humanity, heterosexual identity cannot remain unproblematic. After all, if lesbians are "normal" people, then the heterosexual claim to exclusive normality is dispelled. To facilitate student exploration of heterosexism, several women's studies instructors have initiated heterosexual guest panels. Frequently, instructors use a "Heterosexual Questionnaire" that inverts many of the questions typically asked of lesbian panelists. For example, "When did you first know you were a heterosexual?" or "Since the overwhelming majority of child molesters are heterosexual males, should heterosexual men work at day care centers or as elementary school teachers?"

What becomes most evident in the course of heterosexual panels is the unquestioned power of heterosexual identity. Problems reside not with heterosexual acts or heterosexual actors but with the construction of an identity dependent on diminishing other sexual acts and actors in order to appear as the sole socially acceptable choice. Once heterosexism is challenged, a space is created that allows students to think more reflexively about their own sexual orientation.

Evidence that both types of panels promote self-reflexivity was revealed when one heterosexual student wrote, "I have homosexual friends, lesbians, whom I've talked with about why they are the way they are, but never before have I examined so much the question of why I am the way I am." Another student responded:

> In total honesty—the lesbian panel made me think about my reasons for being a heterosexual and whether I have made the right decision. I'm not sure if I am just curious as to what it is like to be a lesbian or if, maybe, I might have some tendencies towards being a lesbian—I'm just not sure now—and this forces me to really think about it.

A third student wrote, "I am disappointed in myself that I am fearful of being labeled lesbian if I associate with lesbian women—same with my boyfriend and his gay friend—shows a lack of self-esteem."

Speakers, activities, and supportive readings not only undermine a heterosexist/homophobic hegemony that distorts gay and lesbian experiences but also reveal the distortion of heterosexual experiences as well. This function is characterized in Hortense Spillers's (1989) assertion that racial categories and definitions developed by the dominant group "tell us little or nothing about the subject buried beneath them, but a great deal more concerning the psychic and cultural reflexes that invent and invoke them" (p. 166). Heterosexist and homophobic descriptions of lesbians are more often expressions of what heterosexuals are not supposed to be than they are depictions of what lesbians are. For example, branding lesbians as man haters does not describe the experiences of most lesbians but rather serves as a warning to all women not to step out of line (Pharr, 1988).

This form of negative socialization explains the confusion some students report between behavior and identification, and contributes to their inability to recognize personal feelings that don't fit into the norm. Constantly defining oneself in terms of not being like some devalued "other" forces heterosexuals into denying any of the qualities or characteristics they may have in common with homosexuals. Any recognition of commonality almost always seems to us to come by way of the back door: "Homosexuals are just like us," but never, "We are just like homosexuals." Making explicit the interdependence of heterosexual and lesbian identities by exposing their common yet differently distorted experiences creates the possibility for more authentic relationships and moves classroom participants beyond a superficial exploration of difference.

We demonstrate homophobia and heterosexism as culturally debilitating ideas for everyone. By reframing the normative relationships between homosexuals and heterosexuals, we establish the grounds for a relational politics that can break down hierarchical oppositions inherent in the modern construction of sexual identities. In the process of cultivating an explicit interconnectedness, panelists and students hearken to their common ground. As their leverage for criticizing the failure of our democracy to extend equal rights to lesbians, panelists draw on the standard of fairness rhetorically offered to all people through the dominant discourse on democratic ideals. Students generally respond affirmatively to appeals to the rights of life, liberty, and the pursuit of happiness. One student wrote, "Lesbians aren't asking for special rights or privileges just the opportunity to live within mainstream society without being harassed or discriminated against solely because of their sexual orientation."

Yet other students affirm individual choice while denouncing homosexuality. Typical of this position are remarks like, "No I don't agree/ identify with it, but I don't condemn those who do. I believe in freedom of choice in any situation." Another student wrote, "I do not condone homosexuality—that has not changed; however, I feel even more strongly that their rights should be protected. I don't feel I have to support what they do, but I do feel a responsibility to make sure I do not discriminate against them."

This contradiction reflects an implicit hazard in holding the dominant ideology accountable for its promises. When efforts to change stereotypical conceptions occur on hegemonic terrain, lesbians will experience pressures to assimilate in order to be recognized as "normal" and fully human and therefore entitled to basic human rights.

Often, lesbian speakers are acutely aware of editing their personal narratives so as to build emotional bridges between themselves and resistant audiences. Meredith Maran (1990) relates her frustration with the pressure to sanitize:

> As we speak in measured, reasonable tones, another voice begins to speak—and then to yell—inside me. This voice knows half-truths are lies. This voice won't joke or equivocate or prettify; it won't tell "fairy tales" with politically correct endings; it wants the truth to be known. (p. 71)

Once again, the tension of validating lesbian identity as fully human while repairing and rebutting stereotypes can promote defensive protectionism on the part of speakers. Allowing lesbian experience to be evaluated by dominant perceptions of normality and happiness can be a risky undertaking; consequently, many lesbian and gay speakers, scholars, and activists insist upon deconstructing compulsory heterosexuality first (Katz, 1990; Valverde, 1989).

CONCLUSION

In sum, teaching about sexuality humanely and holistically through the use of lesbian and heterosexual people, coming out stories, oral histories, role playing, and films provides a useful opportunity to excavate social contradictions in the construction of women's identities. Within the last few years many feminist writers have commented on the tension between validating stigmatized identities and simultaneously undermining the fragmentation of people into distorted categories (Epstein, 1987; Flax, 1987; Kauffman, 1990; Scott, 1988; Sedgwick, 1990; White, 1990). This paradox is expressed by Alcoff (1988) when she asks her readers, "How do we ground a feminist politics that deconstructs the female subject?" (p. 419). Similarly we ask, How do we ground a sexual politics that deconstructs sexual identity?

Our response in accordance with many of the ideas of De Cecco and Shively (1984) and other social constructionists is that the paradox cannot be resolved on hegemonic terrain. Given that categories of sexual identity brand everyone and accurately describe no one, it seems evident that we must resist the dominant ideology that places us in intolerable hierarchies while making practical the adage "Until all of us are free, none of us is free."

To this end, De Cecco and Shively (1984) challenge the centrality of biology in the modern construction of sexual identity. The authors elaborate:

> It may be asserted, perhaps rather boldly, that the long discourse on sexual identity has been essentially an exercise in exhaustively symbolizing the myriad ways in which sexual relationships can be described as extensions of the biological sex of the partners. (p. 14)

In order to subvert the ideational stranglehold of biological determinism reinforced by heterosexism and homophobia, De Cecco and Shively argue for a contextual shift away from the imposition of categorical identities to the emanation of individual meaning in a socially constructed context. This contextual shift from identity to relationships affects conceptual and moral understandings of sexual identity and methodological approaches to its study.

Our conceptualization of individuals within their historical and social contexts is enhanced when we understand them in relationship to one another, rather than exclusively in relationship to a distorted meaning imposed on their bodies. As the lesbian and heterosexual panels illustrate, these intrapersonal and interpersonal considerations are paramount in creating meaning in our lives and should also be paramount in our teaching and scholarship. Placing people in the context of their community allows for multiple constellations of interactive meanings, including disparities in power.

Despite its debatable usefulness, it would be impractical to abandon the concept of sexual identity (Kauffman, 1990). The inequitable exercise of power based on ranking social differences creates material, psychological, and social oppression that cannot be ignored. Rather, it is imperative that teachers reject the dominant discourse on sexual identities and instead create a space where students may explore how they name themselves. We must offer students both resistance and identification strategies for engaging in personal and social change—resistance against rigid categorization and simultaneous identification with the diversity inherent in humanity (Bauer, 1990).

REFERENCES

Alcoff, L. (1988). Cultural feminism vs post structuralism: The identity crisis in feminist theory. *Signs, 13*(3), 405–436.

Anzaldua, G. (1987). *Borderlands/la frontera*. San Francisco: Spinsters/Aunt Lute.

Anzaldua, G. (1990). *Making face, making soul/haciendo caras: Creative and critical perspectives by women of color*. San Francisco: Aunt Lute.

Asian Women United of California. (1989). *Making waves: An anthology of writings by and about Asian American women.* Boston: Beacon.

Baetz, R. (1980). *Lesbian crossroads: Personal stories of lesbian struggles and triumphs.* New York: Morrow.

Barret, M. (1989). *Invisible lives: The truth about millions of women loving women.* New York: Morrow.

Bauer, D. (1990). The other 'F' word: The feminist in the classroom. *College English, 52*(4), 385–396.

Beck, E. T. (1989). *Nice Jewish girls: A lesbian anthology.* Boston: Beacon.

Berg, A., Kowaleski, J., LeGuin, C., Weinauer, E., & Wolfe, E. (1989). Breaking the silence: Sexual preference in the composition classroom. *Feminist Teacher, 4*(2/3), 29–32.

Bleich, D. (1989). Homophobia and sexism as popular values. *Feminist Teacher, 4*(2/3), 21–28.

Brant, O. (1984). Reclamation: A lesbian Indian story. In T. Darty & S. Potter (Eds.), *Women-identified women* (pp. 97–104). Palo Alto, CA: Mayfield.

Cannon, L. W. (1990). Fostering positive race, class, and gender dynamics in the classroom. *Women's Studies Quarterly, XV*(1/2), 126–134.

Conlon, F., da Silva, R., & Wilson, B. (1986). *The things that divide us.* Seattle: Seal.

Cruikshank, M. (1980). *The lesbian path.* Tallahassee, FL: Naiad.

Cruikshank, M. (1982). *Lesbian studies.* New York: Feminist Press.

Crumpacker, L., & Vander Haegen, E. M. (1987). Pedagogy and prejudice: Strategies for confronting homophobia in the classroom. *Women's Studies Quarterly, XV*(3/4), 65–73.

Daly, M. (1978). *Gyn/ecology: The metaethics of radical feminism.* Boston: Beacon.

Daly, M. (1984). *Pure lust: Elemental feminist philosophy.* Boston: Beacon.

De Cecco, J., & Shively, M. (1984). From sexual identity to sexual relationships: A contextual shift. *Journal of Homosexuality, 9*(2/3), 1–26.

D'Emilio, J. (1984). Capitalism and gay identity. In A. Snitow, C. Stansell, & S. Thompson (Eds.), *Powers of desire: The politics of sexuality* (pp. 101–113). New York: Monthly Review.

Devor, H. (1989). *Gender blending.* Bloomington: Indiana University Press.

Epstein, S. (1987). Gay politics, ethnic identity: The limits of social constructionism. *Socialist Review, 17*(3/4), 9–54.

Flax, J. (1987). Postmodernism and gender relations in feminist theory. *Signs, 12*(4), 621–643.

Grahn, J. (1984). *Another mother tongue: Gay words, gay worlds.* Boston: Beacon.

Gunn, P. A. (1984). Beloved women: The lesbian in American Indian culture. In T. Darty & S. Potter (Eds.), *Women-identified women* (pp. 83–96). Palo Alto, CA: Mayfield.

Herek, G. (1984). Beyond "homophobia": A social psychological perspective on attitudes towards lesbians and gay men. *Journal of Homosexuality, 10*(1/2), 1–25.

Katz, J. (1990). The invention of heterosexuality. *Socialist Review, 20*(1), 7–34.

Kauffman, L. A. (1990). The anti-politics of identity. *Socialist Review, 20*(1), 67–80.

Lorde, A. (1984). *Sister outsider.* Freedom, CA: Crossing.

Maran, M. (1990). Ten for bravery, zero for common sense: Confessions of a speakers bureau speaker. *Outlook, 2*(3), 68–73.

Moraga, C. (1983). *Loving in the war years: Lo que nuca paso or sus labios.* Boston: South End.

Moraga, M., Anzaldua, G. (Eds.). (1981). *This bridge called my back: Writings by radical women of color.* Watertown, MA: Persephone.

Parmeter, S. H., & Reti, I. (1988). *The lesbian in front of the classroom: Writings by lesbian teachers.* Santa Cruz: Herbooks.

Penelope, J., & Valentine, S. (1990). *Finding the lesbians: Personal accounts from around the world.* Freedom, CA: Crossing.

Penelope, J., & Wolfe, S. J. (1989). *The original coming out stories.* Freedom, CA: Crossing.

Pharr, S. (1988). *Homophobia: A weapon of sexism.* Little Rock: Chardon.

Scott, J. (1988). Deconstructing equality-versus-difference: or, the uses of post-structuralist theory for feminism. *Feminist Studies, 14*(1), 33–59.

Sears, J. T. (1989). The impact of gender and race on growing up lesbian and gay in the south. *NWSA Journal, 1*(3), 422–457.

Sedgwick, E. K. (1990). Pedagogy in the context of an antihomophobic project. *The South Atlantic Quarterly, 89*(1), 139–156.

Smith, B. (Ed.). (1983). *Home girls: A black feminist anthology.* New York: Kitchen Table.

Smith-Rosenberg, C. (1975). The female world of love and ritual: Relations between women in nineteenth century America. *Signs, 1*(1), 1–29.

Spillers, H. J. (1989). Notes on an alternative model—neither/nor. In E. Meese & A. Parker (Eds.), *The difference within: feminism and critical theory* (pp. 165–188). Philadelphia: John Benjamins.

Valverde, M. (1989). Beyond gender dangers and private pleasures: Theory and ethics in the sex debates. *Feminist Studies, 15*(2), 237–254.

Vance, C. (1989). Social construction theory: Problems in the history of sexuality. In D. Altman (Ed.), *Homosexuality, which homosexuality?* (pp. 13–34). London: GMP.

White, E. F. (1990). Africa on my mind: Gender, counter discourse and African-American nationalism. *Journal of Women's History, 2*(1), 73–97.

Zandy, J. (1990). *Calling home: Working-class women's writings.* New Brunswick: NJ: Rutgers University Press.

Why Should We Care About Gender and Sexuality in Education?

SUSAN SHURBERG KLEIN

Why should we care about gender and sexuality when we try to improve the school curriculum? What are the key ways in which gender and sexuality interact? What can you do to improve the treatment of sexuality in the formal and informal curricula to benefit females and males? I will try to answer these questions, using insights gained by editing a special issue of the *Peabody Journal of Education* on "Sex Equity and Sexuality in Education" (Klein, 1989), by expanding that journal issue into a book (Klein, in press), and by reading the chapters in Part II of this book.

GENDER, SEXUALITY, AND THE SCHOOL CURRICULUM

After many years of avoidance, why should we care about gender and sexuality when we try to improve the school curriculum? Gender and sexuality are important parts of school life. This is true whether or not educators purposefully include them. It is true even of single-sex schools, but particularly an issue in the mixed-sex schools that predominate in the United States. Gender and sexuality affect the formal and informal curriculum, and how education treats them both *reflects* and *affects* the culture of our society.

If gender and sexuality are so important, how and why were they generally avoided (or sometimes actively suggested as legitimate topics for educators or their students) for so many years? Even today, why is there so much official silence about sexuality and lack of specific attention to discriminatory aspects of treatment by gender? Why are gender and sexuality the hidden curriculum as described by Raphaela Best (1983) in *We've All Got Scars?* Do educators believe that if they don't talk about sex, it will disappear, or are they afraid that if they discuss gender

This commentary was prepared by Susan Klein as a private citizen. Thus, the views are the author's and no support from her employer, the U.S. Department of Education, is intended or should be inferred. Margaret Feldman's insightful comments on earlier drafts are gratefully appreciated.

and sexuality, students will think more about it and engage in more sex discrimination or sexual activity (Fine, 1987; Klein, in press)?

Gender and sexuality have long been neglected aspects of school life. The tradition in America is to desexualize schools, including school staff, students, and the content of what is taught. Sadker, Sadker, and Shakeshaft (1989) report:

> In the 1920s, the lack of sexual knowledge was a criterion for hiring and retention. Contracts often specified that teachers (read only women apply) "were not to keep company with men" and that their employment would be terminated if they should marry . . . Recently court cases have surrounded efforts to remove homosexual teachers from the classroom. Prior to 1972 and the passage of Title IX, pregnant students were barred from attending school. Depending on the culture and climate of the times, different manifestations of sexuality have been seen as educationally taboo. (p. 213)

For example, even after married teachers were allowed, pregnant teachers were barred. Rury (1989) and Tyack and Hansot (1990) discuss how desexualizing schooling helped our society accept coeducation while maintaining sex segregation in physical and vocational education and subtly teaching sex or gender role socialization patterns common to the society of the time.

Most people in our society have been taught to be shy and embarrassed about discussing sexuality—at least publicly. In addition to this constraint, teachers are afraid to address sexuality because of controversies over issues such as sexual intercourse, abortion, and sexual orientation—due in great part to different family and religious beliefs and values (Feldman & Parrot, 1984; Greenberg & Campbell, 1989, in press). In some cases, teachers may even be forbidden to discuss some of these issues or share certain views about sexuality. If they violate these taboos, they may be fired.

It is likely that desexualization in the schools also led to the ignoring of gender equity issues. Similar to the "official" invisibility of sexuality, one of the key ways that women are still discriminated against is to ignore them, their needs, and their accomplishments. This neglect of women ranges from the content of the curriculum to their receiving less educational resources than their male peers. For example, women receive less student financial aid and are less likely to be identified for special education—because unlike many of the males they don't disrupt the class, and therefore are less likely to receive attention from teachers during classroom interactions (Sadker, Sadker & Klein, 1991). Similarly, women's good ideas and accomplishments are often devalued or ignored while less important contributions from males are rewarded. Greenberg and Campbell (1989) point out how this even extends to female fertility, where women and their children are often seen as the valued property of men and their own role and rights in reproduction denigrated.

Today, there are many promising trends to help educators realize the importance of attending openly and comprehensively to issues of gender and sexuality in the schools:

• The mass media are becoming more open and active in dealing with both gender and sexuality issues, and sometimes they even address the intersection of gender and sexuality. Recently reported gender or sex equity issues have included sex differences in dress codes (a Texas boy was removed from his regular class because he refused to cut his ponytail; see "A ponytail," 1990), and sex differences on tests such as the Scholastic Aptitude Test. Sexuality issues are covered in the arts, soap operas, gossip columns, and so forth. In education, articles focusing on the intersection of gender and sexuality typically deal with discussions of sexual harassment or sexual orientation. Thus, gender and sexuality are becoming legitimate topics for public discourse.

• There is substantial public concern about AIDS, teen pregnancy, sexual harassment, and other physical and mental health issues of students, and a concomitant belief that schools should play an active role in addressing these problems. The issues generally deal with the intersection of gender and sexuality and reflect the increased role of the schools in coping with what formerly were "family responsibilities." An example of how people are becoming more aware of sex discrimination as it relates to sexuality issues is illustrated by a recent exchange in the *Washington Post*. In response to an article (Booth, 1990) on increased sexual activity among young girls, a letter to the editor (Raker, 1990) suggested that it was sexist to focus only on females when the study also reported an increase in sexual activity among teen males.

• As shown by recent research (Kaplan 1989; Gallup & Clark, 1987), there is increased public and professional consensus about having schools assume responsibility for sexuality education, but as Whatley (1989) and Trudell and Whatley (in press) point out, there is little attention to making sure that the sex education curricula pays attention to gender equity issues. And the Sex Information and Education Council of the United States (SIECUS) reports that "in 1990, two states rescinded their mandates for sexuality education in response to opposition pressures" (Haffner, 1990).

• During the past 20 years, many laws (such as Title IX of the Education Amendments of 1972, Title VII of the 1964 Civil Rights Act, and state equal opportunity and criminal laws) have helped people realize the importance of paying attention to gender equity and sexuality both separately and together. These laws are based on civil rights, as well as civil and criminal statutes such as in cases of child sexual abuse. Chapter 5 in this volume indicates how interpretations of the 14th Amendment for equal protection are making educators increasingly responsible for maintaining an environment free of sexual harassment.

• The women's and homosexual rights movements and attention to nondiscrimination on the basis of sex and sexual orientation in education and the work force have contributed to increased attention to gender and sexuality issues in education. Much of this education-related work is addressed in this book as well as in Klein (1989, in press). Numerous other books and articles outside of education also contribute to our increased understanding of gender and sexuality.

Despite some recent progress in increased attention to sexuality education and sex equity, we still have a long way to go in accomplishing goals for each, and we need to promote effective approaches. Kirby (1989) synthesizes research on the effectiveness of sexuality education programs and concludes they "can increase knowledge but, like most educational programs, have little measurable impact on behavior" (p. 170).

When feminists think about gender in education, they generally do so in the context of sex equity goals such as those described in *The Handbook for Achieving Sex Equity Through Education* (Klein, 1985). Most sex equity goals have focused on eliminating sex discrimination and decreasing sex stereotyping in educational processes and outcomes to help females achieve parity with males. Recognizing similarities among the sexes, feminist educators such as Greenberg (1985) and Schau (1985) describe how to decrease stereotypical sex role development through the teaching of "opposite sex" scripts. While feminists have been primarily concerned with helping women achieve the advantages traditionally held by males, they emphasize that gender equity also includes having males attain parity with females in areas where females generally excel, such as empathy for others, high school graduation, and writing abilities.

INTERACTION OF GENDER AND SEXUALITY

There are many ways that gender and sexuality interact. This interaction is often detrimental to both females and males. Greenberg and Campbell (in press) state, "Sex[uality] is and has been as central to sexism as are money and power." They and many of the authors in this volume describe the relationships of reproduction and motherhood to patriarchy. This relationship of sexism and sexuality from the larger society carries over to education. Thus, it is increasingly important to

understand the relationship of sexuality to all kinds of educational processes and outcomes. Understanding them may help educators channel
sexuality in positive rather than negative ways to accomplish important
goals such as decreasing teen substance abuse and increasing high
school graduation.

The analyses in "Sex Equity and Sexuality in Education" (Klein,
1989, in press) show how sexuality affects many aspects of gender
equity. For example, while sexuality may be a distraction to learning on
some occasions for both sexes, there is some evidence that the observed
decline in academic achievement of girls from 7th to 12th grade correlates positively with their interest in being attractive to males. Concerns
about sexual interactions may also restrict friendships or mentorships
for students of either gender who could benefit from studying with each
other (Klein, 1988).

Sexual harassment and homophobia also have major negative sex-
differential effects. Females are more likely to be the "victims" of sexual
harassment (Bogart & Stein, 1989). And as Sears suggests in Chapter 7,
often males are more negatively affected by homophobia since our "gendered" society is more accepting of female "tomboys" because the male
"model" is more likely to be highly valued. Additionally, sexual harassment and homophobia often put major limitations on students' choices
of courses, particularly in areas nontraditional for their sex such as auto
mechanics for females. Chapter 8 shows how heterosexuality is a cultural norm that contributes to inequities for those not sharing this sexual
orientation. Sears points out that the more equitable homosexual and
lesbian relationships are, the more they seem a threat to sexists who
prefer to bifurcate roles into butch/femme. Similarly, the equity implications of bisexuality may be more disturbing to some than homosexuality.
It is also interesting to note that sexual harassment may now be defined
as including homophobic types of harassment (a popular way for students—especially young adolescents—to denigrate their peers). This
type of biased behavior has generally been unnamed and unacknowledged by educators and many parents.

Interactions of gender and sexuality are dynamic and change with
generations and cultures. We must be careful that educators' knowledge
of sexuality and gender roles is not totally dependent on their own experiences. For example, while I felt that the sexual scripts described by
Sapon-Shevin and Goodman in Chapter 4 were a good depiction of my
generation and middle-class culture, I doubt that they are generalizable
to many students today.

Sexual activity and orientation influence socially expected sex roles
in all cultures as they provide some "justification" for differential expectations such as female control over male aggression. However, the ties
between sex role development and sexual activity and orientation are

often tenuous. Thus, Sapon-Shevin and Goodman mention how "doing sex" and the "need" to exert heterosexuality and male power influenced the sexual scripts. They also suggest how male power and the isolation of female and male sexual scripts contributed to male lack of sensitivity toward women and to devaluing women's comments.

Although educators who care about gender equity and sexuality education have often been on "separate tracks," some are now joining forces to contribute to sex-equitable sexuality education and to ensure that the way educators address sexuality promotes sex or gender equity (Klein, 1989). Although we have many examples of how gender and sexuality contribute to sex inequities in students' educational interactions and in their eventual outcomes relating to academic and social achievement, we have little knowledge of how educators can use aspects of sexuality such as sexual attraction to influence positively other types of valued educational outcomes.

STRATEGIES TO PROMOTE SEX-EQUITABLE SEXUALITY EDUCATION

What can you do to improve the treatment of sexuality in the formal and informal curricula to benefit females and males? I recommend the following:

• Urge educators and parents to apply Whatley's (1989) nine goals for sex-equitable sexuality education. Examples include eliminating biological determinism by emphasizing "male and female similarities, rather than differences, though with a clear recognition of differences," de-emphasizing "dating and marriage as goals for students and the elimination of the heterosexual assumption; and eliminating double standards "so that males are held responsible for their own sexual behavior, rather than placing that burden on females" (p. 68–69).

• Continue to identity and incorporate feminist approaches to sexuality in all work with gender and sexuality. For example, give high priority to helping students understand equity concepts such as a woman's right to control her own body, including the right to choose abortion, and encourage greater equity in combining parenthood and careers. Also, find creative solutions to sexuality-related constraints as Haring-Hidore and Paludi (1989) have done. They suggest that due to the sexuality issues inherent in traditional male mentor, female protégé relationships, it would be useful to substitute network mentoring based on multiple, but less intense, relationships. Another creative strategy to help males and females experience some of the constraints of pregnancy is to have nonpregnant students wear a heavy "pregnancy belly." Finally, identify and encourage trends like teenage group dating that decrease pressure on establishing intimate dyadic relationships that are likely to lead to sexual intercourse or tensions related to sexual orientation.

• Provide appropriate, consistent ways to talk about and identify sex-equity and sexuality issues. For example, avoid terms like *opposite sex* when discussing females and males. Chapter 4 helps clarify why many feminists object to "learning to be the opposite sex" or stereotypical lessons of sex role development. Feminists object to this socialization because it creates "artificial" differences (classified by sex) and because many of these differences contribute to male power, instead of equal treatment of females and males (which I interchangeably call sex equity or gender equity). Greenberg and Campbell (1989) and Whatley (1989) point out that there are more biological and cultural sex similarities than sex differences even in areas related to physiological sexual functioning. For example, both sexes have sexual desires, the same hormones, and an equal need to control reproduction. In *Beyond Separate Spheres: Feminism and Family Research,* Ferree (1990) equates learning gender roles with sex inequities. She states, "Because the active suppression of similarity and the construction of differences requires social power, the issue of domination is central to gender theory" (p. 868). In addition to avoiding misleading terms it is useful to create new terms such as *sexual harassment* and *date rape*. However, in defining these terms we should make sure that they don't perpetuate bias. Thus, sexual harassment should refer to harassment related to homosexuality as well as to heterosexuality.

• Conduct research and development on important issues that will help to create effective sex-equitable education, and attend to sexuality issues to decrease sex discrimination in education and maximize learning opportunities. For example, what are some effective ways to integrate sex-equitable sexuality education across the formal and informal curricula? How can educators capitalize on positive aspects of sexuality such as "the sexual energy pulsating in even the most boring of classes" noted by Sears in Chapter 7? Sex segregation and isolation contribute to partial education, but are there any justifications for such segregation when helping students achieve sex-equitable sexuality goals? What about using same-sex teachers and students? Also, what are the effects of sex segregation on sexual orientation? How can educators attend to the call in Chapter 4 "to help young adolescents learn how they can become allies rather than aliens to each other?" To what extent should educators condone inequitable sexuality-related behaviors that are culturally based? For example, on a world scale, Molly Yard, president of the National Organization for Women, questioned U.S. support for Kuwait because of its cultural repression of women. She pointed out that the United States would be unlikely to defend a country such as South Africa that has active cultural repression of blacks.

• Include education related to gender equity and sexuality in all types of teacher administrator preparation programs. Sadker, Sadker, and Shakeshaft (1989) point out that "prospective educators can learn more about [sexuality] issues from television and newspapers than from their preparation programs (p. 214). And Stubbs (1988) notes that this training is certainly needed since most educators have limited professional experience dealing with sexuality or sexuality education.

SUMMARY

Gender and sexuality separately and together are important factors in the educational process and outcomes in both formal and informal curricula. Educational researchers and curriculum developers have a continuing responsibility to increase their understanding of how these factors influence all aspects of education, no matter how overt or subtle they may appear. They also have a responsibility to communicate what they have learned to empower other educators, students, and the general public to assume responsibility to ensure that sexuality education will promote sex-equitable attitudes and behaviors. Similarly, all with education responsibilities should learn how to recognize and counteract the factors of gender and sexuality that limit equitable treatment of educators and students, and how to capitalize on those factors, such as sexual attraction, that may increase motivation to perform well.

REFERENCES

Achenbach, J. (1991, July 31). Pee-Wee's nightmare: The kiddie star and the ancient taboo. *Washington Post*, pp. B1, B9.

Best, R. (1983). *We've all got scars: What boys and girls learn in elementary school.* Bloomington: Indiana University Press.

Bogart, K., & Stein, N. (1989). Breaking the silence: Sexual harassment in education. *Peabody Journal of Education, 64*(4), 146–163.

Booth, W. (1990, November 8). Sexual activity of teenage U.S. girls rose in 1980s. *Washington Post*, pp. A1, A11.

Feldman, H., & Parrot, A. (1984). *Human sexuality: Contemporary controversies.* Beverly Hills: Sage.

Ferree, M. M. (1990). Beyond separate spheres: Feminism and family research. *Journal of Marriage and the Family, 52*(4), 866–884.

Fine, M. (1987). Silencing in public schools. *Language Arts, 64*(2), 74.

Gallup, A. M., & Clark, D. L. (1987). The 19th annual Gallup poll of the public's attitude toward the public schools. *Phi Delta Kappan, 68,* 17–30.

Greenberg, S. (1985). Educational equity in early educational environments. In S. S. Klein (Ed.), *Handbook for achieving sex equity through education* (pp. 457–469). Baltimore, MD: Johns Hopkins University Press.

Greenberg, S., & Campbell, P. B. (1989). Sexuality, sexism and education: The views of feminists past and present. *Peabody Journal of Education, 64*(4), 13–24.

Greenberg, S., & Campbell, P. B. (in press). Sexism, sexuality, and education: Feminist thought then and now. In S. S. Klein (Ed.), *Sex equity and sexuality in education.* Albany, NY: SUNY Press.

Haffner, D. W. (1990). *Help SIECUS protect sexual rights* [A "Dear SIECUS Friend" letter]. New York: Sex Information and Education Council of the United States. [Undated but mailed in November.]

Haring-Hidore, M., & Paludi, M. A. (1989). Sexuality and sex in mentoring and tutoring: Implications for women's opportunities and achievement. *Peabody Journal of Education, 64*(4), 164–172.

Kaplan, R. (Ed.). (1989). Sexuality education. *Theory Into Practice, 28*(3).

Kirby, D. (1989). Research on effectiveness of sex education programs. *Theory Into Practice, 28*(3), 165–171.

Klein, S. S. (Ed.). (1985). *Handbook for achieving sex equity through education.* Baltimore, MD: Johns Hopkins University Press.

Klein, S. S. (1988). Sex education and gender equity. *Educational Leadership, 45*(6), 69–74.

Klein, S. S. (Ed.). (1989). Sex equity and sexuality in education [Special issue]. *Peabody Journal of Education, 64*(4).

Klein, S. S. (Ed.). (in press). *Sex equity and sexuality in education.* Albany, NY: SUNY Press.

A ponytail and a principle separate Texas third-grader from schoolmates. (1990, November 25). *Washington Post,* p. A-8. [from the *Dallas Morning News*].

Raker, S. (1990, November 17). Your sexism is showing [Letter to the editor]. *Washington Post,* p. A19.

Rury, J. L. (1989). We teach the girl *repression,* the boy *expression. Peabody Journal of Education, 64*(4), 44–58.

Sadker, M., Sadker, D., & Klein, S. S. (1991). Gender in education. *Review of Research in Education, 17,* 269–333.

Sadker, M., Sadker, D., & Shakeshaft, C. (1989). Sex, sexism, and the preparation of educators. *Peabody Journal of Education, 64*(4), 213–224.

Schau, C. G., with Tittle, C. K. (1985). Educational equity and sex role development. In S. S. Klein (Ed.), *Handbook for achieving sex equity through education* (pp. 78–90). Baltimore, MD: Johns Hopkins University Press.

Stubbs, M. L. (1988). *Sex equitable sex education in elementary and secondary schools: Strategies for engaging practitioners in the topic.* Unpublished manuscript, Wellesley College, Center for Research on Women, Wellesley, MA.

Trudell, B., & Whatley, M. (in press). Sex equity principles for evaluating sexuality education materials. In S. S. Klein (Ed.), *Sex equity and sexuality in education.* Albany, NY: SUNY Press.

Tyack, D., & Hansot, E. (1990). *Learning together: A history of coeducation in American public schools.* New Haven, CT: Yale University Press.

Whatley, M. (1989). Goals for sex equitable sex education. *Peabody Journal of Education, 64*(4). 59–70.

Part III

MAKING MEANING OF SEXUALITY IN THE SCHOOLS

The relationship between the curriculum prescribed by legislation or bureaucratic decree, implemented by a school district or classroom teacher, and interpreted by the student may vary significantly for even the most mundane subject matter. This is particularly true in subject areas of potential controversy such as sexuality education wherein values and politics are more visible. The contributors in this section examine this curricular rupture between what sexual knowledge is officially prescribed or proscribed, what and how that knowledge is formally taught, and the various understandings about this classroom knowledge held by students. Peering into the deep structure of the sexuality curriculum, contributors to this section use a variety of ethnographic methods to illuminate the variety of sexual meanings, messages, acts, and thoughts that lie just below the curricular surface, and to suggest alternate curricular and pedagogical approaches to the teaching of sexuality education within a culturally and ethnically diverse society.

In Chapter 9, Janie Ward and Jill Taylor draw from their extensive data, gathered from focus groups of adolescents and parents representing six different ethnic populations, to examine cultural values and beliefs about human sexuality. Ward and Taylor argue that sexuality education, as it exists in practice today, does not serve the needs of immigrant and minority youth. They assert that sexuality education is based on an understanding of sexuality that is derived from the dominant group in power (white, middle-class), and is thus ethnocentric and culturally biased. The lack of attention to multicultural perspectives serves to silence, dismiss, or denigrate the concerns and life experiences of large groups of minority adolescents. This chapter provides the reader with an understanding of the specific circumstances in which girls and boys make sense of themselves as young adults within their community, their sexuality, and their experiences with school-based sex education programs. In asking, "Whose needs are being met?" Ward and Taylor critique existing sexuality education from the viewpoints of multicultural inclusion and relevancy, developmental psychology, and feminist theory. Chapter 9 concludes with a proposal for the development and implementation of culturally appropriate sex education curriculum that attends to the beliefs, values, worldviews, and life-style patterns of a diverse adolescent population.

Bonnie Trudell, in Chapter 10, illuminates the dynamic, complex, and contradictory process by which traditional versions of appropriate sexual behavior and gender relations are legitimated as well as contested in a ninth-grade, mostly white and Christian Midwestern classroom. Data obtained by daily classroom and school observation as well as teacher and student interviews richly document what happens as the planned curriculum works its way through Mrs. Warren and her students. Trudell's textured description of the curriculum in use suggests possibilities for progressive action within school sexuality education, including "broadening the spectrum of 'acceptable' sexual behavior, affirming the pleasures of sexuality, and encouraging nonexploitive relationships."

In Chapter 11, Diane Brunner reports on her study of the out-of-school experiences of inner-city, African-American adolescents participating in a five-week summer institute. Based upon her interviews and observations of these sixth- through ninth-grade boys and girls, Brunner suggests that "literature may provide a much needed opportunity to repair the break between what is formally taught in sexuality education classes or romanticized by popular culture and how it is interpreted." She demonstrates how focused discussions following the reading of several short stories (written by white authors) can be used to work out their views about sexuality and the images of black teenagers portrayed in these stories. These findings suggest ways in which alternative meanings are constructed when space is provided for confrontational encounters with literature. Further, they suggest the power of dialogue/debate in developing oppositional or alternative meanings.

In their commentary to Part III, Lynn Phillips and Michelle Fine invite readers to partake in a "public conversation about the possibilities and constraints of meaning-making in sexuality education, under the disturbing and saturating cloud of the New Right." From their vantage point as qualitative researchers, teachers, and feminist activists, these commentators challenge us to "not only press the boundaries of sexuality discourse but to move further to confront the forces that impose them."

CHAPTER 9

Sexuality Education for Immigrant and Minority Students

Developing a Culturally Appropriate Curriculum

JANIE VICTORIA WARD AND JILL McLEAN TAYLOR

Over the next decades American health educators will be confronted with two major challenges: to improve the development and dissemination of sexuality education in primary and secondary schools and to impart this information adequately to a student population that is becoming increasingly multicultural. A further challenge lies in how sexuality education can incorporate the view of sexuality as a positive and integral part of human development and experience while at the same time making adolescents aware of the negative consequences of unprotected sexual intercourse.

In this chapter we argue that sexuality education as it is currently taught does not serve the needs of a large percentage of children and adolescents living in America, particularly those from communities of color. Our call for a reconceptualization and redesign of sexuality education curricula is based on the understanding that sexuality education is socially constructed in that it is created within a political and social context that includes the dynamic interplay of race, gender, and class oppression. The social constructionist framework derived from the work of Michel Foucault (1978) and adopted by some feminists (Ferguson, 1984; Rubin, 1984) incorporates the historical and social context of sexual desire and behavior and helps to reveal what has been obscured by the essentialist's biological "drive" or "instinct" view of sexuality. As detailed in Chapters 1, 2, 7, and 8, various cultures interpret, define, and regulate sexuality differently, and cultural group members socialize their children to cultural norms, taboos, and expectations regarding sexual behavior. Yet representations of these cultural determinants of sexuality are absent from the discourse on sexuality education, and their absence draws attention to how the curriculum has failed to incorporate alternative points of view. The norms and consensus guiding the design of sexuality education in the United States privilege a white, middle-class understanding of sexuality. Having rejected the biologically determined view of sexuality that necessarily renders cultural differences unimportant, we take as a theoretical framework the position that sexuality is socially constructed and that most existing sexuality education curricula are limited because they perpetuate a singular world view in a multicultural society.

When sexuality education is viewed from a social constructivist perspective, four interrelated concepts regarding power dynamics in society are revealed. First, sexuality education developed and adopted for use in our schools is ethnocentric and culturally biased and almost always assumes a heterosexual audience. The lack of attention to multicultural perspectives has served to silence, dismiss, or denigrate the concerns and life experiences of large groups of minority adolescents. Second, sexuality education has been based on a traditional understanding of the central development tasks of adolescence in western psychology: separation, individuation, and independence (see, for example, Blos, 1967; Erikson, 1968; Offer, 1969). Feminist theories of adolescent development that question the ethos of individuality provide an alternative understanding of adolescence (Chodorow, 1974; Gilligan, 1982; Miller, 1976). Third, although each group has its own cultural constraints regarding acceptable sex-role behavior (and most groups have their own double standard toward sexuality), existing curricula support both implicitly and explicitly an institutionalized American middle-class double standard toward sexuality. Finally, most sexuality education programs tend to emphasize reproductive biology, particularly the female aspects of reproduction, thus isolating sexuality and its potential outcomes from the context of human relationships.

The following sections provide a review of the recent shifts in demographics and an analysis showing the necessity for the development and dissemination of culturally appropriate sexuality education curricula. Data from a series of focus groups held with adolescents and parents from six different cultural groups discussing issues of sexuality, birth control, parenthood, and sexuality education are provided. We discuss implications of this research for developing alternative, culturally sensitive sexuality education in the United States.

CHANGING STUDENT POPULATIONS

The majority of new immigrants to the United States bring with them a diversity in background, language, and culture from Asia, Central and South America, and the Caribbean Islands. Educational demographers citing trends in enrollment projections indicate that in this decade there will be an increase in the number of minority children attending school. In fact, according to a 1988 report from the National Coalition of Advocates for Students:

> White Americans are aging most rapidly, with a mean age in 1980 of 31.3 years for women and 28.8 for men. When compared with an average age of 25 for Blacks, 23 for Hispanics, and still younger for many recent immigrants, it becomes clear that Whites are moving out of their childbearing years just as other sectors of the population are moving into them. (p. 10)

Across the nation, educators are asking if our teaching and support staff are prepared to address the needs of the diverse group of children and teens who do now and will continue in larger numbers to populate our classrooms. Curriculum developers struggling to bring multicultural perspectives into school call for a curriculum that is inclusive of the unique needs, contributions, and concerns of all racial and ethnic groups (Banks, 1984; Gay, 1983; Morgan, 1986). While models may vary and even conflict, supporters of multicultural education argue for the necessity of children being able to see themselves and their cultures acknowledged positively in what and how they learn (see Cummins, 1986; Sleeter & Grant, 1987; Spener, 1988).

At the same time, educators and public health officials continue to call our attention to the consequences of unprotected sexual activity among adolescents, frequently citing rates of teen pregnancy and sexually transmitted diseases (STDs) that are higher among teens than any other age group of the population and account for more than 25% of the annual reported cases of STDs. More recently, there is a growing concern about transmission of the HIV virus, particularly among inner-city black and Latino young adults. AIDS ranks as the seventh leading cause of death among people ages 15 to 24 in the United States. Even more disturbing is the fact that black children, who constitute 15% of the nation's children, account for 53% of all childhood AIDS cases, while Hispanic children, who represent 10% of U.S. children, account for 23% of all pediatric AIDS cases (Centers for Disease Control, 1989).

Nearly 1 million adolescent girls become pregnant each year, and about half give birth. Although the overall adolescent birthrate has declined since the 1970s, the birth rate for black teens is still twice as high as that for whites, and for Hispanic adolescents, 1.7 times greater than that for whites. However, not all births to adolescents are unplanned or unwanted. While the social and material disadvantages reinforced by racism and classism are assumed to be continued by adolescent childbearing, a growing body of literature demonstrates that becoming a mother in mid-to-late teens may not lead to these detrimental consequences. In fact, as a result of social programs aimed at this group, social and material conditions, particularly access to education and job train-ing, may improve for some low income adolescent mothers, especially when compared to low income women who begin childbearing in their twenties (see, for example, Geronimus, 1986, 1987; McCrate, 1989; Up-church & McCarthy, 1990).

Pregnancy rates for more recently arrived immigrant groups are dif-ficult to collect, especially on a national level, as states differ in how they identify and report rates from different racial and ethnic groups. How-ever, the birth rate among Hispanic teenagers born in the United States closely resembles that of black teenagers, while the birth rate for native-born Hispanic mothers closely resembles that of white teens (Ventura, 1984). This last fact highlights the critical role that culture and accultur-ation play in influencing sexual decision making. In metropolitan areas especially, the attempt to create culturally sensitive and linguistically appropriate programs that address the needs of native born African-American and Latino teens as well as new immigrants, whose youthful-ness is an important characteristic, has drawn attention to the shortcom-ings of existing sexuality education programs in schools.

PERSISTING PROBLEMS WITH SEXUALITY EDUCATION

Although considerably slower than some progressive European na-tions, over the last decade the United States has recognized and re-sponded to the need for increased sexuality education among its school age populations (Jones et al., 1985). According to the Alan Guttmacher Institute (1989), an estimated 93% of the nation's high schools now offer some form of sexuality education and/or AIDS education to students. However, evaluation of sexuality education programs show that most programs are short (10 hours or less) and noncomprehensive (Brooks-Gunn & Furstenberg, 1989; Kirby, 1984). In addition, most sexuality edu-cation programs, while designed for both sexes, are still geared primar-ily toward girls, who are seen as being more vulnerable in terms of con-sequences (Chilman, 1985). In the mid 1980s, as the number of AIDS victims steadily increased, U.S. Surgeon General C. Everett Koop (1988) advocated nationwide sexuality education in schools because of the con-cern about AIDS and STDs. While parents in the United States still differ about the appropriate content of sexuality education and who should teach it, a recent national Harris survey reported that virtually all par-ents want AIDS education in the schools (Meade, cited in Brooks-Gunn & Furstenburg, 1989).

For a number of reasons it has been difficult to assess the extent to which sexuality education programs have been successful for adoles-cents in general and for minority populations in particular. No standardized sexuality education curriculum exists in the United States (and given the diversity in regional populations, this is understandable); most curricula are designed at the initiative of local and/or state education personnel with minimal input from immigrant and minority communities. Typically, these school-based curricula are designed by white, middle-class publishing houses or by educators and instructors who are also white and middle class; rarely are the perspectives of nonwhites solicited. Nationally, there do not appear to be universal goals of sexuality education, although information about human reproduction and methods to reduce the likelihood of unplanned pregnancy are frequently cited (Brooks-Gunn & Furstenberg, 1989). While studies have measured contraceptive and reproductive knowledge (Scott, Shifman, Orr, Owen, & Fawcett, 1988; Scott-Jones & Turner, 1988; Zelnick & Kantner, 1980) and adolescent sexual attitudes and behavior (Zabin, Hirsch, Smith, & Hardy, 1984), culture-specific attitudes about sexuality and sensitivity toward cultural concerns are more difficult to assess and less frequently sought. Finally, apart from the work of Scales and Kirby (1981; Kirby, 1984), Harper (1983), and Reis, Herz, & Slager (1986), little systematic evaluation of information on either school-based or non-school-based sexuality education programs has emerged.

CULTURAL ASPECTS OF SEXUALITY EDUCATION

Most existing school-based sexuality education or "family life education" programs face charges of being ethnocentric and insensitive to different cultural values and beliefs about human sexuality (Espin, 1984; Gibbs, 1989; Medina, 1987). Too often in school-based programs, issues facing cultural and linguistic minority children are either ignored completely, subsumed under majority concerns, or addressed in stereotypical or superficial ways. Sexuality education is seldom introduced in bilingual education classrooms, and children with limited English proficiency may or may not be exposed to sexuality education in school. Despite a growing awareness of the problem, attempts to include minority concerns in commercially produced teaching materials are too often token efforts and may prove to reinforce cultural and sex-role stereotypes. For example, many commercial producers have adopted the practice of "colorizing" their materials, peppering their audiovisual and reading materials with pictures of children of color, yet with little or no reference to the cultural differences represented by their inclusion. In addition, for linguistic minority children, language differences and the necessity of adjusting to the linguistic concepts in a new culture may affect comprehension of sexuality education course content. Even more important for immigrants, the process of acculturation—learning and integrating into a new culture—requires that families make hard decisions regarding which aspects of their former culture will be retained or sacrificed and which aspects of the new culture will be adopted or integrated into their own. Stressors affecting immigrant and minority youth that have implications for sexuality education include the pressure to acculturate, conflicts between their own and the dominant societal values, intergenerational and gender-role conflicts, as well as racism, sexism, and economic disadvantage.

Not only do children and adolescents learn about sexuality from school-based sources, but for some cultural groups, non-school-based sources provide substantial assistance/instruction in this area as well. Community agencies and health facilities, whose staff are more likely to be sensitive to the cultural values of their clients, may offer informal sexuality education or counseling to their constituencies. However, the information disseminated in non-school-based sources may conflict with information disseminated in school-based sexuality education programs. In addition, agency personnel, who are most often bilingual and bicultural adult professionals from the community, may be at a different level of acculturation from school-age populations and thus may be less effective with the adolescent.

Frustrated and concerned minority group members and their advocates, recognizing the need for culturally appropriate curriculum and intervention models, have taken steps to develop their own. Sometimes minority program planners disregard existing and effective intervention approaches for majority populations (seen as culturally inappropriate and "not for us") and instead develop new approaches based upon principles of cultural relevance. Unfortunately, as Orlandi (1986) points out, the gains in cultural sensitivity may not offset the loss in effectiveness incurred by failing to incorporate successful components of previously established interventions.

AN APPROACH TO DEVELOPING A NEW MODEL
OF SEXUALITY EDUCATION

Background Information

The following model for the development of culturally sensitive sexuality education curricula evolved from our work with the Needs Assessment Committee of the Somerville-Cambridge Teen Pregnancy Prevention Coalition. The coalition recognized the need for culturally sensitive programs of sexuality education and agreed that to develop these, we must be informed by adolescents and adults from the different cultural groups represented in these school populations.

The two public high schools of Cambridge and Somerville enroll approximately 4,000 students each year, grades 9 through 12. Both cities are designated as "gateway cities," with over 50 linguistic and cultural minorities represented, and both are ranked among the 20 Massachusetts cities with the highest teen pregnancy rate, with a total of 152 school-age teens giving birth in 1986. In the academic year 1986–87, 43% of pregnancies seen by the Cambridge Rindge and Latin School nurses' office were linguistic minorities, and over 71% of students in the Cambridge Adolescent Parenting Program were from minority backgrounds. Statistics were not kept at Somerville High School until halfway through the 1986–87 school year. In Somerville, 14% of pregnant girls seen in 1986–87 were black, the remaining 86% white. A small but growing number of Southeast Asian girls becoming pregnant was also noted by Somerville school health providers. The numbers reflect the fact that the population in Somerville was, until recently, predominantly white and working class, but also reflect who had access to referral to the teen pregnancy program at the high school. For example, some new school-age immigrants who were pregnant had difficulty with legal documentation, while cultural norms may have prevented others from remaining in high school.

Method

Focus groups are recognized as an effective means of eliciting useful information from target populations because they legitimize the voices of participants and provide insight into the beliefs, attitudes, and experiences of group members (Kisker, 1985; Zane, 1988). The coalition decided to use this method in Cambridge and Somerville and in the spring of 1988 arranged separate focus groups with adolescent boys and girls from six different ethnic populations: Vietnamese, Portuguese,[1] black, white, Haitian, and Hispanic.[2] Focus groups were also held with parents from these ethnic groups, and two culturally diverse groups of adolescent mothers. In total, 21 groups with an average of eight participants in each were held, led, or facilitated by an adult from the same cultural background who spoke the language of the participants.

The focus group approach is essentially collaborative and interactive, involving a series of steps. Prior to the focus groups taking place, our first step (as educators with a particular knowledge of existing sexuality education curricula) was to meet with numerous community leaders and social service providers who work directly with cultural group individuals and family members. In these meetings we collected culturally specific information that we integrated into open-ended questions or scripts designed to elicit focus group discussions of attitudes and behaviors related to dating, sexuality, and cultural perspectives on teen parenting and birth control. Scripts were reviewed by service providers and revised collaboratively following a discussion of how to create questions suitable for each group. For example, the Hispanic and Portuguese professionals suggested that we omit direct questions on abortion as they believed that due to their cultural norms, participants would feel reluctant to share their opinions openly.

The next step involved the coordination of focus groups, which included the identification and training of bilingual and bicultural facilitators or leaders. Next, we recruited adolescents and parents and paid them a small stipend for their participation in the focus groups, which were audiotaped and later translated and transcribed. Finally, we analyzed these transcripts along with community representatives in order to review similarities and differences in themes and to present specific recommendations to various community audiences.

We will present cultural generalizations in an effort to represent salient features of select cultural groups, acknowledging that a multitude of intragroup differences (such as social class and rate of acculturation) can always be identified.

FINDINGS FROM FOCUS GROUPS:
THEMES AND DIFFERENCES ACROSS GROUPS

Although social scientists and health officials remind educators that decisions regarding sexuality, contraceptive use, and family planning are guided by cultural and familial values and beliefs, exclusion of all but the dominant perspective has silenced the voices of cultural and linguistic minority populations and lesbian and gay adolescents (see Chapters 1,7, and 8 in this volume). In this action we present what adolescents and parents said in the focus groups in order to highlight specific cultural understandings of sexuality and sexual behavior. When sexuality education curricula are understood as being socially constructed, it is apparent that sexuality education in the United States tends to be culturally biased; represents a view of development that reflects a white, middle-class, male bias; explicitly supports an institutionalized American middle-class double standard; and overemphasizes reproductive biology.

Adolescent Perceptions of Sexuality Education

The most common response across the focus groups was that sexuality education, while both useful and important, is frequently at odds with what the teens say they want to know in terms of sexuality and relationships. "When you're in sex education class they just tell you what goes on inside your body. They don't tell you what goes *on*" (black girl). A black male defined this issue succinctly when he said, "It doesn't teach you, like, the things you want to know . . . it's hard to explain. You get your own questions and they don't show it in the movies or books or whatever, y'know." This theme was supported by adolescents in other focus groups. "I had sex education. It taught a lot but it doesn't make you change your feelings" (teen mother, white). Students felt that sexuality education does not fit the reality of their lives as it leaves out the feelings, fears and passions, inconvenience, embarrassment, and romance that affect sexual decision making and that occur within a context framed by cultural values and beliefs. Too often, they reported, their questions and concerns regarding how to recognize and manage intimate feelings within relationships or how to negotiate contraception in "the heat of the moment" went largely unanswered and ignored. There was also discussion in some groups about who should teach sexuality education. "It's not easy to trust someone with that [sex education]" (Haitian male). The African-American girls group was clear in stating their preferences, insisting that their black peers "don't want to hear [sex education] from white people," whom they felt could be racist; they recommended more discussions among teenagers rather than classes from (white) adults. Students of color who express distrust of white sexuality education instructors speak to what they perceive as a lack of sensitivity that is rooted most often in cultural ignorance and misunderstanding. For example, students are aware that many assumptions made about them are based on stereotypical beliefs held about their cultural group (e.g., Latino males are "macho," uncaring, and insensitive toward their partners; African-American boys are sexually aggressive and irresponsible; Haitians carry AIDS). The intersection of the sociocultural dynamics of race, ethnicity, and social class inevitably have an effect on interpersonal attitudes and interactions inside the classroom. In our groups the explicit demand for black teachers and the Haitian parents' request for bicultural, bilingual leaders of after-school activities sent a clear message: programs must have culturally diverse staffs who can speak the language, understand the culture, respect the values, and communicate with people from a variety of backgrounds. Exclusively white staffs, no matter how culturally sensitive they try to be, do not suffice.

Participants in several groups saw the goal of their sexuality education classes as "how to protect yourself from illness and pregnancy" (Hispanic male), "learning, like, all about [the] disease" (black male), and "helping us to avoid unpleasant things and danger" (Vietnamese female). The concept of sexual intimacy leading to possible disease as well as social and emotional risks for girls in particular has been identified by Michelle Fine (1988) as "sexuality as victimization." This focus on the negative consequences of sexual behavior for adolescent girls (and

boys) is derived from acceptance of stereotypical assumptions of sex differences and appropriate sexual behavior and is also based on two fundamental assumptions: that sexual expression and behavior are synon-
ymous with sexual intercourse and that sexuality and procreation are
always inextricably linked (Hubbard, 1990; Ruddick, 1991). Furthermore, these notions are tied to an overemphasis on reproductive biology, particularly the female aspects of reproduction, which, as feminist
scholars have argued, isolates and decontextualizes human sexuality
from the rest of human relationships. This overemphasis further perpetuates the notion that responsibility for birth control, pregnancy,
childbearing, and child rearing belongs to females rather than males
(Chilman, 1985; Harper, 1983). Indeed, as one white male explained,
"Females who use birth control are smart. It shows she is protecting herself. She's stupid if she doesn't use it." Unfortunately, this attitude
serves, in effect, to let boys off the hook. In fact, in this same focus
group, while condom use was referred to as an effective deterrent to HIV
transmission, not once were condoms mentioned as a contraceptive
method.

Successful sexuality education, rather than overemphasizing biology and avoiding the complexity of adolescents' social relationships, in-
tegrates specific knowledge regarding sexuality and contraception with
discussions of attitudes and behaviors grounded in the full range of real-
life experience.

Contraception

Ironically, although students reported that the primary focus of
their sexuality education classes was on reproductive biology, they collected a great deal of misinformation and many misconceptions regarding fertility, contraceptive interventions, sexually transmitted diseases,
and AIDS. Females from the Hispanic, Haitian, and African-American
groups possessed incomplete information regarding the pill such as, "It
can give you cancer" and "I heard that you can only use birth control for
seven years and then you have to stop" (African-American girl). Although the withdrawal method is generally discouraged among sex educators, Haitian males spoke of this method as culturally accepted and
claimed they had successfully adopted it as a contraceptive means.

Misinformation about AIDS was particularly disturbing in light of
the current statistics on the rising incidence of AIDS in black and Latino
urban communities. An African-American girl implied that AIDS is easily dealt with—"you can tell who's got it, then just avoid them." Information about the AIDS virus is discussed in almost all sexuality education curricula (Brooks-Gunn & Furstenberg, 1989), yet little attention is

paid to culturally specific determinants of risk-taking behaviors related to HIV infection transmission (Worth, 1989).

Gender and ethnic group membership combined with cultural learning, especially the beliefs and values supporting contraceptive use, must be taken seriously by sex educators dealing with multicultural populations. Contraception is not simply a technical decision, but a decision with moral and emotional dimensions that are embedded in cultural and family expectations (Rains, 1971). Decisions about contraception, in which issues of control and sex-role socialization are implicit, involve motivation, access, knowledge, and skills (Cvetkovich & Grote, 1976). Many of the adolescent focus group participants recognized their own family and cultural norms during the discussion of contraception. For example, in the Vietnamese culture, in which premarital sex is condemned and virginity in a bride is almost mandatory (Hoang & Erickson, 1982), sexuality is not readily discussed even among family members. One Vietnamese female explained that in Vietnamese families, birth control is used only in marriage, and the method used is decided upon in consultation with the parents of the married couple. Vietnamese children are socialized into a network where filial piety and deference to elders are stressed; to expect a Vietnamese individual to make an autonomous contraceptive decision independent of family consultation may go against her or his disposition (Fernandez, 1988) and cause cultural dissonance, tension, and anxiety.

A combination of fear, misinformation, and moral objection combine to make the use and discussion of birth control difficult in other cultural communities. "The Haitian family don't accept you to take the pill. Even a friend may be taking pills but don't tell you" (Haitian girl). On the other hand, the teens who seemed most comfortable discussing birth control were those in the African-American groups—the only groups in which we heard young women say that they would and do carry condoms. However, the level of misinformation within these groups was still high. Scott et al. (1988), in assessing popular beliefs and level of scientific knowledge regarding sexuality and contraception among black and Hispanic inner-city adolescents, determined that two conflicting beliefs were held by these teens simultaneously—that contraception is "good" because it prevents pregnancy, and "bad" because the various birth control methods carry serious health hazards for users. Jemmott and Jemmott's (1990) study supported previous findings that negative attitudes toward contraception were also associated with self-reported risky sexual behaviors. For example, large percentages of African-American males thought that contraception methods are messy and take the enjoyment out of sex or that contraceptive methods do not seem natural.

Within some cultural contexts, the "risks" in discussing sexuality and birth control are very high, not only within romantic relationships but also within one's family. A Hispanic girl said, "I think if I asked my mom anything about sex she would say, 'You ask that either because you are doing it or you've done it'; then she would stop trusting me." Although participants in nearly all groups thought that parents and children should talk to each other about sex, such talk seemed to have occurred within only a few of the American (black and white) families. Many of the parents said they had tried to talk to their children, while others thought that telling their children about birth control would encourage sexual activity. Despite some efforts by parents to speak with their children, all of the recent immigrant adolescents said they could not talk with their parents about sex and recognized a vast set of conditions that inhibited this communication. In the most extreme cases, parents had stayed in their country of origin while their children came to the United States. In other situations, parents and children in various stages of bilingualism did not have a shared vocabulary with which to discuss acceptance of American standards of behavior or did not know how to adjust to differing rates of acculturation within the family. "Back home, an 18-year-old is still under the control of the parents," said one Haitian parent, "but when he comes here, it takes only 6 months for him to change completely."

Relationships, Gender, and Sexual Decision Making

A desire to know more about relationships and how to negotiate them was a recurring theme in the adolescent focus groups, a theme with less cultural variation but more gender variations than the other themes discussed. Girls of all ethnic groups voiced a greater interest in forming and maintaining relationships than did the boys, an observation supported by commonly held knowledge and research findings (for example, Kinsey, Pomeroy, Martin, & Gebhard, 1953; Schofield, 1965). This disparity in thinking about relationships is illustrated by the response from a white teen mother:

> You know what bugs me though? I really cared about the baby's father. It was, like, we went out, like a whole summer. I know that doesn't seem that long but, like, he was open with me. He talked to me. He didn't talk to a lot of people. So I don't know. That's why I went down there—because I really cared about him. He didn't care about me too much. But, that's why I kept going with him. . . . I wanted him to know that I cared . . . that's why I think I ended up having sex with him. Cause like he talked to me and stuff, and I know that he trusted me to talk to me. It was like another way of him showing me that he cared about me.

In contrast, the following exchange involving several respondents took place in the white boy's group: "I don't like lasting relationships . . . too much work involved . . . too much talking on the telephone. . . . You have to spend all your time with her and that fucking sucks, you can't spend it with your friends." "You have to give up your social life, unless I go out with a girl that hangs around with my friends."

These quotes illustrate how adolescent boys and girls, even from the same ethnic group, can attribute very different meanings to their interactions. These differences in expectations and interpretations of experience can involve misunderstandings, emotional pain, and problems in communication. Although girls varied in the criteria they set for sex (some required marriage, some love, some confidence that he was a decent person), all spoke of sex within the context of a relationship.

Miller (1976), Gilligan (1979, 1982), Gilligan, Lyons, and Hanmer (1990), and others challenge developmental theorists to recognize the central place that relationships play in the lives of girls and women. The desire to maintain and strengthen connections and interdependence between people is the organizing framework by which women develop a sense of self and morality (Gilligan, Ward, & Taylor, 1988). Current research suggests that girls acknowledge the difficulties inherent in relationships where the needs of self and others sometimes conflict. In their complex understandings of relationships, girls equate maturity with the ability to balance one's own need with those of others. Interdependence, nurturance, and contextual thought have been largely omitted from discussions of adolescent development as conventional theories have emerged from studies of white, middle-class male experience (Belenky, Clinchy, Goldberger, & Tarule, 1986; Salazar, 1990).

Sexuality education has been based on a definition of adolescence as a time of struggle for autonomy and independence, a recapitulation of the separation and individuation struggles in early childhood (Blos, 1967; Erikson, 1950). This focus upon individuation is found throughout the psychological literature and has profoundly influenced the way we look at adolescents and how and what we teach them. Traditional sexuality education programs reflect the privileging of individuality and independence by stressing as a marker of maturity, autonomous sexual decision making (determining and asserting one's own personal values along with taking personal responsibility for managing one's own sexuality). Not only does this view of development leave out the way adolescent girls experience the world and make decisions, but it also disregards cultural variation in sexual decision making. Research on differences in cultural worldviews suggests that this focus on individuation and autonomy is a uniquely middle-class EuroAmerican phenomenon (Comas-Diaz & Duncan, 1985; Mbiti, 1969; Sue & Morishima, 1982).

Given these alternative constructs of psychological development for adolescent girls and teens from other cultural backgrounds, the current emphasis on individualistic decision making in sexuality education raises serious questions for curriculum developers. Sexuality educators must take into account that previous understandings of development obscured the complexity of decision making within a relational context, especially when cultural values prevent open discussion of sexual feelings and birth control.

Double Standard

Across the six ethnic groups one observation was strikingly similar; all respondents introduced the universal theme of a double standard toward sexual behavior and sex roles that is limiting and oppressive to females. In all groups, boys were generally allowed more freedom and were assumed to be more sexually active than girls. With the possible exception of the Vietnamese boys, who spoke often of tradition, self-discipline, and the expectations of their parents, sexual activity for adolescent males usually met cultural expectations and was generally accepted by adults and peers as part of normal male adolescence. As a Portuguese girl stated, "It's basically that a girl can have one boyfriend and a guy can have all the women he wants. That's like the Portuguese way of life over there, so, um, that's the way, some guys were brought up that way, thinking that they can have everything. But the girl they're going out with should have one man." Both adolescent boys and girls in the Portuguese focus groups report that sexual activity for adolescent females is discouraged prior to marriage and that they are taught that sex is acceptable only within the framework of marriage or a long-term relationship.

This double standard has cultural variations vis-à-vis a range of acceptable behavior for girls, which is the salient point for sexuality education curricula. (Trudell makes a similar point in Chapter 10 in this volume.) In general, women are often seen in terms of their sexual reputation rather than in terms of their personal characteristics (Lees, 1986). For example, Vietnamese girls and boys talked of how boys must ask girls out; if this is reversed, and a girl were to approach a boy, she would soon lose her reputation. For Hispanic, Portuguese, and Haitian girls, reputational concerns were also highlighted in the focus groups, not only in dating patterns but in terms of birth control for Hispanic girls and out-of-wedlock pregnancy for Portuguese, Haitian, and Hispanic girls. The message was clear: sexual activity is dangerous for girls, and premarital pregnancy brings shame and disgrace to the adolescent and her family. "I'd run away because my parents are, like, if you ever get pregnant, just don't ever come back to this house," explained one Portuguese girl. Similarly, as family cohesion is valued in Haitian families, where family honor and reputation are of utmost importance (Hallman, Etienne & Fradd, 1982), the actions of one member can bring glory or disgrace to the whole family. Explained one Haitian male, "Pregnant girls will get beaten" should their transgression be discovered. Both Vietnamese girls and boys explained that sex taints a girl and her family's reputation and, accordingly, if a daughter has done the wrong thing, the parents will kick her out of the house, for "parents have rules and rights too." The values of family honor and familism, the role played by brothers and fathers in protecting a family's image and status, and the resulting conflicts that can arise when daughters and sisters struggle against culturally imposed behaviors have important implications for sexual decision making and contraceptive use. Worth (1989) and Mays and Cochran (1988) highlight the social costs to some minority women, including verbal and physical abuse, when they act assertively in sexual situations (such as asking a partner to use a condom). Comas-Diaz (1987) discusses the difficulty encountered in promoting assertiveness among Hispanic women when such behavior is actively discouraged within their culture. Thus, when girls speak of being swept away by passion and desire, they may be reflecting traditional cultural values saying that females should not learn and know about sexuality (Espin, 1984). The dilemma for educators is how to encourage communication and assertiveness when this runs counter to cultural norms and expectations, particularly those that define female behavior.

CONCLUSION

The concerns expressed in the focus groups by both adolescents and parents from different cultural backgrounds may be addressed in multicultural classrooms by some innovative changes in curriculum content and materials selected to ensure cultural and linguistic sensitivity and relevancy. The need for bicultural and bilingual teachers is obvious but difficult to meet when educators rely exclusively on school personnel. Collaborating with the community so that bilingual and bicultural paraprofessionals teach or augment particular facets of a course is one way of addressing this concern. As a supplement to classroom instruction, support from school systems and communities to establish a peer education network would enable adolescents to share information about sexuality with well-trained peers of the same ethnic group who are 1 to 5 years older. In this way the myths and misinformation evident in the focus groups can be dispelled. The same concept could be extended to parent groups so they too may have a supportive environment to speak and share advice about their struggles to balance traditional family and cultural values with the American mainstream norms regarding sexuality and sexual behavior.

Looking critically at sexuality education raises the question of its overall purpose, and in a multicultural society we must ask, Whose needs are being met? Our critique of existing sexuality education in light of multicultural inclusion and relevancy and from the viewpoint of developmental psychology and feminist theory suggests that the needs of multicultural populations are not being addressed; the developmental needs of young women are not being met; and because sexuality education fails to incorporate the issues and concerns teens themselves say are important, their needs are not being met. The approach to sexuality education that we propose builds upon existing models of multicultural education and includes collaboration with members of diverse cultural groups, including service providers, teachers, adolescents, and parents from those communities. Effective curricula must include an acknowledgment of the context of teens lives and prepare them for the social, cultural, political, and economic realities they will encounter in the world.

NOTES

Acknowledgments. We are indebted to Julia Paley, a doctoral candidate in anthropology at Harvard University, who was employed by the coalition to work with the focus group project. We worked on the project together and regret that Julia was unable to write this paper with us, but she is presently in Chile doing fieldwork for her dissertation. Julia's knowledge, perspective, close attention to cultural issues, and friendship were invaluable both for the project and for us personally. We would also like to thank focus group participants and facilitators, other members of the coalition for their determination to see this project through and for valuable assistance in thinking about the data, Deborah Tolman for comments on early drafts, and Jim Sears for his patience and support.

1. We have used the term *Portuguese* to describe those adolescents and parents who are from Portugal, the Azores, and Brazil. Other Portuguese-speaking people, Cape Verdeans, for example, who live in the communities of Cambridge and Somerville, were not focus group participants.

2. Referring to the 1987 special issue of *Psychology of Women Quarterly,* on Hispanic women and mental health, vol. *11,* (4), we have used the term *Hispanic* to refer to people of Spanish origin, including Mexican, Puerto Rican, Cuban, Central or South American, and Spanish. Hispanics may be of any race.

REFERENCES

Alan Guttmacher Institute. (1989). *Risk and responsibility: Teaching sex education in America's schools today.* New York: Author.

American Medical Association. (1990). *America's adolescents: How healthy are they?* (Profile of Adolescent Health Series, J. Gans, D. Blythe, A. Elster, & L. Gaveras, (Eds.). Chicago: Author.

Banks, J. (1984). *Teaching strategies for ethnic studies.* Boston: Allyn & Bacon.

Belenky, M., Clincy, B., Goldberger, N., & Tarule, J. (1986). *Women's ways of knowing.* New York: Basic.

Blos, P. (1967). The second individuation process of adolescence. In A. Freud (Ed.), *The psychoanalytic study of the child* (Vol. 22, pp. 162–185). New York: International Universities Press.

Brooks-Gunn, J., & Furstenberg, F. (1989). Adolescent sexual behavior. *American Psychologist, 44*(2), 249–257.

Centers for Disease Control, Atlanta, GA. (1989). Reported in the fact sheet "AIDS and Young Children in South Florida." U.S. House of Representatives Select Committee on Children, Youth and Families Hearing. Miami, Florida.

Chilman, C. (1985). Feminist issues in teenage parenting. *Child Welfare, 44*(3), 225–234.

Chodorow, N. (1974). Family structure and feminine personality. In M. Rosaldo & L. Lampiere (Eds.), *Women, culture and society* (pp. 43–66). Palo Alto, CA: Stanford University Press.

Comas-Diaz, L. (1987). Feminist therapy with mainland Puerto Rican women. *Psychology of Women Quarterly, 11*(4), 461–474.

Comas-Diaz, L., & Duncan, J. (1985). The cultural context: A factor in assertiveness training with mainland Puerto Rican women. *Psychology of Women Quarterly, 9*(4), 463–476.

Cummins, J. (1986). Empowering minority students. *Harvard Educational Review, 56*(1), 18–36.

Cvetkovich, G., & Grote, B. (1976). On the psychology of adolescents' use of contraceptives. *Journal of Sex Research, 11,* 256–270.

Erikson, E. (1950). *Childhood and society.* New York: W. W. Norton.

Erikson, E. (1968). *Identity, youth and crisis.* New York: W. W. Norton.

Espin, O. (1984). Cultural and historical influences on sexuality in Hispanic/Latin women: Implications for psychotherapy. In C. S. Vance (Ed.)., *Pleasure and danger: Exploring female sexuality* (pp. 149–164). Boston: Routledge & Kegan Paul.

Espin, O. (1987). Psychological impact of migration on Latinas: Implications for psychotherapeutic practice. *Psychology of Women Quarterly, 11*(4), 489–503.

Ferguson, A. (1984). Sex war: The debate between racial and libertarian feminists. *Signs, 10*(1), 106–112.

Fernandez, M. (1988). Issues in counseling Southeast Asian students. *Journal of Multicultural Counseling and Development, 16,* 157–166.

Fine, M. (1988). Sexuality, schooling and adolescent females: The missing discourse of desire. *Harvard Educational Review, 58*(1), 29–53.

Foucault, M. (1978). *The history of sexuality: Vol. 1. An introduction* (R. Hurley, Trans.). New York: Vintage.

Gay, G. (1983). Multi-ethnic education: Historical developments and future prospects. *Phi Delta Kappan, 64,* 560–563.

Geronimus, A. (1986). The effects of race, residence, and prenatal care on the relationship of maternal age to neonatal mortality. *American Journal of Public Health, 76,* 1416–1421.

Geronimus, A. (1987). Teenage maternity and neonatal mortality: A new look at American patterns and their implications for developing countries. *Population and Development Review, 13*(2), 245–279.

Gibbs, J. (1989). Black adolescents and youth: An update on an endangered species. In R. Jones (Ed.), *Black adolescents* (pp. 3–27). Berkeley, CA: Cobb and Henry.

Gilligan, C. (1979). Women's place in a man's life cycle. *Harvard Educational Review, 47*(4), 481–517.

Gilligan, C. (1982). *In a different voice.* Cambridge: Harvard University Press.

Gilligan, C., Lyons, N., & Hanmer, T. (Eds.). (1990). *Making connections: The relational world of adolescent girls at Emma Willard School.* Cambridge: Harvard University Press.

Gilligan, C., Ward, J. V., & Taylor, J. (Eds.). (1988). *Mapping the moral domain.* Cambridge: Harvard University Press.

Hallman, C., Etienne, M., & Fradd, S. (1982). *Haitian value orientations* (Cultural Monograph No. 2). Gainesville: University of Florida, Bilingual Multicultural Education Training Project for School Psychologists and Guidance Counselors. (ERIC Report No. ED 269 532)

Harper, A. (1983). Teenage sexuality and public policy: An agenda for gender education. In I. Diamond (Ed.), *Families, politics and public policy* (pp. 220–235). New York: Longman.

Hoang, G., & Erickson, R. (1982). Guidelines for providing medical care to Southeast Asian refugees. *JAMA, 248*(6), 710–714.

Hubbard, R. (1990). *The politics of women's biology.* New Brunswick and London: Rutgers University Press.

Jemmott, L., & Jemmott, J. (1990). Sexual knowledge, attitudes, and risky sexual behavior among inner city black male adolescents. *Journal of Adolescent Research, 5*(3), 346–369.

Jones, E. F., Forrest, J., Goldman, N., Henshaw, S., Lincoln, R., Rosoff, J., Westoff, C., & Wulf, D. (1985). Teenage prenancy in developed countries: Determinants and policy implications. *Family Planning Perspectives, 17*(2), 53–62.

Kinsey, A., Pomeroy, W., Martin, C., & Gebhard, P. (1953). *Sexual behavior in the human female.* Philadelphia: W. B. Saunders.

Kirby, D. (1984). *Sexuality education: An evaluation of programs and their effects.* Santa Cruz: Network.

Kisker, E. (1985). Teenagers talk about sex, pregnancy and contraception. *Family Planning Perspectives, 17*(2), 83–90.

Koop, C. E. (1988). *Understanding AIDS.* Rockville, MD: U.S. Public Health Service, Surgeon General and the Centers for Disease Control.

Lees, S. (1986). *Losing out: Sexuality and adolescent girls.* London: Hutchinson Press.

Mays, V. M., & Cochran, S. D. (1988). Issues in the perception of AIDS risk and risk reduction activities by black and Hispanic/Latina Women. *American Psychologist, 43*(11), 949–957.

Mbiti, J. S. (1969). *African religions and philosophy*. New York: Praeger.

McCrate, E. (1989). *Discrimination, returns to education and teenage childbearing* (Working Paper). Cambridge, MA: Mary Ingraham Bunting Institute, Radcliffe Research and Study Center.

Medina, C. (1987). Latino culture and sex education. *SIECUS Report, 15*(3), 1–3.

Miller, J. B. (1976). *Toward a new psychology of women*. Boston: Beacon.

Morgan, S. (1986). *To see ourselves, to see our sisters: The challenge of re-envisioning curriculum change* (Research Clearinghouse and Curriculum Integration Project). Memphis, TN: Memphis State University, Center for Research on Women.

National Coalition of Advocates for Students. (1988). *New voices: Immigrant students in U.S. public schools*. Boston: Author.

Offer, D. (1969). *The psychological world of the teenager*. New York: Basic.

Orlandi, M. (1986). Community-based substance abuse prevention: A multicultural perspective. *Journal of School Health, 56*(9), 394–401.

Rains, P. (1971). *Becoming an unwed mother*. Chicago: Aldine.

Reis, J., Herz, E., & Slager, S. (1986). Family life education in Chicago: A study of programs implemented by nonschool agencies. *Adolescence, 21*(84), 981–990.

Rubin, G. (1984). Thinking sex: Notes for a radical theory of the politics of sexuality. In C. S. Vance (Ed.), *Pleasure and danger: Exploring female sexuality* (pp. 267–319). Boston: Routledge and Kegan Paul.

Ruddick, S. (1991). Educating for procreative choice: The "case" of adolescent women. *Womens Studies Quarterly, 19* (1–2), 102–120.

Salazar, M. (1990). *Women and AIDS: Assessing the factors placing women at risk*. Unpublished manuscript, Harvard University, Cambridge, MA.

Scales, P., & Kirby, D. (1981). A review of exemplary sex education programs for teenagers offered by non-school organizations. *Family Relations, 30*, 238–245.

Schofield, M. (1965). *Sexual behavior of young people*. Boston: Little, Brown.

Scott, C., Shifman, L., Orr, L., Owen, R., & Fawcett, N. (1988). Hispanic and black American adolescents' beliefs relating to sexuality and contraception. *Adolescence, 23*(91), 667–668.

Scott-Jones, D., & Turner, S. (1988). Sex education, contraceptive and reproductive knowledge, and contraceptive use among black adolescent females. *Journal of Adolescent Research, 3*(2), 171–187.

Sleeter, C., & Grant, C. (1987). An analysis of multicultural education in the United States. *Harvard Educational Review, 57*(4), 421–444.

Spener, D. (1988). Transitional bilingual education and the socialization of immigrants. *Harvard Educational Review, 58*(2), 133–153.

Sue, S., & Morishima, J. K. (1982). *The mental health of Asian Americans*. San Francisco: Jossey-Bass.

Upchurch, D., & McCarthy, J. (1990, February). *The effects of the timing of first birth on high school completion*. Paper presented at the annual conference of the American Association for the Advancement of Science, New Orleans, LA.

Ventura, S. (1984). *Trends in teenage childbearing in the U.S., 1970–1981*. National Center for Health Statistics, Washington, DC: 21, 41.

Worth, D. (1989). Sexual decision-making and AIDS: Why condom promotion among vulnerable women is likely to fail. *Studies in Family Planning, 20*(6), 297–307.

Zabin, L., Hirsch, M., Smith, E., & Hardy, J. (1984). Adolescent sexual attitudes and behavior: Are they consistent? *Family Planning Perspectives, 16*(4), 181–185.

Zane, Nancy. (1988). *In their own voices: Young women talk about dropping out.* Washington, DC: Project on Equal Education Rights, NOW Legal Defense and Education Fund.

Zayas, L. (1987). Toward an understanding of suicide risks in young adolescent females. *Journal of Adolescent Research, 2*(1), 1–11.

Zelnick, M., & Kantner, J. (1980). Sexual activity, contraceptive use and pregnancy among metropolitan area teenagers, 1971–1979. *Family Planning Perspectives, 12*(3), 230–237.

CHAPTER 10

Inside a Ninth-Grade Sexuality Classroom

The Process of Knowledge Construction

BONNIE K. TRUDELL

Most public discourse about school sexuality education relates to both its conceptual value and its actual curriculum content. Similarly, most research on the subject is based on reported curricular content and primarily concerned with program effectiveness in reaching goals specified by curriculum planners. Less frequently examined are the assumptions underlying the planned sexuality curriculum as well as what actually happens in the classroom as it works its way through teacher and students in a particular school context (Muraskin, 1986). The following account addresses this research gap by going inside a sexuality education classroom and examining the day-to-day activities and lived experiences of teacher and students.

The chapter is distilled from a more extensive ethnographic investigation of a semester-long health/physical education class that included sexuality education (Trudell, 1988). This work reflects a critical appraisal of the role of education in perpetuating unequal social relationships and conceptualizes school knowledge as socially constructed by teachers and students whose historical, social, and biographical relationships intersect within a particular set of school and social conditions. The research also grows out of my own longstanding involvement in sexuality education and concern with challenging those stereotypical gender relations, traditional antisex norms, and heterosexual assumptions that underpin school-based programs.

The study is primarily concerned with illuminating the process by which knowledge is constructed in one ninth-grade sexuality education classroom. It describes the content and form of sexuality information presented; explores students' classroom responses, revealing some of the ways they acquiesce to, reinterpret, and contest these points of view; and examines factors that affect teacher selection and presentation. This close-up detail on the active, complex, contradictory, and situation-specific process—largely unexamined in the sexuality education literature—reveals some of the mechanisms by which dominant social norms are reproduced and contested in one classroom. It is presented with the hope that both scholars and practitioners will use it to formulate situation-specific strategies to make classroom discussion more relevant to students' lives, broaden the spectrum of "acceptable" sexual behavior, encourage nonexploitive and mutually responsible sexual relationships, and affirm the pleasures of sexuality.

The study reveals both the progressive and regressive possibilities for sexuality education in schools. Such programs have the potential to either reinforce or alter dominant social norms of heterosexuality, intercourse in the context of marriage, and inequitable gender relations. Additionally, no matter how restrictive or progressive, the planned curriculum or teaching materials may acquire alternate cultural meanings as they work their way through teacher and students in a particular context. As teachers are well aware, the privacy of the classroom offers considerable space for educators to maneuver; progressive teachers can subvert a restrictive official curriculum of materials (Fine, 1988), and vice versa. Furthermore, the study suggests that students themselves can both open up and close down possibilities for relevant, meaningful discussion.

As Koch (Chapter 12), Sears (Chapters 1 and 7), and others in this volume suggest, skilled and creative teachers can play a major role in relevant and critically based sexuality education. Nevertheless, this chapter documents that a school's organization and the conditions in which teachers work are major factors in the fragmented, technical classroom coverage of mostly noncontroversial topics related to sexuality. It illustrates that even the most well-intentioned and "sexuality affirming" teacher (Scales, 1987) might be constrained in the classroom setting. Yet the day-to-day realities of teachers' working conditions (e.g., sexuality incorporated into a lengthy required health syllabus, teaching schedules that allow little time for reflective planning, large classes in which open discussion is difficult) are often ignored by those of us outside the classroom who advocate for more comprehensive and relevant sexuality education.[1] We must beware of a narrow, critical focus on individual practitioners as personally responsible for content and teaching strategies that we may regard as unsatisfactory—including some described in this chapter. We must be cognizant of the constraints and possibilities that even the most progressive, personally comfortable, and academically well-prepared teachers will encounter on a daily basis and prepare teachers for this reality by critically examining both constraints and possibilities in preservice and in-service education. Thus, in detailing the process of knowledge construction in Mrs. Warren's classroom, it is not my intent or major purpose to criticize her teaching strategies. I portray them rather as active attempts to deal with dilemmas and contradictions created by institutional constraints, student classroom responses, and her own social positioning by gender, marital status, and motherhood.

I will begin by briefly describing the classroom context in terms of the community and school setting, the health course format, and the teacher and students, including their classroom behavior as well as their interpretation of classroom experience. Then I will discuss teaching strategies, factors that influenced these curricular choices, and the lived curriculum.

CULTURAL AND INSTITUTIONAL CONTEXT

The setting for the study was a Midwestern city (Woodland) of about 170,000. The school (Van Buren) is located on the less affluent side of Woodland in a relatively modest residential area. This community is largely homogeneous in terms of race (mostly white) and religion (mostly Christian, including some fundamentalist groups). Most families of Van Buren students are supported by state/city government, small business, or blue-collar workers. Traditional values and hierarchical gender arrangements are an integral part of the immediate community and everyday school life at Van Buren. Key aspects of the context—the school (comprehensive public high school of about 1,800), incorporation of sexuality education in a physical education department, and teacher (certified in both physical education and health, with 12 years teaching experience)—are similar to those in other U.S. contexts where school sexuality education is offered (Orr, 1982; Sonenstein & Pittman, 1984). Data were obtained during the fall semester of 1985 by daily classroom and school observation as well as interviews with the teacher, 25 of 27 students in the class, and other school and district staff. Parent permissions were obtained for student interviews, and names given here to the community, school, teacher, and students are fictitious.

The Specific Health Course

The ninth-grade health classes met daily for a full semester on an alternate classroom/activity basis, that is, even-numbered days in the classroom and odd-numbered days in physical activity. The class was a state requirement for high school graduation. Classroom components of the lengthy official district curriculum included healthy life-styles, physical fitness, nutrition, mental health, human sexuality, personal safety and emergency care, and alcohol and other drugs; physical activity components included jogging, biking, swimming, and weight training. With so many topics to cover, Mrs. Warren said she can only "touch on" most of them if she is to "get through" the syllabus. Since this is the only required health offering at the high school level, inclusion of all topics is valued by both school and district.

School organization and conditions in which she worked played a central role in Mrs. Warren's teaching strategies. These include the students' need to pass this required course, alternate-day arrangements, sexuality squeezed into a long and ever-expanding district health syllabus, fragmented teaching duties (including three health classes, four grade levels of physical education, and an "adapted" class for special education students), little planning time, large number of students (225 per week, 40 in some classes), and school administrative concern with discipline and avoiding parent complaints. Although it is less focused on here, pressures related to gender (especially patriarchal authority relations of the school and dual demands of work and family) were also factors in her teaching. Fatigue and stress were major outcomes of these heavy demands. In Mrs. Warren's words, "I'm always behind and rushing around"; "I'm runnin' on empty."

Teacher

Mrs. Warren, the classroom teacher, is a white woman in her mid-thirties who functioned in the multiple roles of teacher, mother, and wife. She majored in physical education and minored (earning two credits short of a major) in health education at a state university, where she did well academically. Mrs. Warren married while in college and has two children, ages 8 and 4, for whom she has major caretaking responsibility. With the exception of two maternity leaves, she had been teaching physical education and health at Van Buren for the previous 12 years. She assisted in developing the original districtwide ninth-grade health curriculum in 1975–76. Mrs. Warren is a committed, hard-working teacher who is highly regarded among school and district administrative staff and students; this good reputation as a sexuality educator was an important element in her selection for the study.

Students

The 27 students (17 females an 10 males) in Mrs. Warren's class were not a unified, coherent group; they formed smaller, sometimes overlapping, groups with a variety of identities related to gender, class, race, and so on. Thus, the classroom may be thought of as a social arena permeated by the contradictions and tensions within and between these groups. Whatever the information about sexuality and gender relations or the form of its presentation, it is interpreted through students' varied and sometimes contradictory cultural responses and may acquire alternate meanings.

About three fourths of the students could be described as "participators" who took academic work fairly seriously (seven had grade averages of 3.5 or higher) and took part in school-sanctioned extracurricular activities. Most were what Mrs. Warren referred to as "good kids"—those who generally met expectations of Van Buren administrators and teachers. The remaining students did not fit dominant norms, including three African-American students and two white young women Mrs. Warren privately referred to as "dirts."

These students actively participated in constructing their own versions of the curriculum. For most participators, this meant outwardly acquiescing to classroom information and procedures to get a good grade in the required course and avoid embarrassment, while inwardly (as revealed by subsequent interviews) not accepting classroom versions of appropriate sexual behavior. For more marginalized students, it meant infusing the classroom with humor and interjecting their own language and lived cultural experience into the discourse.

In general, students offered few straightforward challenges to information Mrs. Warren presented or to her agenda, although the classroom atmosphere was informal, with much banter. Student quips, digressions, and muted conversations were generally good-natured and humorous rather than belligerent, and usually kept within limits of informality and jocularity acceptable to Mrs. Warren. Dealing with student classroom responses (particularly from members of more marginalized groups) and maintaining boundaries of acceptable behavior from all students were important factors in Mrs. Warren's teaching strategies.

Classroom Observations

Three African-American students (Andrew, Carrie, and Dawn) did not visibly fit prevailing norms at Van Buren (where only 7% are students of color), although they shared characteristics of "participators." Andrew and Carrie frequently engaged in humor and mutual insults that symbolized their bond of intimacy and understanding around race, calling each other "nappy-headed reject from Africa," "African boody-scratcher," and so on. Carrie and Dawn usually exhibited similar racial solidarity. Yet while they shared two aspects of identity (gender and race), there were undercurrents of tension and sometimes caustic classroom exchanges between them.

Carrie and Dawn, along with two other young women, were also part of an all-female social grouping that played the most prominent role in classroom dynamics. The other two (Toni and Paula) had been identified privately to me by Mrs. Warren as "dirts," this school's term for students who smoked and drank. Both came from working-class families; Paula had been picked up by the police during that semester for juvenile drinking, and Toni (as well as her older siblings) had a record of encounters with school and law enforcement authorities. Carrie, Dawn, Toni, and Paula usually sat near each other, engaging in muted conversation.

When Mrs. Warren separated them, they would simply talk over another student who was between them or switch seats the following session.

These four asserted a particular form of "femaleness" in the classroom, cultivating a sophisticated and sexy image. Paula had long and tousled bleached blond hair, wore heavy makeup, and polished her long, manicured nails in class. She and Dawn both dressed in ways that accentuated their sexuality, frequently wearing high-heeled boots or pumps and tight pants and sweaters. During nearly every class session Dawn engaged in a low, hip-gyrating stroll to the front of the room (to sharpen a pencil, use the wastebasket), sometimes accompanied by a long leisurely arm stretch. Toni dressed mostly in tight jeans, a T-shirt (including one with the words, "I got this body from lifting weights—12 ozs. at a time") or hooded sweatshirt, and sneakers.

These three and Carrie (who was fat[2] and wore looser clothing) also interjected their sexiness into the classroom in audible ways. For instance, when Mrs. Warren asked students to list their "favorite activities," Paula asked with feigned innocence, "Can we list things we *really* like to do and not get in trouble?" to which Carrie whispered loudly to Toni, "She'd write 'give blow.'" A few sessions later, when Mrs. Warren solicited qualities looked for in a date, Toni quipped, "We *could* get into details, but I don't think you'd like it." On another occasion, Carrie and Dawn burst into a spontaneous chorus of "I Can't Get No Satisfaction" (with "satis-*fuck*-tion" laughingly substituted by one).

Throughout the semester, Carrie kept up a steady stream of humorous digressions and risqué one-liners that perpetuated a sexy image. For example:

> "Do we get to practice?" [at the beginning of the sexuality education unit]
> A loud "Oh yeah!" at Mrs. Warren's mention of the female clitoris.
> "I'm a sex fiend" (in response to Toni's comment that she had seen Carrie at a shopping mall with several guys).

These quips did not necessarily reflect Carrie's experience but seemed more an attempt at affiliating with other students and making the classroom more livable. She told me during the interview that such comments were "kind of an act for me. I can put on all kinds of faces. Sometimes I talk about serious stuff in a humorous way so people get into it." Carrie also used brashness and humor to cultivate a more personal relationship with Mrs. Warren—asking questions about her family, using familiar terms of address ("buddy," "babe," "teach," "woman") and offering compliments ("You're pretty hip for an old lady").

Finally, Carrie, Dawn, Paula, and Toni resisted activity sessions in a variety of ways—walking instead of jogging, forgetting their gym clothes or swimsuits, skipping class, fooling around, recording inflated scores for each other during the physical fitness tests, and so on. They did not attempt to hide their dislike for activity and participated mainly because they were required to pass—especially Toni, a sophomore who had failed the year before with another teacher, mostly for refusing to get into the swimming pool. None of them was very good at most activities.

This apparent lack of interest and skill, minimal enthusiasm, and occasional sullenness during activity was a concern for Mrs. Warren; she saw these four young women as a real "challenge" and genuinely tried to help them pass the course. For example, she allowed Dawn to retake a failed exam, ignored some of Paula's skipping activity periods, and— after repeated unsuccessful attempts during the semester—finally coaxed Toni into the pool to "pass" the swimming test at a special lunch-period session just before semester grades were due. Mrs. Warren was also cognizant of the dual difficulties Carrie faced as an African-American, fat young woman at Van Buren; she attempted throughout the semester to make school life somewhat easier by showing a special interest in Carrie, offering encouragement for her often unsuccessful attempts at physical activity and tolerating her classroom quips. It is a testimony to her ability to relate effectively with this student that Carrie considered Mrs. Warren an ally and sought her out to talk about personal concerns—even after the semester was over.

Students' Understanding of Their Classroom Role

Subsequent interviews revealed that most students were silently but actively calculating their own best interests in choosing for the most part to go along with classroom arrangements, albeit in an informal and bantering way. They regarded the class as easy, and seemed aware that their grade in this required course depended on a combination of test scores and "attitude" (defined variously by them as "paying attention," "if you try, listen in class and stuff," "if you don't goof around," and so on). Twenty-one of the 27 exerted enough effort to get A's and B's; no one failed. Furthermore, they recognized Mrs. Warren's efforts to help them do well in the class. As Andrew said: "Even the lowest person—if they don't do really bad—will pass. A lotta teachers don't want to flunk kids, but some teachers are more prone to *do* something about it. If you know something in health, you'll pass—and Mrs. Warren helps you get a better score." Students overwhelmingly expressed satisfaction with the class and Mrs. Warren. For example, when asked what they would tell friends about the class, 15 (including Carrie, Dawn, and Paula) responded with superlatives such as "The teacher's real cool," "Mrs. Warren is the nicest teacher," "I hope you [the friend] get Mrs. Warren," and "It was fun—one of my best classes," and so on.

Embarrassment—or at least the potential for it—seemed to be another factor in the bantering but generally acquiescent classroom behavior, with 19 of the students (80% of females, 70% of males) commenting on this without solicitation from me. Because questions and/or personal disclosure may have had more potential risks than benefits in the eyes of these students, they did not participate openly or seriously in large group discussion. Michelle Fine (1988) found that fear of being ostracized affected the personal disclosure of many students—young women who were heterosexually active, heterosexual virgins, as well as gays, bisexuals, and lesbians. In Mrs. Warren's class humorous fragments or muted exchanges with nearby friends were culturally acceptable ways to "discuss" sexuality, which had the collective reward of laughter from peers. This seemed to represent an active decision to participate in a way that avoided embarrassment.

For example, one young woman "participator" (for whom this was a first class on sexuality education) was quiet, looked bored, and was perceived by Mrs. Warren as disinterested. Yet, this student told me she learned a great deal from the class and offered the following insight on student classroom behavior: "Everybody's putting on this cool act to give the impression you don't really—you don't need to care because you're 'Jack Cool.' But if you look too interested, that's not good either. People will wonder what you're doing." Although she asked several questions about it during the interview, she said, "I'm not gonna stand up in the middle of class and say, 'I wanna know about birth control.' They'd think I was using it." She believed this would give her a "bad reputation." While other young women were similarly concerned that others might interpret signs of interest as evidence of "too much" sexual experience, young men seemed more concerned about being perceived as having "too little."

Even the most vocal students revealed very little of their personal behavior and opinion, and some expressed concern over possible interpretations of their interest and questions by Mrs. Warren or other students. For example, Dawn said she chose not to ask questions about birth control for the following reasons:

> *Dawn:* Students might react or have a reaction. I'm not comfortable saying it in front of an adult—unless they don't know who I am. They might think I'm doing something. [pause] The teacher might wonder why you asked and do something.
>
> *Interviewer:* Do you mean refer you to a guidance counselor—something like that?
>
> *Dawn:* Yes.

Because parent permission had to be obtained for the interviews, I did not specifically ask students about their own sexual behavior. However, nearly 75% of the young women and 50% of the young men elaborated in what seemed a comfortable way on several questions about peer sexual behavior and attitudes as well as their own attitudes toward sexuality. In general, their levels of ease and disclosure with a relatively unfamiliar adult were similar to those of adolescents I had talked to in other school and community settings.[3] Adults concerned with school sexuality education might well explore creative ways to provide such one-to-one opportunities, including programs in which young people are trained to act as a resource for peers. In addition, concerns about embarrassment and relevance of classroom information to students' lives might be met by providing opportunities for them to write questions anonymously, with answers provided in class. Expanding the role of students on district advisory committees (in sufficient numbers so they are not overwhelmed by adults) and in classroom planning (through ascertaining anonymously what they want to know) might also contribute to more relevant school sexuality education.

TEACHING STRATEGIES

Before describing Mrs. Warren's teaching strategies, it is worth repeating that my intent is not to criticize them but to describe them as active attempts to deal with underlying dilemmas and contradictions created by organizational constraints, student classroom responses, and her social position. Given the organizational constraints and student cultural responses just outlined, Mrs. Warren was faced with a dilemma. She needed to cover material on a lengthy district syllabus yet make the work easy enough for all students to do well; she needed to maintain classroom control while being enough of a "buddy" to secure student participation in alternate-day physical activities in which they—especially the young women—had no particular interest. In this context, Mrs. Warren minimized student resistance to the required course and maintained a congenial authority by making the class easy and utilizing what McNeil (1986) calls "defensive teaching" strategies. These included selecting noncontroversial topics, simplifying content, presenting mostly fragments of technical detail geared toward passing the exam, and limiting discussion. Such strategies had the effect of reducing rich and diverse knowledge about sexuality to a narrow range of technical school knowledge with little relevance to students. As expressed by one young woman, course content on sexuality was "just stuff you had to know. I don't know if we'll ever use it." This white female's perception of content irrelevance is strikingly similar to a black male student's assertion in Chapter 9 that sexuality education "doesn't teach you, like, the things you want to know."

Selecting Less Controversial Topics

Sexuality education was the last and shortest classroom unit of study in the health course, with only about 5 ½ hours of time spent on it. Like respondents in large survey research samples (Alan Guttmacher Institute, 1983; Orr, 1982; Sonenstein & Pittman, 1984), Mrs. Warren spent most time on the least "controversial" sexuality education topics: sexually transmitted diseases, consequences of teenage pregnancy, adolescent body changes, and reproductive anatomy and physiology. She also spent a comparatively large amount of time on other less controversial topics not mentioned in that research: communicating with parents, dating, and marriage and family. Similar to 75% of teachers in a later study (Alan Guttmacher Institute, 1989), she spent time on birth control. Finally, like respondents in all these surveys who reported they less frequently covered the issues of sexual response/pleasure, masturbation, abortion, or homosexuality, Mrs. Warren barely mentioned these more controversial topics.

Presenting Fragments Geared to the Exam

Nearly all information was conveyed by Mrs. Warren as fact or detail, with no elaboration beyond a few sentences. Additionally, the seemingly random order in which she presented various classroom topics (e.g., the menstrual cycle before reproductive anatomy), the absence of transitions between them, and the two-week Christmas vacation all contributed to an overall impression of fragmentation. Because of the alternate-day format, daily sessions were further fragmented by Mrs. Warren's giving directions, answering questions, or presenting material regarding the next day's physical activities. For example, the film on teenage pregnancy had to be reserved early in the semester for all the Van Buren health teachers, and thus was shown the day before classes were scheduled to begin using the weight training room. In order to make maximum use of this equipment on activity day, Mrs. Warren (and the other two teachers) did a 25-minute classroom presentation on muscle groups before showing the film (Trudell, 1990).

Furthermore, Mrs. Warren told students from the semester's beginning that she would point out information on which they would be tested: "You don't have to take notes on reading because I'll give you notes in class. . . . Anything I put on the board is important." This strategy continued throughout the semester. The following quotes are typical:

"There are three terms from the male reproductive sheet I need you to know."

"You need to know that the pill, IUD, and diaphragm are prescription methods. You need to be able to list this."

"Chlamydia is the number one sexually transmitted disease. I want you to know that for sure."

Pointing out specific information on which students would be tested reached a peak in the last few classroom sessions before each exam. They received a "review sheet," and Mrs. Warren read brief explanations of each word or concept (while students copied them), as well as questions from the upcoming exam. Students learned they could "do well" on exams by saving handouts, jotting down details as Mrs. Warren emphasized them, or—more easily—simply filling in the review sheet. Therefore, during the review sessions, they were especially quiet and attentive—talking and bantering less among themselves, asking fewer questions (digressive or otherwise), and dutifully taking notes.

Mrs. Warren presented information in bits and pieces in part because of her belief that "you can't get too detailed or you lose them [students]." She also saw good grades as a form of encouragement that could "help that person feel good about themselves," giving Paula a C − − −, instead of a D on the sexuality exam. In short, she felt responsible for helping students "do well" on unit exams, particularly since passing the health course was a state and district requirement for graduation.

Mrs. Warren frequently conveyed fragments of information by reading aloud while students recorded them on worksheets. Coverage of sexually transmitted diseases, female/male reproductive anatomy, pregnancy/birth, and contraception was handled this way. For example, she gave students a worksheet that listed 10 sexually transmitted diseases and was divided into four columns ("symptoms," "complications," "transmission," "cure/treatment"). Mrs. Warren had typed information pertaining to each disease in the "complications" column and read details for students to write in others. Such piecemeal information was fragmented even further when she began by listing the symptoms of chlamydia, gonorrhea, syphilis, and herpes before discussing these diseases as separate entities. "Prevention" was not one of the columns, and condoms were not mentioned in this regard.

Information on contraception was conveyed via a handout in a similarly truncated and technical way. During a 7-minute display of contraceptives, students had brief glimpses of several forms of birth control, including an *unopened* condom packet. They received no instructions on condom or other contraceptive use. When subsequently asked about why she did not take the condom out of the packet, Mrs. Warren replied that "lack of time" due to limited availability of the shared contraceptive kit was the reason. Nevertheless, she had earlier described a parent complaint about a condom being passed around the room. Following a much later reading of a research draft, Mrs. Warren revealed other factors in her decision not to show the condom itself, including a student classroom response some years earlier that led to her losing control of the class. She was pregnant at the time, and as she took a condom out of the packet, it accidentally made a loud snapping noise. Two male students "just went nuts" with laughter, she got "red-faced," and everyone in the room (including her) began to laugh. In her words, "I lost it [classroom control] completely."

Simplifying Complex Issues

In addition to providing fragmented details, Mrs. Warren frequently simplified complex issues by reading verbatim from informational handouts she gave students. These included "Ann Landers' 18,000 Lines Used by Boys on the Make," "Eight Popular Reasons for Having Intercourse . . . That No Smart Teenager Would Use," "How to Say 'No,'" "What is AIDS?" (Network Publications, 1985) and other material such as sexual abuse laws and newspaper clippings.[4] Coverage of sexual assault and AIDS, both additions to the Woodland ninth-grade health curriculum that year (1985), were handled almost entirely in this way. Mrs. Warren felt pressure to include them but uncertain about how to deal with them in her own words.

Sexual Assault. In referring to sexual assault during an interview, Mrs. Warren said: "You want to say it just the right way because everyone's going to take it differently. You have to be so careful how you deliver things—especially with this stuff. You can't joke about it, and you can't laugh it off because it's not funny." Given this uncertainty as well as limited time for planning and presentation, she presented the topic to students in the following way:

> Mrs. Warren reads a memo from the Woodland health coordinator that expressed a concern about sexual assault and the district's intent to deal seriously with incidents of it when they occur at school.
>> *Andrew* (to Carrie): Their rules are so strict, though. You couldn't even say "hi" without getting accused.
>> *Carrie* (to Andrew): You can't even touch someone on the shoulder anymore.
> Mrs. Warren finishes reading the memo and then reads a legal definition of fourth degree sexual assault.

> *Andrew* (louder, for all to hear): You can't even touch someone on the shoulder anymore.
>
> *Mrs. Warren:* If a girl is enticing—going, "come on, come on"—that's different.
>
> *Andrew:* What if you do it accidentally?
>
> *Mrs. Warren:* Your body is private. (She explains that people don't have to "put up" with being touched in ways they don't want to be.) It's not right if guys get aggressive.
>
> *Andrew:* What if she's wearing a one piece bikini?
>
> *Dawn:* It doesn't matter what kind of clothing a girl wears—they say on TV.
>
> *Mrs. Warren:* Girls can ask for it. Let's get on with this. I'll read you something else.
>
> She reads an article from the Woodland daily paper reporting sexual assault incidents in local schools.

Beyond these comments, students did not press for expanded discussion of this 9-minute presentation. However, several students indicated during the interviews that they would have preferred more coverage.

Mrs. Warren herself seemed to convey contradictory points of view: sexual assault is wrong and has serious legal consequences; males should not "get aggressive," but avoiding it is primarily the responsibility of females, who should not be "enticing" or "ask for it." Rather than exploring these contradictions, Mrs. Warren limited discussion and retained classroom control by "get[ting] on with" reading aloud and "getting through" the syllabus. Like other teachers, she sought safety and control during these potentially uncomfortable and controversial moments (Ellsworth, in press). While there can be no set formula for dealing with such pedagogical situations, Mrs. Warren might have been assisted by greater understanding of this complex issue and familiarity with resources, including classroom speakers from community organizations, that cover it in more depth. Furthermore, given the prevalence of sexual assault in our culture, Mrs. Warren (or one of her students) could have been the estimated one in three women or one in seven men molested before the age of 18 (Bass & Davis, 1988). If such had been the case, her reading aloud and moving quickly would take on very different meanings. Teachers who are themselves survivors of sexual violence may be less than willing or able to teach about it; those of us involved in teacher preparation and in-service must be aware of this possibility and realize that brief "how to teach" training sessions may be totally inadequate (Trudell & Whatley, 1988).

Homosexuality. "Become accepting of an individual whose sexual orientation differs from their own" is an official objective in Woodland district's ninth-grade health curriculum; nevertheless, this did not translate into classroom practice. The topic was first mentioned while Mrs. Warren was reading from a handout on "saying 'no'" to intercourse. One of the "lines" that "guys" use to convince young women to have intercourse was: "I've heard that you're 'lezzie.' If you aren't, prove it." This statement was greeted by loud laughter and echoes of the word "lezzie" from many students of both sexes, while Mrs. Warren simply went on with her reading.

The major reference to homosexuality was made briefly in the context of AIDS, with Mrs. Warren reading from a handout that was distributed at a district in-service that referred to gay and bisexual men as follows: "So far in the United States, gay and bisexual men have been most at risk of getting AIDS. More than 70% of reported cases are in these 2 groups" (Network Publications, 1985). She then added in her own words: "Because it [AIDS] involves gay people, many others say, 'Don't do anything about it.' But they're human too. There hasn't been enough money spent on it." Although it was not further pursued, this last comment illustrates a moment in which Mrs. Warren opened up possibilities for critical discussion of dominant heterosexual norms and homophobia as they affect social policy.

The potential for derisive student response seemed to be a factor in Mrs. Warren's omission of the topic except in the context of AIDS; their laughter at the word "lezzie" confirmed her belief that "most students wouldn't handle it right. I think they're not mature enough." She went on to say, "I'm comfortable with it myself, but I still haven't found a way that I can say it to ninth-grade girls and boys to make it sound like I'm not out in left field." Organizational constraints (overloaded syllabus, lack of planning time, and administrative concern with parental reaction in the context of dominant heterosexual norms of school and community) also played a role in the minimal classroom coverage of homosexuality. Finally, Mrs. Warren's heterosexual assumptions, based on her own taken-for-granted social position, seemed to be a factor in this curricular decision. Such an assumption was clearly evident in other class content and presentation. One emphatic example occurred just before she explained the menstrual cycle, when Andrew asked whether it was "necessary" to cover this. Mrs. Warren replied, "You're gonna get married or at least have a girlfriend."

Nevertheless, 17 of the 25 interviewed students indicated that homosexuality ought to have been discussed more thoroughly. Most suggested that students do not know enough about it; five pointed out that homosexuality is a current real-life issue, that is, "It's a thing that's kind of hitting America today. People should be aware of what's going on." Two other students explicitly stated that homosexuality is not necessarily "wrong" and argued for greater tolerance, and two of the seven who believed the topic should not be included said it would be too "embarrassing," although one added that "it might be useful." Males were more reluctant to include it than females; 40% of males and 20% of females expressed disapproval.

No student made an overtly homophobic comment during the interviews; however, the classroom "loner," a nonathletic and soft-spoken young man, was frequently the target of name-calling (including "fag" and "queer" on at least two occasions) and insults from other students—particularly one of the most popular male athletes. Thus, although student interview responses generally indicated support for the inclusion of homosexuality in the curriculum, it is difficult to judge the degree to which this support is permeated with homophobia. Furthermore, these moments of name-calling might have provided Mrs. Warren with opportunities for interruption or discussion. However, her attention was directed elsewhere when they occurred, and they went unchallenged.

Limiting Student Discussion

Like Mrs. Warren's explanations, wider class discussion consisted mainly of fragments, with some students—particularly those from more marginalized groups—calling out brief remarks related to her discussion-starting questions, while others made muted comments to those sitting nearby. Most participated by simply calling out brief responses that revealed little information about their personal attitudes or behavior, protected them from embarrassment, and minimally met Mrs. Warren's behavioral expectations. I observed no substantive or ongoing discussion in which students expressed varying points of view and no teacher-organized small group discussion.

For example, after the film on teenage pregnancy (with only 8 minutes of class left) Mrs. Warren asked students what they thought of it. Carrie and Dawn pointed out that the girl in the film might have chosen to have an abortion instead of giving birth, but several other students had begun talking among themselves, and a group focus never materialized. Mrs. Warren then attempted to redirect discussion by asking students to put themselves in the "girl" or "guy's place" in the film. This time, the two white young women described by Mrs. Warren as "dirts" (Paula and Toni) joined the two black young women (Carrie and Dawn) in interjecting their lived experience:

> *Toni:* I'd slap him [the teenage father] up.
> *Carrie* (sarcastically): I'd be the sweetest girl in the world.
> *Paula* (defiantly): My mom was seventeen when she had me.
> *Toni:* My mom was married when she was eighteen, and she got married because she had my sister.

Carrie: My sister had a baby when she was fourteen.
Dawn: My cousin had a baby when she was fourteen.

They more or less called their comments out into the air, while several other students began to talk with each other. Mrs. Warren spoke with a small group of young women in the front, and the group focus vanished again.

The film portrayed giving birth and keeping the baby as a preferred option for teenage pregnancy, mentioning adoption and abortion only as choices rejected by its two major female characters. This excerpt also illustrates a moment when Carrie and Dawn opened up possibilities for discussing abortion as an option—a moment that Mrs. Warren did not pursue. In fact, Mrs. Warren told me that she is against abortion, a stance she described as "pro-life." During a subsequent session on pregnancy and prenatal development, she consciously showed pictures of fetal development and referred to the fetus as "baby" as a means to convey that perspective, although she never said explicitly in class that abortion was wrong or the choice least preferred by her. While personal beliefs did play a role in these curricular choices, other considerations such as availability of resources that portray pregnancy options in a balanced way, time to locate them, and a sense that school administration and community shared her views seemed more salient.

When Mrs. Warren created space for students to include their own lived experience in classroom discussion by asking them for qualities they looked for in a date, only a few, especially Carrie and Andrew, contributed to the list Mrs. Warren put on the board. However, several students shared more muted list suggestions; those heard in my immediate vicinity of the classroom included "someone who knows you inside and out" (the double meaning was not lost on other students), "take what you can get," "beaver," and so on. Furthermore, some audible comments were ignored by Mrs. Warren:

Dawn: Good kisser—good smacker.
Carrie: Not a wham-bam-thank-you-ma'am.

After spending 15 minutes this way, Mrs. Warren summarized by saying that the lists largely exemplified "infatuation" and defined the term for students to write in their notebooks: "Just understand it's physical." Next she read several brief definitions of "love," telling students, "You don't have to write this down."

Overall, Mrs. Warren kept her own language in the medical/technical realm. When students interjected their informal version of language, she generally either ignored or rephrased their words into "classroom" language. For example: when Dawn pronounced *epididymis* as "epi-titty-miss," Mrs. Warren simply said, "Not *titty—didy*" and moved on to the next item of male reproductive anatomy. Later, in labeling a diagram, Mrs. Warren used the word *anus* and then added, "I'm sure you have other words." Several students snickered but no one audibly used the terms. Students mostly confined classroom use of generally less acceptable sexual language (*dick, fuck, suck, beaver*, to name a few I heard) to muted interactions with each other. If Mrs. Warren overheard such remarks between students during the sexuality education unit, she did not acknowledge them.

Most students said during the interviews that they would have liked a little more time for small group work—especially if they could have chosen their "own mixture," that is, people with whom they were at ease, could trust, or didn't "goof around." Mrs. Warren had expressed very different ideals for her own teaching at the beginning of the semester, when she told me she planned to use small-group discussion as students became more "comfortable." Later, she attributed her nonuse of this teaching method to time constraints (small groups "take a lot of time to prepare"), discipline ("kids play and fool around in small groups"), and efficiency ("a lot doesn't get done"). Thus, as McNeil (1986) also notes, defensive teaching had the contradictory outcome of splitting teaching ideals from actual practice. While Mrs. Warren said she would "like to get away from talking," talking represented the most effective way to get through the lengthy syllabus and control students.

Personal Asides

In contrast to the economics teachers in McNeil's study (1986), who split off personal information from lecture content, Mrs. Warren sometimes interjected personal experience into the classroom, including brief comments on her marriage, pregnancy, childbirth, parenting, and sterilization experiences as well as her own early ignorance about sex.

It is noteworthy that Mrs. Warren's socially sanctioned status as heterosexual, wife, and mother probably made such disclosure easier for her and more acceptable to students than if she had been a lesbian or heterosexually active yet unmarried female teacher. Thus, most of Mrs. Warren's personal asides implicitly conferred status on dominant cultural values, particularly since students liked her and the class. Nevertheless, some of her comments (e.g., she makes more money than her husband, their children are in day care, and so on) did contradict traditional gender arrangements.

The following excerpt involving personal disclosure typifies several aspects of classroom dynamics: the mostly fragmented way Mrs. Warren incorporated personal experiences, the generally bantering classroom atmosphere (in which substantive student questions were sometimes lost), the use of a worksheet to limit discussion, and participation of students from marginalized groups. However, it is *not* typical in that most of Mrs. Warren's other descriptions of her childbirth experiences referred to their difficulty (pain, stitches, and so on).

> Mrs. Warren defines afterbirth (a term on the handout) as "placenta [previously defined] and everything left over after the baby is born." She says her doctor asked her if she wanted to see it, but she said, "No thanks."
>
> *Paula:* What's it like?
> *Carrie:* Like having a mass period.
> *Mrs. Warren:* It's a little worse than that.
> *Paula:* How many things are delivered?
> Mrs. Warren says that the placenta is the third stage of delivery and that the amniotic fluid didn't come so "the doctor went in there with a fish hook thing to break the sac." She goes on to say that the baby comes second and then "everything else."
> *Paula:* What else?
> *Carrie:* A Christmas present from your gramma.
> There is loud laughter from the rest of the students, who have been listening intently. Mrs. Warren says that giving birth is a "beautiful experience. Having kids is very special." She says she feels a lot of love for her children.
> *Carrie:* We know you beat 'em.
> *Mrs. Warren:* Well, Greg [her son] gets more spankings than Judy [her daughter].
> Students begin talking among themselves, and there is a noisy interlude of about 20 seconds while Mrs. Warren talks with young women near the front.
> *Mrs. Warren* (to the whole group): Amniocentesis (next word on the handout) is a test for birth defects.
> *Andrew:* You can check for the baby's sex too.
> *Paula:* Did you worry before the baby was born?
> *Mrs. Warren:* Only about whether it was a boy or girl.
> *Andrew:* What did you want first?
> *Mrs. Warren:* A boy.
> Students begin talking with each other again, and Mrs. Warren directs other comments about her children to those near the front. Some students tell her to bring her children to school. After a minute, Mrs. Warren addresses the large group and defines the next word on the handout.

LIVED SEXUALITY CURRICULUM

Taken together, course content, teaching strategies, and classroom interaction invited students to adopt various points of view about sexual behavior and gender relations—mostly coinciding with but sometimes contradicting dominant social norms. For example, students were offered an overall picture of the problematic and dangerous outcome of adolescent sexuality (teenage pregnancy and sexually transmitted diseases) rather than of its pleasures. Nevertheless, the relaxed, humorous, and bantering atmosphere in the classroom could have gone a long way toward contradicting this impression of sexuality as a grave and potentially dangerous aspect of life.

Although limited by the heterosexist assumptions underlying course content, students might have perceived contradictory points of view about "responsible" sexual behavior. First, since love, marriage, and parenting provided much of the context for the discussion of sexuality, students were offered encouragement to postpone intercourse until they are "in love" (nebulously defined in opposition to "infatuation," i.e., physical attraction) or married (with "love" as a major "ingredient"). Students of both sexes were urged not to "go too far" (an expression that was never defined) and to "say 'no.'" Although Mrs. Warren prefaced the "say 'no'" materials by remarking that young women sometimes use similar "lines" to convince young men to have intercourse, most of the content suggested it is the young woman's role to say "no" and (as Mrs. Warren reiterated twice during the session) not to be a "tease." Along these same lines, she told students to write down "abstinence" as the "best" method of birth control. Thus, they might infer that avoiding pregnancy is a very important reason for not having intercourse.

However, students were also told, "If you're not ready for birth control, you're not ready for intercourse" and given some information about the various forms of contraception. Thus, in contrast to the "say 'no'" message, they were also offered the possibility that having intercourse constitutes "responsible" sexual behavior *if* birth control is used. Nevertheless, information about birth control was neither accurate nor complete enough to enable them to make an informed choice about a method or to use it effectively.

Mrs. Warren also pointed out that most of the birth control devices shown students are used by the female and added, "It shouldn't really be that way." Even so, she spent a total of only 30 seconds describing condoms and did not show them to students, implicitly reinforcing female responsibility for pregnancy prevention. Furthermore, condoms were never mentioned as a form of prevention for sexually transmitted diseases. Finally, the film seen by students did point out male responsibility in preventing pregnancy; however, it seemed to position males in a protective and, thus, more powerful role than females, i.e., a "responsible" male should "take care of" a young woman by using a condom.

It is noteworthy that Mrs. Warren personally believed that ninth-graders are "too young" to be having intercourse, although she was not against premarital intercourse in general. Nevertheless, in the classroom she did not focus exclusively on abstinence but provided information on birth control. Taken together, this and observations regarding homosexuality and abortion suggest that Mrs. Warren's personal beliefs did consciously enter into some curricular decisions but seemed to have less of an effect than factors related to school and district organization and student classroom responses.

Although most students did not openly challenge classroom versions of "responsible" sexual behaviors, interviews revealed contradictory and complex interpretations, rather than simple acceptance. When students were asked, "According to the message you got about sexuality and relationships, how do you think the class would like you to behave sexually at this time?" they responded with the following:

- *Wait to have intercourse* (7 females, 6 males). "Maybe the beginning of the ninth grade is a little too young." "You shouldn't do anything." "Supposed to wait for a while—until someone really special and you're in love with him." "Kinda keepin' it casual—not real active and gettin' some girl pregnant."
- *Better to wait but use birth control if you don't* (4 females). "Intercourse is not really OK, but if you're going to they told us different things to prevent pregnancy." "If you're going to be involved, take the right precautions."
- *OK not to wait but use birth control yourself* (1 female, 1 male). "They didn't tell us in the class 'don't' and stuff—they just said use birth control." "Using birth control and using a safe method—not withdrawal or rhythm."
- *Old enough to make the choice yourself* (3 females). "You're able to make you own choice now." "It depends on a person's maturity. Girls are usually more mature right now."
- *Not certain* (2 males).

While 13 students perceived the major message as "wait," only 5 (3 females/2 males) thought other Van Buren students would agree with this message. Thus, dominant classroom messages seemed to be contradicted by the wider cultural setting.

IMPLICATIONS

This description and analysis of the process of knowledge construction in one sexuality education classroom reveals complexity and contradiction, instead of simple prescriptions, for those of us concerned with broadening the spectrum of "acceptable" sexual behavior, affirming the pleasures of sexuality, and encouraging nonexploitative relationships. The study suggests that such classes may reinforce or alter traditional antisex and patriarchal norms and reveals multiple possibilities for situation-specific action. Therefore, feminist and progressive educators need to be precise about the *kind* of school sexuality education we advocate, rather than uncritically supporting the general concept or mandates that require its inclusion in the curriculum. We must work toward school programs that analyze sexuality in the context of wider power relations, thus uncovering gender, class, racial, and other inequalities that put low-income women (with a disproportionate number being women of color) at greatest risk for pregnancy, sexually transmitted diseases, and harassment (Fine, 1988).

More specifically, Mariamne Whatley (1989) has articulated some goals for "sex equitable" sexuality education. These include

- Replacing biologically determined sex roles with more flexible, socially constructed gender roles
- Emphasizing female/male similarities rather than differences
- Recognizing female sexual pleasure and desire
- Presenting intercourse as one of many possible forms of sexual expression
- Eliminating heterosexual assumptions
- Establishing common standards of sexual behavior/responsibility for both sexes
- Providing education about violence that applies to both potential victims and perpetrators

As scholars and practitioners who share these goals, we might also be involved in developing curricular materials, including audiovisuals as well as pre-service and in-service education workshops for teachers. Instead of blaming individual teachers, we need to work collectively to circumvent and change the institutional constraints made visible in the study. Considering these constraints, smaller and less structured community-based programs developed for and with young people may offer more realistic possibilities for honest and open discussions about sexuality. For example, members of the AIDS Coalition to Unleash Power (ACT UP) are staffing storefront walk-in centers in New York City neighborhoods to distribute condoms and talk about safer sex in frank street language.

Finally, we should recognize that even the best school sexuality education offers an *individualistic* solution to broad social problems like teenage pregnancy and AIDS. Such programs can obscure consideration of how inequality in education, employment, and material benefits in a capitalistic, patriarchal, and racist society might actually contribute to these problems, particularly among members of social groups affected in multiple ways—such as poor teenage women of color. Given this recognition of social and economic issues, progressive educators must not abandon the field of school sexuality education to those who advocate "saying 'no' to sex." Instead, we must continue our work in and outside classrooms to change the social and economic conditions that keep women and men from maximizing their potential as fully human, sexual beings.

NOTES

Acknowledgments. Special thanks to Elizabeth Ellsworth and Mariamne Whatley for their support and helpful suggestions regarding this chapter.

1. For example, in her important and otherwise excellent analysis of "the missing discourse of desire" in school sexuality education, Michelle Fine (1988) ignores the organizational setting; she accuses teachers of "systematic refusal to name issues" that make them uncomfortable and of projecting their discomfort onto students (p. 38).

2. I use the word "fat" deliberately, rather than other euphemisms, because I believe "fat" needs to be reclaimed as a descriptive rather than perjorative term.

3. One young woman (with whom I became quite well acquainted during the semester) actually disclosed that she had been sexually abused as a child, saying I was the first adult she had told. Fortunately, because of my past work experience, I was able to respond in an appropriate and supportive way, ultimately facilitating a series of sessions between her and the school psychologist. The dilemma created by this disclosure might be problematic for teachers as well. Specifically, teachers and various school support staff are mandated in all states to report child sexual abuse to authorities; in the state where I conducted research, anyone under age 16 is legally incapable of consenting to sexual activity. Thus, if teachers become aware of such activity between two 15-year-olds (perhaps by being sought out for contraceptive advice), they must report it. Although Mrs. Warren did not express this dilemma, it has been my experience that teachers' concerns over mandatory reporting are widespread and behind a great deal of reluctance to get involved with sexual abuse prevention and sexuality education. See Trudell and Whatley (1988).

4. I must acknowledge my role in making these "saying 'no'" materials available to teachers during a workshop I conducted as community educator for a family planning agency in 1981, four years prior to my classroom observations. In making these materials part of a resource packet, I had not—at that point—given sufficient consideration to the emphasis that might be placed on this approach or the possibility that they would be read aloud to students.

REFERENCES

Alan Guttmacher Institute. (1983). *Issues in Brief, 3*(3).

Alan Guttmacher Institute. (1989). *Risk and responsibility: Teaching sex education in America's schools today.* New York: Author.

Bass, E., & Davis, L. (1988). *The courage to heal.* New York: Harper.

Ellsworth, E. (in press). Teaching to support unassimilated difference. *Radical Teacher.*

Fine, M. (1988). Sexuality, schooling, and adolescent females: The missing discourse of desire. *Harvard Educational Review, 58*(1), 29–53.

McNeil, L. (1986). *Contradictions of control: School structure and school knowledge.* Boston: Routledge & Kegan Paul.

Muraskin, L. (1986). Sex education mandates: Are they the answer? *Family Planning Perspectives, 18*(4), 171–174.

Network Publications. (1985). What is AIDS? Santa Cruz, CA: Author.

Orr, M. T. (1982). Sex education and contraceptive education in U.S. public high schools. *Family Planning Perspectives, 14*(6), 305–313.

Scales, P. (1987). How we can prevent teen pregnancy (and why it's not the real problem). *Journal of Sex Education and Therapy, 13*(1), 12–15.

Sonenstein, F. L., & Pittman, K. J. (1984). The availability of sex education in large city school districts. *Family Planning Perspectives, 16*(1), 19–25.

Trudell, B. (1988). *Constructing the sexuality curriculum-in-use: An ethnographic study of a ninth-grade school sex education class.* Unpublished doctoral dissertation, University of Wisconsin–Madison.

Trudell, B. (1990). Selection, presentation, and student interpretation of an educational film on teenage pregnancy: A critical, ethnographic investigation. In E. Ellsworth & M. Whatley (Eds.), *The ideology of images in educational media: Hidden curriculums in the classroom* (pp. 74–106). New York: Teachers College Press.

Trudell, B., & Whatley, M. (1988). School sexual abuse prevention: Unintended consequences and dilemmas. *Child Abuse and Neglect, 12*(1), 103–113.

Whatley, M. (1989). Goals for equitable sex education. *Peabody Journal of Education, 64*(4), 59–70.

CHAPTER 11

Discussing Sexuality in a Language Arts Class

Alternative Meaning-Making and Meaning-Making as an Alternative

DIANE D. BRUNNER

Even in schools that have a strong program of sexuality education, students are frequently left alone to make sense of complicated and often highly contrary sexual notions. Bombarded with sexual stimuli from movies, television, music, the clothing industry, and books, students seldom receive sound sexual knowledge or sexual understanding. In short, students are deprived of opportunities for guided meaning-making or knowledge construed from educative social interaction that might result in understanding, particularly with respect to *social* aspects of sexuality (e.g., sex roles, relationships, behavior patterns and lifestyles). Elizabeth Roberts (1980) calls this kind of understanding "sexual learning" because it does not come from factual information alone but assumes a social construction of knowledge.

Observational learning only, the kind that derives from television, for example, often results in a "sex-appropriate" perception of sexuality defined by Feshbach, Dillman, and Jordan (1979) as the development of sex roles through culturally approved male/female characteristics. Moreover, from a variety of media as well as personal experiences, young people learn that male/female sexual behaviors are linked with systems of power, and they especially learn that "power" is most often white, middle-class, and male (see, for example, Foucault, 1990).

On the other hand, most students are not limited to observational learning. In grades 6 through 12, sexuality education classes present factual information on venereal disease, contraception, and reproduction. However, such classes pay little if any attention to aspects of sexuality that have to do with relationships or with understanding other *dimensions of sexuality* (e.g., masturbation, kissing, petting, orgasm, wet dreams, sexual preference, and sexual physiology) that might lead to

226

enjoying one's sexuality (Roberts, 1980; Trudell also makes a similar point in Chapter 10 of this volume).

My position on issues of control by inclusion/exclusion of curricular content is informed by critical social theories that illumine the relation between school knowledge or "official knowledge" and codes of power and control (Apple, 1982; Bernstein, 1975; Wexler, 1982, 1987; Whitty, 1985; Williams, 1977). These theories suggest that the society in which we live "channels, guides, and limits our imagination in sexual as well as other matters" (Hubbard, 1990, p. 135). Moreover, practices that exclude all but traditional content and/or viewpoints ensure that some groups are never served (Apple, 1982; McNeil, 1988; Williams, 1977). It is these groups about whom I am most concerned.

Treating topics of sexuality more like "disaster prevention" or "remedial treatment" tends only to reinforce notions that sexual issues are not legitimate subjects for inquiry or discussion and inhibit sexual learning (particularly learning that includes culturally diverse perspectives) in sanctioned situations. In fact, rarely do young people have the opportunity to discuss sexual concerns openly with parents or teachers. While adults deal out curricular controls to limit discussions that could lead to sexual learning, children pay the price. Children develop most of their sexual orientation in streetwise conversation (Roberts, 1980). Therefore, any opportunity for meaning-making, in and of itself, constitutes an alternative to the typical protocol of sexuality education—especially when it calls for an understanding that does not legitimate dominant class interests or is not the "accepted, official knowledge" passed on in schools. When what passes for knowledge is assumed to be that which can be transmitted rather than constructed, and when that knowledge valorizes one particular worldview over another, schools control not only the content of instruction, but they attempt to control the outcome of students' learning. Thus, the narrow focus on "sex for procreation" (Hubbard, 1990) perpetuates a view of sex as separate and isolated from other human experience.

For these reasons, discussions around the reading of culturally diverse literature may provide a much needed opportunity to repair the break between what is formally taught in sexuality education classes or romanticized by popular culture and how it is interpreted.[1] If, for example, black students only learn about sex from a white, middle-class perspective and their experiences do not match this taught knowledge, then both they and their white peers may regard these experiences negatively. They may not recognize that cultural diversity and social or circumstantial phenomena contribute to differences in sexual experiences. Further, these young people are unlikely to recognize that the sexual orientation formally taught in school is designed largely to serve dominant class interests and intended to perpetuate the status quo. However, opportunities for open discussion around the reading of culturally diverse literature can enhance possibilities for students' sexual learning that authenticates cultural knowledge and diversity as it challenges existing systems of power.

AN ALTERNATIVE TO INFORMATION-ONLY CLASSES IN SEXUALITY EDUCATION

In this chapter I suggest possibilities for sexual learning in the language arts curriculum via literature-based discussions. Two rationales permit my making this recommendation. First, because literature offers a full range of opportunities for learning about the human condition, it provides a space for encouraging young people to consider all of the dimensions of sexuality—physical, psychological, social, and cultural. Vicarious experiences through literature (i.e., entering the fiction world—becoming the characters) allow readers to question certain assumptions and test out certain attitudes and behaviors in a safe, nonthreatening medium (Rosenblatt, 1938/1976).

Additionally, data drawn from a small response study reveal adolescents' willingness to deal with issues of teen pregnancy and to openly discuss sexual topics ranging from contraception to abortion and adoption, to financial responsibilities related to child care. That these data are drawn from an all black population (this was not a public school program) also provides insight into cultural perspectives that embody alternative points of view. Further, these data support Ward and Taylor's position (see Chapter 9 in this volume) that sexual curricula have often failed to serve the needs of minority students by privileging a white middle-class perspective.

In the available professional literature on sexuality and the curriculum, no materials for teaching sexuality beyond the traditional sexuality education class could be found. Though curricular materials are available for developing programs with a similar pedagogical orientation, none of these programs deal directly with sexuality education. Even with the recent focus on women's studies, my search through several volumes discussing feminist approaches to teaching literature in the middle and high schools found none with a sexuality focus. Therefore, this chapter suggests an alternative curriculum for accomplishing goals related to sexuality education, and at the end of this volume a list of annotated resources is provided for those who wish to build such a program.

CONTEXT, METHODS, AND CONTENT

This study took place at the Institute for Neighborhood Academic Development located in an inner-city community in the Midwest. The institute is not so much an alternative program as it is a supplement to public school efforts, providing otherwise "latchkey kids" with a place to be after school and during the summer. The institute offers both academic and recreational services to hundreds of minority students (mostly black and Hispanic), with activities ranging from after-school tutorials to science and African-American/history clubs to varsity scouting and a "be a star" program. The study took place during a 5-week summer enrichment program offering courses in math, history, and language arts. Though all the students in the reading/literature class that I visited were black, they came from diverse social, economic, and political backgrounds, and their responses to the readings represented that mix. (Student names appearing in this chapter are fictitious.)

For example, Tyrone told me he had recently visited the Detroit Institute of Art to see the Cleopatra exhibit, and he talked of the science and industry exhibits at the museum in Chicago. A fifth-grader, Edgar, spoke of a visit to Jekyll Island, Georgia. Still another student, Loretta, talked of living in a run-down garage that is cold in the winter and hot in the summer. Students conversed about self-government and decision making, staying off drugs (one student said, "Black people have to pay more to get out of jail than white people, especially for drug busts"), standing up for one's own rights, boycotting Coke products, and self-discipline. Ronnie, an eighth-grader, wrote in a journal: "To control your attitude means to have respect for people. Don't crack any jokes like if something is wrong with their hair cause [you] would like them to respect you."

Twenty males and 16 females ranging from ages 10 to 15 inhabited this classroom. The age ranges were adequately accounted for because students worked together in cooperative learning groups in which students of mixed ability and various ages collaborated on projects of their choice. For example, one group of students assembled in a corner to work on a drawing that illustrated a story; another group read silently; and a third group, all female, engaged in what appeared to be somewhat inflammatory social conversation. When I joined them for one hour per day during the summer program, we all sat on the floor in a large circle to discuss and/or read literature.

For the project, students read three books on their own—*Drop-out*, by Jeanette Eyerly (1963), *Fast Sam, Cool Clyde, and Stuff*, by Walter Dean Myers (1975), and *A Hero Ain't Nothing But a Sandwich*, by Alice Childress (1973)—and I read two stories to them—"In the Heat," by Robert Cormier (1984) and "Welcome," by Ouida Sebestyen. (See Annotated Resources at the end of this volume for bibliographic information on other books containing themes related to sexuality.) On some occasions students wrote in journals following the reading. The regular teacher (a black woman attending classes at a nearby university) took notes and audiotaped each session. All taped data were transcribed.

This study goes beyond traditional literary analyses (Anyon, 1981; Taxel, 1981, 1984) by assessing readers' own reactions to ideological tensions within texts, by examining dynamics in an actual classroom, and by attempting to understand these responses and social dynamics against actual instructional methods used. Regarding the importance of studying social dynamics, Ira Shor (1987) writes:

> The strongest potential of education lies in studying the politics and student cultures affecting the classroom. It is politically naive or simply "technocratic" to see the classroom as a world apart where inequality, ideology, and economic policy don't affect learning. (p. 14)

In other words, students' responses in this study are examined against the context or learning environment created out of a particular pedagogical stance that is both student centered and cooperative. This stance assumes that every student is also a teacher and has much to contribute. Student responses depend entirely upon how students perceive the text in question (not on teacher interpretations) and often upon how they perceive the context or situation in which the text is read. Reading theorists (Bleich, 1978; Iser, 1978; Rosenblatt, 1978) describe such a transaction as being what the reader brings to the event, or the unique reading of a text resulting from the reader's own special background of experience. And reading response researchers (Galda, 1983; Holland, 1968) argue the validity of response research as a means of understanding idiosyncratic factors in readers' interests, expectations, and anxieties, which can affect how and what a reader perceives. Because of the multiplicity of possible readings within the texts used in this study, then, not all data collected related to sexuality. However, since one of the goals of the study was to collect responses via classroom discussion, data reflecting classroom dynamics around the instructional methods used are as important a data source as the response data. Though responses regarding sexuality are limited, discussion data illustrate instructional protocol that allows students to make sense of what they read through an open forum of debate or dialogue (for a discussion of "dialogical teaching" see Freire, 1970; Shor & Freire, 1987) and, in this case, provides an alternative method for sexuality education/learning.

Prior to each day's reading or discussion, I asked students simply to listen for anything in the story that made them happy, sad, or mad, and then say why. I also asked, "What connections to your own life can you make?" Discussions following my reading of Ouida Sebestyen's story "Welcome" (1984) yielded the most information regarding students' thinking about sexuality, especially with respect to aspects of teenage pregnancy. A synopsis of that story precedes their conversational interpretations of the text.

"Welcome" shares themes of teenage pregnancy, divorce, and mental retardation. Mary is the mother of Tina, the 14-year-old central character in the story. Mary and Tina travel by car to visit Mary's parents after a failed marriage. During the trip, Tina tells her mother about Sharon, Tina's best friend, who is also 14 and pregnant (Mary calls Sharon "a bubble-headed blonde" and students call her a "white girl"). On the surface the central conflict appears to be related to Tina's close association with an unwed, pregnant teenager who has nowhere else to turn. Tina's family is black and Sharon's is white. Tina invites Sharon to stay in her home while she is away visiting relatives. Without consulting her mother first, Tina simply gives Sharon the keys to the house. This action seems to set the tone for the story. A greater problem, however, centers around the splintering of the family, and the changes (emotional and financial) that divorce can bring. "Keys" tend to be an overriding metaphor for changes both Mary and Tina wish either to lock in or lock out.

When Mary decides to make a detour to visit some aunts on her husband's side of the family, she is reminded of how they had once taken her in, "no questions, just welcome." Tina is hoping her mother will react with similar graciousness to Sharon, and eventually she does come through. Tina is also bitter about her mother and father's separation, but both Tina and Mary are able to come to terms with their feelings while visiting the aunts. They meet Arley, Aunt Noella's mentally retarded "man-child," and he helps them to see through some of their fears and understand the pain each feels.

Conversation: Reflective Thinking or Just Talk?

The format for discussion was an open dialogue with each respondent reacting to something in the text. This was not simply a question-answer session; students were free to react, ask each other questions, and direct comments to one another. The first conversation following this reading had to do with Sharon's parents being unwilling to help her (the grade of the students is given after their name).

> *Rafaleh* (8th): It was kinda stupid that they didn'want to take care of the girl that was pregnant. Plus why she [Tina] want her parents to be taking care of her friend's baby? She [should] let her [Sharon] own parents take care of it or the baby's father.
> *Ahmad* (6th): Yeah, we always take care of our own.

David (6th): Why they have to move off and leave her?

Donnie (6th): Well, it a sin to have sex without being married.

Lucretia (8th): Anyway, it's stupid to get pregnant when you can't afford it.

David (6th): Especially if you got to go live with a family that ain't yours. She a white girl too. Why should Tina's mother [provide care] when her husband gone and probably won't pay no child support or anything?

Lucinda (7th): Well, I'd get pregnant right now, if I knew I could support it.

Shifting from evaluation of the situation to consideration of important perspectives regarding the "support" and care of a baby led students into a new topic. In this conversation they look at economic concerns:

Shane (6th): How can you get a job at 11, 12, 13, or 14 to support a baby? What kind of job can you get?

Kristin (7th): Baby-sitting. Sometimes you make over two dollars an hour.

Lucretia (8th): That's nothing! How you gone feed, clothe, and educate that kid on two dollars an hour?

Shane (6th): That's a box of Pampers.

The previous brief dialogue seems especially oppositional in light of stereotypical portraits of blacks reproducing carelessly and going on welfare or increasing an already-in-place welfare subsidy.

In a discussion of whose responsibility it was to care for a baby, this very brief exchange occurred:

Rafaleh (8th): The baby's father should get a job.

David (8th): Well, if he'd been wearing a rubber . . . You gonna have sex, you better protect yourself.

Often, in order to expand students' thinking, help students make connections, or just bring other nonparticipating students into the conversation, I rephrased students' comments and reiterated other pertinent reactions, responding myself when appropriate. This step helped to decenter the discussion and make students more aware of the many possible ways of thinking about the subject. It also helped them see the importance of their ideas and helped them extend those ideas beyond the text in question. In this next conversation students override a topic change I try to make in order to continue their discussion of pregnancy and some of its outcomes or alternatives.

Brunner: What about identity? As you get older you will begin to ask yourself, "Who am I? What individual am I in this world?" You won't want to be just your mother's child or your father's child.

Rafaleh (8th): It illegal to have abortions.

Yvonne (7th): It was illegal to have abortions a long time ago and now it is again.

Janine (8th): Well, if a person want an abortion, they should be able to get it. *It her own body.* No one got the right to say what should and shouldn't be, really. If you wants an abortion, you just get one anyway. My sister friend got an abortion. *Man, she in pain—* more before than after.

Brunner: Several of you have mentioned abortion as a solution to unwanted pregnancies. Besides abortions, are there other solutions?

Rafaleh (8th): A lot of people don't want to take their baby out into the world so they put it up for adoption.

Gaiya (8th): Yeah, that another solution. But sometime it ain't we don't want the baby, it that we got no way to care for it ceptin goin on the welfare. And maybe we don't want that.

Tyrone (6th): (pointing his finger) Anyway, it a sin to have sex without being married.

Lucretia (8th): What are you, a preacher? [followed by laughter and jibes]

Brunner: Well, that may be something to consider. [No one took up that subject, thus topic was closed.]

Structuring Dialogue

Most students were eager to speak. In fact, the most challenging aspect of this form of class discussion was to get students to talk one at a time. I said several times that what each student had to say was important but that no one could be heard if more than one person spoke at a time. This verbal declaration of the importance of each student's contribution to the conversation seemed to have the greatest effect on the manner in which the discussion continued. Students began to regulate each other, and when more than one student spoke at a time, another would remind the one talking out of turn that the group could only hear one of them.

Given the opportunity, students raised questions and suggested alternatives. In doing so, they broadened meanings and understandings of the text in question as they made their own alternative meanings— not necessarily ones the school or even Sebestyen, the author of the story, might have had in mind. I simply facilitated this process; discus-

sion techniques and texts made possible the conditions for critical thinking, and the students did the rest.

What made this discussion educative? First, the topic was of interest
to everyone in the room, and students were allowed to maintain the
discussion as long as it was productive. In fact, when I attempted a topic
change by asking several questions and offering a clarifying statement,
students refused to relinquish topic control and returned to the subject
of teen pregnancy and its multilayered, problematic nature, extending
the text and reporting their own understandings. A second and important consideration had to do with the structure of the text.

Social Dynamics in the Classroom

I noted the following about classroom dynamics: First, students
understood that the discussion was theirs. By allowing students to discuss what mattered to them, I apparently sent a message that I believed
they made an important contribution. Second, students' unwillingness
to change topics, instead extending the subject of teenage pregnancy to
abortion and then to adoption, illustrates their capacity for problem-
solving. Third, females tended to hold the floor longer than males. The
speech exchange seemed uneven, with males sometimes having to insert their statements more forcefully and often with gestures (e.g.,
pointing a finger and calling premarital sex a sin). I assumed this was
partly related to the age and physical size of males and females in the
group (most of the preteen and 13-year-old females were larger than
males in the class). Because speech acts are often predicated upon power
relations within any group, this unevenness seemed also to indicate a
resistance by females to indulging the male members of the group—
rather than indulging males as Dale Spender's *Man Made Language* (1980)
suggests females often do, simply keep the conversation going. Spender's research shows males and females interacting in ways that suggest
females tend to take on the role of accommodater in order to keep the
conversation going. That is, women more often ask questions to which
they know men will respond with detail. The females in this study
seemed to resist such behavior.

The Role of the Text

Having considered the implications of this kind of teaching versus
standard instruction, a second consideration as to why an open-ended,
student-regulated discussion can be educative has to do with the structure of the text in question (Barthes, 1974; Eco, 1979; Iser, 1978; Williams,
1977). Both the form and content of the text we were discussing lent
itself to oppositional meanings. Tina's mother, Mary, used statements of

traditional sentiment, while Tina countered with a somewhat less traditional, more enlightened view. Williams (1977) calls meanings associated with the mother's language "residual," and he calls the opposing or extended meanings "emergent." Residual meanings are seen in lines like this one from Mary, after she learned of Tina's offer of refuge to her pregnant friend, Sharon: "The last thing I need is a tenth-grade dropout with a fatherless child on the way." The meaning conveyed here is consistent with what many parents, teachers, and much of society considers appropriate: A pregnant teenager is certain to be a dropout, someone to be scorned, and certainly not a good influence to have around the house. Without problematizing such a statement, adolescents would likely draw generalizations that suggest that such is the *sexual experience* of a particular group of people (unwed teenagers). The mother's statement is followed by this one from Tina: "There's always a father. . . . She just doesn't want him around. . . . He's a creep. She doesn't really like him." Tina's retort points out two things: First, that Tina is not stupid; she knows there is a father. Second, loving/liking someone is important, especially if that person is to help raise your child. Tina's language provides a sense of the emergence of new meanings associated with what some teenagers know about life and pregnancy.

On the other hand, Tina is not blinded by Sharon's infatuation over having "something really truly her very own." Tina's fear shows in her knowledge that Sharon is about to "gulp down whole chunks of life" that she "hadn't even dared to taste." Contradictions between language and action (between form and content) seem to represent those present in a society that claims to value change but tends to reward stasis, status quo, and sameness. This view actually mirrors the story's most contradictory elements.

For example, only two references suggest that Tina and her family are black and Sharon is white. In the second paragraph of the story an 80-year-old aunt is described as having "corn-row hair she must have made with a real hoe," and later in the story Tina's mother calls Sharon a "bubble-headed blonde," a stereotypical swipe at (caucasian) blonde females. Language and idiomatic expressions are consonant with what is frequently used in the rural South or Southwest, a life-style the author knew because of her own family background.

However, a biographical sketch at the end of the story states, "Like 'Welcome,' all of Sebestyen's stories end on a warm, upbeat note. Also like 'Welcome,' much of her writing reflects her own [white] Southern heritage and early life in a small Texas town" (Sebestyen, 1984, p. 59). And like Rudine Sims (1980) in an article entitled "Words by Heart: A Black Perspective" published in the *Interracial Books for Children Bulletin*, I have to ask, why write about a black family and not about her own?

This author may have created subtle racist overtones in her story.

For example, we learn that Sharon's mother is "in Florida with four step-children and her dad got an ultimatum from his girl friend." Tina then asks, "Who's she supposed to turn to besides us?" Something subtle here suggests that Sharon is a poor white from a class that would naturally have more in common with a black family. Since Sebestyen is a white author, with Sims I wonder why she created a black family in the first place. If Tina's family had also been white, readers would have had yet another opportunity to learn more about white families who struggle. In other words, readers need more stories that depict poor whites who struggle because literature traditionally depicts (and thus perpetuates the notion that it is) African Americans or Mexican Americans who struggle to survive. Or why let it seem as though teenage, out-of-wedlock pregnancy occurs only among a certain class of people? Would a black author writing this story have chosen to emphasize the same things? Or does it matter, given the fact that students reacted well to the story in a class discussion? How might they have reacted without a forum in which to discuss some of the subtleties within this text?

These textual contradictions, combined with open discussion, allow for the construction of a sensibility drawn out of students' own diverse experiences—a sensibility that does not suggest a singular teenage experience with sexuality and/or pregnancy. (See, e.g., in this volume, Chapter 4 on "scripting" and Chapter 7 on the "impact of culture and ideology" on the construction of one's sexuality). In the following student's journal we can see how unique experiences tend to create such a sensibility.

Journal Response

I proposed a journal assignment at the close of our discussion of "Welcome" since there were a number of students who had not participated. Loretta, a ninth-grader, is the only student who responded in her journal. Her response, which follows, is in the form of a letter.

My dreams are shattered and my life is in a cocoon. My child is now without a father or a friend. I do sometimes wish that I didn't have her anymore[;] she cries so much and uses up so much money. . . . She erased any hope for me to meet another man in my life forever. . . . To me my life is wrecked and I have no one to turn to for moral support and to try to keep me and my baby alive I must bumb and dig in trash cans. . . . I think I will [give] my baby up or leave her stranded in a trash can or on the doorsteps of some-ones house that I think can take care of her even though I couldn't. Then I can . . . start a new life of my own not having to worry about the welfare of my baby because I know that she will be in a very good home and she will be okay. I am writing this letter and attaching this letter to my baby because I want you to know that I do so really love my baby with all my heart and soul[,] and if I wasn't so poor I would never have given my baby up. I know you are going to be really nice parents to my baby[;] I have watched you. Thank you for the support. Give her to a good foster home if you don't want to keep my baby. GOOD BYE. SINCERELY YOURS FOREVER, S. T. R. MOTHER

Loretta entitled this journal entry "GRIEF."

Particularly for many black and other minority students, this picture is not uncommon. An unwanted pregnancy, whether the person is married or not, often creates a financial burden of mammoth proportions. When the construction of one's sexuality is predicated upon one's race and the specific set of economic constraints that may follow, the birthing experience, like any other experience, takes on a unique dimension. In such an instance choices may be more associated with survival than with desire.

A study conducted by Betty Bardige (1988) affirms adolescents' sensibilities in terms of moral development. Her data, which show adolescents having a "profoundly moral sense of justice and concern for others," suggest categories of thinking that are a departure from theories that posit a strong developmental link between cognitive ability and moral development (p. 93). Bardige's point here is that students' sensibilities were revealed during journal writing and discussion, very different intellectual processes from the usual problem-solving or sentence completion task. Data from the present study support her findings.

Perspectival Thinking

Taking a stand while creating a more complete scenario that includes responsibility could be considered a form of perspective-taking. Flavell, Botkin, Fry, Wright, and Jarvis (1975) discuss perspectival thinking with regard to role-taking abilities in children. Perspective-taking seems to be characterized by a larger worldview that considers other people and their perspectives and recognizes the importance of decision making. On at least three subjects related to pregnancy (birth control, abortion, and adoption), students in this study appeared to display this kind of thinking.

Comments like those from David (e.g., "You gonna have sex, you better protect yourself") that were not countered by any other students suggest that at least some young black males consider birth control not just the female's responsibility. At the very least, this thinking may represent a degree of sophistication and maturity not expected in young teenagers. Though many would agree with Ruth Hubbard (1990) that "teenagers do not act 'responsibly'—teenage pregnancies and abortions are on the rise and teenage fathers do not acknowledge and support their partners and babies" (p. 130), the social responsibility intimated in statements like David's suggests yet another alternative worldview considering his age, race, and social class.

Residual and Emergent Meanings

Like the text, some of the messages students conveyed about sexuality indicated residual and emergent meanings—those contrary notions that need lots of discussion in order for understanding to occur. For example, Tyrone's pointed statement, "It a sin to have sex without being married," suggests traditional meanings regarding sexuality. Lots more discussion could and should have followed that statement, as well as a statement like "It's stupid to get pregnant when you can't afford it," which indicates that Lucretia considers other problems beyond the traditional religious code. Emergent meanings can also be seen in students' discussion of abortion and adoption, and in Loretta's journal writing in particular.

Those meanings that reflect a nontraditional view are often seen in terms of student resistance to the power and control of dominant interests. Studies (Lubeck, 1988; Ogbu, 1988; Weis, 1985; Willis, 1977) suggest that whether consciously or not, some minority students reject the official knowledge of schooling. Sally Lubeck's study (1988), though speaking of black *teachers* in particular, shows their "values and attitudes" in the classroom to be "congruent with experiences outside of school" (p. 53). This seemed to be particularly evident in student responses in this study.

CONCLUSION

Critical thinking and/or dialogue about a subject as important as sexuality, and in this particular instance teen pregnancy, presents some real challenges, including how to get younger adolescent students to have an educative discussion about sex. A genuine dialogue suggests the importance of sexuality as a relevant subject in their lives that deserves attention—a subject that even preadolescents already have a good deal of personal knowledge about, as this study indicates. Young people need the opportunity to work through their notions and their experiences with sex, accepting and even discussing themselves as sexual beings.

In this chapter I have discussed the importance of including sexuality education in any area of the curriculum where educative discussion might occur, especially language arts. My data-based illustrations of discussions around literature as opportunities for students to better understand complex issues related to sexuality suggests that taking a collective approach to teaching—multiple voices rather than one privileged voice—is possible, but not easy (Apple, 1982). My findings also suggest the importance of providing meaning-making opportunities, especially regarding sexuality, which are most likely absent in traditional settings.

NOTES

Acknowledgments. I want to extend my gratitude to Rashidah Jaami' Muhammad for allowing me to enter her classroom to conduct the response study on which this chapter is based and for her assistance and valuable feedback both during the study and throughout the writing of this chapter. Many of the book titles and annotations included in the annotated resources at the end of the book are courtesy of Peter Butts, a local middle school librarian who has completed an extensive compilation in gender studies.

1. Much of the discussion around issues of sexuality that occurred in relation to stories read for this response study would not have been possible in many/most public school language arts classrooms. In Michigan, for example, only in cases where the language arts instructor is also certified in health/sexuality education would such conversation be permissible in public schools (L. Shapiro, personal communication, December 8, 1990). Because this was a summer enrichment program that took place in a school setting other than public school, I was allowed greater flexibility in both form and content of discussion and materials chosen for the study. Again, the institute does not consider itself an alternative school; its programs are supplemental. On the other hand, the Barbara Taylor School described in Chapter 6 by Christine LaCerva is an alternative school that advocates sexuality education across its curriculum.

REFERENCES

Anyon, J. M. (1981). Social class and school knowledge. *Curriculum Inquiry, 11*, 3–42.

Apple, M. W. (1982). *Education and power.* Boston, MA: Routledge and Kegan Paul.

Bardige, B. (1988). Things so finely human: Moral sensibilities at risk in adolescence. In C. Gilligan, J. Ward, J. Taylor, with B. Bardige (Eds.), *Mapping the moral domain* (pp. 87–110). Cambridge, MA: Harvard University Press.

Barthes, R. (1974). *S/Z*. New York: Hill & Wang.

Bernstein, B. (1975). *Class, codes, and control: Towards a theory of educational transmissions.* London: Routledge & Kegan Paul.

Bleich, D. (1978). *Subjective criticism.* Baltimore, MD: Johns Hopkins University Press.

Childress, A. (1973). *A hero ain't nothing but a sandwich*. New York: Avon.

Cormier, R. (1984). In the heat. In D. Gallo (Ed.), *Sixteen* (pp. 154–162). New York: Dell.

Eco, U. (1979). *The role of the reader: Explorations in the semiotics of texts*. Bloomington: Indiana University Press.

Eyerly, J. (1963). *Drop-out*. Philadelphia: Lippincott.

Feshbach, N., Dillman, A., & Jordan, T. (1979). Portrait of a female on television: Some possible effects on children. In C. Kopp with M. Kirkpatrick (Eds.), *Becoming female* (pp. 363–385). New York: Plenum.

Flavell, J. H., Botkin, P. T., Fry, C. L., Wright, J. W., & Jarvis, P. E. (1975). *The development of role-taking communication skills in children*. Huntington, NY: Robert E. Krieger.

Foucault, M. (1990). *The history of sexuality: Vol. 2. The use of pleasure* (R. Hurley, Trans.). New York: Random House.

Freire, P. (1970). *Pedagogy of the oppressed* (M. B. Ramos, Trans.). New York: Continuum.

Galda, L. (1983). Research in response to literature. *Journal of Research and Development in Education, 16*, 1–7.

Holland, N. H. (1968). *The dynamics of literary response*. New York: W. W. Norton.

Hubbard, R. (1990). *The politics of women's biology*. New Brunswick, NJ: Rutgers University Press.

Iser, W. (1978). *The art of reading: A theory of aesthetic response*. Baltimore, MD: Johns Hopkins University Press.

Lubeck, S. (1988). Nested contexts. In L. Weiss (Ed.), *Class, race, and gender in American education* (pp. 43–62). Albany: SUNY Press.

McNeil, L. M. (1988). *Contradictions of control: School structure and school knowledge*. New York: Routledge, Chapman and Hall.

Myers, W. D. (1975). *Fast Sam, Cool Clyde, and stuff*. New York: Viking.

Ogbu, J. U. (1988). Class stratification, racial stratification, and schooling. In L. Weis (Ed.), *Class, race, and gender in American education* (pp. 163–182). Albany: SUNY Press.

Roberts, E. J. (1980). Sexuality and social policy: The unwritten curriculum. In E. Robets (Ed.), *Childhood sexual learning* (pp, 259–278). Cambridge, MA: Ballinger.

Rosenblatt, L. M. (1976). *Literature as exploration*. New York: Noble and Noble. (Original work published 1938)

Rosenblatt, L. M. (1978). *The reader, the text, the poem: The transactional theory of the literary work*. Carbondale: Southern Illinois University Press.

Sebestyen, O. (1984). Welcome. In D. Gallo (Ed.), *Sixteen* (pp. 48–59). New York: Dell.

Shor, I. (1987). Educating the educators: A Freirean approach to the crisis in teacher education. In I. Shor (Ed.), *Freire for the classroom: A sourcebook for liberatory teaching* (pp. 7–32). Portsmouth: Heinemann.

Shor, I., & Freire, P. (1987). What is the "dialogical method" of teaching? In I. Shor & P. Freire (Eds.), *A pedagogy for liberation* (pp. 97–119). South Hadley, MA: Bergin & Garvey.

Sims, R. (1980). Words by heart: A black perspective. *Interracial Books for Children Bulletin, 12*(7), 12–15, 17.

Spender, D. (1980). *Man made language.* Boston: Routledge & Kegan Paul.

Taxel, J. (1981). The outsiders of the American revolution: The selective tradition in children's fiction. *Interchange, 12,* 206–228.

Taxel, J. (1984). The American revolution in children's fiction: An analysis of historical meaning and narrative structure. *Curriculum Inquiry, 14,* 7–55.

Weis, L. (1985). Excellence and student class, race, and gender cultures. In P. Altbach, G. Kelly, & L. Weis (Eds.), *Excellence in education: Perspective on policy and practice* (pp. 217–232). Buffalo, NY: Prometheus Press.

Wexler, P. (1982). Structure, text, and subject: A critical sociology of school knowledge. In M. W. Apple (Ed.), *Cultural and economic reproduction in education: Essays on class, ideology, and the state* (pp. 275–303). London: Routledge & Kegan Paul.

Wexler, P. (1987). *Social analysis of education: After the new sociology.* London: Routledge & Kegan Paul.

Whitty, G. (1985). *Sociology and school knowledge: Curriculum theory, research and politics.* London: Methuen.

Williams, R. (1977). *Marxism and literature.* London: Oxford University Press.

Willis, P. (1977). *Learning to labor: How working class kids get working class jobs.* Lexington, MA: D. C. Heath.

What's "Left" in Sexuality Education?

LYNN PHILLIPS AND MICHELLE FINE

As feminist educators, we teach and write about the politics of gender, race, class, and sexuality, and about the politics of teaching itself. We spend much of our time reflecting on teaching *about* the political, and on teaching *as* the political. And we take part in a variety of conversations, both "official" and "behind closed doors," discussing the various shapes and directions that sexuality education should take. And so, when asked to comment on these essays on meaning-making in sexuality education, we eagerly anticipated writing our visions of the best of "what could be."

Stepping into the task, however, we find ourselves instead quite sobered. It is increasingly clear that given the past decade's dramatic national shift to the Right, it makes little sense to offer up "ideal visions" without interrogating critically the pedagogical implications of a political climate that is fundamentally hostile to a textured exploration of sexuality, outraged by feminism, and well financed to undermine efforts to advocate critically for and educate with students. This essay, therefore, is less an exploration of "the ideal," and more an invitation to a public conversation about the possibilities and constraints of meaning-making in sexuality education, under the disturbing and saturating cloud of the New Right.

We impart three related, though sometimes conflicting, frames to our analyses of sexuality education. We are qualitative researchers who want to know how adolescents construct and make meaning of their own sexual subjectivities, and how teaches and schools might midwife that process. We are also teachers, interested in facilitating collective meaning-making, committed to offering students deep and critical slices of social knowledge, and eager to foster a collective sense of entitlement to imagine, create, and select life possibilities critically and carefully. Finally, we are feminist activists, interested in interrupting structured silences and pressing the boundaries of public sexuality talk.

Lately, we find ourselves musing together about the growing space between and among these three stances in our conversations about sexuality education. Reflecting on this space, we worry that our activist voices, usually strong and at home in the classroom, are being quietly pushed into the private realm. As faculty at a private university, we face few explicit institutional constraints relative to teachers in elementary and secondary schools. And yet as more and more students, even at our university, preface their comments with, "It's against my religion to take part in discussion of . . . ," we worry that we are becoming complicit in our own silencing. A growing national and institutional climate of conservatism constricts our language, the topics we allow ourselves to address within the classroom, and the ambiguities we invite ourselves to muck around with publicly. We worry that conversations about ambivalence and contradiction have retreated into the privacy of our offices. These are the very conversations we have always needed to have in our classrooms—indeed, they are the very conversations we openly invited in our classrooms only a few years ago, before they were watered down and silenced by the roaring tide of the Right. Our colleagues in public elementary and secondary schools experience, more powerfully than we, the Right's efforts to silence the discourse surrounding sexuality— especially adolescent female sexuality. Thus, creating the space for ambiguities, critique, and analysis in the classroom becomes increasingly difficult at precisely the moment that it takes on such acute importance.

We are particularly concerned about how this silencing results in a narrowed and increasingly biologized construction of "what counts" as sexuality and sexuality education, and in a constraining of our abilities as concerned educators to offer meaningful support to students who come to us in need of information and advocacy, whether in class or in private.

WHAT COUNTS?

Sexuality education in public schools is typically constructed around an "official curriculum" that "structures in" hegemonic silences, orchestrates the preservation of cultural power arrangements, and denies social taboos in the name of being value-free. As a consequence, taboos include the naming and exploration of abortion, masturbation, adolescent (particularly female) desire, homosexuality, and, despite the rhetoric of concern about teen pregnancy, contraception. Even as educators strive to push beyond the official curriculum, we know from reports of public school teachers that they are evaluated on the basis of a "value-free" discourse that privileges and "naturalizes" chastity, marriage, and heterosexuality; that denigrates teen motherhood; and that hesitates to discuss abortion lest they be "leading" the young woman (as if *not mentioning* is not "leading").

The official curriculum typically severs notions and discussions of sexuality from constructions of gender politics, violence, heterosexism, and the economics of reproduction. It is, simply, a curriculum that in its sparcity teaches a reproductive heterosexuality serving dominant interests. Teaching "only the facts" means teaching male pleasure and heterosexual privilege (as if that in and of itself were sexuality), absent from critique, distinguished as if separable from violence, and devoid of female desire. This curriculum is one that students and teachers need to critique actively in order to understand how language, silences, and ideologies maintain certain sexual arrangements and practices as legitimate, while exporting others to the categories of Deviance, Disgust, and Disease. Centrally, such a curriculum ignores the real contexts of students' lived sexualities and reproductive concerns.

ADVOCACY AND CRITICAL PEDAGOGY—NEEDED AND WITHHELD

Such a paring down of the sexuality curriculum constricts not only the content (un)covered, but also the depth and authenticity of teachers' pedagogical interactions with adolescents. One suburban educator, for instance, recently explained to us that while she feels free, within her school, to show students a film on AIDS, her district has decided that "we don't do condoms." She was instructed, therefore, to turn off the film 10 minutes before its end, when condoms were being discussed. Unable to stray too far for fear of "opening" topics that they are unable or unwilling to engage (analogous to women's fear of "arousing" without "satisfying"), educators in such settings convey a message of taboo that is all too clear to their students. Critical reflections on both the politics and the practices of sexualities are thereby rendered moot/mute.

The constricting of sexuality education has further implications for teachers' ability to advocate with students who are facing complex and important sexuality-related decisions. At a recent informal meeting of public school educators, for example, a group of teachers began discussing, "What are we allowed to say to a young girl who comes to us, is pregnant, and wants an abortion?" The consensus among these 15 very committed and connected urban educators was that they had to say, "Well, I can't really talk to you about this, but . . ." One progressive woman added, "You can tell them to call the —— hotline." This hotline is a local resource offering women information about all of their reproductive options. But it does not offer abortion services itself. It is, therefore, "OK" according to Board regulations. Referrals to Planned Parenthood, however, would be prohibited by Board policy. Such a deep censoring of teachers requires that they self-consciously remove themselves as critical adults from conversation with adolescents about decisions vital to students' health. Teachers' active (if imposed) silence in such cases supports the likelihood that an adolescent will continue her pregnancy with information about neither abortions nor prenatal care. We understand how, in the midst of conservative pressures, silence may seem "safer." But we know, of course, that our silence speaks loudly. It always supports the status quo. And it literally endangers students' lives.

REFLECTIONS ON MEANING-MAKING IN SEXUALITY EDUCATION

Within this politically suffocating context, long-standing concerns in sexuality education take on new dimensions of complexity. We find ourselves grappling with increasingly complicated questions and unforeseen dilemmas. Here, we examine—and reexamine—our own thoughts on a set of particularly compelling themes raised by the provocative chapters in this section:

1. The role of *multicultural perspectives* in the development of sexuality education
2. The notion that *"democratic education"* should involve giving information and fostering a sense of entitlement so that students can move individually toward "informed decisions"
3. The desire for a critical surfacing of *student voices* in classrooms committed to adolescent meaning-making.

We devote the remainder of this essay, then, to a consideration of the tensions and implications of each of these themes within sexuality education.

On Multicultural Education

Like Ward and Taylor in Chapter 9, we believe that sexuality education must authentically infuse the beliefs, practices, and values of multiple cultures. In order to speak to (and be heard with/by) a student population that is richly multicultural, sexuality curricula must be shaped in collaboration with members of students' own cultures and communities. Such collaboration, we would hope, could not only make sexuality education more culturally relevant for students, but could also begin to unravel and problematize dominant cultural constructions of "sexuality."

Inspired as we are by this vision, however, we also find ourselves concerned—concerned that in the very process of trying to expand sexuality discourse beyond the prevailing conservative categories, we may, ironically, exacerbate the silencing. First, we struggle with the question of who represents which "culture." Often, community members who get to speak *for* their cultures are selected as the Official Representatives of (sometimes quite conservative) community institutions, who deliver packaged positions, rarely rich in contradiction. They are neither necessarily empowering for students, nor particularly representative of the students' or the full community's concerns and desires. We are not sure what we should do if the values of these representatives dictate that we *not teach* information (such as access to contraception, abortion, and STD prevention) or attitudes (such as entitlement to choice, sexual equality, and desire) that we as educators consider vital to a fuller understanding of sexuality and critical to health. When conflicts arise, who, ultimately, decides what students "really need"?

We worry, too, about the political implications of having "culture" represented by organized religious groups. On the one hand, community members may consider the voice of organized religion to be the most authentic rendering of their cultural concerns. On the other hand, however, many gains supported by progressive educators rest on the separation of church and state in public schooling. In the midst of the New Right's efforts to replace discussions of sexuality, contraception, abortion, and even evolution with mandatory prayer and readings of Genesis, we rely heavily on the argument that diverse religious beliefs are respected and studied, but are not, themselves, shapers of the classroom text.

We are by no means suggesting that the costs of multicultural sexuality education outweigh its importance. We are, however, reminded of the need to incite conversations about which public is being invited in—and for what. How do we decipher "culture" and still problematize the dominant culture? How do we begin a conversation rich in the tensions we face and yet critical of the potential for multicultural perspectives to be used to buttress a conservative and silencing Right? What principles do we have to buy into in order for a full and pluralistic conversation to commence? And *whose* principles are these?

On Democratic Education

As educators, our primary goal is to engage students in deep, critical, and democratic conversations geared toward unraveling multiple, partial, informed frames on their worlds. We seek, through this process, to foster students' sense of entitlement to know/ask/critique/decide, both individually and collectively. We take seriously Patti Lather's (1990) warning against trying to teach *to* a particular outcome, or *toward* a particular process. And yet, given the powerful silencing of the Right, we cannot sit comfortably inside a pedagogy of relativism.

The notion of simply offering students "the facts," or even "all choices," as if they were evenly weighted options makes little sense to us when students and teachers confront institutional and social climates that privilege certain options and refuse to examine those privileges critically. Today there is no fair playing field. Public schools are, for some students, the *only* place in which some options, such as abortion, can (and therefore must) be discussed aloud. This needs to happen *before* a young woman is faced with a pregnancy. The layers of silencing are so textured that young women rarely get to interview a peer who has experienced an abortion. And yet they often meet peers who have children. They rarely get to hear that "abortion is the best thing that ever happened to me." They do not hear that young women in Baltimore who have had abortions are personally and academically far more successful than those who have had babies in their teen years (Zabin, Hirsch, & Boscia, 1990). Yet they ritualistically hear from peers of the delights and dilemmas of teen motherhood, and, of course, they hear from the broader official culture of the joys of chastity. They rarely get to hear that women who masturbate report greater pleasure in their sexuality with partners and higher self-esteem. Yet, they receive countless messages that their bodies are dirty and their desires are dangerous. Under such conditions, presenting students with a menu of options cast in relativistic terms amounts, as Bonnie Trudell suggests in Chapter 10, to an endorsement of only those options supported by the dominant culture, and a refusal to engage conversations about power. We agree with Donna Haraway (1988) when she writes,

> The alternative to relativism is not totalization and single vision, which is always finally the unmarked category whose power depends on systematic narrowing and obscuring. The alternative to relativism is partial, locatable, critical knowledges sustaining the possibility of webs of connection called solidarity in politics and shared conversations in epistemology. (p. 584)

We are concerned, further, that the liberal strategy of "giving students information and a sense of entitlement, and then leaving them alone to decide" essentially reifies an androcentric notion that development, decisions, and moral dilemmas are worked out within the minds of isolated, autonomous individuals, rather than in the context of relationships, responsibilities, conversations, and consequences. In light of the general androcentric bias that runs throughout schooling, and in light of our goal within sexuality education to pierce sexuality discourse with conversations around power, we are compelled to explore ways of supporting students' decision making as they search for deep, contextualized, temporal, and transitive meanings.

On Privileging Student Voices

Finally, we agree with Diane Brunner who argues in Chapter 11 that sexuality education must engage students and begin from their voiced perspectives, facilitating and reframing their individual and collective constructions of meanings. Student-centered classrooms that authorize student voices, stories, and interpretations allow for much-needed active exploration and ongoing explicit critique of ideas.

While we embrace such pedagogies with enthusiasm, we also recognize the need to question what it is that we think we are "getting" when we listen to students' stories in our classrooms. Is this their culture? Their uncontaminated, raw meanings? Their public display of "adolescent cultural understandings" of sexuality? Their hegemonic voicing of the ideas and assumptions of the dominant culture? That is, while it is critical to understand and teach from where students are "at," it is also important not to essentialize that which students display as "pure" anything.

We often hear assumptions that student voices will stand automatically in critical opposition to the dominant culture, if only we let *them* shine through in the classroom. But given the social nature of the construction of meaning, and given the increasingly pervasive and persuasive influence of the Right, it would be short-sighted to assume that adolescents have developed perspectives that are somehow "untainted" by, even transcendent of, the dominant discourse of sexuality.

In light of accusations that progressive educators are trying to "brainwash" students, it may be tempting to wish that student voices would automatically speak with critique. But we have much evidence to suggest that adolescents, like the rest of society, deeply support homophobia, date rape, and narrow, male-centered biological notions of (hetero)sexuality. Educators need to be prepared to attend carefully, respectfully, and dramatically to students' understandings, while never subverting our role *as educators*, which is to press students to challenge and reframe their own, as well as others', constructed meanings.

REFLECTIONS ON OUR REFLECTIONS

We really didn't write this essay to toss the sexuality debates back a decade. Nor did we intend to silence ourselves further. We sought to narrate, from both distressing and delicious experiences, the openings to conversations that we think feminist educators of sexuality need to be having together, and with our students, about the politics of our classroom talk.

While we must continue to assert our responsibility to infuse considerations of ethnicity and culture, student voices, and activism into sexuality education, such assertions won't replace deep, ongoing, and transformative conversations about the powers of silencing, language, and social change as they lace with our lived sexualities. Perhaps our most hopeful notion is that we can carve out educational contexts in which students are researching precisely the questions and dilemmas we have posed in this essay: investigating how and why public talk about abortion, parental consent, masturbation, and homosexuality is so unsettling; studying how social "problems" such as teen pregnancy are represented in the popular press with respect to race, class, and gender bias; unearthing the multiple and contradictory positions on sexuality that loiter within every racial/ethnic/religious community; analyzing the tests and assumptions of state parental consent legislation; interviewing progressive and conservative activists and educators about the impact of the New Right on sexuality work. Such projects invite students not only to press the boundaries of sexuality discourse but also to move further to confront the forces that impose them.

If we, as feminist theorists and educators, have anything to impart, it is the capacity and courage to look critically at social arrangements, to chart out spaces for rigorous analyses of power, and to seek out intellectual and political surprises. Perhaps this is the greatest gift we can give our students—the invitation to interrupt the structured silences that deprive them of the critical sexuality educations they so desperately need and deserve.

REFERENCES

Haraway, D. (1988). Situated knowledges: The science question in feminism and the privilege of partial perspectives. *Feminist Studies, 4,* 575–597.

Lather, P. (1990). *Staying dumb? Student resistance to liberatory curriculum.* Paper presented at the annual meeting of the American Educational Research Association, Boston.

Zabin, L. S., Hirsch, M. B., & Boscia, J. A. (1990). Differential characteristics of adolescent pregnancy test patients: Abortion, childbearing and negative test groups. *Journal of Adolescent Health Care, 11,* 107–113.

Part IV

PROBLEMATICS OF CHANGE

Operating from a variety of theoretical frameworks, the authors contributing to this section detail alternative approaches to sexuality education. Seven reflective practitioners outline suggestive curricular content, instructional approaches, and reform strategies for sexuality educators who share our belief in the necessity of reconceptualizing sexuality and the curriculum to extend beyond its cognitive and behavioral focus. Based upon the theoretical and research insights presented in previous chapters, these contributors invite the reader to reflectively examine: the what and how of teaching sexuality to preschool age children, physically disabled young adults, and children with mental retardations; the alternatives to the narrow preventive focus of contemporary sexuality education aimed at the reduction of HIV/AIDS cases and the number of teenage pregnancies; and the public arenas wherein resistance and contestation and "open multiple arenas for dialogue and action," culminating in curricular, social, and personal change.

The ultimate goal of sexuality education, asserts Patricia Koch in Chapter 12, is the adoption of sexual practices that promote and enhance satisfying and healthy sexual expression among *all* persons. Seldom does sexuality education meet this goal. Too frequently sexuality education fails to integrate the cognitive (facts, data, information) with the affective (feelings, values, and attitudes) and the behavioral (skills to communicate effectively and make responsible decisions) domains. While Koch cautions that "there is no cookbook of easy 'recipes' for sexuality education," she aptly illustrates a variety of "multidimensional holistic learning experiences" rooted in existential psychology and contemporary curriculum thinking. Chapter 12 details some of these experiences for three populations not yet addressed in this text: preschool age children, children with mental disabilities, and young adults with physical disabilities.

Locating HIV/AIDS education within the history of school-based sexuality education and the broader context of public health efforts to control sexually transmitted diseases, Jonathan Silin in Chapter 13 describes and evaluates the instrumentalist assumptions underlying current information- and skills-based approaches to HIV/AIDS education. Silin argues that an approach to HIV//AIDS education that emphasizes adolescent sexual knowledge and behavior will "not make us safe from the effects of HIV. . . . Preventing the transmission of HIV involves not only learning about condoms and spermicides and negotiating sex; it also means developing tools of political analysis, a commitment to social change, and an ethic of caring and responsibility." This chapter outlines the elements of this alternative curricular approach.

Building upon Silin's concern for an ethic of caring and responsibility, Diane Lee and Louise Berman in Chapter 14 present recommendations for rethinking teenage pregnancy by emphasizing potentiality, caring, and communication. These authors say the issue of teenage sexuality, pregnancy, and childbearing is conventionally viewed as a *well-structured* problem that can be solved through anatomical discussion. But they see it as an *ill-structured* problem—a problem with broad parameters and for which there is no single correct solution. Framed this way, appropriate sex education curricula need to be comprehensive and involve professionals form many fields as well as teens, their parents, and the community. The authors discuss several comprehensive school-based, mentoring, and alternative school programs that "offer solutions far beyond sex education."

The final chapter in Part IV is an analysis of three arenas of interest and power within which sexuality education policies are debated, designed, and implemented: the legislature, the state educational agency, and the local school district. From their vantage point as participant observers in a long-term effort to develop a sexuality education curriculum, Ruth Earls, Joanne Fraser, and Bambi Sumpter detail the events and actions within each of these arenas in this provocative case study. Chapter 15 details the contestations within each of these three arenas and discusses these arenas' inherent limitations and potentialities for reform-oriented, critically minded change agents. In the process they examine how political, economic, and cultural forces influence efforts to institutionalize a sexuality curriculum in a region of the country in which centralization has been a dominant feature of educational settings.

In the commentary to Part IV, Charol Shakeshaft details how sexual issues—a topic with which most administrators feel uncomfortable—shapes management strategies including hiring practices and organizational climate. Shakeshaft also discusses how this administrative uncomfortability "narrows and weakens policies and practices directly related to students," including the perpetuation of a hostile sexualized climate and the failure to address issues of sexual abuse.

CHAPTER 12

Integrating Cognitive, Affective, and Behavioral Approaches Into Learning Experiences for Sexuality Education

PATRICIA BARTHALOW KOCH

Sexuality encompasses the sexual knowledge, beliefs, feelings, atti-tudes, values, intentions, and behaviors of individuals (Sex Information and Education Council of the United States, 1990) and is certainly not limited to what a person does with her or his genitals. While sexuality involves anatomy, physiology, and biochemistry, it also includes self-concept, body concept, gender roles, relationships, life-styles, religious beliefs, societal mores, and much more. Sexual learning begins at the moment of one's birth and continues throughout one's life: from womb to tomb. This sexual learning is influenced directly and indirectly by a myriad of people (including parents, siblings, friends, peers, teachers, clergy, and partners) and occurs through innumerable planned and un-planned life experiences.

Too often both the formal and informal sexuality education that an individual receives in our society is inaccurate, fragmented, and dimin-ishing. Such incomplete and negative sexuality education has taken its physical, emotional, and social toll on individuals, as well as our society collectively. This is evidenced by such epidemic problems as unplanned teenage pregnancies, sexual dissatisfaction and dysfunction, sexual abuse, committed relationship dissolution, and infections of sexually transmissible diseases, including AIDS (Bell & Holmes, 1984; Bottom, 1980; Centers for Disease Control, 1988; Hall & Flannery, 1985; Jones et al., 1985; Koch, 1988; Strunin & Hingson, 1987). While many agree that parents ought to be the primary sexuality educators of their children, research finds the sexuality education that takes place in the home lack-ing (Fox, 1981; Hass, 1979).

The schools, from preschools to community colleges and universi-ties, can fill this void by providing comprehensive, accurate, positive, and enhancing sexuality education to our children, adolescents, and adults. The potential rippling effect of this education would be tremen-dous: Not only would students develop knowledge and understanding important to their present growth and development, but they would also be preparing to become sexuality educators in their future parental, professional, and/or community roles.

The Sex Information and Education Council of the United States (SIECUS) represents a variety of professionals, scholars, and organizations that believe the general objectives of sexuality education should be

> to provide students with accurate, relevant information; to provide students with educational opportunities to explore their sexual values, behaviors, and attitudes; to increase their self-esteem; and to provide them with a foundation for acquiring decision-making and communication skills in preparation for responsible adult sexual lives. (de Mauro, 1990, p. 2)

Yet even the best-intentioned teachers who are currently providing sexuality education in our schools are faced with formidable internal and external barriers to meeting these objectives, many of which are well articulated in Chapters 10 and 15 of this book. One of these barriers is the lack of preparation and support given teachers regarding sexuality education philosophy and methodologies (Kenney, Guardade, & Brown, 1989). This surely contributes to problems expressed by teachers of sexuality education such as student lack of interest or negative reactions, personal discomfort, and lack of materials upon which to base their lessons (Forrest & Silverman, 1989). The following discussion of philosophy and teaching is aimed at providing a solid foundation upon which sexuality education teachers can *create* meaningful learning experiences with their students.

PHILOSOPHICAL BASIS FOR SEXUALITY EDUCATION CURRICULUM

The philosophy upon which a curriculum is based is the driving force and soul of that curriculum and is of utmost importance when dealing with sexuality education. To be consistent with the goals and objectives of sexuality education previously described, an existential philosophy of education must be adopted. In this philosophical approach, as explained by Schubert (1986), curricula can be best described as journeys of learning experiences in which one engages in a process of critically questioning oneself and the world in which one lives. Learning becomes a series of personal encounters about ideas, feelings, and skills with other people, social institutions, and oneself. Human beings are understood as the creators of knowledge and agents of their own learning; students, therefore, must be active developers, not just passive receivers, of their own learning experiences and curriculum.

Through examination of one's own experiences, self-realization serves as the motivation for choice and action. Values are developed or accepted through conscious reflection, not held purely for the sake of tradition. Communicative action evolves between people who seem quite different in many ways but discover a bond of common human values (Habermas, 1984). Students, through small and large group discussions, become more "wide awake" and open to multiple perspectives that make the familiar strange and the strange familiar (Greene, 1978). One begins to perceive through different lenses by listening to others' thoughts and feelings. From this orientation, diversity and pluralism are both the means to learning about sexuality and ends to the curriculum.

Democratic action emerges within this model as each individual, studying his or her own needs, realizes that these are similar to the needs of others and that we can assist one another in meeting our needs more fully. Thus, "When subject matter moves teachers and learners from discord toward harmony, from monotony to variety, and from constraint to expansion, it has moved them in the direction of moral action" (Schubert, 1986, p. 295). Moral action pertaining to one's sexuality would include the adoption of sexual practices that promote satisfying, healthy, and enhancing sexual expression rather than those that are hurtful (e.g., abusive relationships, sexual assault, and rape), unhealthy (e.g., unsafe sex leading to sexually transmissible diseases, including AIDS), and diminishing (e.g., sexism and homophobia).

TEACHING IN THE SEXUALITY CURRICULUM

Teaching occurs through interaction with students, subject matter (curriculum) and environmental context. It can be viewed as "the artistry of every day intuition and decision making in the educational milieu [determined by the curriculum] by those who have the experience to be connoisseurs of their craft" (Schubert, 1986, p. 248). Indeed, much teaching occurs from curriculum enacted "on the spot" in response to what is happening in the classroom at the moment (Berman, 1990).

The teacher's primary role should not be one of a credentialed expert but rather one of a scientist and artist who develops insight into students' needs, interests, and purposes. A teacher should be able to lead her or his students in the creation of a "classroom society" in which learning experiences are relevant and interesting (Thelen, 1981).

The goal of learning experiences is less the acquisition of subject-specific content than the development of greater knowledge and understanding. To reach this goal, teacher and students must engage in reflective dialogue based on trust and mutual respect; the teacher, as a co-learner, joins other members of the classroom society in their openness to the transformation of individual experience. "The student, operating from a position of trust, must be willing to share embryonic and emerging thoughts and to reflect on them logically and psychologically" (Doll, 1990, p. 45). By engaging in this process, students "enfold themselves into the curriculum and unfold themselves to others in class" (Sears & Marshall, 1990, p. 38), as good teachers teach the process of empowerment while empowering their students. "When students share the burden of the classroom dialectic, classrooms become incubators in which ideas are germinated, shared, nurtured, argued, acted upon, and often transformed by teacher and students alike" (Marshall & Sears, 1990, p. 18).

LEARNING EXPERIENCES IN THE SEXUALITY CURRICULUM

The most effective strategy for facilitating learning is to relate subject matter to students' interests, needs, and experiences so that they are able to attach personal meaning to what is learned. From this perspective, "curriculum needs to be defined in terms of personal, lived experiences, rather than through some set of objectives, strategies, notions of scope and sequence, and artificial scenarios" designed by persons far removed from the students' lives (Kantor, 1990, p. 71). In these ways, a learning experience is much more meaningful and growth enhancing than the mere acquisition of subject matter of the participation in learning activities that are planned and executed on the basis of behavioral objectives.

Truly holistic learning experiences include the integration of elements from the cognitive, affective, and behavioral domains. In the sexuality curriculum, such integrated experiences help students gain a holistic understanding of sexuality (Carrera & Calderone, 1976; Moglia, 1990). Included in the cognitive domain are facts, data, information, concepts, and theories. The affective domain deals with one's feelings, attitudes, and values toward sexuality. In the behavioral domain, one acquires and practices the skills necessary for positive sexual expression, such as communication, assertiveness, decision making, and problem-solving. Various disciplines, including psychology (Fazio, 1990; Fishbein & Ajzen, 1975) and health education (Green, Kreuter, Deeds, & Patridge, 1980; Maiman & Becker, 1974) offer theories regarding the important relationships among cognition, affect, skills, and behavior. Empirical research investigating factors significantly related to sexual behaviors and sexual health practices support these theoretical frameworks (Hester & Macrina, 1985; McKusick, Wiley, Coates, & Morin, 1986; Simon & Das, 1984; St. Lawrence, Kelley, Hood, & Brasfield, 1987; Young, Koch, & Preston, 1989). In short, theoretical, empirical, and experiential evidence all indicate that the cognitive, affective, and behavioral domains work in consort to affect one's behavior and that dealing with any domain in isolation significantly reduces the impact of the learning experience.

Such multidimensional holistic learning experiences can be created to represent any sexuality topic with learners of any age, in any setting. Other authors in this book advocate for such learning experiences: in teaching college students about sexual identity (Chapter 8), in teaching sexuality education to immigrant and minority adolescents (Chapter 9), in redesigning HIV education (Chapter 13), and in restructuring programs on teenage pregnancy (Chapter 14). The rest of this chapter is devoted to providing specific illustrative examples of such learning experiences on a variety of topics with learners of differing ages.

Body Concept for Preschoolers

Our body concept is an important aspect of our total self-concept (Champion, Austin, & Tzeng, 1982; Fisher & Cleveland, 1968; Secord & Jourard, 1953), including our sexual self-esteem (Hutchinson, 1982). According to Koch and Young (1986), body concept includes:

1. Evaluation of the attractiveness of one's own body (often referred to as body image)
2. Evaluation of the functioning of one's own body
3. Feelings toward one's own body (e.g., disgust, acceptance, pride)
4. Feelings experienced from one's own body (e.g., pleasure, pain, fatigue)

The nature of one's body concept is learned, beginning in the earliest years, and is variable depending on life experiences. Unfortunately, many people have negative body concepts—females significantly more so than males (Berscheid, Walster, & Bohrnstedt, 1973; Lerner, Karabenick, & Stuart, 1973). In addition to lower self-esteem, poorer body concept is also related to poorer social relationships (Krantz & Friedberg, 1985); poorer academic performance (Lerner & Lerner, 1977); poorer health practices (Norris, 1970); and poorer physical health (Kurtz & Hirt, 1970). Therefore, it is crucial that the development of a positive body concept be an important goal of all sexuality curricula, beginning in our early childhood education programs.

Too few preschools and kindergartens include "formal" learning experiences about body concept, or any other aspects of sexuality for that matter. Yet, we send numerous indirect and negative messages to young children daily in these settings when we reprimand or even punish them for saying words like "dick," touching their "private parts," or engaging in body exploration with their peers. These learning experiences must be replaced by ones that are planned to help children learn the names of *all* of their body parts (cognitive domain), to feel good about all of these parts (affective domain), and to be able to use communication skills in expressing the different aspects of their body concept (behavioral domain). Following are examples of such learning experiences (Brick et al., 1989: Koch, 1985).

Children should be involved in experiences that teach the difference between public and private body parts—a distinction that can be illustrated using female and male dolls (preferably with genitals) clothed in bathing suits. Children can learn that the areas clothed are considered private in our society, but that private does not mean nasty, dirty, or funny. As the dolls are unclothed, children can learn the correct terms for these parts of the body. Typically, children use slang terms for these body parts ("boobs" for breasts, "pee-wee" for penis); as they are encouraged to use the correct, "grown-up" words, they will develop a sense of pride and competence in realizing that they are growing up.

Since young children love songs, chants, and games, and teachers already use many about "acceptable" body parts, they can be easily expanded to include the "private" parts, such as the breasts, buttocks, penis, and vulva.

> Little One, touch your nose.
> Little One, touch your buttocks.
> Little One, turn around.
> Little One, touch the ground.
> Little One, touch your breast.
> Little One, quietly sit down again.

> "Simon Sez" point to your ear, breast, ankle [substitute different parts of the body].
> "Simon Sez" point to the part you see with, you taste with, you urinate with [and so forth].

Throughout these activities, the children will probably make many nonverbal expressions of feelings (giggling, making faces, and so forth), since they may have already learned uneasiness or embarrassment about bodies. Such feelings should not be ignored, but rather students should be encouraged to express them in appropriate ways as the entire group explores why people have differing feelings about their bodies. Within these discussions, it is important that nudity be presented as something natural that is reserved in our society for private places. Children can be shown photographs of public (e.g., park, school, restaurant) and private (e.g., bathroom, bedroom) places to sort into piles. They can also be encouraged to draw their own pictures of these places.

When these activities, discussions, games, chants, and songs are incorporated naturally throughout the child's day and are treated as any other topic, the children will absorb the most critical message of all: Our bodies are an important, positive aspect of our lives that we should take care of, understand, and enjoy.

Sexual Abuse Prevention for Mentally Retarded Children

Many people have a split image of the mentally retarded person as being, on the one hand, sexless and, on the other hand, oversexed and as such, a threat to the community. In reality, mentally retarded people are not that much different from the rest of the population in terms of their range of sexual interests, needs, and desires. There does not seem to be a very high correlation between sex IQ and general IQ (Johnson, 1973). On the other hand, nearly everyone is "retarded" when it comes to sexual understanding, with one's intellectual capabilities decreasing and one's emotionality taking over. Mentally retarded persons have just as much right and need for sexuality education as everyone else, and research indicates that they can effectively learn a variety of sexual concepts (Zelman & Typer, 1976). Particular emphasis should be placed on the use of repetition, concrete materials, modeling and examples, clear nonverbal messages, and language appropriate to the learner's level. The Scarborough Method is useful in organizing concepts and skills for learning experiences from the most basic to the more complicated (Goldstein, 1972).

One area in which mentally retarded people are particularly in need of education is sexual abuse prevention, since they are especially vulnerable to exploitation (Kempton, 1975). Any sexual abuse prevention program, regardless of its intended audience, must be grounded in a comprehensive sexuality education curriculum so that students do not become frightened of sexual expression altogether. The learning experiences on setting sexual limits described below should follow other experiences about body awareness, relationships, and positive sexual expression (Koch, 1985). As with any other group of students, information, feelings and attitudes, and skills need to be addressed in the sexuality education of mentally retarded persons.

Children must learn that their bodies belong to them. The teacher can emphasize this by pointing to various parts of the student's body and stressing that this part belongs to him or her: "This is Maria's ear and it belongs to Maria; this is Max's penis and it belongs to Max." Ask the student, "Who does this ear/penis belong to?" and have them respond with an emphatic "Me"! The teacher can create a variety of games using the concept, such as

- *Guess Who.* Each person takes a turn describing something about someone else's body in class, like "I see someone with blond hair, guess who." When the class guesses, the teacher reinforces the concept by asking, "Who does the blond hair belong to?" or "Who owns the blond hair?"

• *In the Looking Glass.* Each student looks in a full-length mirror, points to and names all the body parts that belong to him or her. This is a good time to explore with the student how she or he feels about the parts of the body, too.

After students have assimilated this concept of body ownership, they can progress to the concept of getting, giving, or not giving permission to touch or be touched in various situations. Role-playing is a valuable technique for teaching this concept. The teacher can begin by role-playing a situation in which someone did not ask permission to touch someone else (e.g., playing with someone's long hair) and allowing the consequences of the action to be played out (e.g., fighting, hurt feelings). The teacher should be sure to explore with the students what types of feelings the people involved in this situation might have. The teacher must emphasize that people need to gain permission before touching someone else's body and should reenact the role-play, this time asking permission to touch the other person's hair. In one version of the role-play, the person may respond "Yes," while in another version, the person may respond "No." The outcomes and feelings involved in each situation should be fully explored.

Students need to be taught to say "No" emphatically when they do not want to be touched. They also need to be told what to do (e.g., yell, get away, resist, tell) when someone tries to force them to do something they don't want to. In order to practice these protective skills, the teacher and students should generate and act out other scenarios, such as:

• While you're walking down the street, someone that you don't know walks up to you and puts his or her arm around you.
• When you're at the movies, the person sitting next to you starts patting your leg.
• While your uncle is reading you a bedtime story, he touches your vulva or penis.

It is important to emphasize that being an adult, friend, or family member does not give someone the right to touch you when you don't want to be touched.

As sexuality educators, we must always keep in mind that while it is important to teach mentally retarded people about sexual abuse prevention, our goal is not to eliminate their sexual feelings and behaviors. Sexual abuse prevention should be one small part of a total educational program for mentally retarded people directed at developing sexually fulfilled persons who can understand and appropriately express their sexuality.

Sexuality and Physical Disabilities for Young Adults

Too often persons with physical disabilities (about 10% of our population) are treated as asexual beings who should have more important things to worry about than their sexual expression and functioning. But disabled people *are* sexual beings as demonstrated by the second most frequently asked question by men experiencing a paralytic trauma: "What are my sexual responses like now?" (Cole, 1976). Yet while persons with disabilities hunger for sexuality education regarding the specific effects of their particular disability on their sexual functioning, expression, and relationships, they continue to have restricted access to information and few opportunities to form partnerships and loving relationships (Chipouras, 1981). The goals of sexuality education for disabled (and able-bodied) persons are eloquently described by Susan Daniels (1981), a scholar in this field who also happens to have a disability:

> Hopefully, we will begin to discover that each human being has an unlimited potential for sexual well-being that is not related to neurology, the cardiovascular system, or the skeletal-muscular system. We will find out that we all have an unlimited capacity to give and receive, to belong in the world of each other, to respect ourselves as sexual persons, and to enjoy the pleasure that life gives us, be that with ourselves or with other people. We will begin to see the effects of disability not as how they impinge on certain neurological conditions or how certain muscles respond, but how they might limit or change the way we respond to other people. If we begin to understand those issues, we might begin to see sexuality as part of the total person as opposed to limiting it to the genital area. (p. 7)

The following holistic learning experience on becoming sexually abled attempts to approach these goals through integration of the cognitive, affective, and behavioral learning domains. While persons with varying disabilities have found this to be a very beneficial experience, it also is extremely effective in a mixed group of disabled and able-bodied persons.

As this experience begins, the participants are asked to describe, on a piece of paper, what constitutes a healthy, happy sexual relationship. These papers are collected (without names) and redistributed. As the descriptions are read aloud, the elements of satisfying sexual relationships that are emphasized generally include getting in touch with one's own body and feelings as well as one's partner's; exploring new sensations and experimenting with sexual pleasuring techniques like sensate focus; openly communicating; not focusing solely on vaginal/penile intercourse; being less goal-oriented; relaxing gender-role stereotypes and other assumptions; and developing other aspects of the relationship. After all of the group's points are made, the teacher can then focus the discussion on the kinds of knowledge, attitudes, and skills a sexually abled person would need in order to create such relationships.

The next step is to have the participants imagine that they have incurred a particular disability (e.g., paraplegia, blindness, deafness, renal failure). Depending on the group, for some or all of the participants this fantasy journey may actually be grounded in reality. (Various disabilities may be explored at different times.) Each person should be encouraged to share personal feelings and beliefs as to exactly how this disability would affect his or her sexual functioning, expression, and relationships. Once people have voiced all of their concerns, the participants should be encouraged to suggest adaptations that can be made in order to overcome obstacles. The teacher should provide information and resource suggestions when appropriate.

In closing this experience, the teacher makes apparent that the adaptations that physically disabled persons may be "forced" to make in their sexual lives (e.g., freer experimentation and communication) can be positive forces and actually help them to become more sexually abled. In fact, most sexually disabled persons are not physically disabled. As Susan Daniels (1981) described this phenomenon:

> We need to bring the lessons we have recently learned about sexuality and disability to our nondisabled brothers and sisters. We have not yet fulfilled our own potential to be loving sexual partners, nor have they. . . . I also think that our nondisabled brothers and sisters may not have the security of knowing that sexuality does not exist in the perfect body but in the pleasing body. We can help them overcome their handicaps. (p. 9)

CONCLUSION

The effectiveness, meaning, and worth of learning experiences in the sexuality curriculum are greatly enhanced when teachers integrate approaches from the cognitive, affective, and behavioral domains of learning. It is hoped that this chapter stimulates ideas for such integration across *all* sexual topics, not simply those discussed here or in other chapters of this book. Ultimately, there is no "cookbook" of easy recipes for sexuality education: The creation of learning experiences must be guided by the needs and interests of the students and teacher and not the political agendas of school boards or the "moral" agendas of vocal conservative groups. Teachers must battle against the deskilling aspects of restrictive, mechanistic curricula developed by those far removed from classrooms and must recapture their leadership in development of curricula and learning experiences for sexuality education. They must empower themselves to teach! When this happens, the possibilities of growth-enhancing learning experiences are bounded only by the teacher's creativity and skill and the students' vigor and imagination. By experiencing a holistic process of sexual learning in the classroom, students will be better able to integrate the cognitive, affective, and behavioral aspects of their own sexuality and empower themselves as fully human sexual beings.

REFERENCES

Bell, T. A., & Holmes, K. K. (1984). Age-specific risks of syphilis, gonorrhea, and hospitalized pelvic inflammatory disease in sexually experienced U.S. women. *Sexually Transmitted Disease, 11,* 291–295.

Berman, L. M. (1990). Toward a continuing dialogue. In J. T. Sears & J. D. Marshall (Eds.), *Teaching and thinking about curriculum: Critical inquiries* (pp. 280–286). New York: Teachers College Press.

Berscheid, E., Walster, E., & Bohrnstedt, G. (1973). Body image: A *Psychology Today* questionnaire. *Psychology Today, 6,* 58–66.

Bottom, F. J., Jr., (1980). *The pregnant adolescent: Problems of premature parenthood.* Beverly Hills, CA: Sage.

Brick, P., Davis, N., Fischel, M., Lupo, T., MacVicar, A., & Marshall, J. (1989). *Bodies, birth, & babies.* Hackensack, NJ: The Center for Family Life Education.

Carrera, M. A., & Calderone, M. S. (1976). Training of health professionals in education for sexual health. *SIECUS Report, 4*(4), 1–2.

Centers for Disease Control. (1988). HIV-related beliefs, knowledge, and behaviors among high school students. *JAMA, 260,* 3567–3568.

Champion, V. L., Austin, J., & Tzeng, O. (1982). Assessment of relationship between self-concept and body image using multivariate techniques. *Issues in Mental Health Nursing, 4*(4), 299–315.

Chipouras, S. (1981). Sexuality-related services for disabled people: A needs assessment. In D. G. Bullard & S. E. Knight (Eds.), *Sexuality and physical disability: Personal perspectives* (pp. 223–227). St. Louis, MO: C. V. Mosby.

Cole, T. M. (1976). Sexuality and the spinal cord injured. In R. Green (Ed.), *Human sexuality: A health practitioner's text* (pp. 142–170). Baltimore: Williams & Wilkins.

Daniels, S. M. (1981). Critical issues in sexuality and disability. In D. G. Bullard & S. E. Knight (Eds.), *Sexuality and physical disability: Personal perspectives* (pp. 5–10). St. Louis, MO: C. V. Mosby.

de Mauro, D. (1990). Sexuality education 1990: A review of state sexuality and AIDS education curricula. *SIECUS Report, 18*(2), 1–9.

Doll, W. E., Jr. (1990). Teaching a post-modern curriculum. In J. T. Sears & J. D.

Marshall (Eds.), *Teaching and thinking about curriculum: Critical inquiries* (pp. 39–47). New York: Teachers College Press.

Fazio, R. H. (1990). Multiple processes by which attitudes guide behavior: The mode model as an integrative framework. *Advances in Experimental Social Psychology, 23,* 75–109.

Fishbein, M., & Ajzen, S. (1975). *Beliefs, attitudes, intention, and behavior.* Reading, MA: Addison-Wesley.

Fisher, S., & Cleveland, S. E. (1968). *Body image and personality.* New York: Dover.

Forrest, J. D., & Silverman, J. (1989). What public school teachers teach about preventing pregnancy, AIDS, and sexually transmitted diseases. *Family Planning Perspectives, 21*(2), 65–72.

Fox, G. L. (1981). The family's role in adolescent sexual behavior. In T. Ooms (Ed.), *Teenage pregnancy in a family context* (pp. 73–130). Philadelphia: Temple University Press.

Goldstein, J. (1972). Sex education and the trainable. In M. S. Bass & M. Gelof (Eds.), *Sexual rights and responsibilities of the mentally retarded* (pp. 150–154). New York: Association for Voluntary Sterilization, Inc.

Green, L., Kreuter, M., Deeds, S., & Patridge, K. (1980). *Health education planning: A diagnostic approach.* Palo Alto, CA: Mayfield.

Greene, M. (1978). *Landscapes of learning.* New York: Teachers College Press.

Habermas, J. (1984). *The theory of communicative action.* Boston: Beacon.

Hall, E. R., & Flannery, P. J. (1985). Prevalence and correlates of sexual assault experiences in adolescents. *Victimology, 9,* 398–406.

Hass, A. (1979). *Teenage sexuality.* New York: Macmillan.

Hester, N. R., & Macrina, D. M. (1985). The Health Belief Model and the contraceptive behavior of college women: Implications for health education. *Journal of the American College Health Association, 33,* 245–252.

Hutchinson, M. (1982). *Transforming body image: Your body, friend or foe?* New York: Haworth.

Johnson, W. R. (1973). *Sex education and counseling of special groups: The mentally and physically handicapped, ill, and elderly.* Springfield, IL: Charles C. Thomas.

Jones, E. F., Forrest, J. D., Goldman, N., Henshaw, S. K., Lincoln, R., Rosoff, J. I., Westoff, C. F., & Wulf, D. (1985). Teenage pregnancy in developed countries: Determinants and policy implications. *Family Planning Perspectives, 17*(2), 53–62.

Kantor, K. (1990). Both sides now: Teaching English, teaching curriculum. In J. T. Sears & J. D. Marshall (Eds.), *Teaching and thinking about curriculum: Critical inquiries* (pp. 61–74). New York: Teachers College Press.

Kempton, W. (1975). *A teacher's guide to sex education for persons with learning disabilities.* North Scituate, MA: Duxbury Press.

Kenney, A. M., Guardado, S., & Brown, L. (1989). Sex education and AIDS education in the schools: What states and large school districts are doing. *Family Planning Perspectives, 21*(2), 56–64.

Koch, P. B. (1985). *Self-awareness and sexuality for the mentally retarded person: A comprehensive program (child through adult).* University Park: Pennsylvania State University.

Koch, P. B. (1988). The relationship of first intercourse to later sexual functioning concerns of adolescents. *Journal of Adolescent Research, 3,* 345–363.

Koch, P. B., & Young, E. W. (1986). *Body concept and responsible health practices.* University Park: Pennsylvania State University, Center for the Study of Child and Adolescent Development.

Krantz, M., & Friedberg, J. (1985). Physical attractiveness and popularity: The mediating role of self-perception. *The Journal of Psychology, 199,* 219–223.

Kurtz, R., & Hirt, M. (1970). Body attitude and physical health. *Journal of Clinical Psychology, 26,* 471–474.

Lerner, R., Karabenick, S., & Stuart, J. (1973). Relations among physical attractiveness, body attitudes, and self-concept in male and female college students. *Journal of Psychology, 85,* 119–129.

Lerner, R. M., & Lerner, J. V. (1977). Effects of age, sex, and physical attractiveness on child-peer relations, academic performance, and elementary school adjustment. *Developmental Psychology, 13,* 585–590.

Maiman, L., & Becker, M. (1974). The health belief model: Origins and correlates in psychological theory. *Health Education Monographs, 2,* 336–353.

Marshall, J. D., & Sears, J. T. (1990). An evolutionary and metaphorical journey into teaching and thinking about curriculum. In J. T. Sears and J. D. Marshall (Eds.), *Teaching and thinking about curriculum: Critical inquiries* (pp. 15–32). New York: Teachers College Press.

McKusick, L., Wiley, J., Coates, T., & Morin, S. (1986). *Predictors of AIDS and behavioral risk reduction: The AIDS Behavioral Research Project.* Paper presented at the meeting of the New Zealand AIDS Foundation, Auckland.

Moglia, R. (1990). The professional preparation of sexuality educators: A pivotal factor for sexuality education. *SIECUS Report, 18*(2), 13–15.

Norris, C. (1970). The professional nurse and body image. In C. Carlson (Ed.), *Behavioral concepts and nursing intervention* (pp. 39–59). Philadelphia: J. B. Lippincott.

St. Lawrence, J., Kelley, J., Hood, H., & Brasfield, T. (1987). *The relationship of AIDS risk knowledge to actual risk behavior among homosexuality-active men.* Paper presented at the Third International Conference on AIDS, Washington, DC.

Schubert, W. H. (1986). *Curriculum: Perspective, paradigm, and possibility.* New York: Macmillan.

Sears, J. T., & Marshall, J. D. (Eds.). (1990). *Teaching and thinking about curriculum: Critical inquiries.* New York: Teachers College Press.

Secord, P., & Jourard, S. (1953). The appraisal of body-cathexis: Body cathexis and the self. *Journal of Consulting Psychology, 17,* 343–347.

Sex Information and Education Council of the United States. (1990). Position statements 1990. *SIECUS Report, 4*(4), 10–12.

Simon, K., & Das, A. (1984). An application of the health belief model toward educational diagnosis for VD education. *Health Education Quarterly, 11,* 403–418.

Strunin, L., & Hingson, R. (1987). Acquired immunodeficiency syndrome and adolescents: Knowledge, beliefs, attitudes, and behaviors. *Pediatrics, 79,* 825–828.

Thelen, H. A. (1981). *The classroom society: The construction of educational experience.* New York: Wiley.

Young, E. W., Koch, P. B., & Preston, D. B. (1989). AIDS and homosexuality: A longitudinal study of knowledge and attitude change among rural nurses. *Journal of Community Health Nursing, 6*(4), 189–196.

Zelman, D. B., & Typer, K. (1976). *Essential adult sex education curriculum.* Pasadena, CA: James Stanfield Fiem.

CHAPTER 13

School-Based HIV/AIDS Education

Is There Safety in Safer Sex?

JONATHAN G. SILIN

AIDS is a disease of contradictions. It is a disease that is not a disease, a biological reality that has had a greater impact on sociopolitical practices than on medical care, an illness of hiddenness that has led to irreversible changes in public discourse.[1] Unfortunately, HIV infection has also become a disease of adolescence, a period characterized in our society by its own unique logic—moments of sudden growth and regression, open search and certain definition, of personal power and extreme susceptibility to the influence of others. It is understandable that adults have been reluctant to admit the presence of a complex, wily virus such as HIV in a chameleonlike population that itself often appears to have no other goal than to test the limits of human possibility.

During the earliest years of the epidemic, the years of GRID (gay related immunodeficiency) and the gay cancer, this reluctance to view young people as vulnerable to HIV infection was reinforced by the dominant risk-group vocabulary, which suggested that the virus would be contained within specific populations. The social and political marginalization of gay men and intravenous drug users allowed many to discount their experiences. Today, despite widespread denial of the existence of gay-identified youth in our classrooms, we see greater acceptance of the fact that any teenager may experiment with behaviors or accede to peer pressure in such a way as to place himself/herself at risk for contracting HIV. Indeed, these very attributes are most frequently cited as the reasons it is so difficult to conduct effective HIV/AIDS education.

Whether motivated by irrational fear or realistic assessment of the problem, a strong national consensus exists in favor of HIV/AIDS education for young people (Center for Population Options, 1989). In response to this consensus, over half of the states have mandated HIV/AIDS education in their schools and most others strongly recommend it. However only 13 states have established complete programs including published curricula, training, or certification requirements and in-service education for staff (Kenney, Guardado, & Brown, 1989). The absence of resources for staff development is especially notable given recent calls for greater teacher autonomy to increase school effectiveness and the proliferation of experiments in teacher-based school governance. In many of the nation's largest school districts education about HIV has begun to take precedence over sexuality education as a focus of pedagogical attention. While the majority of schools address both topics, the transitional and often confusing nature of the moment is evidenced by the number of sites that offer HIV/AIDS education but not sexuality education and others where the situation is reversed.

HIV-related curricula tend to have a strong prevention focus. Not surprisingly, the prevention method of choice is clearly abstinence. Of the 27 state-approved curricula, only 8 address abstinence and strategies appropriate for sexually active students in a balanced manner and provide comprehensive information about the epidemic. Indeed, the subject of safer sex is one of the least likely to be discussed with students. While teachers blame their own discomfort with this topic on parental and administrative constraints, lack of appropriate materials, and the embarrassment with which students approach discussions of sexuality, they report little difficulty teaching abstinence and sexual decision making (Kerr, Allensworth, & Gayle, 1989). This suggests that the latter topic is not so much about learning to make choices from a world of possibilities as about deciding to say no to sex, based on a predetermined set of behavioral rules. That decision making has become a code phrase for a "just say no" message is underlined by the fact that surveyed teachers have an almost universal commitment to programs that enable students to examine and develop their own values, while at the same time they believe that students should be explicitly taught not to have sex (Forrest & Silverman, 1989). The values clarification discussion becomes the critical vehicle for persuading students to own the adult perspective.

Despite media and school-based efforts, teenagers remain woefully ignorant about HIV and ill-disposed toward people with AIDS (Brooks-Gunn, Boyer, & Hein, 1988). AIDS cases among 13- to 19-year-olds increased by 51% between 1988 and 1989. Other studies indicate that 7% of homeless and runaway youth and 1% of all teenagers in high-incidence cities like New York and Miami may have already contracted HIV (Center for Population Options, 1989; Kolata, 1989). Most disturbingly, over one fifth of people with AIDS are in their 20s. Because the average latency period between initial infection with HIV and the onset of AIDS is 10 years or more, it can be inferred that many of these people contracted the virus as teenagers.

In order to create more effective HIV education programs, many curriculum makers have begun to focus on what they perceive as a critical gap between information and behavioral change (Basch, 1989). By creating experientially based programs that teach a variety of "social skills," they hope to enable students to negotiate more successfully the new terrain of safer sex. Yet if young people aren't getting the message about HIV infection, and this is clearly what the statistics are telling us, then we must examine not only how the message is being delivered but also the nature of the message itself. This chapter explores the multiple meanings contained in both information- and skills-based curricula as well as the theoretical gap between information and behavioral change that the latter seek to overcome. In the process it raises questions about the premises behind HIV prevention education that require a detour into the heart of the epidemic itself as we seek to understand why safer sex education alone will not be sufficient to prevent the transmission of HIV.

HIV/AIDS EDUCATION IN THE SCHOOLS

Information-Based Curricula

State-approved HIV curricula usually give priority to information about healthful life-styles, communicable diseases, and HIV transmission and prevention. But many pose constraints to the discussion of subjects that might be interpreted as facilitating sexual activity—contraception, safer sex, and sexuality. The *AIDS Instructional Guide* (New York State Education Department, 1987) is one example of the technocratic mind-set that undermines the teacher's own role as decision maker. Although only a guide, it is worth considering in detail, since many districts adopted it in toto as the curriculum in order to avoid controversy and save time. An interesting political document, this guide requires local districts to create community review panels to assure decency permits parents to withdraw children from lessons on HIV prevention, and consistently denies the sexual realities of teenagers' lives. To educators, however, the guide may appear as an even more curious pedagogical document for the way that it parcels out information across the grades.

An underlying assumption of this guide seems to be that children's minds are compartmentalized, able to deal with AIDS information in a logical, sequential order that permits them, for example, to discuss how HIV is *not* transmitted, while holding in abeyance for several lessons and/or years how it is transmitted or how to prevent its spread. There appears to be no need to assess the knowledge with which children arrive at school, information they may have garnered on the street, from the media, or at the family dinner table. The child is read as a tabula rasa when it comes to AIDS.

In the New York State *AIDS Instructional Guide* the social and economic consequences of AIDS are confined to a single lesson in the Grade 9–12 cluster. This lesson structures a student debate, concluding with a class vote, over the advisability of mandatory HIV-antibody testing. Although other lessons are geared to elicit sympathy for people with AIDS (and thus attempt to curb potential discrimination), never does the curriculum address underlying issues like homophobia, racism, and addictophobia that form the basis for much of the AIDS hysteria the curriculum is trying to dispel. This superficial approach to "humanizing" the disease belies the guide's extensive introductory comments about the importance of pluralism and democratic values. Like so many others, this curriculum guide denies the fundamental reality of HIV infection in our country—that is has disproportionately affected groups of people who have been marginalized and subjected to various forms of physical and psychological violence (Fraser, 1989). Convincing students to listen to any messages about HIV and to begin to understand personal vulnerability cannot be accomplished without interrupting the "us versus them" mentality that pervades our social thinking.[2]

While theoretical analysis of information-based curricula reveals their political biases, empirical evidence is also beginning to suggest their lack of practical efficacy. Studies conducted 2 years after implementation of specific curricula point to little or no change in student knowledge (New York City Board of Education, 1990). Needless to say, the misunderstandings of many students can be lethal. A study conducted in the Boston public schools indicated that half of the students do not know that HIV can be transmitted during sex with someone who appears healthy; 16% do not know about sexual transmission between men; 8% do not know about transmission between men and women; and 7% do not know about transmission when sharing needles (Hingson & Strunin, 1989).

Skills-Based Programs

Other educators have also begun to look at the growing gap between the HIV information that young people do possess and their willingness and/or ability to change specific behaviors that may place them at risk for infection (Edgar, 1988; Mangan, 1988). Increasingly, HIV/sexuality education curricula emphasize an ill-defined cluster of behaviors variously labeled as "life skills," "coping skills," or "problem-solving skills." Depending on the commitment of the particular curriculum, it is claimed that these skills will enable teenagers to remain abstinent until marriage, delay intercourse until an unspecified time in the future, or negotiate safer sex practices as necessary. Through active participation in role-playing, brainstorming sessions, and games, students are taught resistance or refusal skills so that they will not succumb to pressures from peers. These skills are often reduced to a set of sharp retorts that permit students to say no to sexual activity without losing face among their friends. In some instances a few lessons are added to more traditional, direct instruction curricula, while in others information is interwoven into a consistently interactive format (Brick, 1989).

Skill-based programs are frequently built on the understanding that the lack of a positive self-image is the biggest factor preventing teenagers from making healthy decisions. Nationally distributed curricula such as *Project Charlie* (Charest, Gwinn, Reinisch, Terrien, & Strawbridge, 1987) and *Growing Healthy* (National Center for Health Education, 1985) are being described as panaceas to a wide variety of problems including high school dropout rates, lowered academic performance, widespread alcohol and substance abuse, and teenage pregnancy. As in similar programs designed to improve adult productivity in the workplace, the focus on changes in self-perception and interpersonal skills masks material barriers to real equity and autonomy (Steinberg, 1990; Williams, 1990).

Although self-esteem has become a popular buzzword for efforts to promote better psychological adjustment, cognitive social learning theory has long been used as the basis for smoking and pregnancy prevention programs. Comprehensive in design, these programs attempt to account for the reciprocal relationships among cognitive, affective, physiological, and environmental influences. Flora and Thoresen (1988) suggest that this model be combined with a social-marketing perspective to target specific audiences by race, gender, ethnicity, and other social demographic differences.

While there is much to be learned from cognitive social learning theory (e.g., active engagement of students, multiple levels of learning, and variable strategies), its limitations are highlighted by turning to the experience of the gay community, where safer sex instruction first began (Silin, 1987a). Safer sex organizing was initiated hurriedly, in response to an immediate community crisis. Theoretical frameworks were developed only as programs became more professionalized and sought government funding. Gordon (1988) uses a tri-phasic map of health education, including behavioral change, self-empowerment, and collective action models, in order to make sense of the many programs now in existence. He raises questions about the long-range effectiveness and ethical implications of programs that stress individual behavioral change and self-empowerment, questions as relevant to school-based as to community-based education.

The underlying assumption behind behavioral change and self-empowerment models for gay men and direct instruction and experientially based programs for teenagers is that increased information about HIV transmission, or the practice of specific skills, will result in a decrease of high risk behaviors. This in turn will translate into a reduced number of new HIV infections (Eckland, 1989). The linear reasoning embedded in these approaches is highlighted when they are juxtaposed against a collective action model of health education. In addition to addressing the need for information and communication skills, the collective action approach encourages organizing to transform the social and political forces that shape and give meaning to individual behavior.

If the links between health status and issues such as poverty, employment, low income, and social class are fully recognized, then socioeconomic factors would appear to have greater significance for health than individual practices. These factors are best addressed through collective action in the political process. While this position is consistent with radical definitions of health and illness (Illich, 1976), it threatens the official governmental position on disease causation, as summarized by the Presidential Commission on the Human Immunodeficiency Virus Epidemic (1988), which is that "the heaviest burden of illness in the technically advanced countries today is related to individual behavior, especially the long-term patterns of behavior often referred to as 'life-style'" (p. 89). Paradoxically, it is this attempt to define critical social issues as private and personal rather than as public and political that heightens the very bigotry that the Presidential Commission seeks to dispel (Silin, 1987b).

Even the seemingly humanistic techniques of self-empowerment models can become a means to reproduce the hegemonic ideology and ensure the colonization of the student's life world (Berenstein, 1975; Young, 1990). This occurs, for example, when the press to ensure safer sex, whether condom use for gay men or abstinence for teenagers, impels facilitators to assume responsibility *for* group members rather than *toward* them. The most sympathetic educators may fail to exercise pedagogical tact when confronting HIV. Programs are coercive to the degree that they compromise the participants' abilities to draw their own conclusions from experiences that take place within a context that specifically proclaims the importance of individual choice. Experiential learning becomes a means to an end rather than an open exploration of possibility, including the potential rejection of safer sex practices.

Both individual behavior change and self-empowerment models are based on the instrumentalist assumption that behavior can be abstracted, analyzed, and understood apart from the socioeconomic context in which it occurs—an assumption that negates the necessity of addressing issues of the differential distribution of economic and cultural capital. Brandt (1987) comments:

> These assumptions with which we still live regarding health-related behavior rest upon an essentially naive, simplistic view of human nature. If any-

thing has become clear in the course of the twentieth century it is that behavior is subject to complex forces, internal psychologies, and external
pressures all not subject to immediate modifications, or, arguably, to modi-
fication at all. (p. 202)

The historical record documents that narrow approaches to the control
of sexually transmitted diseases have not only failed, they have also, to
a great degree, been constructed upon a set of moralistic judgments
about the nature of sexual activity (Fee & Fox, 1988).

As progressive educators have asserted since the last century
(Dewey, 1956) and others have reminded us more recently, children
learn most effectively when in the midst of meaningful activities (Lee,
1989). Programs that abstract social skills provide neither the motivation
nor intentionality required for substantive learning. A curriculum that
attempts, in a few brief lessons, to teach students how to make critical
decisions cannot make up for years of education that have denied them
the right to become autonomous, self-determining learners. Friday
afternoon "magic circles" to build self-esteem or Monday morning
rehearsals of refusal skills divert our attention from the realities of contemporary children, who too seldom have the opportunity to make
meaningful choices, follow through on them, and reflect on their consequences.

The difficulties posed by safer sex education suggest that we need
to look more carefully not only at the sources of health-related behavior
but also at what it is that we are attempting to prevent through AIDS
education. What exactly is HIV? Can safer sex really make us safe?

DEFINING HIV/AIDS, STRUCTURING THE CURRICULUM

AIDS makes no sense. However, the proliferation of curricula that
seek to control human behavior in order to avoid HIV speaks to our very
real desire to claim epistemological rationality and epidemiological certainty in a world plagued by a new and as yet incurable disease. In defining HIV as a biomedical phenomenon that can be addressed only by
those trained in science and health education, we attempt to make it safe
for children, contained within a specific discipline, so that it will not
contaminate other areas of study. Thus sanitized, teachers and students
are protected from the truly unhealthy aspects of society that might otherwise be revealed; the status quo is ensured.

Even those with liberatory goals join in this effort to make compre-
hensible that which is ultimately beyond reason. Susan Sontag (1988),
for one, claims that AIDS is just an illness, or more accurately, a medical
condition whose consequences are a spectrum of illnesses. She writes in

order to reveal and criticize the metaphors in which we couch our references to AIDS and thus imbue it with meaning. Language can be deadly when it fosters shame, embarrassment, and a sense of blame, turning people into passive victims rather than active participants in their own care. By freeing AIDS of its metaphors, Sontag hopes to disabuse us of the apocalyptic thinking that breeds irrational fears and programmatic paralysis. Ironically, however, she also manages to minimize, even eliminate, the actual pain and suffering that HIV infection imposes on the individual.

Others argue that there is no reality to be uncovered through critical analysis of the AIDS discourse but rather that the disease is only known through its socially defined meanings (Crimp, 1988). This is not to deny the existence of viruses, opportunistic infections, or the all-too-real suffering they have caused, but to seek control of the epidemic in new arenas. The classic statement of this relativist position was made by Delaporte (1986) in a study of the history of cholera. He argues "that 'disease' does not exist. It is therefore illusory to think that one can 'develop beliefs' about it or 'respond' to it. What does exist is not disease but practices" (p. 6). From this perspective, medical knowledge is not discovered but constructed, not objectively "out there," a reflection of physical reality, but socially negotiated to enhance an arbitrary set of economic arrangements and distribution of power.

This position has been used to create an incisive critique of the media and governmental responses to HIV and to provide the theoretical underpinnings of much of the radical activist response to the disease. Familiarity with how the disease has been constructed has suggested opportunities for how it might be deconstructed—small moments that reveal the larger interests served by specific representations and programs. Those who are most committed to changing immediate circumstances and, in many instances, also living with the disease are engaged by an analysis that emphasizes the social over the biological, the subjective over the objective, the phenomenological over the material.

HIV/AIDS: An Epidemic of Signification

Treichler (1987) calls AIDS an epidemic of signification. In a detailed look at the scientific and popular discourse on HIV/AIDS, she explores the ways in which these ostensibly discrete realms of speech are in fact interactive and mutually determinative, thus undermining the once privileged position held by scientific language. We can no longer assume, as does Sontag (1988), that science defines an objective base of information upon which we build a symbolic superstructure that distorts reality. Rather, it is the scientific enterprise itself that comes under closest scrutiny, becoming one of many equally valid perspectives. Treichler (1987) adopts a complex attitude toward the presence of HIV in our world, one that is theory based while ever mindful of the needs of practice:

> We must learn to live—indeed, *must* learn to live—as though there are such things as viruses. The virus—a constructed scientific object—is also a historical subject, a "human immunodeficiency virus," a real source of illness and death that can be passed from one person to another under certain conditions that we can apparently—individually and collectively—influence. The trick is to learn to live with this disjunction, but the lesson is imperative. Dr. Rieux, the physician-narrator of Camus' novel, acknowledges that by dealing medically with the plague he is allowing himself the luxury of "living in a world of abstractions." But not indefinitely; for "when abstraction sets to killing you, you've got to get busy with it." (p. 69)

Treichler's practical intent is clear. What AIDS signifies cannot be determined by the narratives of experts—scientific, religious, or political. A democratically structured discourse must be initiated that will encourage all those who have been directly affected by HIV to enter the dialogue and tell their stories. Hopefully, this will serve to counter many of the mythical stories generated by those who have attempted to control and explain the meaning of HIV rather than to bear witness to its natural history. The original and perhaps most significant of these fictions has arisen from the attempt to read the story of AIDS from the text of the male homosexual body, a text that has heretofore been largely unspoken in the public, if not the scientific, domain. This is a text that has been read simultaneously as absence and presence. It is the absence of natural male characteristics and, by implication, the presence of female qualities, in themselves read as void, that leave the homosexual without family and children. He is thus missing the requisite commitment to socially responsible behaviors and concern for others. In turn, an excessive sexual drive propels the homosexual into a life of promiscuity, self-absorption, and the recruitment of innocent victims.

The gay man with AIDS is represented on the one hand as someone who continues to put others at risk through a vindictive refusal to practice safer sex and on the other as the now repentant and rightfully punished sinner advocating the wonders of monogamy and "life in the slow lane." Most prominent are the images of the isolated and hapless victim abandoned by family and friends, wasting away in a hospital bed—an image that cruelly deflects attention from the real abandonment by government and media.

But the gay story, as well as representations of heterosexually transmitted HIV, must be placed in the context of "a crisis of representation itself, a crisis over the entire framing of knowledge about the human body and its capacities for sexual pleasure" (Whatney, 1987, p. 9). HIV/

AIDS does not represent a unique moment of moral panic. It is instead, part of an ongoing struggle by competing forces to define the meaning of the body that has most recently been framed by discussions of reproductive technologies, definitions of the family, abuse, and incest. HIV is embedded in a system of representations constituted by ideologically defined dichotomies—male/female, heterosexual/homosexual, adult/child. The transmission of HIV through anal intercourse has been used by many professionals to intensify their efforts to control human sexuality. The possibility of nonreproductive pleasure from a bodily organ associated with waste and pre-oedipal erotic satisfactions may be particularly threatening. The continual denial of heterosexual involvement in this practice remains emblematic of our erotophobic attitudes (Hocquenghem, 1978). Unfortunately, it is teachers of adolescents who are most cognizant of the extent to which anal intercourse is used to preserve virginity and avoid pregnancy among young girls.

Essentialist Sexual Pedagogy

Although contemporary media provide a vehicle for the more complete socialization into medicalized morality, this process was set in motion during the 19th century with the proliferation of professional discourses on sexuality, the female body, and child rearing that are discussed by Carlson in Chapter 2 of this book. In America, the first proponents of an expanded pedagogy of sexuality were social purity crusaders who saw unregulated sexuality as a threat to family and thus to the social and economic stability that was the basis of national integrity. While open discussion of sex was viewed by many as a radical disruption of the social order that would increase licentiousness and more appropriately belonged in the home, the message was always a traditional one sanctifying fidelity within the monogamous, heterosexual union.

The social hygiene movement widely publicized the need for school-based sex education but was most successful in securing new public policies, including premarital blood testing, mandatory reporting of venereal disease, and contact notification (D'Emilio & Freedman, 1988). Not surprisingly, public health officials have sought to reconstruct these same ineffective, quick-fix strategies in their attempt to control HIV. Diseases transmitted through sex continue to be viewed as diseases of behavior, punishment for those who take risks, and an indication of personal maladjustment and societal decay. Echoing earlier campaigns to control venereal diseases in the military that played on the prospect of "innocent" infections among wives and children, popular media typologies have portrayed people with HIV along a continuum of innocence and guilt—children and recipients of blood products are characterized as innocent bystanders deserving of sympathy; Haitians are suspected of being closet homosexuals, drug users, or prostitutes; gay men and drug users are guilty for knowing participation in nonnormative behaviors.

Despite a shift in emphasis away from sexually transmitted diseases to the prevention of teenage pregnancy and now AIDS, pedagogy for most remains a tool for solving complex social problems. Underlying this view is an ahistorical assumption about the nature of sexuality and disease. For example, curricula that focus on contraception, though suggesting that sex and reproduction can be separated, implicitly teach teenagers that intercourse is the only real form of sex (Diorio, 1985). Ignoring constructivist arguments that posit the social negotiation of sexual meanings, sex educators too often assume an essentialist position that reifies sexuality as an unchanging, transhistorical phenomenon (Epstein, 1987). When sexual pleasure is automatically equated with heterosexual intercourse, educators close down options for students and reinforce the patriarchal power structure by valorizing a heterosexual, male-authored definition of sex as universal. Sex education becomes part of a state apparatus through which control of the body assures control of the body politic.

Assessing the impact of a curriculum on students requires an exploration of the knowledge assumptions on which it is based. This assessment is critical to dispelling the myths about sexual identity and behavior that prevent effective HIV/AIDS education. Adrienne Rich (1980) argues "that heterosexuality, like motherhood, needs to be recognized and studied as a *political institution*" (p. 637). While such a project is unlikely to occur within mainstream educational research, some have already begun to act on this injunction. Katz (1990), for example, through careful historical documentation, describes the invention of the modern heterosexual. Noting that homosexuality entered the public discourse well before heterosexuality, he makes problematic that which is otherwise taken for granted. Fine's (1988) ethnography of sex education in an urban school looks not only at the suppression of a discourse of female desire and the promotion of female sexual victimization but also at the privileging of married heterosexuality over other forms of sexual practice. Thus, through the efforts of sex educators, the dominance of what French feminists have called "The Law of the Father" is assured—it is the male who seeks to fulfill desire and the female who must protect herself. Controversies that have erupted among American feminists in the last 2 decades over pornography, s/m, butch/femme roles, and the right of women to explore openly sexual pleasure regardless of traditional standards of political correctness further attest not only to the degree to which erotophobic attitudes are internalized by everyone but also to the transformative power of social constructivist perspectives (Rubin, 1984).

SEX, HIV, AND THE PERMEABLE CURRICULUM

This chapter began by asserting that AIDS is a disease of contradictions. A review of prevention programs suggests an additional conundrum: safer sex will not make us safe from the effects of HIV. The complexity of HIV itself mandates a multifaceted approach. Reconceptualizing HIV/AIDS education means abandoning the instrumentalist assumptions of information- and skills-based programs that have led many to theorize the problem of HIV/AIDS education as one of bridging a gap between adolescent knowledge and behavior. Preventing the transmission of HIV involves not only learning about condoms and spermicides and negotiating sex; it also means developing tools of political analysis, a commitment to social change, and an ethic of caring and responsibility. In short, we must shift our attention from HIV prevention narrowly defined as a means of behavioral control to a broader focus that would more accurately reflect our students' life worlds. But what are the elements of such an approach? Where are we to begin?

Effective sexuality education itself, education that empowers students by building their sense of entitlement and decreasing their vulnerability, must be based on our willingness to listen to and work with the experiences students bring with them. This requires giving up presuppositions about the nature of sexuality and the outcomes of our efforts in favor of a sociohistorical appreciation of the ways in which sexual meanings are constructed and changed. Safer sex can be less about the limitations imposed by HIV and the inculcation of specific behaviors and more about exploring multiple zones of bodily pleasures and the transformation of culturally determined constraints (Patton, 1985). In the time of HIV, a discursive analysis becomes essential to reimagining sexual practices in life-affirming, sex-positive ways.

Our goal should be to replace isolated lessons calculated to build self-esteem and social skills with an ongoing discourse of desire that problematizes violence and victimization. The assumption is that if we valorize the experiences of our students, they will be better able to understand the sources of pleasure and danger in their own lives. Such a process begins when students find a safe place in which they can tell their own stories. To accept these narratives is not only to foster respect for individual differences but also to reveal their distance from officially given versions of human sexuality, a distance that is clearly identified by

Ward and Taylor in Chapter 9 and Trudell in Chapter 10. At the same time it is impossible to ignore externally imposed constraints to liberation, for even the best-intended pedagogic efforts may have little impact without increased life options for poorer students and easy access to birth control materials, health clinics, and substance abuse treatment for everyone.

But HIV/AIDS curricula cannot be reduced to sexuality and drug education; they must also give an equal emphasis to the economic, political, social, and biomedical strands that make up the Gordian knot of AIDS (Johnston, 1986). Fear-based appeals have proven unsuccessful in the past. Greater familiarity with HIV, not less, is needed in order to break down the distancing mechanisms that allow us to feel that we can remain untouched by the epidemic. In Chapter 11 Brunner describes the use of language arts to provoke meaningful discussion of teenage sexuality. HIV/AIDS curricula, too, should reflect the growing response to the disease in literature, music, and the plastic arts, for the richness of these imaginative reconstructions offer alternative routes to understanding the presence of HIV in our world (Engler, 1988; Klein, 1989; Preston, 1989).

HIV/AIDS education also needs to begin with the youngest children and permeate the curriculum in order to break down the taboos with which it is associated and to make the subject a more comfortable one for discussion (Quackenbush & Villarreal, 1988; Silin, 1990). All our HIV curricula should be informed by a concern for democratic values, as well as by an appreciation of the experiential base and developmental levels of different groups of students. Equal attention must be given to individual responsibility for transmitting HIV and for changing the social context in which it thrives. Therefore, curricula should depict active responses by all kinds of citizens, especially people living with HIV (Navarre, 1987). Images of diversity remind us that people with HIV are a part of all of our lives.

Just as effective sexuality education is based on an entire school experience that encourages decision making, problem-solving, and self-worth, successful education about HIV is built on a continuing appreciation of equity and pluralism in society. It cannot be assumed that the absence of negative comment signifies a lack of bias or commitment to social justice (Croteau & Morgan, 1989; Vance, 1984). Educators must take an active role in bringing the full spectrum of human difference to the classroom, acknowledging the ways that these have become sources of conflict and domination as well as the ways that they enrich and form the basis of participatory democracy. A curriculum that is permeable to the impact of children, one through which they can learn the skills of responsible citizenship, lays the groundwork for all AIDS education. For the history of HIV constantly reminds us not only of individual suffering and pain but also of the power and creativity that reside in a collective response.

NOTES

1. AIDS is not a single disease but rather a syndrome, a pattern of symptoms pointing to a "morbid state." A syndrome points to or signifies the underlying disease process(es); a disease is constituted in and by those processes. Because AIDS refers only to the last stage of the disease, signaled by the presence of a major opportunistic infection, most doctors have adopted the term *HIV disease/illness* to refer to the spectrum of infection associated with the human immunodeficiency virus.

2. Such interruption may occur for some when they understand that 34% of teenagers with AIDS are African-American and 18% Latino, although it is minority adolescents, in comparison with their white peers, who are less knowledgeable about HIV, overall, and particularly ill-informed about the effectiveness of condoms for HIV prevention (DiClemente, Boyer, & Morales, 1988). For others it may occur when they realize that 18% of teenagers with AIDS are females, 9% have been infected through heterosexual contact, 47% through homosexual or bisexual male transmission, 12% through intravenous drug use, and 8% through intravenous drug use combined with homosexual/bisexual male contact (Nettles & Scott-Jones, 1989).

REFERENCES

Basch, C. E. (1989). Preventing AIDS through education: Concepts, strategies, and research priorities. *Journal of School Health, 59,* 296–300.

Bernstein, B. (1975). *Class, codes and control* (Vol. 3). London: Routledge & Kegan Paul.

Brandt, A. M. (1987). *No magic bullet: A social history of venereal disease in the United States since 1880.* New York: Oxford University Press.

Brick, P. (1989). *Teaching safer sex.* Hackensack, NJ: Planned Parenthood of Bergen County.

Brooks-Gunn, J., Boyer, C. B., & Hein, K. (1988). Preventing HIV infection and AIDS in children and adolescents: Behavioral research and intervention strategies. *American Psychologist, 43,* 958–965.

Center for Population Options. (1989). *Adolescents, AIDS and HIV: A community wide responsibility.* (Available from Center for Population Options, 1012 14th Street, N.W., Washington, DC)

Charest, P., Gwinn, T., Reinisch, N., Terrien, J., & Strawbridge, C. (1987). *Project Charlie.* (Available from Storefront/Youth Action, 4570 West 77th Street, Edina, MN 55435.)

Crimp, D. (Ed.). (1988). *AIDS: Cultural analysis/cultural activism.* Cambridge, MA: MIT Press.

Croteau, J. M., & Morgan, S. (1989). Combating homophobia in AIDS education. *Journal of Counseling & Development, 68*, 86–91.

Delaporte, F. (1986). *Disease and civilization: The cholera in Paris, 1832* (A. Goldhammer, Trans.). Cambridge, MA: MIT Press.

D'Emilio, J., & Freedman, E. B. (1988). *Intimate matters: A history of sexuality in America.* New York: Harper & Row.

Dewey, J. (1956). *The child and the curriculum/The school and society.* Chicago: University of Chicago Press. (Original works published 1902/1900).

DiClemente, R. J., Boyer, C. B., & Morales, E. D. (1988). Minorities and AIDS: Knowledge, attitudes and misconceptions among black and Latino adolescents. *American Journal of Public Health, 78*, 55–57.

Diorio, J. (1985). Contraception, copulation, domination, and the theoretical barrenness of sex education literature. *Educational Theory, 35*, 239–255.

Eckland, J. D. (1989). Policy choices for AIDS education in the public schools. *Education Evaluation and Policy Analysis, 11*, 377–387.

Edgar, T. (1988). Communicating the AIDS risk to college students: The problem of motivating change. *Health Education Research: Theory and Practice, 3*(1), 59–65.

Engler, R. K. (1988, October). *Safe sex and dangerous poems: AIDS, literature and the gay and lesbian community college student.* Paper presented at the Annual National Literature Conference, Chicago.

Epstein, S. (1987). Gay politics, ethnic identity: The limits of social constructionism. *Socialist Review, 17*(93–94), 9–54.

Fee, E., & Fox, D. M. (1988). *AIDS: The burdens of history.* Berkeley: University of California Press.

Fine, M. (1988). Sexuality, schooling, and adolescent females: The missing discourse of desire. *Harvard Educational Review, 58*(1), 29–53.

Flora, J. A., & Thoresen, C. E. (1988). Reducing the risk of AIDS in adolescents. *American Psychologist, 43*, 965–971.

Forrest, J. D. & Silverman, J. (1989). What public school teachers teach about preventing pregnancy, AIDS and sexually transmitted diseases. *Family Planning Perspectives, 21*(2), 65–72.

Fraser, K. (1989). *Someone at school has AIDS.* Alexandria, VA: National Association of State Boards of Education.

Gordon, P. (1988). *A review of safer sex education workshops for gay and bisexual men.* Unpublished manuscript.

Hingson, R., & Strunin, L. (1989). *Summary of results: Boston schools baseline surveys, spring 1988, 1989.* Unpublished manuscript, Boston University, School of Public Health.

Hocquenghem, G. (1978). *Homosexual desire.* London: Allison & Busby.

Illich, I. (1976). *Medical nemesis: The expropriation of health.* New York: Pantheon.

Johnston, R. (1986). *Medical, psychological, and social implications of AIDS: A curriculum for young adults.* Stony Brook: SUNY Press.

Katz, J. N. (1990). The invention of heterosexuality. *Socialist Review, 21*(1), 7–34.

Kenney, A. M., Guardado, S., & Brown, L. (1989). Sex education and AIDS education in the schools: What states and large school districts are doing. *Family Planning Perspectives, 21*(2), 56–64.

Kerr, D. L., Allensworth, D. D., & Gayle, J. A. (1989). The ASHA national HIV education needs assessment of health and education professionals. *Journal of School Health, 59,* 301–305.

Klein, M. (1989). *Poets for life: Seventy-six poets respond to AIDS.* New York: Crown.

Kolata, G. (1989, October 8). AIDS is spreading in teen-agers, a new trend alarming to experts. *The New York Times,* sec. 1, pp. 1, 30.

Lee, P. (1989). Is the young child egocentric or sociocentric? *Teachers College Record, 90*(3), 375–391.

Mangan, K. S. (1988, September 28). Sexually active students found failing to take precautions against AIDS. *Chronicle of Higher Education, 35*(5), 32, 33.

National Center for Health Education. (1985). *Growing healthy.* (Available from the National Center for Health Education, 30 East 29th Street, New York, NY 10016.)

Navarre, M. (1987). Fighting the victim label. *October, 43,* 143–147.

Nettles, S. M., & Scott-Jones, D. (1989). The role of sexuality and sex equity in the education of minority adolescents. *Peabody Journal of Education, 64*(4), 183–198.

New York City Board of Education, Office of Research, Evaluation, and Assessment. (1990). *AIDS education project: Evaluation section report.* New York: Author.

New York State Education Department. (1987). *AIDS instructional guide.* Albany: Author.

Patton, C. (1985). *Sex and germs: The politics of AIDS.* Boston: South End.

Presidential Commission on the Human Immunodeficiency Virus Epidemic. (1988). *Report of the Presidential Commission on the Human Immunodeficiency Virus Epidemic.* Washington, DC: U.S. Government Printing Office.

Preston, J. (1989). *Dispatches.* Boston: Alyson.

Quackenbush, M., & Villarreal, S. (1988). *"Does AIDS hurt?" Educating young children about AIDS.* Santa Cruz, CA: Network.

Rich, A. (1980). Compulsory heterosexuality and lesbian existence. *Signs, 5,* 631–660.

Rubin, G. (1984). Thinking sex: Notes for a radical theory of the politics of sexuality. In C. S. Vance (Ed.), *Pleasure and danger: Exploring female sexuality* (pp. 267–320). Boston: Routledge & Kegan Paul.

Silin, J. G. (1987a). Dangerous knowledge. *Christopher Street, 10*(5), 34–42.

Silin, J. G. (1987b). The language of AIDS: Public fears, pedagogical responsibilities. *Teachers College Record, 89,* 3–19.

Silin, J. G. (1990, April). *Children, teachers and the AIDS curriculum.* Paper presented at the annual meeting of the American Educational Research Association, Boston.

Sontag, S. (1988). *AIDS and its metaphors.* New York: Farrar, Straus and Giroux.

Steinberg, C. (1990, February 18). How "magic circles" build self-esteem. *The New York Times,* sec. 12, p. 1.

Treichler, P. A. (1987). AIDS, homophobia, and biomedical discourse: An epidemic of signification. *October 43,* 31–71.

Vance, C. S. (1984). Pleasure and danger: Toward a politics of sexuality. In C. S. Vance (Ed.), *Pleasure and danger: Exploring female sexuality* (pp. 1–29). Boston: Routledge & Kegan Paul.

Whatney, S. (1987). *Policing desire: Pornography, AIDS and the media.* Minneapolis: University of Minnesota Press.

Williams, L. (1990, March 28). Using self-esteem to fix society's ills. *The New York Times*, pp. C1, C10.

Young, R. (1990). *A critical theory of education.* New York: Teachers College Press.

CHAPTER 14

Ill-Structured Problems

Reconsidering Teenage Sexuality

DIANE LEE AND LOUISE M. BERMAN

Teenage sexuality, pregnancy, and childbearing gained recognition as a social problem in the early 1970s. To this day, however, debate continues about the nature of this problem and how it should be posed. Whose problem is it? What exactly is the problem: Teens engaging in sexual intercourse? Teens having intercourse outside of marriage? Teens having babies? Teens choosing to rear babies? Teens having abortions? The rising incidence of these occurrences?

Early responses to these questions tended to define and view the problem narrowly. The most common response was to offer sex education classes in which instruction was limited to less than 10 hours and content was focused on anatomy (Sonnenstein & Pittman, 1982). This limited kind of problem posing typifies what many call a well-structured problem (Churchman, 1971; Lee, 1989; Wood, 1983).

Well-structured problems are usefully thought of as "puzzles," that is, as problems having only one correct solution. That solution can be found through application of explicit rules within a closed system. The boundaries for considering what might be relevant information are well defined, and the selection of parameters to include is finite. Solutions are derived using the logical and analytical strategies common to mathematics and Newtonian physics. Once a solution has been adopted, strategies and skills are set in motion in a mechanical way. Interpersonal and intrapersonal knowledge is considered subjective knowledge that is ordinarily eliminated from the problem space. Thus, issues of value and responsibility are not permitted in analyses of well-structured problems.

Since 1973, with the advent and rise of comprehensive school-based programs, responses to questions about teen sexuality reflect more closely those related to ill-structured problemization. Ill-structured problems, also known as "wicked" problems (Churchman, 1971), are the messy problems typically found in everyday life. These are the problems for which no simple set of rules or single correct answers are available; rather, they have multiple causes demanding multiple responses, thereby requiring one to consider several interwoven problems simultaneously. As ill-structured problems are investigated, certainty breaks down, and the relativistic, dynamic, and personal nature of knowledge is realized. Contradiction is considered a necessary feature of reality as persons from varied walks of life gather to work collaboratively toward tenable solutions. Indeed, contradictions are resolved through consensus in order to achieve new systems of increasingly adaptive knowledge. In this process context is relevant. Thus, selection of elements to include in the problem space is broad and ongoing, as meanings are generated through creative interpretation; problems are defined and redefined, formulated and reformulated.

Throughout this process problem solvers unearth values and subjectively identify responsibilities as self-referential thought and interpersonal knowing enter analyses. As noted by Meacham and Emont (1989), ill-structured problems invite issues of value and responsibility in at least three junctures: (1) the choice of goals for human action, (2) the need for justification of those goals, and (3) the definition of means for achieving those goals. Within this framework, a dialectic involving logical, pragmatic, creative, ethical, and affective dimensions is established.

The complex subjective concerns and questions surrounding teen sexuality suggest that it might usefully be framed as an ill-structured problem. Some programmatic responses do attempt to address the complexity and inclusive demands of wicked problems but fall short of meeting all the criteria or possibilities inherent in this approach. One purpose of this chapter is to review current efforts illustrative of some of the parameters identified within an ill-structured problem-solving framework. A second purpose is to explore more fully the potential meanings of an ill-structured orientation for curriculum. The recommendations following are grounded in the conviction that all persons are worthy of being treated with respect and dignity, that educational practice must be embedded within an ethic of care as well as rights, and that programs built upon a principle of care must simultaneously be situation-specific and give attention to values and guidelines that may transcend local settings.

EXISTING RESPONSES TO TEEN SEXUALITY

Nonmarital coitus among teenagers is tied to interactive socioeconomic, social-psychological, and situational characteristics. Many teens, especially those from disadvantaged backgrounds, see no reason to delay intercourse or parenthood; they see their own potential as limited and their future as void of quality life options (Berlin & Sum, 1988; Wilson, 1987). These are the teens who express negative attitudes toward school, have a high truancy rate, and are likely to fail in and withdraw from school (Abrahamse, Morrison, & Waite, 1988; Dryfoos, 1987; Hofferth & Hayes, 1987). The same youths are prone to substance abuse, to suffer with sexually transmitted diseases, and to be officially labeled as delinquents (Cates & Rauh, 1985; Dryfoos, 1987). Not surprisingly, this same population is more frequently diagnosed as more clinically depressed than peers who do not fit this profile (Abrahamse, Morrison, & Waite, 1988). They are also most likely to parent prior to their 20th birthday (Dryfoos, 1987).

In short, those attending to the persons whom this profile represents must address a complex range of social problems. A comprehensive school-based program is an approach that goes beyond sex education to include a wide range of services provided by professionals from varied disciplines. Underscoring this approach is the recognition that teen sexuality is a complex issue for which there is no single correct answer or quick fix.

Comprehensive School-Based Programs

Most comprehensive programs are housed within schools. Professionals see these programs as offering the most promising approach to pregnancy prevention and reduction of high risk pregnancies among teens while not encouraging sexual activity among those not already sexually active (Dryfoos, 1988; Pigg, 1989). Most school-based programs offer athletic physicals, general health assessments, treatment for minor illnesses and injuries, laboratory and diagnostic screenings (including those for sexually transmitted diseases), immunizations, first aid and hygiene information, Early and Periodic Screening, Diagnosis, and Treatment testing, family planning counseling and referral, prenatal and postpartum care, drug and alcohol abuse programs, nutrition and weight reduction programs, family counseling, and information and referral for those health and social services not provided (Hayes, 1987). These school-based clinics serve both males and females and usually provide services at little or no cost. Parents are typically required to sign a blanket permission form at the beginning of the academic year, and students' visits are totally confidential.

Among the most well known comprehensive programs are the St. Paul Ramsey Adolescent Health Service Project in Minnesota (Edwards, Steinman, Arnold, & Hakanson, 1989) and the Johns Hopkins Self Center in Baltimore (Zabin et al., 1988).

The St. Paul Project is perhaps the best-known comprehensive school-based program and the prototype for many others. In keeping with the holistic approach called for with ill-structured problems, all of the services described above, as well as job and school physicals, treatment for venereal disease, and infant day care at some sites, are offered here. Counseling for relationship problems, career planning, and financial concerns is also available. Services are provided by professionals including educators, health practitioners, psychologists, and social workers. Because members of the community participate in planning programs for the teens, "best fits" are carefully negotiated, context is taken into account, and tenable solutions enacted.

The Self Center provides a slightly different model; in addition to the wide range of services usually available at school-based clinics, the Center offers full contraceptive services at a nearby storefront clinic after school hours. All services are free. Not restricted to the school calendar, the clinic limits its services to students enrolled in either of two target schools. Teens experiencing pregnancies are referred to several agencies, including the Johns Hopkins Adolescent Pregnancy Program, for prenatal health care.

In comprehensive school-based programs such as the St. Paul Program and the Self Center, priority is given to providing multiple responses at one site to problems associated with teen sexuality. While professionals from many fields offer a myriad of services for teens, seldom are teens given responsibility for their own decision making or opportunities to role-play hypothetical "what would happen if" scenarios.

A program that does focus on developing teens' decision making and communication skills by building upon their personal knowledge and beliefs related to sexuality is the Life Skills Counseling Program. This program is limited in focus, however, and does not offer the wide range of services found at others.

The stated goal of the Life Skills Counseling Program is to strengthen teens' ability to deal safely with their own sexuality and risk-related choices and situations by developing their decision making and communication skills (Gilchrist, 1981). The program has three major components: information input, cognitive and behavioral skills training, and structured practice both within and outside of the group setting.

Factual information is presented within a "relational thinking" framework. Teens are expected to transform abstract information into their everyday reality by being actively involved in information gathering that supplements traditional curricular offerings. For instance, students are asked to interview persons at community agencies and to conduct mini-surveys. They are also given experiential exercises requiring verbalization of facts and choices in personal terms, such as "Each time I have sex and don't use birth control, I risk pregnancy" (Gilchrist, 1981, p. 4).

Skills training is focused on decision-making strategies leading one to consider multiple sides of an issue, to consider consequences, to select objectives and weigh factors, and to generate and evaluate evidence. Assertive communication skills emphasize verbal and nonverbal aspects of good communication. Teens may initiate difficult interactions, self-disclose positive and negative feelings, refuse unreasonable demands, request changes in another's behavior, ask others for relevant information and feedback, and negotiate mutually acceptable solutions.

Students have varied opportunities to practice these skills and take part in extended role-play interactions in class. Outside of class, students complete assignments such as imagining a partner and a setting where sex is possible and creating a complete dialogue in which the two discuss the possibility of intercourse and the desirability of birth control. These dialogues are often used in role-play exercises. Additional "homework" may involve purchasing over-the-counter contraceptives, meeting with a family planning counselor, and actually discussing birth control with a dating partner.

Teens in this program have freedom to voice their own conceptions of reality and to participate in defining the problem and possible solutions. Thus, issues of value and responsibility that are omitted in most programs are examined. Intrapersonal and interpersonal knowledge is prominent, and context is considered.

In ill-structured problem situations, subjective knowing serves as a point of reference for helping persons make sense of experience. Curriculum conceived within a broad frame of person/world relationships, as opposed to a skills orientation, permits our probing of what it is to be human, to become more fully human, and to act more humanely (Aoki, 1979). In the next section, programs emphasizing the role of interpersonal knowing situated within caring relationships will be discussed.

Mentoring Programs

The development of caring relationships is of particular importance to teens who might become parents as well as to those who are already parents. Dysfunctional relationships, particularly in the family, are consistently associated with teens' participation in nonmarital intercourse without contraceptive protection (Brooks-Gunn & Furstenberg, 1989). In general, high risk teens often have difficulty developing "connectedness" with adults and with adult society. Indeed, young parents will often refer to the need to have someone to love and to love them in return as the primary reason for having, keeping, and/or rearing a baby (Marek, 1989).

Noddings (1984) states that caring is embedded in "receptivity, relatedness, and responsiveness" (p. 6). Work with teens must reflect care that emancipates, values, and respects the persons being cared for; care that smothers or emanates from judgment alienates recipients from providers and erodes the worth of any program. With this in mind, many programs go beyond the services described earlier and pair teens with other individuals so that a close relationship can develop between them. Project Redirection, sponsored by the Manpower Development Research Corporation in New York, is one such program.

Project Redirection, which offers comprehensive services to low-income teenage mothers and pregnant teens across the United States (Nickel & Delany, 1985; Polit, 1989), was one of the first comprehensive programs to include a mentoring component. Mentors are advocates, confidants, friends, models, teachers, and at times, even parent figures (Nickel & Delany, 1985). These volunteers, unlike staff, are readily available outside of the center and offer services beyond the confines of the program. As a result, they can form more personal and intimate bonds with the teens than those typically deemed appropriate for professional staff (p. 65). The caring and supportive involvement of these mentors enriches the lives of the teens and their children and adds a personal dimension to the provision of services.

With well-structured problemization, subjectivity may not enter the problem space, nor may problem solvers go to others for help. Had subjectivity been devalued or support from an intimate other not been available, Project Redirection would certainly be less successful. For example, in a 5-year follow-up, the program's strongest effects were exhibited in measures of maternal warmth, affection, and acceptance and in language stimulation in the home, suggesting the generativity of caring connections (Nickel & Delany, 1985; Polit, 1989).

The efforts described thus far were designed primarily by professionals for teens. In keeping with an ill-structured approach, teens should participate fully in defining problems related to their own sexuality and in designing programmatic and curricular responses to those problems. When giving voice to their visions, teens describe a comprehensive and challenging program that goes beyond sexuality issues to respond more fully to the totality of their needs.

ALTERNATIVE HIGH SCHOOL

Teen parents attending an alternative school for disaffected youth who were asked what they wanted in a school-based program called for the traditional mandated curriculum as well as vocational training, particularly with apprenticeships connected to employment opportunities in their community (Lee & Berman, 1987). Recognizing the relationship between school failure and limited options, these teens further called for remediation in the form of on-site tutoring, small group instruction, and individual pacing.

Students also asked for classes related to child development and parenting to be available to all students, male and female, with and without children. They noted, in addition, that an in-house day care facility would provide children with whom the teens could actually work while studying child development and child care, and serve as a convenient location for the offspring of teens with children. In this way teen parents could bring their children to school and interact with them during the day. Finally, these "disaffected youth" noted a need for practical assistance in the forms of medical care; nutritional, vocational, emotional, and substance abuse guidance; transportation services; and financial assistance.

Like the students given voice in several of the chapters in this book (see Chapters 4, 6, 8, and 9), these students were reliable witnesses of their own experience. They described a program that went well beyond the status quo. As their ideas unfolded, their voices reflected the passion that is situated in participatory freedom. Their visions were described thoughtfully and often emerged slowly. They were quite willing to share responsibility for creating and living a curriculum that would be truly empowering and that transcended any singular curricular orientation.

The programs and curricula described thus far respond to teen sexuality and related sequelae as ill-structured problems and offer solutions far beyond sex education. They are more integrated, holistic, and personally penetrating than would be possible within a well-structured approach. Even so, the full and far-ranging meanings provided by this conceptualization are not evidenced. In the next section, the salient features of ill-structured problems are considered more fully as a basis for curriculum.

TOWARD THE FUTURE: ILL-STRUCTURED PROBLEMS AS A BASIS FOR CURRICULUM

Ill-structured or "wicked" problems indeed seem to be a useful organizing concept for thinking about school curricula, for life in a democracy presupposes thoughtful persons who are energized and enchanted by working their ways through dilemmas that may be fuzzy in character and to which no simple or single solution is evident. Thus, although Chapter 15 presents a scenario of a state in which attempts are made to forego fundamental consideration of the varied meanings of sexuality, we would like to suggest that the essence of participatory democracy lies within the continuous probing, challenging, uncovering, and dealing with problematic areas of human existence. Sexuality is one such area. To think about curricula for sexuality, however, means thinking about curricula for the total person, for sexuality is not separate from a person's being.

Curricula for the person, then, sexuality being one lens through which to view the person, must of necessity take into account the various facets of the person's being. Complexity of the person means complexity in curricula. Using ill-structured problems as a base permits attention to individual meanings, community values, and the individual and public knowledge found in books and documents. In a sense, ill-structured problems transcend any one curricular perspective as described by curriculum writers (Schubert, 1986) and invite fresh ways of uncovering personal meanings, dealing with values, and treating public knowledge.

Characteristics of ill-structured problems include (1) multiple responses to a problem, (2) multiple causes as well as multiple solutions, (3) the impact of context on the problem, and (4) the involvement of interpersonal as well as intrapersonal knowledge in dealing with problems. Each of these qualities is briefly considered below in terms of its meaning for curricula.

Multiple Responses to a Problem

A major consideration for curriculum is the nature of knowledge that the school sets out to teach. In curricula that focus upon single solutions to problems, knowledge becomes unproblematic. Topics for inclusion within the curriculum are ones to which the community ordinarily has a single response. Making possible multiple responses to problems raises a number of curricular issues.

First, what is the nature of the problem and to whom is the problem important? For example, the *topic* of teenage pregnancy is problematic to different persons in different ways. The mother of a teenager may ask, "How will I hold on to my job with an infant in the household?" while the teenager wonders how to continue school with a baby. The teacher may ask, "How will the child with a child progress in a reasonable way in the school program?" while the state is concerned about the financial responsibility for the newborn. Each question or problem is legitimate; each questioner has a different problem to which no single answer is adequate. Problem-posing and problem-solving are integral to the single case and the single person. As Miel and Brogan (1957) note, "The school is sometimes the only institution that may be counted upon to encourage [students] to take the first important step of sensing that they have a problem and that they can work on it with help" (p. 260). Seeing, working, and believing that a better rather than a single solution may emerge is important to dealing with ill-structured problems.

When problems to be considered are seen as the concerns of those who sense them, attention needs to be given to helping persons act upon the ownership of problems or dilemmas important to them. We see this second curriculum issue represented vividly in the belief that persons go to school to educate themselves—not to be educated (Henri, 1951). If this statement of ownership were seen as significant, we would provide opportunities for people to define matters of concern to them, to search for possible solutions, and to hold themselves responsible for problems and solutions. This theme is evident in several of the chapters in this volume, particularly Chapters 4, 8, and 9. Answers would not be handed to individuals for whom no problem was sensed or owned.

A third curriculum issue arises because such a stance demands that we recognize and value the process of reflection within the total school curriculum. Reflection places one in the sphere of self-reference and self-awareness, the place where conscience and action are directed (Scheffler, 1985). By encouraging thoughtful conversation through dialogue journals or autobiographies, we bridge the gap between public and private, visible and invisible. Reflection calls upon lived experience. Teens who find their own words to make meaning of their experiences integrate actions with analysis (Erdman, 1990); analysis may not necessarily be a breaking down but rather a "re-creation" of the subject under study (Grudin, 1990). In the case of teenage sexuality, and more specifically, teenage pregnancy and parenting, students may do more than break down issues; through reflection, they may re-create their lives in ways that allow them to see the complexity of the dilemmas that they face and the absence of a "correct" answer. Students who learn to unharness their own creative powers through articulating the power of their own "inner energies" come to know the challenge of prolonged concentration and the beauty of reformulating old problems in new ways (Grudin, 1990).

Various Causes, Various Solutions

The causes of ill-structured problems may be many and their possible solutions, or at least ways of dealing with them, varied. Again, reflection can help students recognize the causes of and solutions to problems in their own lives.

Reflection demands solitude. Storr (1988) reminds us that solitude promotes insight as well as change, that the capacity to be alone "becomes linked with self-discovery and self-realization, with becoming aware of one's deepest needs, feelings, and impulses" (p. 21). He also recalls Winnicott's description of "being alone in the presence of"; that is, being able to concentrate on one's inner self even in the presence of other people (p. 26). These ideas suggest that time must be set aside for students to recognize and eventually tell their stories. Time may be allocated during the school day or after school. Persons working with teens need to help them create optimum settings for reflection and to underscore that all of our inner lives, thoughts, values, hopes, and dreams are important. One premise of this chapter, and many others in this volume, is that teens have an obligation to develop and are entitled to tell their own stories before they can become the authors of their own lives.

We cannot emphasize enough the importance of providing reflective opportunities for teens who are at risk of becoming parents. When asked, most teenage parents say that they had never intended to get pregnant and have a baby; it just happened (Hayes, 1987). Might things have been different had they had the opportunity to think about their actions, to see alternative solutions to problems they face, and to share their reflections openly in conversation? Reflection enables persons to rise above the hubbub of everyday life and hear the call of conscience. "It is only because we are so deafened by what 'they' are saying that when we do sometimes hear the genuine call of conscience, it seems to us so strange that we think it must have originated 'out there' " (Macquarrie, 1983, p. 130).

Planning for multiple causes and multiple solutions requires our attention to insights gained from the various fields of knowledge, as evidenced in comprehensive school-based programs. In other words, thought might be given to perspectives from different fields that can be brought to bear on problems related to teenage sexuality, pregnancy, and parenting. Using teen pregnancy as a referent, many questions emerge:

- What does research in physiology indicate about child rearing for 14-year-olds?
- What insights to ethicists have about teenagers rearing the young?
- What light might economists shed on the problem?
- How might an anthropologist study cultures in which the teenage pregnancy rate is high? Low?
- What theological thought has bearing on youth pregnancy? On youth's sexuality in general?
- How might psychology or sociology or psychoanalysis help youth understand their problems?

Such cross-disciplinary linkages provide broader bases for dealing with the intricate issues associated with teenage sexuality and invite students to search within the various fields of knowledge for possible answers to problems they pose.

Context Significance

Persons grow up and live within contexts. Some persons seek to shape these contexts to their ambitions, longings, desires, and dreams, while others permit the contexts to shape them. Most of us are some-where in between: we shape but also are shaped by our contexts.

Recognizing these contexts is extraordinarily important when we attend to curriculum development, particularly curriculum develop-ment with a focus on teenage sexuality as an ill-structured problem.

- Can we empower students to recognize, understand, and tran-scend their contexts in order to enhance their well-being?
- What kinds of experiences does it take and what new contexts do students need to create if they are to see their own lives as worth-while?
- What opportunities can we provide so that students can make de-cisions as to how they will live ethically, or as Verhoeven extends the meaning, to "inhabit the earth" (1972, p. 140)?

As noted in several chapters in this book (Chapters 1, 2, 6, 7, and 8, for example), inhabiting various spaces and contexts can be productive or destructive to individuals. A major curricular issue, then, is how to pro-vide opportunities for students to realize the significance of their con-texts and work to change them when necessary.

A follow-up question might be: How can students learn how to make increasingly wise decisions in relation to their contexts? Reflection enables students to evaluate their decisions as to whether they are black and white, relativistic, or based upon careful thought and considered values. As students uncover their values, decisions may become more fitting and decision making become a recursive process in which stu-dents take into account contradictions and competing values in more telling ways. As students improve their ability to make decisions and uncover what is important to them, they become fluent in dealing with ill-structured problems.

Intrapersonal and Interpersonal Knowing

One cannot use a particular five- or six-step process to solve all problems, especially ill-structured problems, whose solutions require the use of interpersonal and intrapersonal skills. Persons are not linear when dealing with themselves or others but rather are complex beings possessing both idiosyncratic as well as reasonably predictable qualities. Recognizing that our lives are complex and intertwined with those of others, teachers and students should see themselves as co-participants in all of life—including the learning process. Being co-participants does not mean that teachers abdicate responsibility, but rather that teachers and students together share their joys, frustrations, questions, realiza-tions, and desires as they together engage in life's journey. Such interrelationships among persons of different ages allow compassion and caring to become integral to being together. A concerned watchfulness allows persons to feel the joys and satisfactions that come from caring and being cared for. In a curriculum based upon ill-structured problems, persons are encouraged to help and support each other.

Through a variety of interactive situations persons come to understand themselves better. Individuals describe their journeys, questions, and reactions to their world (see Chapter 12). Reflecting upon what each person brings to a relationship permits students to uncover the meanings of their own lives, the metaphors that guide their thinking, and the ethics that determine their actions. Freedom may take on new meaning as persons search not so much for freedom *from* as for freedom *with*, the freedom to accomplish satisfying activities with others.

Sexuality topics of utmost concern to teenagers are usually omitted from formal curricula: Contraception and abortion options, the language of desire, and diversity in sexual orientations are, in our current "call to silence," excluded from conversations (Fine, 1988). Muting of the female voice in such conversations is of particular concern, for the silencing of the "feminine" reflects a loss of a woman's inheritance (Jacobus, 1979), autonomy, and power (Petchesky, 1980), and ultimately her self (Heilbrun, 1988). As noted by Fine (1988), "While too few safe spaces exist for adolescent women's exploration of sexual subjectivities, there are all too many dangerous spots for their exploitation" (p. 35).

Although such conversations may be absent from the "official" curricula, they are not absent from teens' lived experiences or out-of-class discussions. The unfortunate result is that the persons excluded from meaningful dialogue about the most important and controversial issues related to sexuality are adults—parents, teachers, guidance counselors, and other service providers—precisely the people who should be invited into dialogue with teens of both genders.

The importance of providing forums for dialogue and critique cannot be overstated. Teens who are able to participate in discourse that goes beyond "just say no" are better equipped to make informed choices, to identify values that are personally relevant and thus likely to undergird their actions as well as their decisions, and to understand better their own feelings about themselves as fully human and sexual beings.

Curricular Priorities

In conclusion, curricula based on dealing with ill-structured problems may have a number of characteristics.

First, curriculum development begins with the meanings students bring to the issue—in this case human sexuality, particularly as it relates to teenage pregnancy. One may use the tools of the ethicist, the anthropologist, or the sociologist to uncover both individual meanings and the sedimented meanings of the community. By delving into these meanings, one can determine ownership for ill-structured problems:

- Does the outsider looking in see a problem?
- Does the community with clear standards of right and wrong see a problem?
- How does the dilemma of teenage sexuality seem to those from communities in which mores for sexual behavior are less explicit?

Second, students need opportunities to learn the consequences of their actions relative to sexuality. Information needs to be available about the consequences of limited education for a teenage mother, about the consequences of raising a child without adequate resources, and about the consequences of giving in to desire without knowledge of the outcomes. Although information alone may not change behavior, information that helps students transcend current meanings and develop new ones can make a difference. Information that is available when students are seeking answers to their own questions has more meaning than information given when they have not posed a problem.

Third, ill-structured problems are recursive in nature, that is, persons who deal with them may develop skill in thinking about them. In addition, they may handle problems better as they develop a mind-set that moves them from seeking singular responses, realizing that many problems are beyond single solutions. Solving problems, evaluating the process, and solving new problems is a growth process.

Fourth, curriculum development necessitates attention to staff, whose qualities should include an ability to care. Persons need to be well versed in the literature on adolescence as a life period, tolerant of those who vacillate between adultlike and childlike behaviors, and able to set limits while remaining patient and nonjudgmental. In addition, staff need to be reliable, in doing what they say and not promising more than they can deliver, and flexible, in responding to unusual requests. A capacity and willingness to function in a variety of roles is necessary. They need to care genuinely for the teens with whom they will be involved (Nickel & Delany, 1985). Staff need to think through their own definitions of healthy teenage sexuality, to clarify their own values, and to define the boundaries that curtail their ability to be respectful of values and aspirations not consonant with their own. Staff should rely on this self-knowledge when selecting a position working with teens. If caring relationships are to develop, they must be built upon reciprocal value, regard, and respect.

The involvement of community volunteers, especially those who were teen mothers themselves, provides a unique dimension to the caring connection, an expression of care based upon shared lived experiences. Noddings (1984) speaks of this kind of empathic caring when she reminds us that caring is a "stepping out of one's own personal frame of reference into the other's" (p. 24). It is easier at times to "step out" when the place of origin is shared.

Fifth, sexuality in general needs a new look in education. Sexuality denotes differences. A consideration of likenesses and differences among persons can help place sexuality and teenage pregnancy in perspective. What calls persons to engage in sexual activity leading to pregnancy? To abstinence? To sexual activity with precaution? As students come to understand themselves and others in terms of different attitudes toward sexuality, they may raise their consciousness toward what leads to teenage pregnancy and see more integrative approaches to life.

Ill-structured problems seemingly are endemic to life in a democracy. Societies that exclude dealing with ill-structured problems from their day-by-day experiences may be substituting more authoritarian ways of thinking and feeling for democratic ones. Such is not appropriate for life in a democracy. Curriculum development that is problematic and leads the young to make increasingly better normative decisions is essential if we are to maintain a humane, caring citizenry (Berman, in press).

Miguel de Unamuno (1954) talks about the "tragic sense of life." In a sense education is tragic also. Persons are imperfect, education is imperfect, educators are imperfect.

> By maintaining the tragic sense, we admit to ourselves and to those engaged with us in an activity the inherent difficulties and uncertainties of our efforts—which may in fact bind us together more strongly, inspire more persistence and conscientious effort, and help us maintain a more realistic appraisal of the worth of what we are trying to accomplish. (Burbules, 1990, p. 471)

The tragic sense may be the glory of education in a democracy. Dealing with ill-structured problems provides enchantment to what may be seen as tough and wicked dilemmas.

REFERENCES

Abrahamse, A. F., Morrison, P. A., & Waite, L. J. (1988). Teenagers willing to consider single parenthood: Who is at greatest risk? *Family Planning Perspectives, 20*(1), 13–18.

Aoki, T. (1979, April). *Toward curriculum inquiry in a new key.* Paper presented at the Conference on Phenomenological Description: Potential for Research in

Art Education, Montreal, Canada. (ERIC Document Reproduction Service No. ED 182 808)

Berlin, G., & Sum, A. (1988). *Toward a more perfect union: Basic skills, poor families, and our economic future* (Occasional Paper 3). New York: Ford Foundation.

Berman, L. M. (in press). Problematic curriculum development: Normative inquiry in curriculum. In E. Short (Ed.), *Forms of curriculum inquiry: Guidelines for conducting educational research*. Albany: SUNY Press.

Brooks-Gunn, J., & Furstenberg, F., Jr. (1989). Adolescent sexual behavior. *American Psychologist, 44*(2), 249–257.

Burbules, M. C. (1990). The tragic sense of education. *Teachers College Record, 91*(4), 469–479.

Cates, W., Jr., & Rauh, J. L. (1985). Adolescents and sexually transmitted diseases: An expanding problem. *Journal of Adolescent Health Care, 6*, 1–5.

Churchman, C. W. (1971). *The design of inquiring systems: Basic concepts of systems and organization*. New York: Basic.

de Unamuno, M. (1954). *Tragic sense of life*. New York: Dover.

Dryfoos, J. G. (1987). *Youth-at-risk: One in four in jeopardy*, Report to Carnegie Corporation, New York: Carnegie Corporation.

Dryfoos, J. G. (1988). School-based health clinics: Three years of experience. *Family Planning Perspectives, 20*(4), 193–200.

Edwards, L., Steinman, M., Arnold, K., & Hakanson, E. (1980). Adolescent pregnancy prevention services in high school clinics. *Family Planning Perspectives, 12*(1), 6–14.

Erdman, J. I. (1990). Curriculum and community: A feminist perspective. In J. T. Sears & J. D. Marshall (Eds.), *Teaching and thinking about curriculum: Critical inquiries* (pp. 172–186). New York: Teachers College Press.

Fine, M. (1988). Sexuality, schooling, and adolescent females: The Missing discourse of desire. *Harvard Educational Review, 58*(1), 29–53.

Gilchrist, L. D. (1981). Group procedures for helping adolescents cope with sex, *Behavior Group Therapy, 3*(2), 3–10.

Grudin, R. (1990). *The grace of great things*. New York: Ticknor & Fields.

Hayes, C. D. (Ed.). (1987). *Risking the future* (Vol. 1). Washington, DC: National Academy.

Heilbrun, C. G. (1988). *Writing a woman's life*. New York: Ballantine.

Henri, R. (1951). *The art spirit*. New York: Harper & Row.

Hofferth, S. L., & Hayes, C. D. (Eds.). (1987). *Risking the future* (Vol. 2). Washington, DC: National Academy.

Jacobus, M. (1979). *Women writing and writing about women*. New York: Barnes & Noble.

Lee, D. M. (1989). Everyday problem solving: Implications for education. In J. D. Sinnott (Ed.), *Everyday problem solving: Theory and applications* (pp. 251–265). New York: Praeger.

Lee, D. M., & Berman, L. M. (1987). Teen-age parents talk about school: Meanings for the curriculum. *The Educational Forum, 51*(4), 355–375.

Macquarrie, J. (1983). *In search of humanity*. New York: Crossroads.

Marek, E. (1989, April). The lives of teenage mothers: School-books, boyfriends, and babies. *Harper's*, pp. 56–62.

Meacham, J. A., & Emont, N. C. (1989). The interpersonal basis of everyday problem solving. In Jan D. Sinnott (Ed.), *Everyday problem solving: Theory and applications* (pp. 7–23). New York: Praeger.

Miel, A., & Brogan, P. (1957). *More than social studies.* Englewood Cliffs, NJ: Prentice-Hall.

Nickel, P. S., & Delany, H. (1985). *Working with teen parents: A survey of promising approaches.* Chicago: Family Focus & Family Resource Coalition.

Noddings, N. (1984). *Caring.* Berkeley: University of California Press.

Petchesky, R. P. (1980). Reproductive freedom: Beyond "a woman's right to choose." In C. R. Stimpson & E. S. Person (Eds.), *Women: Sex and sexuality* (pp. 92–116). Chicago: University of Chicago Press.

Pigg, R. M., Jr. (1989). The contribution of school health programs to the broader goals of public health: The American experience. *Journal of School Health, 59*(1), 25–30.

Polit, D. F. (1989). Effects of a comprehensive program for teenage parents: Five years after project redirection. *Family Planning Perspectives, 21*(4), 164–187.

Scheffler, I. (1985). *Of human potential: An essay in the philosophy of education.* Boston: Routledge and Kegan Paul.

Schubert, W. H. (1986). *Curriculum: Perspective, paradigm, and possibility.* New York: Macmillan.

Sonenstein, F. L., & Pittman, K. J. (1982). The availability of sex education in large city school districts. *Family Planning Perspectives, 16*(1), 19–25.

Storr, A. (1988). *Solitude: A return to the self.* New York: Ballantine.

Verhoeven, C. (1972). *The philosophy of wonder* (M. Foran, Trans.), New York: Macmillan.

Wilson, W. (1987). *The truly disadvantaged.* Chicago: University of Chicago Press.

Wood, P. K. (1983). Inquiring systems and problem structure: Implications for cognitive development. *Human Development, 26*(5), 249–265.

Zabin, L. S., Hirsch, M. B., Streett, R., Emerson, M. R., Smith, M., Hardy, J. B., & King, T. M. (1988). The Baltimore pregnancy prevention program for urban teenagers: How did it work? *Family Planning Perspectives, 20*(4), 182–187.

CHAPTER 15

Sexuality Education—In Whose Interest?

An Analysis of Legislative, State Agency, and Local Change Arenas

RUTH F. EARLS, JOANNE FRASER, AND BAMBI SUMPTER

When it comes to public education, sexuality curriculum is mired in conflicting influences. The power of education is vested in the state; in many states this power is ubiquitous, while in others it is delegated to counties or local education agencies. The locus of authority to control curriculum usually reflects a state's historical conditions and the respective tax dollars contributed by state or local agencies. In the South, the locus of curriculum control tends to be centralized. This pattern of control has been intensified in the wake of school desegregation, accountability, and the reform efforts of the 1980s. South Carolina, cited as a model of educational reform, provides a case study of the institutionalization of sexuality education in the South. When a conservative southern state attempts to institutionalize a sexuality curriculum, it is important to examine the unequal political, economic, and cultural interests that surround the effort and thus influence school curriculum and change efforts at both state and local levels. To understand the complexity of such curriculum change, Apple (1990) urges that we see it situated within the context of the larger society so that we can analyze where educational actions and approaches come from, and who benefits from them. In whose interest is sexuality education?

An appropriate mode for such analysis is critical theory, a mode that is inseparable from action. Grounded in praxis or reflective action and based on open dialogue, it combines hermeneutic understanding with grass roots action (Schubert, 1986). Critical theory has an explicit value orientation toward liberation: The aim of liberation is one "of freeing persons from the parochialness of their specific times and places and opening up possibilities for persons to create themselves and their societies" (Macdonald, 1977, p. 17). Critical theory elicits emancipatory models of curriculum rather than technological control models (Apple & Weis, 1983; Habermas, 1973). From this perspective, the role of the controlling state mandating a new curriculum is complicated by resistant and contradictory events at all levels.

An overview of the history and culture of the state and antecedent events prior to state-mandated sexuality education sets the stage for examining the legislative strategies. Following the passage of legislation, the actions of the state education agency to implement the curriculum and teacher preparation requirements through the typical technological control model are contrasted with resulting contradictory impulses within the state agency and at the local level. The technological control model, as described by Bullough, Goldstein, & Holt (1984), derives from the historical conditions of industrial capitalism and permeates our society and our schools, pervasively influencing human interactions by its taken-for-granted understandings of power, legitimacy, age, race, and sex differentiation and roles. At both the state agency and local levels, resistance to a control model of sexuality education included community upheavals, silent voices who paid no heed to the regulations, confrontational and vocally belligerent administrators and teaching personnel, and district educators who viewed the sexuality education mandates as anathema to the emancipatory models they had been using for many years. The events and interactions arising from the advent of legislated sexuality education through its implementation stage are described as three separate arenas:

Arena 1. The realities of sexuality education legislation
Arena 2. The realities of state education agency implementation
Arena 3. The realities of local implementation

A description of the actions and interactions occurring in each arena serves to illustrate the ideological conflicts and examine actions that support the technical mindset and reproduction of the existing structure and status quo. Each tale also describes overt and subtle resistances to the taken-for-granted reality and hidden curriculum interactions existing in all arenas of human interest (Apple & Weis, 1983; Jackson, 1990).

Generally, in southern states, the state education agency is empowered to enact the changes mandated and funded by the state legislature. Thus, the agency is situated between those with power to mandate and those in local districts who are charged with implementation. The dilemma created by mandating sexuality education provides those "in the middle" with the observational perspective to analyze change strategies and effects. We work in the middle—as curriculum, staff development, and teaching consultants in subject-oriented content areas.

Two years after the mandate for sexuality education, we arrived by serendipity in the same agency and shared some common commitments to knowledge, health, sexuality issues, curriculum, teaching, and students. Our employment or previous work roles placed each of us, directly and centrally, in at least one arena of conflict as a participant observer. In sharing and reflecting on our experiences in institutionalizing sexuality education, we remain immersed in the hermeneutic circle of inquiry and hope that we have uncovered some generative themes (Friere, 1970, 1985) that may help other states steeped in conflicting sexual ideologies to restructure efforts and critical praxis toward what we consider more emancipatory models of sexuality education. Although we recognize that events and interactions are specific incidences in an analysis of one southern state, South Carolina, we also acknowledge that conservative ideology is not germane only to southern states; it permeates American culture.

HISTORICAL ANTECEDENTS TO SEXUALITY EDUCATION LEGISLATION

South Carolina has a recent history of educational reform ("How to tackle," 1989). The 1984 Educational Improvement Act, which placed an increased penny of sales tax in the state education coffer, has raised SAT scores 48 points (the largest gain in the nation), tripled advance placement enrollment, provided accountable basic skills tests and high school exit exams, and lowered students absences. The gains in education were led by a state superintendent who "took care to build a consensus among business leaders, educators, politicians and parents and understood that improved education would need to be a generational commitment in order to build a literate work force" ("How to tackle," 1989, p. 47). We find it worthy of note that the stated focus for educational reform is a literate work force. Habermas (1971) suggests that the human interest of work tends to place persons in a model of technological rationality that views human resources as capital in the economic system. This technological control ideology permeates our political, economic, and cultural contexts and indirectly influences educational reform efforts.

Like many southern states, South Carolina is economically poor, has a large black population, ranks low on health status indicators, and has a highly conservative religious climate and strong family and locality values. Passage of a mandated sexuality education bill seems aberrant in this climate. How did this happen?

Throughout the last decade, health officials have documented the poor health status of South Carolina citizens. The statistics relating to children and teens and sexuality issues were alarming: The state stood ninth in teenage births, fifth in the rate of gonorrhea cases, seventh in syphilis cases, and third in the nation in cases of sexually transmitted diseases among children aged five to nine. The rape and sexual abuse incidence, as well as extraordinarily high infant mortality and low birth weight rates, suggested a call to action and pragmatic solutions. Teen family planning services were available in every county, but local attitudes, budget cutbacks in Title X, and Reagan administration pressures to restrict teen access to family planning, including parental notice regulations, discouraged efforts to expand teen outreach initiatives. Thus, health advocates sought other avenues to curb teen pregnancy and urged that school health education programs become comprehensive and include family life and sexuality education. Prompted by a coalition of teen pregnancy prevention advocates, the state education agency convened a Comprehensive Health Education Advisory Committee in 1981. This committee recommended a five step action plan for improving health education, but no broad action was taken as the acknowledgment that teens were sexually active was perceived as too controversial. Yet the agency, in cooperation with the state medical association, produced and distributed a video series entitled *Growing Up*, which confined sexuality education to anatomy and changes of puberty (Mitcham, 1983). The series' graphics of the body were so thoroughly censored that one student viewer commented that she thought the ovaries were in the throat!

Other resulting attempts to address sexuality education failed as well. For example, in the late 1970s one affluent school distict tried to offer an elective values clarification course and was scathingly denounced by offended and highly vocal parents; the "sinful" health educator resigned to work in public health (Personal communication, October 1987). Elsewhere, an advocate of early sexuality education and researcher from the state university attempted to open a clinic in a capital city high school without school board approval. The clinic was rejected and he took it to Myrtle Beach, successfully providing education and contraceptives to sunning and runaway teens for several years. The same researcher has chronicled the sexual behaviors of college freshmen in the state over a decade, noting that the average age of first intercourse has remained steady at 16 while sexuality knowledge and effective use of contraceptives has declined (Vincent, Faulkenberry, James, & Johnson, 1987). This sexual behavior parallels declines noted nationally (Trussell, 1988).

In 1979 in the rural Pee Dee region, a public health educator developed a reproductive health education curriculum and teacher training program acceptable to the conservative community. Called RHETTA, its acceptability was found in its reproductive health (rather than sexuality education) focus, strong promotion of abstinence as the healthiest choice for young teens, clear identification of the risks of early teen sexuality activity, and overt instruction in the values of respect, responsibility, and restraint in relationships. Parent evaluations showed overwhelming acceptance of the program, and a 3-year follow-up of student participants noted continued retention of high levels of reproductive health knowledge (Thomas et al., 1985). Increases in teen family planning enrollment and declines in the county teen pregnancy rates were also noted. Based on this success, the state health department received a federal grant in 1985 to disseminate the RHETTA program to other school districts in rural counties with high teen pregnancy rates. The acceptance of the program by 23 school boards may be attributed to its discovery of consensus values in the school and parent community (Fraser, 1990).

In 1983 the Office of Adolescent Pregnancy Prevention at the U.S. Department of Health and Human Services funded a school community intervention program to reduce teen pregnancy in another rural South Carolina county (Centers for Disease Control, 1988). Over a 3-year period, the county showed a 54% decrease in the pregnancy rate among 14- to 17-year-olds, as compared to three similarly rural counties (Vincent, Clearie, & Schluchter, 1987). Both this program and RHETTA used school-based sexuality education as a basic intervention component, and featured community and parental participation and involvement directed toward local ownership and institutionalization of the programs.

While initiatives occurred in rual districts, sexuality education was nearly nonexistent in the urban schools. Except for a few brave teachers who invited a public health nurse to present methods of birth control, the urban school districts did not address pregnancy prevention. Yet, all three of the state's large urban districts had alternative programs for teen parents, and school nurses in a number of districts provided early pregnancy tests and referrals to family planning or prenatal services. These efforts were belatedly and expensively directed toward ameliorating consequences rather than preventing problems (Orton, 1983; McGee, 1982; Moore, Werthernier, & Holden, 1981).

One important actor thoughout the decade was Governor Richard Riley whose 8-year tenure stimulated passage of significant education and health reform bills that specifically served the poor and children. Teen pregnancy, which has severe consequences for those caught in the poverty cycle, was a logical target for his leadership. Solutions to the escalating teen pregnancy concern, however, were highly controversial since they meant admitting that teenagers were sexually active and that contraception was needed. Racial issues also complicated the controversy since the black teen pregnancy rate was double the white rate (80 vs. 43 per 1000 teen girls in 1988), and over 90% of black teen births were out of wedlock. Furthermore, the state experienced a twofold increase in the white out of wedlock birthrate since 1981 (South Carolina Department of Health and Environmental Control, 1987).

The data on teen pregnancy and its public sector costs (over $26 million annually) were brought to public discussion by state health department reports that targeted the age cohort of 14- to 17-year-olds and presented pregnancy, birth, and abortion rates by county, race, and rankings (South Carolina Department of Health and Environmental Control, 1983, 1985, 1987). These reports also assessed available intervention programs and found them insufficient, underfunded, uncoordinated, and lacking in primary prevention focus. It was the governor who brought the issue to the forefront of public policy and the legislative arena; in 1986, he created the Governor's Task Force on the Prevention of Teenage Pregnancy, which was charged with developing recommendations to prevent and ameliorate the adverse effects of teenage pregnancy.

Nowhere in this chronicle was note taken of the importance of sexuality education for healthy life-styles, for aiding adolescent developmental tasks, or for providing knowledge for its own sake. It seemed that sexuality in South Carolina was not an acceptable topic for public discussion, let alone for public policy discussion, and was certainly not appropriate for teen discussion; teens were not supposed to be sexual.

Historical and cultural antecedents to South Carolina's mandated sexuality education reflect disparate efforts and conflicting ideologies of sexuality education in general. Some actions stemmed from the maintenance of the traditional ideology of sexuality such as that described by Carlson in Chapter 2, manifested in many southern states in religious conservatism, patriarchal leadership in government and economics, paternalistic ties through an "old boys" network, and subordinate roles for females and people of color. Other actions emanated from a progressive ideology based on social utilitarianism, also described in Chapter 2, and motivated by the political and economic consequences of teen pregnancy. Carlson also suggests that both ideologies largely accept the current distribution of class, gender, and sex preference power, and focus attention upon various problems that threaten the stability of the current system. Both ideologies have been fueled by the technological control model of curriculum disseminated through federal health initiatives and grants issued to reduce teen pregnancy. Economy is often the necessary spur to both political and curriculum decisions.

To more closely examine ideology, we now turn to the progression of events and actions that took place surrounding South Carolina's sexuality education curriculum, employing the structural concept of action arenas introduced earlier—legislative, state agency, and local school district.

ARENA 1: THE REALITIES OF SEXUALITY EDUCATION LEGISLATION

In Arena 1 conflict occurs between persons who hold a traditional ideology and those who advocate a progressive ideology. In the South, legislators commonly represent a traditional ideology of patriarchy, paternalistic ties, and Bible Belt values, while health advocates espouse a progressive ideology of sexuality that views access to knowledge as critical to solving the social problem of teen pregnancy and empowering persons in a democratic society. The conflict and struggle in Arena 1 illustrate whose interests are served by these competing ideologies.

Constructing the Legislation

In 1986, the recommendations of the Governor's Task Force on the Prevention of Teenage Pregnancy were announced, proclaiming the magnitude of public sector costs of teen pregnancy and citing model programs in the state. The task force composition was deliberate, providing a broad spectrum of opinion to support the subsequent legislative recommendations. Members included religious, community, health, education, and business leaders and representation from the antiabortion groups, black and white churches, women's groups, and parent organizations. The spokesperson for the task force was selected for his credibility in the interacting constituencies.

The task force recommendations never mentioned sexuality education, but called for *primary* prevention legislation requiring comprehensive health education that included reproductive health, family life, and pregnancy prevention education beginning in the middle school grades and again in high school. All proposed requirements within the legislation were couched in the context of extending the current requirements for comprehensive health education programs in schools. The media, however, quickly identified the legislation as a call for mandated sexuality education. Public dialogue and debate ensued.

The task force also recommended *secondary* teen pregnancy prevention initiatives, such as school clinics and provision of family planning services to sexually active teens in school settings, which caused a cry of outrage from highly vocal opposition ("Plan recommends," 1986). Although school-based service interventions were known to be the most effective in reducing teen pregnancy, they were also receiving severe criticism nationally from the radical right and pro-family organizations, which said the interventions encouraged teen sexuality and usurped parental rights (Mosbacher, 1987). The disinformation circulated by local opposition groups echoed this view; any mention of the task force plan triggered accusations of handing out birth control pills and condoms, and providing abortion referrals ("Group lashes out," 1986). The opposition argued that "sex education is beginning to look like major attempt to bamboozle parents, children and taxpayers" ("Ten year moratorium," 1986, p. 2C). Demonstrators even protested the plan at the annual National Governor's Conference held in Charleston ("Picketers draw attention," 1986).

Four members of the task force issued a Minority Report (Adams, Chardos, Swanson, & Tyler, 1987) objecting to the inclusion of contraceptive education and presenting distorted citations from "research" that indicated contraception caused teen pregnancy. Their report, which recommended adoption of an abstinence-only curriculum, was sent to every legislator ("Abstinence stressed," 1987). Shock sheets and tracts describing explicit sexual fantasies and practices that children would be taught, such as putting condoms on broomsticks and using masturbation to explore sexual feelings, were circulated in churches, real estate offices, and laundromats ("Pornography in schoolrooms," 1986). Other opposition strategies included seven simultaneous press conferences organized by the South Carolina chapter of Eagle Forum and other pro-life organizations to protest the recommendations of the governor's plan. The Eagle Forum chapter issued a press release calling for a "ten-year moratorium" on sexuality education programs until researchers could study the effects of sexuality education on the initiation of sexual activity.

> A statewide parent's group lashed out Monday against a sex education plan for the public schools that members say would promote rather than curb teenage sexual activity. . . . Under the governor's plan, contraceptives could be issued at the schools, abortion referrals could be made and discussions could include masturbation, homosexuality and "all kinds of sexual activity." ("Group lashes out," 1986, p. 2C)

Those opposing the plan were urged to write to public officials and newspapers, and their letters to newspaper editors across the state became a fairly accurate barometer of misinformation and the general attitude of opponents to school sexuality programs (Fraser, 1987).

Opposition to sexuality education and the views of opponents were analyzed by a local district director of curriculum and instruction. Sherbine (1989) categorized opponents into three general views of sexuality education and his interpretation seemed to parallel the opposition views at the state level. As we examined shock sheets, flyers, and other materials circulated by protesters, their concerns and arguments provided further examples of these three perspectives. The following general views depict the ideological conflicts occurring in the legislative arena.

1. *Sex, and sex education, is sinful.* Sex is basically bad, a manifestation of the sins of the flesh, and thus a temptation that only the strong and spiritual are able to reject and only the married are allowed to indulge in. The weak, the developing youths, must not be exposed to anything sensual or tempting; sex education, talking about sex or sexuality, is deliberately exposing youth to sexual arousal, thus tempting them to sin.

To have the authority figures in schools conducting this discussion "condones" and puts the stamp of official approval on teen sexual behavior.

> I know what talking about sex does to me and I don't want my daughter sitting next to an aroused young guy in class. (South Carolina state representative, personal communication, February 17, 1988)

> The major goal of nearly all sex education curricula being taught in the schools is to teach teenagers how to enjoy fornication without having a baby and without feeling guilty. (Schlafly, 1981)

> When you tell teens they should use birth control if they are sexually active, you're telling them it's OK to have sex. ("Plan recommends," 1986, p. 1A)

> NORMA GABLER: school textbook authority stated that one text used the word, masturbation, 43 times on 2 pages, encouraging it. ("Pornography in schoolrooms," 1986)

2. *Sex education undermines parental/church authority.* Sex education is yet another example of government, society, the public school, and the health department being involved in an aggressive attempt (a conspiracy and Communist plot) to supersede the authority delegated to parental figures by God, the Bible, and Judeo-Christian culture. It is another example of secular humanism, a force placing human will and locus of control above that of God's, thus threatening the authority of God, home, and family. Sex education gives today's children a value-less system of factual information that undermines the strength of our nation. In other words, knowledge, unless provided within the "correct" value framework, will corrupt impressionable youth.

> The Communist Program calls for getting the young interested in sex so that they will be superficial, unable to understand what is happening to their country, easy to push over. The perverted sex programs that are coming into schools fit in exactly. ("Pornography in schoolrooms," 1986)

> Don't let government destroy the family. . . . Promiscuity not permitted here. ("Picketers draw attention," 1986, p. 1)

> Values clarification [sexuality decisions] usually tell young people that they can do anything they want to with little or no regard for parental or societal inhibitions. (American Family Association, 1990, p. 20)

> Three R's [RHETTA] . . . undermines parental authority and suggests to our children that they may feel the need to tune out their [parents'] voices. ("School board should," 1986, p. 4)

3. *Sex education is necessary but must be censored.* Sex education is of value and is needed in today's world, as long as certain topics are not

discussed in school. These topics must be censored because they arouse differences of opinion and only certain opinions should be presented as fact to children. Taboo topics include birth control, abortion, homosexuality, living together, sex outside of marriage, sexual deviance, and pornography. This view espouses beliefs in teacher-as-authority and instruction as "telling," and reflects the inability to distinguish fact from opinion.

> Birth control should not be discussed since recognition of its effectiveness can be interpreted by students as giving them the right to engage in sexual activity without having to be concerned about the consequences of meaningless relationships, promiscuous lifestyles, and general immoral attitudes. Abortion should not be mentioned since discussion can't be controlled and might convey support or acceptance of this activity. (Sherbine, 1989, p. 18)

> If the subject of homosexuality is included as part of the instructional unit, the information on homosexuality must present homosexual behavior as unnatural, unhealthy and illegal and may not include information that promotes the behavior. (Journal of the House of Representatives of the State of South Carolina. February 18, 1988, Am. # 18, p. 1276)

Eventually these three views influenced the language of the legislation, some provisions of the bill, and the types of compromises that were needed in order to get the legislation passed. For example, just prior to the sexuality legislation, a new, conservative governor had been elected and he promoted very specific language in the bill. This language essentially redirected the original intent of the legislation: instead of putting sexuality education in the context of comprehensive health, he reworded the law's purpose to specifically promote his vision of healthy *sexual* behaviors and abstinence from sexual activity until marriage. Our consideration of the synergistic effects of these views of sexuality education suggests an ultraconservative traditional ideology that serves the interests of cultural reproduction and structural maintainance of public versus private knowledge. Such interests retain the meritocracy of power and authority through religious belief in a controlling God, male, father figure.

In order to co-opt these three views of sexuality education, advocates of a more progressive sexuality education promoted the importance of maintaining family options and local control in selection of curriculum materials. Consequently, the bill included provisions for a community advisory structure and for parental exemption of children if desired. The latter was important legally since court challenges to sexuality education in other states had proved fruitless in the face of allowed parental exemption (Smith v. Ricci, 1982). In other words, as long as opposed parents could choose for their own children, they had no right to impose their values on the children of others.

Passing the Legislation

Gaining the active commitment of and providing factual information to sponsoring legislators was critical to passage of the legislation since sponsors had to navigate the legislative tactics of opposition legislators as well as counter the disinformation received by their colleagues. Advocates demonstrated that the bill represented the majority view and had strong public support by organizing a broad-based coalition of 55 endorsing organizations (South Carolina Commission on Women, 1988). They also cultivated "informed expert" relationships with legislative staff members and key legislators, because accurate facts that conflict with Bible Belt ideology are sometimes suspect (Fraser, 1988).

Overt support by religious interests helped to convince legislators that sexuality education was acceptable. The South Carolina Baptist Convention endorsed the bill, and *The State* ("Facts of life," 1987) newspaper analyzed a statewide public opinion poll on sex education by religious affiliation of respondents, showing that 80% of members of major denominations, even Catholics, supprted the bill's inclusion of contraceptive information and use of condoms to prevent STDs.

As the Comprehensive Health Education Bill went before the respective legislative bodies, bargains and trade-offs emerged. In the Senate one member's objection was removed with a promise for an additional state police officer for his county (state senator, personal communication, February 4, 1988). Since language rewording by the governor had already been incorporated into the legislation, most other efforts to amend the bill were defeated. A 750-minute requirement of reproductive health and pregnancy prevention for all high school students was the compromise for an unacceptable Carnegie unit of health education. And one senator, who apparently believed the antiabortionists' claim that 77 physical complications were associated with abortion (Kotasek, 1975), provided an accepted amendment allowing the risk and potential complications of abortions to be taught (Journal of the Senate of the State of South Carolina, February 3, 1988. Doc. No. 0816J, p. 32).

The House debate was extremely lively; with 48 amendments introduced, some got passed by sheer persistence. Strong amending efforts were made first to eliminate contraceptive education, then restrict it to the 12th grade, and finally to require a community referendum on its inclusion in the curriculum. Opposition again clearly represented the three views of sexuality previously identified. In the end, the belief that sexual knowledge is sinful, embarrassing, and somehow not suitable for mixed company, coupled with the view that contraceptive knowledge encourages sexual activity (Adams et al, 1987), resulted in an amendment requiring that pregnancy prevention information be presented in sex-segregated classes (Comprehensive Health Education Act of 1988, Sect. 59–32–20F).

Concern for the undermining of parental authority surfaced in amendments to require parental permission for the instruction, an *opt-in* requirement rather than the exemption noted earlier. These amendments were defeated largely because they would create extra paperwork; some also argued that the very youngsters needing the information would be the least likely to get permission, a confirmation of parental irresponsibility. At the same time the exemption clause is evidence of the tension between public versus private knowledge; its language and wording clearly evoke suspicion, fear, and rejection of knowledge as liberating if not set in a prescribed value framework or traditional ideology.

Most of the amendments, were presented by two die-hard legislators and centered on curriculum control of perceived controversial issues: homosexuality, abortion, and depiction of sexual intercourse, termed "pornography" in instructional materials. Homosexuality, for example, was to be characterized as "unnatural, unhealthy, and illegal"; legislative compromise relegated its discussion to units on STDs, reflecting belief in its inseparable relationship to AIDS instruction. STD education was prohibited below the sixth grade. Cloture on more amendments was invoked by the House leadership because they "did not want to see this embarrassing debate on the news" any longer (J. Rogers, personal communication, February 18, 1988).

In February of 1988, sexuality education bills passed both houses with differing amendments; four supporters and two opponents were named to a conference committee, thus successfully defeating additional debilitating changes. On April 6, 1988, the legislature passed the bill and appropriated $692,000 for textbooks and teacher training and the governor signed the bill into law (Comprehensive Health Education Act of 1988).

To us, the conflict in the legislative arena was worth the effort. Our quest to promote K-12 sexuality knowledge and education at the legislative level attempted to provide legislators with research facts and data to alter the misperception that adolescent sexual activity is nonexistent. Teen pregnancy data clearly showed the lie; teens are sexually active and need access to knowledge that is relevant to their lives. We believe that if this knowledge is denied in the home, church, and general society, ignorance will continue to create victims. This legislative effort, though ultimately in the interest of student lives, contradicted the state's Bible Belt ideology that "good" teens are not sexually active. The legislature resolved to support sexuality education in order to protect reproductive health. Ultimately, substitution of the term *reproductive health* in place of *sexuality* assisted this effort. In other words, state policymakers essentially gave the local education agencies permission to move beyond the denial stage to talk about sexuality and thus to improve students' access to relevant knowledge.

One of the valuable insights gained from our experience in the legislative arena was that opposition to sexuality education always comes from a small, highly vocal minority. The new South Carolina law supplies protection of the right to a minority opinion through its inclusion of a prenatal exemption clause. But the equally democratic principle of not allowing a minority to impose their values on the majority had strong appeal to fair-minded legislators. Persons working to institutionalize sexuality education need to sustain their efforts to assess and communicate majority support and not barter away the "inalienable rights" of most students.

ARENA 2: THE REALITIES OF STATE EDUCATION AGENCY IMPLEMENTATION

In Arena 2 conflict exists between the agency that embodies a dominant technological control model of curriculum and health advocates and state consultants who possess both health content expertise and experience working and teaching in local districts. Arena 2 is laden with slightly different sexuality ideologies than those in the legislative arena, and although issues span social, political, ethical, and educational dimensions, conflicts often get reduced to technical questions. The concern within the state agency becomes not what should be done but rather *how* it can be done (Bullough et al., 1984).

The South Carolina Department of Education was the state agency empowered to enact the mandates of the Comprehensive Health Education Act (CHE Act). The agency is situated between the ideology of those who mandate and those who enact. The CHE Act addressed all topical areas of health, requiring a program of reproductive health in grades 6 to 8 and 750 minutes of reproductive health and pregnancy prevention in grades 9 to 12. The State Board of Education, through the state education agency, was responsible for three major components of the act:

1. To select or develop an instructional unit with separate components addressing the subjects of reproductive health, family life education, pregnancy prevention, and sexually transmitted diseases and to make the instructional unit available to local school districts

2. To provide staff development
3. To monitor implementation of the specifics of the act. (Comprehensive Health Education Act of 1988)

In Arena 2, actions reflecting both reproduction and resistance illustrate the conflict between the bureaucratic mind-set and machinery of the state agency, which serves the technical control model of curriculum and the progressive sexuality ideology of health advocates, educators, and state employees, who were seeking to implement legislation in an emancipatory form.

The conflict and critical components of contention in the passage of the CHE Act reoccur at the state agency level. We see these conflicts as evidence of the "tightness of control" maintained in the bill to retain the dominant ideology of those "benevolent patriarchs" empowered to control both the status and kind of available knowledge within the institution of schools. At the core of any analysis of these events lies the question: Knowledge in whose interest? Several specific mandates of the Comprehensive Health Education Act are used as sample generative themes to examine and analyze the conflicts and actions that occurred in the state agency arena and relate them to critical theory. Friere (1973, 1970) describes generative themes as universal themes encompassing concrete and specific thematic program content enabling authentic dialogue and experiential awareness and consciousness within a community. Generative themes may be considered one methodology of praxis. Conflicts in the state agency arena suggest these generative themes:

1. The status of knowledge and structural limitations in schools
2. Content censorship, prescribed textbooks, and time constraints
3. Technological efficiency, deskilling and work intensification

These themes provide a framework for analyzing the "push and pull" that occurs within a state agency, the mediator between legislative and local action; tensions between state ideology and local practice provide the substance of praxis.

Status of Knowledge and Structural Limitations in Schools

The legislation is specific to the subject area of health, but health is traditionally nonacademic and has low status in schools. One way to assess the status of subject area knowledge is to look at its required time allocations within the school curriculum. Health is given minimal time allocation in the defined minimum program for grades 1 to 8 and is offered as an elective, not a required course, in the program for grades 9 to 12. In fact, time allocation for health is about 25% of that for reading or math.

We might ask why this low status is accorded to health. First, health knowledge and skills represent an applied rather than a pure science. The application of the biological and behavioral sciences in educational settings is not seen as rigorous or academic; health knowledge, in particular, has come packaged in local newspapers and women's magazines. Teens share their pedestrian sexual health information or misinformation in locker rooms and at sleep-over parties. Second, health knowledge and maintenance is traditionally a family concern; specifically, nutrition, hygiene, and accessing medical care are a mother's responsibility. In other words, the minimal importance of health knowledge may be a reflection of its class of advocates, primarily women, whose power, efficacy, and access to policy-making have been minimal. Today, health is a multibillion dollar business, yet conflict remains regarding the policy of health knowledge and whether this knowledge is the province of family, church, school, or the business world. Health knowledge and skills are vital, but relevancy of subject matter to the lives of students has seldom been a criterion for inclusion in the school curriculum. All of these factors contribute to acknowledging that if schools and curricula are agencies of social legitimation as Anyon (1988) suggests, then neither health nor sexuality have been considered appropriate content for endorsing the prevailing political, cultural, or economic interests of the dominant ideology.

The Comprehensive Health Education Act is laudatory, despite attempts to soften its efficacy in each and every arena of confrontation. The act places health (specifically reproductive health education) within the preexisting time requirements of the health curriculum in grades 1 to 8. Although the law specifies 750 minutes of reproductive health and pregnancy prevention in high school, it prescribed no Carnegie unit equivalent in order to receive a state diploma (this requirement was lost in the compromise bartering of the legislative process). The state's education agency is required to provide the actual instructional unit along with teacher training but in reality provides few examples of where or how to incorporate comprehensive health education within local high school curriculum reequirements. As a result, the low status of health knowledge remains, for it is still not measured on basic skills or exit exams.

Ultimately, the vital decision of how to meet the Comprehensive Health Education mandates falls on the local district, creating a dilemma of local autonomy and leadership from the state agency. In fact, when several local districts in the state decided that a required half unit of health credit for graduation would best meet the mandates of the act (and the needs of their students), they received a noncommittal written response from the accreditation section of the agency. The agency response indicated that in order for students to receive an official state diploma, they must meet only the state-specified credits for graduation (R. Fulmer, correspondence with Greenville School District, December 15, 1989). Several districts, sensing little support from the state agency for a Carnegie unit in health, abandoned the idea; the whole area of reproductive health was too controversial to take on if the state agency seemed reluctant to be supportive. In spite of this, several districts have decided to add a local requirement above and beyond the state diploma requirements.

Implementation provisions for the CHE Act were given to the division of the agency responsible for curriculum materials and teacher training, while the monitoring process belonged with the accreditation division. The state accreditation process, primarily a paper audit that counts the number of credit offerings, makes the monitoring of an illusive 9–12 integrated comprehensive health program cumbersome at best. Thus, separation of responsibilities and lack of communication between various segments of the state agency reduce legislative effectiveness and triggers an ameliorative reaction of mere minimal compliance in most local districts. In fact, five high schools have documented their noncompliance with the law, apparently sensing the agency can impose few consequences.

Content Censorship, Prescribed Textbooks, and Time Constraints

Another theme for examining the reproduction/resistance motif is the specific limitations on content, textbook adoptions, and time constraints surrounding sexuality instruction. Both adopting and developing materials at the state level represents a form of state control and censorship, and the potential denial of access to content knowledge. State agencies tend to follow a technological control model of curriculum for reasons of efficiency; the role of the agency is to figure out *how* to carry out the legislation in a timely manner. Resistance actions can occur at local levels because both legislators and policymakers tend to forget that textbooks and curriculum materials are not the only sources of content in the classroom and do not completely control the teacher's script or classroom interactions. On the other hand, the structural constraints of schooling, content delimitations for sexuality education, time constraints, age appropriateness of content, and gender-separate classes all influence the hegemonic relationships of hidden power and authority among bodies of knowledge and classes of people in school settings (Anyon, 1988; Apple, 1986).

Examples of state ideological control through technological rationality can be seen, here, through textbook adoptions and time constraints. The time constraints placed on the Comprehensive Health Education Advisory Committee for state-adopted materials practically dictated the selection of a textbook rather than the examination or development of other curriculum materials for grades 6 to 8. Publishers and other vendors were invited to submit appropriate curriculum materials to the committee for review. The state advisory committee reviewed the two series of current state-adopted textbooks and found both comprehensive in scope except in reproductive health, family life education, pregnancy prevention, and sexually transmitted disease. Therefore, to provide resources for these new topics, two additional booklets were adopted. Local boards were required to supplement these with lessons on child adoption and state laws relating to the sexual conduct of minors, including criminal sexual conduct such as rape and incest. Ninety-five percent of the local districts opted to use the supplementary booklets on sexuality education; the remaining school districts chose to receive an equivalent amount in funds for resources chosen at the local level.

In the CHE Act, pregnancy prevention in grades 6 to 8 is an optional component subject to local decision. The two state recommended supplementary booklets provided perforated pages containing contraceptive information. The state advisory committee viewed this format as appropriately adaptable for local districts because they could choose to include or exclude the contraceptive information as the law prescribed. Controversy arose over the perforated pages when the advisory committee learned that a resolution was presented by the South Carolina Association of School Librarians to the Region V Caucus of the Affiliate Assembly of the American Association of School Librarians (AASL) on June 25, 1989. The resolution, addressed to the publishing community, strongly objected to the whole idea of pages that could be removed from the booklets (A. Slater, personal communication, June 1988). The AASL resolution implies that this practice promotes censorship (American Association of School Librarians, 1989).

In the second year of implementation the state advisory committee, unable to locate a textbook that adequately met the content mandates of the 9–12 instructional unit, persuaded the publisher of the text that came closest to meeting the law's content guidelines to provide a special state edition of its text. The publisher removed references to homosexuality and moved the information on abortion so as to disassociate it from contraception (South Carolina State Board of Education, 1989, Attachment N). In short, controversial facts were omitted, and language was restructured to fit within the legislative mandates. The work of Michael Apple (1986) on the profit motive of publishing companies may help explain the willingness of publishers to adapt content and provide special state editions.

Technological Efficiency, Deskilling, and Work Intensification

A final theme in the state agency arena of conflict is the recurring problem of efficiency and the struggle pitting bureaucratic mind-set and technological control against the internal disharmony and dis-ease of personnel. This internal conflict occurs not only among health advocates and agency consultants, but reoccurs among teachers at the local level.

Apple (1983), in his analysis of the ideology of technological control, notes that in curriculum work, when faced with a separation between conception and execution in developing learning experiences, teachers feel disempowered, deskilled, and treated as technicians. Their internal conflict becomes another mechanism operating in favor of technological rationality and cultural reproduction; while a prescriptive curriculum may protect the teacher from dismissal, it also creates a deskilling condition by separating planning actions from actual teaching.

The early months and years of implementing the mandated CHE Act took its toll on everyone in the state agency. Other subject area consultants fussed because to them it seemed the dominant focus of the curriculum section was "sexuality education" (personal communication, September 15, 1988). In addition, two new health educators were hired by the agency to provide on-site teacher training through a mobile health van. The consultants produced a handout entitled "Thou shall not," which presented to teachers all the issues in the CHE Act that should *not* be addressed. Intended to alleviate fears and set limits for teachers worried about their jobs, it took a negative tone. Teachers seemed to be treated as just another cog in the wheel of knowledge transmission from the "correct" value framework.

One consultant was a specialist in AIDS education. As a grass-roots person and advocate for responsible sexuality education, she raised awareness and knowledge among personnel. Awareness of sexuality issues and taboo topics were no longer hidden within the agency, and as awareness and knowledge became overt, less restrictive models of sexuality education were shared in the agency and in local districts. Yet, just as positive impacts were occurring, the agency paused and delayed replacing a health consultant who resigned from sheer work overload. This diminished the agency's guidance to local districts for over 6 crucial months during implementation. Although no one believes this action was intentional, finding someone to bridge the ideological differences and provide pivotal leadership toward more liberating models was no easy task for a director entangled in the bureaucratic mind-set and technological control of efficiency and cost.

The effects of the low status knowledge of health, supplementary textbook adoption and censorship, monitoring an illusive 9–12 integrated, comprehensive health program, one-shot in-services intended

to allieviate fear but projecting the serious consequences of noncompliance, and work intensification were all issues of conflict between reproduction and resistance within the arena of the state agency and in the
dissemination to local schools.

Within the agency itself, positive actions toward emancipatory
praxis sometimes seemed minimal. The agency did carry out the mandates in a timely manner, but its actions reflected its embeddedness in
the technological control model of curriculum and were reminiscent of
the control ideology of efficiency that permeates Western culture and
most state agencies. Pragmatic adoption of state textbooks avoided additional controversy over written curriculum development while the
agency continued to interpret the new legislation in the most conservative way.

Choices or options that may have enhanced the intent of the legislation were, for the most part, neglected due to time pressures created
by the delay of the legislation in the compromise committee and the refusal of legislators to phase in implementation. State agency personnel
had less than 2 months to have curriculum materials for grades 6 to 8 in
place for the opening of school. Still, the agency might well have translated the 750 minutes of high school reproductive health education into
broader directional goals, student outcomes, or recommended criteria
for judging adequate implementation practices. Such practices could
have strengthened the hastily developed reproductive modules, regardless of the subject in which they were placed in the traditional curriculum.

The state department of education, in response to the law, could
have taken the position that it was appropriate and necessary to properly assess and evaluate the needs of local districts and their potential
barriers to implementation before recommending models of implementation or teacher training for the legislation. However, no provisions
were made for planning and needs assessment; rather, we provided service on a first-come, first-served basis—an action considered to be an
equitable practice. Action occurred without adequate planning, and the
expertise of state consultants was never fully utilized.

ARENA 3: THE REALITIES OF LOCAL IMPLEMENTATION

In Arena 3 the local level conflict is one of reproduction and resistance described by critical theorists like Willis (1977), Apple (1986), and
Anyon (1988). The resistance to the technological control model is seen
as opposition to the legislation, to the state agency, and to local administrators enforcing the law, and coming sometimes from the community,
sometimes from teachers, and sometimes from students. Each subordi-

nate level of persons in the hierarchy of power opposes and blames the other. Here, community consensus or conflict reflects the same ideological consensus or conflict that occurred in the legislative and state agency arenas. This arena depicts a collage of skirmishes at the local level that stem from conflicting ideologies combined with a state control model creating a condition of powerlessness for true local autonomy and subsequent curriculum decisions. The collage also portrays resistance to content acquisition teacher training models, student access or denial to relevant sexuality information, and content and structural delimitations in school settings. Sexuality education is a controversial matter now open to the public forum. Certainly, this is a first step toward more emancipatory models.

Although public dialogue was allowable, the traditional Bible Belt ideology seemed to serve as the "standard" for all those in local communities who chose to follow its tenets and affected the lives of citizens who chose other paths to awareness or "spirituality." Hence, the conflict between traditional ideology, which disallows acceptance of children as sexual beings, and public dialogue acknowledging sexuality and teen pregnancy was waged with great intensity. It soon became apparent that reactions from local school boards were fueled by perceived fears resulting from differing ideologies that tested the roots of southern tradition. Based on our personal observations, three major issues serve as examples illustrating the underlying ideological conflicts: (1) curriculum, (2) censorship, and (3) teacher autonomy and selection. Larson (1982) identified similar issues in his analysis of ideological conflicts in one Ohio school district. These conflicts perpetuate both community and personal dissonance and fear, and affect curriculum decisions.

Curriculum Issues

Several school sites will serve as examples of how conflicting ideologies were played out in local district arenas. In one school district in the "low country," teachers signed a petition with X's to indicate their support for dissolving an abstinence-only curriculum that students perceived as being "a big joke." "Pet your dog . . . not your date" was not the message these teens felt would deter early sexual involvement and other risk-taking behaviors occurring among themselves or their peers. The local school board, ignoring recommendations of its advisory board, directed the superintendent to implement the abstinence curriculum nonetheless and made it very clear that despite petitions from 3000 parents and community members, teachers failing to adhere to this curriculum would be fired on the spot. About 80% of the students and their parents voted with their feet and walked out, choosing to use the "exemption clause" in the law to protest material they felt was juvenile. An editorial in *The State* newspaper, recounting the incident, advised voters to "just say no" to the school board at the next election ("Islanders," 1990).

In four school districts in the "up country," the provision for local autonomy was clearly invoked by the local advisory committee. The provision of the CHE Act called for local advisory committees comprised of 13 representative community and school members including three clergy. The local committee recommended to the board that state supplementary materials be rejected and that the money be used for more conservative materials stressing abstinence (South Carolina Department of Education, 1990). In addition, in one district they placed the 750 minutes of high school reproductive health and pregnancy prevention education into the physical education curriculum, where often the sport mentality and strict sex-role stereotypes abound. This decision precipitated some rather negative attitudes, since many teachers who value teaching sport skills were forced to teach sexuality education, often in gymnasium spaces (Spartanburg physical education teacher, personal communication, November 2, 1990). Another major drawback to this local action was that it overlooked the need to develop a selection process to acquire the most interested and effective physical education teachers for the job. Consequently, even some teachers holding appropriate certification expressed fear and discomfort when appointed to teach sexuality education (Lexington physical education teacher, personal communication, January 19, 1990).

In other regions, opposition to the mandated sexuality legislation was more overt. In one district two-thirds of the seniors opted out of the 750-minute requirement, and in another the pregnancy prevention component was never taught (South Carolina Department of Education, 1990).

Censorship Issues

In other communities fear and Bible Belt ideology rooted in the law were apparent. By law, the Health Department was barred from conducting education within the school setting without specific school board permission. Other organizations such as Planned Parenthood, which previously served as valuable resources for many sexuality teachers, realized similar restraints. Such groups were singled out because of fears and rumors that they were passing out condoms, promoting masturbation as an alternative to pregnancy, or because of their association with abortion rights ("Ten year moratorium," 1986). The state department's position was generally one of neutrality, frequently reminding local school districts that they had the option to do whatever they felt was best as long as it fit within the mandates of the law.

Earlier oppositon directed at the state government level resurfaced in various school districts as vocal minorities equated comprehensive health education with sexuality education, resulting in teacher fears, censorship issues, and separation of the sexes during instruction. Parents, fearing that access to knowledge would precipitate early sexual involvement, set about the task of controlling and intimidating local school boards and censoring knowledge ("Sex education opponents," 1987). One district school board member received a phone call stating that "if sex education was placed in local schools, he would bomb them" ("Caller threatens," 1986).

Prior to the sixth grade, students could not receive any type of instruction about sexually transmitted diseases. Although the law required the separation of sexes only during instruction in pregnancy prevention, some school districts, fearing the wrath of the local "moral majority," elected to separate the sexes for all instruction in human sexuality. Never once were students asked their opinion, and it was not uncommon to hear them express frustrations with this arrangement. One eighth-grade female told a state consultant: "It is ridiculous to separate boys and girls. If we have so many problems with infant death and disease, teen pregnancy, and STD rates, it's just stupid. We need to hear what the other sex thinks so we can make better decisions" (Richland student, personal communication, April 10, 1989).

Some local school advisory boards established additional "guidelines" for superintendents, principals, and teachers. In one district, the superintendent was required to ensure that the AIDS hot-line number was crossed out of the state-adopted supplementary text with a black magic marker. Librarians in the same district sought guidance from the state Department of Education when they contemplated removing books that merely mentioned homosexuality (J. Mahaffey, personal correspondence, May 5, 1989). A few districts removed pages from the state-adopted text that discussed condoms. While we were examining local curriculum materials, we noted that in order to satisfy conservatives several districts in the upper region of the state had entire sections of textbooks rewritten, then retyped, and transposed them back into the original text.

While some local boards and communities were frantic, students' concerns were apparently different. Even the bland and fairly conservative state-approved text for reproductive health was in high demand in some communities. Upon arrival of the state health van and consultant at one school site, one teacher threw up her hands and said, "When can we get some more of the sexuality texts? The students have stolen nearly all of them" (Spartanburg teacher, personal communication, September 9, 1989). So despite local censorship in schools, sexuality knowledge relevant to the lives of students was needed and apparently not being taught in the homes. As one fourth-grade girl, starving for information, said so eloquently to a state consultant, "Yo, lady, I want to thank you for talking to us about that uterus thing 'cause I've been asking my grandma about it for a long time and she don't know nothin." (Hampton student, personal communication, October 21, 1990).

Teacher Autonomy and Selection Issues

In the few districts where early community and school intervention and sexuality programs had been established prior to the law, teachers with long histories of providing human sexuality education cherished their previously developed curricula. Nonetheless, these same teachers were deskilled and mandated to use prespecified texts and lessons selected to deter controversy. Curriculum decisions based on racial/cultural differences were never a consideration since all children should be the same—nonsexual until their teens, but preferably until marriage.

Sexuality instructors from the "old school" were infuriated to learn they could no longer discuss abortion as a method of birth control within their pregnancy prevention unit, but could only bring up the subject within the context of complications during pregnancy, as the law now mandated. They could no longer increase awareness and sensitivity about homosexuality unless they used the term within the context of diseases, mainly HIV/AIDS. As one Lexington teacher noted, the "word gay or homosexual creates a negative stigma and perpetuates the myth that sexual orientation is related to the incidence or likelihood of contracting sexually transmitted diseases and not related to sexual preference behavior as we know it to be" (personal communication, September 25, 1989).

Teachers forced to teach against their will created a whole new set of challenges. One teacher attended a sexuality education training session with his attorney, who was there to scrutinize and advise his client on the legal liability of teaching human sexuality. Health education consultants at the State Department of Education were met frequently by fearful, disgruntled, and angry teachers who had little or no training in teaching human sexuality, and had too many other job assignments to perform. Female teachers frequently voiced their fears and anger resulting from issues related to gender, class, and racial discrimination, while battling their own sexuality issues. Male teachers were unsure how they would discuss intimate sexuality issues with young and "budding" women. Thus, it became clear that the tuition reimbursed, content-knowledge courses provided by the state to ensure the mandates of the CHE Act were either inadequate for meeting the needs of teachers, or the districts did not assign their trained teachers to teach. The choice of who teaches human sexuality appears to be as important as the selection of a text.

Despite the conflicts in the local arena that stemmed from ideological differences; censorship of sexuality content; inadequate identification, selection, and training of teachers; and the structural constraints with the schools, such as sex-segregated classes and curricular "location" of sexuality education, the Comprehensive Health Education Act had many positive impacts on sexuality education at the local level. Funding for teacher training provided over 808 teachers with courses in comprehensive health and sexuality education, and many teachers who may never teach health or sexuality have been exposed to personal and pragmatic knowledge that they probably never got in school or in the home. In addition, school districts that once operated in perpetual fear of implementing sexuality education could now do so without fear of legal or employment consequences.

Certainly, increased communication about sexuality education occurred between the school and the community in all school districts, although some programs encouraged more communication between parents and students. Many, if not all, students received more sexuality knowledge. Dialogue is often a precursor to action.

SEXUALITY EDUCATION—IN WHOSE INTEREST?

The events described in each of the three arenas of action depict ideological struggles analogous to those described by Friere (1973). In his efforts to empower illiterates, Friere suggested that liberation occurs through praxis in which both the powerful and the powerless become part of the dialogue, for each creates the condition. Our experience confirms the need to address awareness, dialogue, and action as critical elements in all arenas, from the legislative floor to the lives of students. The interest served must ultimately be that of young people; sexuality education should not be bartered but rather emerge from the scripts of students' lives. Each arena is a worthy place to step into the dissonance of conflict and create dialogue.

In recounting this story of our efforts to assist in institutionalizing a sexuality curriculum, we hope we have shared the ideological struggles and the bureaucratic and technical models that pervade our curriculum work. We have done this in order to gain a broader understanding and reflection for action. Apple (1990) urges that we not divorce our work as educators from the larger society and that we analyze where educational actions and approaches come from, who benefits from them, and what actions we must take to stem the current conservative restoration in our society. "To the extent that we create a critically reflective community with our students and colleagues and then extend that community to those bearing the brunt of inequalities that dominate our society, we will be acting in a way that is of no little importance not just educationally but socially as well" (p. 188).

Sexuality education can be in the interest of all. It must not be stymied by retrogressive tendencies and actions in the interest of enforcing and controlling the dominant ideology. Rather, it can be connected in identifiable ways to similar actions in the larger society. To be unaware is to be blinded by the relationships and connections between ideology, the growth of the technological and bureaucratic models of controlling education, and the fact that the knowledge of dominant groups tends to be taught in the school curriculum (Apple, 1986).

Institutionalizing and providing sexuality education in one southern state is an important first step. It opens multiple arenas for dialogue and action. Few other Southern states have chosen to open this door of educational reform with such bold steps. This reform effort, like others in the state, is a generational commitment, for we all know that ideological changes are infinitely slow and technological rationality is so pervasive in our institutions. Recognizing whose interests are served by various actions can lead to the critically reflective community and liberating models needed to create sexuality education in the interest of all.

REFERENCES

Abstinence stressed for sex education programs. (1987, February 5). *The Evening Post* (Charleston, SC), p. 8C.

Adams, S., Chardos, H., Swanson, S., & Tyler, C. (1987, January). *Minority report: Governor's Task Force on the Prevention of Teenage Pregnancy.* Columbia: State of South Caroliina, Office of the Governor.

American Association of School Librarians. (1989, January 25). Resolution presented by South Carolina Association of School Librarians to Region V Caucus of the American Association of School Librarians Affiliate Assembly. Dallas, Texas.

American Family Association. (1990). *Public school sex education: A report.* Tupelo, MS: Author.

Anyon, J. (1988). Schools as agencies of social legitimation. In W. Pinar (Ed.), *Contemporary curriculum discourses* (pp. 175–200). Scottsdale, AZ: Gorsuch Scarisbrick.

Apple, M. W. (1983). Work, gender and teaching. *Teachers College Record, 84*(3), 611–625.

Apple, M. W. (1986). *Teachers and texts: A political economy of class and gender relations in education.* New York: Routledge & Kegan Paul.

Apple, M. W. (1990). Teaching the politics of curriculum. In J. Sears & J. D. Marshall (Eds.), *Teaching and thinking about curriculum* (pp. 186–190). New York: Teachers College Press.

Apple, M. W., & Weis, L. (1983). *Ideology and practice in schooling.* Philadelphia: Temple University Press.

Bullough, R. V., Goldstein, S. L., & Holt, L. (1984). *Human interest in the curriculum: Teaching and learning in a technological society.* New York: Teachers College Press.

Caller threatens to bomb schools over sex-ed plan. (1986, July 21). *Beaufort Gazette,* p. 1A.

Centers for Disease Control. (1988). *Reducing unintended adolescent pregnancy through school/community educational intervention: A South Carolina case study.* Atlanta: U.S. Department of Health and Human Services, Public Health Service, Centers for Disease Control.

Comprehensive Health Education Act of 1988. *South Carolina Code of Laws, 1976,* as amended. Sec. 59–32–10 through 59–32–90.

Facts of life. (1987, March 22). *The State,* p. 1A.

Fraser, J. G. (1987, November). *Sex education in the South: Battling the New Right.* Paper presented at the meeting of the American Public Health Association, New Orleans, LA.

Fraser, J. G. (1988, December). *Successful advocacy mandates for comprehensive health and sex education in South Carolina public schools.* Paper presented at the meeting of the American School Health Association, Orlando, FL.

Fraser, J. G. (1990). *South Carolina adolescent reproductive risk reduction project.* (Report MCJ 453702–01–0). Washington, DC: U.S. Public Health Service, Bureau of Maternal and Child Health.

Friere, P. (1970). *Pedagogy of the oppressed.* New York: Seabury.

Friere, P. (1973). *Education for critical consciousness.* New York: Seabury.

Friere, P. (1985). *The politics of education, culture, power, and liberation.* South Hadley, MA: Bergin & Garvey.

Governor's Task Force on the Prevention of Teenage Pregnancy. (1986, May). *State plan for the prevention of teenage pregnancy.* Columbia: State of South Carolina, Office of the Governor, Division of Health and Human Services.

Group lashes out at sex education. (1986, September 16). *The State,* p. 2C.

Habermas, J. B. (1971). *Knowledge and human interest.* Boston: Beacon.

Habermas, J. B. (1973). *Theory and praxis.* Boston: Beacon.

How to tackle school reform. (1989, August 14). *Time,* p. 47.

Islanders "just say no." (1990, February 19). *The State,* p. 8.

Jackson, P. (1990). *Life in classrooms* (reissued). New York: Teachers College Press.

Journal of the House of Representatives of the State of South Carolina. (1988, February 18). *23* Columbia: State of South Carolina.

Journal of the Senate of the State of South Carolina. (1988, February 3). *14,* Columbia: State of South Carolina.

Kotasek, A. (1975, January). *Medical consequences of induced abortions and its effect on subsequent pregnancy.* Paper presented at the Fourth International Conference on Perinatal Medicine in Prague.

Larson, J. R. (1982). The new right: Its agenda for education. *American Secondary Education, 11*(4), 52–56.

Macdonald, J. B. (1977). Value bases and issues for curriculum. In A. Molner & J. Zahorik (Eds.), *Curriculum Theory* (pp. 10–21). Washington, DC: Association of Supervision and Curriculum Development.

McGee, E. A. (1982). *Too little, too late: Services for teenage parents.* New York: Ford Foundation.

Mitcham, J. (Ed.). (1983). *Growing up: A T.V. series* [Videotape]. Columbia: South Carolina Department of Education and South Carolina Medical Association.

Moore, K. A., Werthernier, R., & Holden, R. (1981). *Teenage childbearing: Public sector costs.* Washington DC: National Institute of Health, Center for Population Control.

Mosbacher, B. (1987). *Teen pregnancy and school based health clinics.* Washington, DC: Family Research Council.

Orton, B. B. (1983). Public sector costs of teen pregnancy and childbirth. In *Teenage pregnancy in South Carolina: Everybody's problem* (Vol. 1, pp. 34–44). Columbia: South Carolina Department of Health and Environmental Control, Office of Health Education and Division of Family Planning.

Picketers draw attention to views on sex education in public schools. (1986, August 25). *Island Packet* (Hilton Head), p. 1.

Plan recommends required sex education. (1986, July 30). *The State*, p. 1A.

Pornography in schoolrooms: H.E.L.P.—Help eradicate liberal pronography in schools. (1986, November 11). (Available from R. Jordal, 702 Wisteria Lane, Piedmont, SC 29673)

Schlafly, P. (1981, February). What's wrong with sex education. *The Phyllis Schlafly Report, 14.* Alton, IL: Author.

School board should adopt sex education program. (1986, July 22). [Letter to the editor]. *Beaufort Gazette*, p. 4.

Schubert, W. H. (1986). *Curriculum: Perspective, paradigm, and possibility.* New York: Macmillan.

Sex education opponents offensive. (1987, March 17). [Letter to the editor]. *Greenville Piedmont*, p. 4A.

Sex education plan addresses urgent issue. (1986, July 31). *The State*, p. 9.

Sherbine, D. (1989). Views of the opposition. In *Adolescent reproductive risk reduction: Implementation guide* (p. 18). Columbia: SC Department of Health and Environmental Control.

Smith, v. Ricci, 89 N.J. 514, 446A.2d 501 (1982), appeal denied 459 U.S. 962.

South Carolina Commission on Women. (1988). *A good answer to hard questions: Comprehensive health education.* Columbia, SC: Author.

South Carolina Department of Education. (1990, May). *South Carolina Comprehensive Health Act of 1988 and AIDS survey.* Columbia, SC: Author.

South Carolina Department of Health and Environmental Control, Office of Health Education and Division of Family Planning. (1983, 1985, 1987). *Teenage pregnancy in South Carolina: Everybody's problem* (Vols. 1–3). Columbia, SC: Author.

South Carolina State Board of Education (1989, March 8). Minutes of meeting. Columbia, SC: Author.

Ten year moratorium. (1986, December 16). *The State*, p. 2C.

Thomas, L. L., Long, S. E., Whitten K., Hamilton, B., Fraser, J., & Askins, R. V. (1985). High school students long term retention of sex education information. *Journal of School Health, 55*(7), 274–278.

Trussell, J. (1988). Teenage pregnancy in the United States. *Family Planning Perspectives, 20*(6), 262–272.

Vincent, M. L., Clearie, A. F., & Schluchter, A. D. (1987). Reducing adolescent pregnancy through school and community-based education. *Journal of the American Medical Association, 257,* 3382–3386.

Vincent, M. L., Faulkenberry, R., James, A., & Johnson, W. (1987). Cognitive behavior, attitudes and knowledge of students who experience early coitus. *Adolescence, 22,* 321–332.

Willis, P. (1977). *Learning to labor,* Lexington, MA: D. C. Heath.

Administrators as Barriers to Change?

CHAROL SHAKESHAFT

The chapters in this section examine the problems faced by those who wish to introduce sexuality into the curriculum. Because schools are political organizations as well as educational ones, the barriers that confront those who wish to expand the curriculum are not only academic. Any examination of the barriers must confront the political context in which these changes are proposed. Central to the understanding of the political process of the organization of schools are administrators. The ways in which administrators, as the formal leaders of schools, conceptualize the issue of sexuality will determine what gets into the curriculum and how. Whether introducing a sexuality curriculum into a southern state or developing a comprehensive approach to HIV education, administrators are a part of the politcal and academic equation.

Thus, in reflecting upon the barriers that prevent the addition of sexuality to the curriculum that were discussed in the chapters in this section, my thoughts turn to the role administrators play in this process. While I do not think that all the problems center on administrative resistance, and while I am aware that administrators—like everyone else in schools—are both products and representatives of society at large, I would like to examine some of the reasons why I believe administrators block a healthy exploration of sexual issues in the curriculum.

I believe administrators, like many of us, are not comfortable with sexaul issues. It is this discomfort and lack of awareness about sexuality—their own and others'—that keep administrators from feeling secure and comfortable enough to support and promote educational experiences and courses in sexuality in their schools and districts.

Obviously, one of the reasons that administrators are uncomfortable with sexual issues is that they were raised in an environment that reinforced or taught this discomfort. Examining administrative discomfort, then, not only helps us understand the range and depth of administrative resistance to sexuality in the curriculum, it also serves as a case study of what we become as adults if we haven't been exposed to ideas and information about sexuality as children. I'd like, then, to share the evidence that convinces me that administrators are uncomfortable with their sexuality, exploring the effects of this discomfort on their administrative style as well as on policies and practices for students.

SEXUALITY AND ADMINISTRATIVE BEHAVIOR

While administrators often joke about sex, they seldom examine how their attitudes and beliefs about their own sexuality guide their administrative behavior. While both males and females are uncomfortable with sexual issues, male discomfort serves as a larger impediment to effective administration than does female discomfort for three reasons:

1. There are more male administrators at every level in schools than there are female administrators.
2. Females have had to learn to understand a white male world to succeed in it, and therefore, are more likely to have already dealt with issues of sexuality.
3. Women and men have been socialized differently around the issues of sexuality, and women's socialization is less likely to be the kind that impairs effective administrative functioning than is men's socialization.

Sexual issues shape many management strategies. For instance, hiring practices, organizational climate and team building are all affected by fears, discomfort, or displays of sexuality. The following examines briefly how sexuality interacts with some typical management behaviors and, more specifically, how male discomfort with the sexual self impedes effective management.

Hiring Practices

An example of how beliefs about sexuality affect administrative behavior can be found in an examination of who male administrators hire and why. In a study of the hiring practices of male superintendents (Shakeshaft, 1989), we asked these superintendents if they would hire an attractive female. Almost all of the superintendents in our study said, "Sure, I'd hire an attractive woman." When we asked for what job, almost all had her slotted for an elementary principalship. When we followed up and asked if these superintendents would hire this imaginary woman as an assistant superintendent, in a role that worked very closely with the superintendent, very few of the superintendents said they would. The issue for them was the combination of the intensity of the working relationship and the attractiveness of the woman. Most admitted that they felt uncomfortable in a close working relationship with an attractive woman.

Some, however, not only did not feel uncomfortable, but said they had, indeed, hired a woman to work closely with them, usually as assistant superintendent. We interviewed both groups of superintendents about their beliefs or experiences with hiring women in an attempt to get an understanding of some of the issues that might surface when men think about working closely with women.

The first reason superintendents gave for not hiring women to work closely with them was their concern that school board members would see something unseemly in the relationship and that this perception would threaten the superintendents' effectiveness with their boards. We interviewed those superintendents who had hired a woman and asked them if they had received negative feedback from board members. While a few reported suggestive comments or sexual jokes from board members, they all said that they in no way felt that working with a woman had hurt their reputations or threatened their effectiveness in the eyes of the board.

The second reason the superintendents gave for not hiring attractive women was their worry that it would cause marital friction, and few wanted "trouble on the home front" added to their already stressful lives. Interviews with those superintendents who had hired women indicated they didn't find this a problem. None of these superintendents reported the jealousy or friction that their colleagues anticipated. However, the fear of jealousy wasn't confined to superintendents who didn't hire women. The women assistant superintendents worried about the possibility and reported that they made a special effort to build a relationship with the wife of their "boss." In an attempt to "avoid problems," these women tried to ensure that the wives of the men to whom they reported would not worry about romantic relationships developing at work.

Most of the male superintendents said they wouldn't feel comfortable working closely with an attractive woman because they weren't sure they wouldn't be sexually attracted to her. And if they were attracted, it would seem to be a no-win situation. If a female subordinate didn't return the feelings, the superintendent felt he ran the risk of being charged with sexual harassment. On the other hand, if she were similarly attracted, the superintendent's first two fears (school board disapproval and marital discord) might become reality. Thus, fear of their own lack of sexual control led these superintendents to a position that it was better not to work closely with women. As it turned out, the issue of attractiveness was not central because all women had the potential to become sexually attractive to these men. The superintendents who had hired women didn't deny that they might become sexually attracted to the women who worked with them, but they didn't believe that feeling attracted to a woman meant they had to act on it.

Thus, in this study, most male superintendents did not want to work closely with women because they saw them as a threat. Because of the superintendents' gender expectations that women are for sex and that women thus constitute a sexual danger, most men in our study said they would not hire a woman. This example demonstrates how male discomfort with sexuality and how male socialization of what it is to be a man keep women from positions in school administration.

Team Building

The sexual issues discussed in hiring practices are also found in the creation of work groups. Even if a woman is hired into a position, male discomfort with his own sexuality may cause him not to include her in a team situation. From the woman's perspective, the issue of sexuality is also a problem. Women administrators report being cautious and suspicious of attention from male superordinates, unclear about what the underlying message is. Whether or not there is a spoken or unspoken sexual message, women process the possibility and think about their responses and actions in light of that possibility. Administrative action is influenced by gender expectations based upon the stereotype that when men and women are together the outcome is sexual.

Again, this isn't surprising. Sex integration rarely occurs in American school systems. Starting in about the second grade, boys and girls move apart and segregate themselves along sex lines (Best, 1983). Little is done to change this pattern of sex isolation, and observations of classrooms and playgrounds find ample evidence of spelling bees or athletic contests pitting boys against girls.

When males and females do come together again during late adolescence, it is for sexual or romantic reasons. Men and women have very little training or practice in working together as people, rather than as representatives of another sex. It's not surprising, then, that sexuality (and particularly heterosexuality) gets in the way of easy working relationships between women and men. These patterns in the absence of a curriculum that helps students explore their own sexuality ensure that when students become adults, they, too, will have difficulty working with members of the other sex. This is how a curriculum that does not include sexuality is a threat to a well-functioning work force.

Organizational Climate

Male socialization has contributed to behavior that creates an organizational climate not welcoming to women. Sexual jokes, references to female anatomy or appearance, and sexual innuendo are behaviors that women say make them uncomfortable and create a climate that is experienced by them as hostile.

A not uncommon example of ways in which male administrators allow male teachers to create a hostile environment, using sexuality as a tool, can be found in the following example from a school district on Long Island:

> The male teachers pasted a nude centerfold over a poster announcing Women's History Week. The message was not only that Women's History Week is unimportant, but also that it is acceptable and humorous to equate Women's History Week with the viewing of women as sex objects. [When women teachers complained to the administration they] were told that they lacked a sense of humor if they didn't laugh. (Shakeshaft, 1986, p. 502)

This is just one of the many ways women report that a hostile environment is created, using sexuality to make women uncomfortable.

Women are often coded by men as sexual objects, whether or not they have chosen to present themselves in this way. Research by Abbey (1982; Abbey & Melby, 1986; Abbey, Cozzorelli, McLaughlin, & Harnish, 1987) indicates that men interpret women's behavior as sexual even if women mean the behavior to be friendly. These misinterpretations by men (along with hostility toward women by some men) may then lead to unwanted and threatening sexual advances to women teachers and administrators. Interviews with women administrators indicate that most can report at least one incident of unwanted sexual advancement by male colleagues or board members (Shakeshaft, unpublished data). These women describe having to be careful how they present themselves—both physically and verbally—in order to make sure that unwanted sexual advances by men don't occur. And when they do occur, the women report that they are frightened, for their jobs and their physical safety. Thus, the school world for women employees is one that has elements of sexual fear and threat—in other words, a world that is unsafe and hostile.

SEXUALITY AND PRACTICES THAT AFFECT STUDENTS

Discomfort with sexuality not only impairs administrative functioning, it also narrows and weakens policies and practices directly related to students. In addition to the obvious result of administrative sexual discomfort—failure to support and nourish a sexuality curriculum—administrators who are not comfortable with sexuality build an education environment that is hostile to women students, fail to respond adequately to sexual abuse of students, and encourage practices that put distance between teachers and students, particularly female students.

Hostile Sexualized Climate for All Females and Male Homosexuals

Administrators uncomfortable with their own sexuality or those who view sexual comments, jokes, and "come-ons" as a natural part of male development are administrators who allow an environment hostile to women students to exist. As in the case of women employees, this hostility takes the form of both physical and verbal abuse.

Administrators who aren't clear about their sexuality don't punish behavior that puts down females. They allow boys to rate girls on their anatomy and call them bitches and cunts. These administrators themselves use female-identified words to insult both males and females. Words such as pussy, pussywhipped, pansy, and sissy are all aimed at humiliating another male by equating him with a female. Male homophobic language has its roots in equating a male homosexual with a female. This language humiliates females as well, who understand clearly that female is the worst thing a male can be accused of being.

This hostile sexualized climate is one that either encourages or permits physical sexual abuse of females by both male students and male staff. In schools and districts where this climate prevails, female students are harassed by male peers. In a study of sexual harassment by peers, Bogart and Stein (1989) found that

> young women are much more likely to be victims of sexual harassment than their male counterparts, especially in the more severe forms of unwanted sexual attention, including acquaintance rape and gang rape; that student to student sexual harassment is more prevalent than teacher to student sexual harassment; that peer to peer sexual harassment, including cases in which the harasser is both known to or identifiable to the victim or not known, ranged from verbal and written comments to physical assault and attempted rape. (p. 152)

Representative of the kinds of physical abuse reported by Bogart and Stein were

> A young woman who had been cheerleader at our school received threatening notes and phone calles with sexual innuendoes, in school and at home. After football season was over, this young woman was told, after track practice one day, that her mother had gotten into an accident right near the school. The young woman, tricked into believing it was true, ran outside and was knocked out and assaulted, but not raped. The female student suffered terrible fear after the situation and missed a lot of school due to both physical and emotional reactions to this incident. (p. 153)

Peers aren't the only people who sexually abuse and harass female students. A study of allegations of sexual abuse of students by faculty

and staff in 184 school districts in New York found that of the 300 reported incidents in elementary, middle/junior high, and high schools,
97% of the faculty/staff abusers were heterosexual males and 74% of the
victims were female students (Shakeshaft & Cohan, 1990).

Thus, discomfort with and lack of knowledge about sexuality result
in administrative structures that support and/or nurture an environment
in which female students are verbally or physically/sexually abused by
male students and faculty/staff.

Inadequacy in Dealing with Reports of Sexual Abuse

Administrative discomfort with sexuality also constructs an environment in which response to sexual abuse is inadequate. In a previously reported study of how superintendents responded to allegations
that school employees were sexually abusing students, we found that
many superintendents were not only unclear about what constituted
sexual abuse but also unsure what their response to these allegations
should be (Shakeshaft & Cohan, 1990).

When sexual abuse of students by staff was reported to the superintendent—usually by parents—school district response was most often
slow and confused. Superintendents indicated competing loyalties for
the accused teachers and the student victims. While superintendents reported they knew exactly what to do if a student reported abuse by a
father or uncle, they confessed confusion about what course of action
they should take when the alleged abuser was a colleague with whom
they had worked. They often stated that while what the staff member
had done was "wrong," they could understand how it had happened.
More often than not, they said that the teacher had shown a lack of judgment but that it wasn't all that terrible, particularly if the victim was a
teenage female.

Further, in cases in which a male teacher or coach was reported to
abuse a female student, superintendents told us that victims were often
ostracized within districts and made to feel that they had been the cause
of a "terrible tragedy." Because many of the abusers were popular teachers and coaches, the female victims were seen as villains who had
"blown everything out of proportion." On the other hand, male students who were sexually abused were seen as "real" victims. This response demonstrates how male beliefs about female sexual power and
males' own inability to control their sexuality make them unable to deal
effectively with sexual abuse of students. Further, it suggests that men
who are not clear about these issues may unwittingly foster a climate
that encourages both staff and students to abuse females.

Policies Limiting Teacher/Student Time Together

The study of sexual abuse of students by teachers and staff also highlighted another damaging practice that may occur because of lack of knowledge of healthy sexuality. Superintendents in this study perceived that reports of allegations of sexual abuse caused anxiety in other educational professionals within the system, prompting less physical interaction between teachers and students. This behavior was prompted by the fear that teachers would be unfairly accused of sexual abuse, despite data that indicate that false accusations are rare. Again, fear of the power of female sexuality and fear of dangerous females who would wrongly accuse teachers out of spite, shaped policies and practices in schools.

Further, not one of the 184 districts in this study made an effort to present the reality of these issues, working at ways to decrease irrational fears while still protecting students. No district provided any formal educative or in-service experience to counter these perceived changes in teaching practice. However, many superintendents felt that less physical contact robbed students (particularly in the early school years) of an important ingredient of teacher attention. Nevertheless, these superintendents reported either telling teachers directly not to touch or interact with students, particularly female students, or indirectly fostering such an environment, in an effort to be "safe."

CONCLUSION

It's no wonder that administrators, particularly male administrators, have not been facilitators in introducing sexuality into the curriculum. Like most other members of American society, administrators are uncomfortable with sexuality, their own and others. This discomfort shapes behaviors and influences administrative styles as well as policies and practices that affect students.

Dealing with sexuality in administrative training programs might improve administrative practice, both in terms of management and curriculum decisions. It might also help administrators be part of a team that encourages a healthy approach to sexuality in the curriculum. In the long run, such changes in our school might ensure that those in the formal leadership of schools in the future are aware of how their own discomfort with sexuality has the potential to affect everything they do on the job.

REFERENCES

Abbey, A. (1982). Sex differences in attribution for friendly behavior: Do males misperceive females' friendliness? *Journal of Personality and Social Psychology, 42*(5), 830–838.

Abbey, A., Cozzorelli, C., McLaughlin, K., & Harnish, R. (1987). The effects of clothing and dyad sex composition on perceptions of sexual intent: Do women and men evaluate these cues differently? *Journal of Applied Social Psychology, 17*, 108–126.

Abbey, A., & Melby, C. (1986). The effects of nonverbal cues on gender differences in perceptions of sexual intent. *Sex Roles, 15*(5/6), 283–298.

Best, R. (1983). *We've all got scars*. Bloomington: Indiana University Press.

Bogart, K., & Stein, N. (1989). Breaking the silence: Sexual harassment in education. *Peabody Journal of Education, 64*(4), 146–163.

Shakeshaft, C. (1986). A gender at risk. *Phi Delta Kappan, 67*(7), 499–503.

Shakeshaft, C. (1989). The gender gap in research in educational administration. *Educational Administration Quarterly, 25*(3), 324–337.

Shakeshaft, C., & Cohan, A. (1990, April). *In loco parentis: Sexual abuse of students by staff*. Paper presented at the annual meeting of the American Educational Research Association, Boston.

Shakeshaft, C. (n.d.). Unpublished data.

ANNOTATED RESOURCES

ORGANIZATIONS

Alan Guttmacher Institute, 360 Park Ave. South, New York, NY 10010. Conducts research and disseminates information in the fields of population and fertility regulation. The institute also encourages responsible family planning through policy analysis, research, and education.

American Association of Sex Educators, Counselors, and Therapists (AASECT), 435 North Michigan Ave., Suite 1717, Chicago, IL 60611. National organization providing professional development opportunities and certification based on academic preparation, continuing education, work experience, and supervision. Membership dues ($130) include a monthly newsletter and the quarterly journal *Journal of Sex Education and Therapy.*

American Library Association, Office for Intellectual Freedom, 50 East Huron St., Chicago, IL 60611. The ALA and its Intellectual Freedom Committee are active leaders and promoters of academic freedom for teachers and students as well as librarians and readers. The Office for Intellectual Freedom is perhaps the best clearinghouse for information on developments in this area and can help make contacts with a broad range of groups supporting intellectual freedom in schools, libraries, and the commercial marketplace.

Coalition on Sexuality and Disability, 122 East 23rd St., New York, NY 10010. The coalition is an all-volunteer not-for-profit organization committed to the advancement of full social integration of people with disabilities through educational programs, advocacy work, and as a resource information clearinghouse. Individual membership, $25; organizational membership, $50. Quarterly newsletter.

International Council of Sex Education and Parenthood (ICSEP),

Special thanks to the following persons for contributing annotations: Peggy Brick, Dianne Brunner, Peter Butts, Ruth Earls, Mary Margaret Fonow, Leslie Walker-Hirsch, Patricia Koch, Diane Lee, Eleanor Linn, Jonathan Silin, Bonnie Trudell, Janie Ward, and Anthony Whitson. These annotations represent an abbreviated list; for a more complete and up-to-date list, write: GLARP, P.O. Box 5085, Columbia, SC 29250 and include a check or purchase order for $5.

5010 Wisconsin Ave., Washington, DC 20016. Professionals working in the fields of medicine, psychology, social work, and family planning in 44 countries interested in providing training, program development, and research in family health and relations. Conducts research and surveys in family life and sex education, develops curricula and technical materials for countries, and provides materials for educational and clinical use.

Planned Parenthood Federation of America, 810 7th Ave., New York, NY 10019. Provides leadership in family planning through its 190 affiliates in 45 states. Activities include reproductive health services, training, public information and education, reproductive rights advocacy. Publishes several newsletters and occasional papers.

Sex Information and Education Council of the U.S. (SIECUS), 130 W. 42nd St., Suite 2500, New York, NY 10036. Serves as a clearinghouse of information about human sexuality as well as a referral service for institutions and individuals. In addition to the publication of its bimonthly newsletter, *SIECUS Report,* it maintains a resource center and library. Annual dues are $75 ($35 for students and $135 for organizations).

The Society for the Scientific Study of Sex (SSSS), PO Box 208, Mount Vernon, IA 52314. Founded in 1957, this professional society of psychiatrists, psychologists, physicians, educators, and others promotes scientific research in sexuality and organizes symposia, seminars, and workshops at its meetings.

NETWORKS AND INSTITUTIONAL RESOURCES

The Campaign to End Homophobia, PO Box 819, Cambridge, MA 02139. National network of antihomophobia educators that hosts a national conference, serves as a resource clearinghouse, and consults on educational strategies. Membership dues, $5 and up.

Education, Training and Research Associates/Network Publications, PO Box 1830, Santa Cruz, CA 95061-1830. Publishes and distributes a wide range of materials on sexuality ("family life") education, HIV/AIDS prevention, sexual abuse, and comprehensive health education. Catalogue with over 550 titles available. ETR also offers on-site trainings on designing and implementing sexuality and health education programs.

Human Sexuality Computer Service (HSX), Clinical Communications, Inc., 132 Hutchin Hill, Shady, NY 12409. HSX is the largest online utility for sex education and self-help and is available to subscribers of the CompuServ videotex network. It provides the Human Sexuality Information and Advisory Service, an electronic magazine offering over

2,000 manuals, articles, and interviews with experts. It also offers a hot line, HSX Support Groups, and a variety of forums.

Men Stopping Rape, Box 316, 306 N. Brooks St., Madison, WI 53715. Community-based group of men working to stop rape through workshops/presentations and educational materials. They publish a brochure, "What One Man Can Do to Help Stop Rape," a rape myth poster series, and a video, *Gentleness Is Strength.*

Network Publications, PO Box 1830, Santa Cruz, CA 95061-1830. Provides useful curriculum materials and books for sexuality education and offers workshops throughout the country to train sexuality educators.

Sex Equity in Education, c/o Women's Action Alliance, 370 Lexington Ave., Room 603, New York, NY 10017. Program to create a nonsexist environment for children by providing nonsexist activities for elementary and secondary age children. Creates and distributes educational materials, conducts research and development projects, and offers training and technical assistance.

MATERIALS

Adolescents, AIDS and HIV: Resources for Educators. An annotated bibliography of print, video, and audio materials for AIDS education and HIV prevention. The Center for Population Options, 1012 14th St., NW, Washington, DC 20005.

Bodies, Birth and Babies: Sexuality Education in Early Childhood Programs. A manual for schools and teachers identifying specific ways to promote healthy sexual development. Planned Parenthood of Bergen County, 575 Main St., Hackensack, NJ 07601.

Can We Talk: Myths About Lesbians and Gays. A 180-slide presentation with audiotape and bibliography compiled from the slide library at Kai Visionworks, PO Box 5490, Station A, Toronto, Ontario, M5W 1N7, Canada.

Childhood Sexual Learning: The Unwritten Curriculum. Cambridge, MA: Bollinger. A superb study of the vital part played by parents, schools, and the total environment in shaping the young child's idea of self as a sexual being.

Circles. This innovative tool helps the mentally handicapped learner to organize his or her social/sexual behavior around six color-coded, concentric circles that represent varying degrees of intimacy and social distance. A life-size set of circles in a floor graphic provide concrete practice environment to enact role-plays upon and to attract and maintain learner interest. Thirteen basic topics are addressed in relation to this self-esteem-oriented multisensory teaching tool. James Stanfield & Co., PO Box 41058, Santa Barbara, CA 91340.

Early Adolescent Sexuality: Resources for Parents, Professionals, and Young People. Cites materials on several early adolescent issues, including general reading, bibliographies, and periodicals for parents and professionals. Additionally, lists curricula for use with adults and young adolescents, general fiction and nonfiction reading for young adolescents, and films for young adolescents. ERIC Reproduction Clearing House ED 238 584.

The Facts of Love in the Library: Making Sexuality Information Relevant and Accessible to Young People. A provocative video featuring Ruth Westheimer. American Library Association, 50 East Huron St., Chicago, IL 60611.

In Every Classroom: The Report of the President's Select Committee for Lesbian and Gay Concerns. A useful compilation of statistics, essays, and suggestions for teaching staff concerned about the quality of campus life for lesbian and gay students. Rutgers University, 301 Van Nest Hall, New Brunswick, NJ 08903.

It's Not Funny If It Hurts and *Think About It . . . It Won't Go Away* are two 10-minute filmstrips for students and educators, respectively, that give viewers a good introduction to why sexual harassment is an important issue that warrants serious attention. Sex Equity Office, California Department of Education, 721 Capitol Mall, Sacramento, CA 95814.

Life Horizons is a visually oriented set of teaching stimulus slides with guidebook/facilitators guide that is the most recent expanded edition of the earlier *Sexuality and the Mentally Handicapped* curriculum. Part 1 focuses on physiological and emotional aspects of sexuality; Part 2 emphasizes the moral, social, and legal aspects. James Stanfield & Co., PO Box 41058, Santa Barbara, CA 93140.

Medical, Psychological, and Social Implications of AIDS: A Curriculum for Young Adults. A comprehensive curriculum that can be adapted for use with junior high school, high school, and college age students. AIDS Education and Resource Center, School of Allied Health Professions, Health Science Center, State University of New York, Stony Brook, NY 11794.

No Laughing Matter: High School Students and Sexual Harassment is a 25-minute videotape docudrama that presents the stories of three young high school women who encounter sexual harassment in school and in the workplace. Their stories are interspersed with conversations with teachers and administrators who discuss strategies for the prevention and elimination of sexual harassment. Massachusetts Department of Education, Bureau of Educational Resources and Television, 1385 Hancock St., Quincy, MA 02169.

Not All Parents Are Straight. A film examining the various questions surrounding the issue of children raised by gay, lesbian, or bisexual parents. Cinema Guild, 1697 Broadway, New York, NY 10019.

Peer Leadership: Preventing AIDS. A useful curriculum that assists educators and youth workers in preparing selected high school age teens to serve as peer educators for other young people. AIDS Education Project, The Medical Foundation, 29 Commonwealth Ave., Boston, MA 02116.

Prisms. A multicultural play about growing up lesbian and gay designed for readers' theater presentation with follow-up questions for group discussion. Appropriate for high school and college students. Gay and Lesbian Advocacy Research Project, PO Box 5085, Columbia, SC 29208.

Raising Sexually Healthy Children: A Loving Guide for Parents, Teachers, and Care-Givers. New York: Rawson Associates. An upbeat book affirming sexuality and urging adults not to miss the daily "golden opportunities" for initiating talk with children.

Rappin', Teens, Sex and AIDS. A comic book written in the language of adolescents in which African-American and Latino youth visit a health educator who speaks frankly to them about sexual issues. Multi-Cultural Training Resource Center, 1540 Market St., Suite 320, San Francisco, CA 94102.

Sexual Harassment: It's Uncool is an eye-catching poster showing a young woman recoiling from the ambiguous look of a young man as she is reflected in his mirrored sunglasses. They are racially and ethnically unidentifiable. Project Esteem, Hawaii Department of Education, 1390 Miller St., Suite 416, Honolulu, HI 96813.

Stepping Out of Line: A Workbook on Lesbianism and Feminism. A book designed to take lesbianism "out of the realm of misinformation and fear." Includes the script for a 2-day consciousness-raising workshop on lesbianism and feminism, adaptable to students, trade unions, professional and other mixed groups. "Organizing for Change," the second half, is a compilation of personal stories and analysis by lesbians covering everything from lovers and sexuality to the media, religion, and violence. Press Gang Publishers, Vancouver, Canada.

Sticks, Stones, and Stereotypes. This film gives viewers an appreciation of difference by examining the negative effects of name calling and the desire for assimilation. Equity Institute, 48 N. Pleasant St., Amherst, MA 01002.

Tune In to Your Rights: A Guide for Teenagers About Turning Off Sexual Harassment is a 24-page booklet written at a sixth-grade reading level and designed in a magazine format. Definitions, advice, warning signals, and school guidelines are presented in the context of a girl's diary and a third-party letter-writing complaint management resolution. Students are shown in racially unidentifiable silhouette. *Agarra la Onda de Tus De-*

rechos and *Iaraf Hookuk* are culturally sensitive translations of *Tune In to Your Rights* in which the support network portrayed and feelings described by both victim and perpetrator incorporate the ideas of a group of Hispanic or Arab-American teenagers and educators. Programs for Educational Opportunity, 1005 School of Education, University of Michigan, Ann Arbor, MI 48109.

Who's Hurt and Who's Liable: Sexual Harassment in Massachusetts Schools, A Curriculum and Guide for School Personnel is an 87-page book containing legal guidelines, theoretical discussion, intervention strategies, and 2-day and 5-day curriculum outlines useful for students or the training of complaint managers. Activities include a questionnaire, a series of escalating vignettes, and role-plays. Massachusetts Department of Education, Chapter 622 Project, Bureau of Equity and Language Services, 1385 Hancock St., Quincy, MA 02169.

SCHOLARLY AND PRACTITIONER-ORIENTED JOURNALS, MAGAZINES, AND NEWSLETTERS

AIDS Education and Prevention. Guilford Publications, 72 Spring St., New York, NY 10012. Published quarterly, this journal highlights existing and theoretical models of AIDS education and HIV prevention, including their development, implementation, and evaluation.

Changing Men. 306 N. Brooks St., Madison, WI 53715. Published essays and reviews on gender, sex, and politics. $16 for two years ($30, institutions).

Curriculum Inquiry. Subscription Department, John Wiley & Sons, 605 Third Ave., New York, NY 10158. Quarterly journal that features distinct and opposing ideas penned by curriculum specialists, evaluators, historians, psychologists, and anthropologists. $54 per year.

Empathy. PO Box 5085, Columbia, SC 29208. Published twice a year, this interdisciplinary journal for individuals working to end oppression based on sexual identities includes scholarly essays, prose and poetry, practitioner articles, anecdotal essays, research reports, as well as annotated bibliographies. $15 per year ($25 for institutions).

Family Life Educator. PO Box 1830, Santa Cruz, CA 95061-1830. Quarterly publication of Network Publications providing updates on sexuality topics, teaching tools for sexuality educators, and abstracts of timely articles from the Network library. $35 per year.

Family Planning Perspective. 111 Fifth Ave., New York, NY 10003. Bimonthly professional journal publishing scholarly research conducted by the Alan Guttmacher Institute and other social scientists on reproductive health issues. $28 per year ($38, institutions).

Feminist Teacher. 442 Ballantine Hall, Indiana University, Bloomington, IN 47405. Publishes three times a year interdisciplinary essays and reviews targeted for K–college specialists interested in using women's studies and feminist pedagogy to combat sexism and other forms of oppression in the classroom. $20 per year.

Health Education. American Alliance for Health, Physical Education, Recreation, and Dance, 1900 Associate Dr., Reston, VA 22091. Bimonthly journal that provides articles and features on a wide spectrum of issues and topics related to teaching and promoting health. Free to association members ($50, institutions).

Health Education Quarterly. Subscription Department, John Wiley & Sons, 605 Third Ave., New York, NY 10158. Monthly journal that includes research papers, commentaries, essays, teaching techniques, and health services applications related to or affecting health promotion in the schools. $43 per year ($86, institutions).

Journal of Curriculum Theorizing. 53 Falstaff Rd., Rochester, NY 14609. An interdisciplinary quarterly journal of curriculum studies, including essays, political notes, book reviews, and poetry. $35 per year.

Journal of the History of Sexuality. University of Chicago Press, Journal Division, PO Box 37005, Chicago, IL 60637. A cross-disciplinary journal of essays and reviews on the history of sexuality from ancient times to the present. $29 per year.

Journal of Homosexuality. Haworth Press, 10 Alice St., Binghamton, NY 13904-1580. Quarterly interdisciplinary journal devoted to scholarly research on homosexuality, including sexual practices and gender roles and their cultural, historical, interpersonal, and modern social contexts. $40 per year ($95 for institutions and $175 for libraries).

Journal of Sex Education and Therapy. Guilford Publications, 72 Spring St., 4th Floor, New York, NY 10012. Journal of the American Association of Sex Educators, Counselors, and Therapists that presents research and clinical articles, field reports and reviews of new materials. $30 per year ($50, institutions).

Journal of Sex Research. PO Box 208, Mount Vernon, IA 52314. Quarterly journal published by the Society for the Scientific Study of Sex containing book reviews and case studies. $45 per year ($70, libraries).

Matrices: Lesbian Feminist Resource Network. Women's Studies Department, University of Minnesota, 492 Ford Hall, Minneapolis, MN 55455. A quarterly publication containing book and film reviews, dissertation abstracts, lesbian features in journals and newspapers, directory of lesbian periodicals and archives, conference calls, and brief descriptions of new books.

Sexuality and Disability. Human Sciences Press, 72 Fifth Ave., New York, NY 10011. Published by the Coalition on Sexuality and Disability, this quarterly journal is devoted to the study of sex and physical and mental illness. $38 ($102 institutions).

SELECTED NOVELS FOR CHILDREN AND YOUNG ADULTS

Bradford, R. (1952). *Red Sky at Morning*. Philadelphia: Lippincott. Josh Arnold and his fragile "Southern Belle" mother spend World War II at a summer retreat in the mountains of New Mexico when his father leaves his Mobile, Alabama, shipyard to serve in the navy. Josh experiences public schools for the first time (with Hispanic majority), and learns about dating and himself.

Chambers, A. (1982). *Dance on My Grave*. New York: Harper & Row. Hal Robinson has been looking for the ideal friendship since he was young. Barry Gorman promises to fulfill that dream, but the inevitable conflict of needs and miscommunication lead to tragedy. This is a compelling, positive account of a first gay experience with emphasis on friendship.

Donovan, J. (1969). *I'll Get There, It Better Be Worth the Trip*. New York: Harper & Row. Davy comes from a broken home: Deserted by both his alcoholic mother and his father who has remarried, he lives with his grandmother. His only real interest is his dog. When his mother brings him to New York, Davy meets Altshuler. Their friendship is spoiled when a brief sexual encounter coincides with the death of Davy's dog.

Etheridge, K. (1985). *Toothpick*. New York: Holiday. Jamie "Needle" Amont is a tall, skinny, shy kid. He admires the school beauty queen from afar and finally with the help of Janice, whose cystic fibrosis has left her even skinnier than Needle, he gets the courage to approach the girl of his dreams.

Garden, N. (1982). *Annie on My Mind*. New York: Farrar, Straus & Giroux. Liza Winthrop is an intelligent and successful high school senior from a wealthy section of Brooklyn. She meets Annie Kenyon, a working-class girl, who attends a public school in the city. The two quickly become friends, then slowly and sometimes painfully acknowledge that their relationship has both a romantic and a sexual component.

Mazer, N. (1986). *Three sisters*. New York: Scholastic. Karen's misplaced romantic feelings for her sister Liz's boyfriend threaten to alienate Liz, but a disturbing revelation from the third sister in the family promises to bind them all together again.

Myers, W. (1975). *Fast Sam, Cool Clyde, and Stuff*. New York: Viking. The adventures of three African-American friends in New York City: exposure to drugs, pressures for sex, police harassment, and divorce in a light, upbeat manner.

Rees, D. (1980). *The Lighthouse*. New York: Dobson. Victoria, a young woman from the Greek island of Mykonos who is about to go to school at Cambridge, meets Leslie, a physically attractive Englishman.

Sebestyen, O. (1984). "Welcome." In D. Gallo (Ed.), *Sixteen* (pp. 47–

58). New York: Dell. Tina's best friend, Sharon, is 14 and pregnant. Sharon's parents don't want her around so Tina offers to let Sharon move in with her and her mom. Tina is black; Sharon is white. Their friendship creates conflict between Tina and her mother, which is eventually resolved.

Voight, C. (1985). *The Runner.* New York: Fawcett. Young adult fiction on sports and interpersonal relationships.

Voight, C. (1990). *Solitary Blue.* New York: Fawcett. Fast-paced young adult fiction on divorce and father/son relationships.

Zindell, P. (1969). *My Darling, My Hamburger.* New York: Harper & Row. Explores the world of four high school seniors who get caught between fear and a desire for intimacy.

About the Editor and the Contributors

James T. Sears is an associate professor in the Department of Educational Leadership and Policies at the University of South Carolina. He is also a senior research associate for the South Carolina Educational Policy Center. Completing graduate degrees at the University of Wisconsin–Madison and at Indiana University, Professor Sears' academic interests are curriculum and sexuality. His books include *Teaching and Thinking About Curriculum: Critical Inquiries* (with J. Dan Marshall), and the critically acclaimed *Growing up Gay in the South: Race, Gender, and Journeys of the Spirit*. He is currently completing an ethnography that details how persons belonging to various cultural communities within the United States understand sexuality and the implications for sexuality education. Professor Sears' writings have appeared in a variety of scholarly journals and popular magazines and he serves as co-editor of *Teaching Education* and editor of *Empathy*. He holds leadership positions in national organizations including the Association of Supervision and Curriculum Development and the American Educational Research Association. Additionally, he serves on the editorial boards of *Journal of Curriculum Theorizing* and the *Journal of Homosexuality*.

Louise M. Berman is professor, Department of Education Policy, Planning, and Administration at the University of Maryland, College Park. Her field is curriculum theory and development. Her B.A. degree is from Wheaton College, Illinois, and her M.A. and Ed.D. are from Teachers College, Columbia University. Interested in cross-national exploration of educational issues, she is past president of the World Council for Curriculum and Instruction and is active in a number of other professional organizations. Author of various publications, she also serves on editorial boards of professional journals.

Diane D. Brunner, assistant professor of English at Michigan State University, earned her doctorate at University of Georgia. She is an English educator interested in multicultural literacy and feminist pedagogy. Professor Brunner's work with teachers led to her forthcoming book tentatively titled *Teaching Toward Reflective Practice: A Role for Literature and the Arts in Teacher Education*.

347

Dennis L. Carlson is a member of the faculty, Department of Educational Leadership at Miami University. He received his Ph.D. from the University of Wisconsin-Madison and has previously taught at Hobart and William Smith Colleges and Rutgers University. He has published in a number of scholarly journals and is completing work on a book about the urban school crisis.

Saundra L. Davis, in the California Department of Education, Office of Gender Equity, provides leadership, assistance, and resources to schools and organizations concerned with gender equity and implementation of the federal Title IX law and the state Sex Equity in Education Act. As an educator since the early 1970s, she has been involved in access, advocacy, equity, employment, and training issues for reentry women, pregnant teens, and minority students.

Ruth F. Earls received her doctorate in curriculum and instruction from the University of North Carolina at Greensboro, received her M.S. in administration from the college of health and human services at Northeastern University, and got her B.S. in health and physical education from Springfield College. She is currently employed as the state physical education consultant for health or physical education or both in state education agencies in Ohio and New Hampshire. She has also been employed as a teacher educator at five universities and taught for 7 years in public schools.

Michelle Fine is the Goldie Anna Charitable Trust Professor of Psychology in Education at the University of Pennsylvania and a consultant with the Philadelphia Schools Collaborative. Her recent books include *Framing Dropouts: Notes on the Politics of an Urban High School* and *Silenced Voices: Race, Class, and Gender in U.S. Schools* (co-edited with Lois Weis).

Mary Margaret Fonow is a sociologist and assistant director of the Center for Women's Studies at Ohio State University. She has published in the area of feminist epistemology and methodology, feminist pedagogy, and rape prevention. She is co-editor of *Beyond Methodology: Feminist Scholarship as Lived Research* and serves on the editorial board of *Empathy.*

Joanne G. Fraser received the B.S. degree in education from the University of Illinois, M.A. in curriculum and Ed.D. in curriculum research from the University of Alabama. She is currently the state health education consultant for the South Carolina Department of Education. From 1985 to 1989 she was director of the South Carolina Adolescent Reproductive Risk Reduction (3R) Project, helping rural school districts implement a reproductive health education curriculum for middle school students.

Jesse Goodman received his Ph.D. degree in 1982 from the University of Wisconsin–Madison, and he is now an associate professor at Indiana University in Bloomington. His primary interests include teacher education/socialization and the development and implementation of emancipatory pedagogy. He has had over 25 articles on these topics published in a variety of scholarly journals. Since 1986, his research of teacher socialization has received four national awards for distinguished scholarship.

Susan Shurberg Klein is a senior research associate in the Office of Educational Research and Improvement, U.S. Department of Education, where she has recently provided assistance to the staff of the Select Education Subcommittee in the U.S. House of Representatives. She also worked in the Department's Women's Research Team and the National Advisory Council on Women's Educational Programs. She is the editor of *Handbook for Achieving Sex Equity through Education* and *Sex Equity and Sexuality in Education*. Dr. Klein chaired the American Educational Research Association Women's Committee and its Special Interest Group: Research on Women and Education and received their Willystine Goodsell Award. Her 1970 doctorate is in educational psychology from Temple University.

Patricia Barthalow Koch is an assistant professor in the Department of Health Education at Pennsylvania State University. She earned a B.S. degree from Indiana University of Pennsylvania in elementary education and an M.S. degree in health education from New York University. She taught in the public schools before earning a doctorate in health education from Pennsylvania State University and then teaching and conducting research in academia. Her areas of specialization include sexuality education, enhancement of sexual development and health, and AIDS prevention. Professor Koch has served as a consultant to the American Academy of Pediatrics and is the president-elect for the Eastern Region of the Society for the Scientific Study of Sex. She has published numerous articles in journals and has contributed to health education textbooks.

Christine LaCerva, as the educational director of the Barbara Taylor School, has designed and implemented the curriculum and pedagogical methods that help teachers create a nonabusive developmental environment in the classroom. She has received a master's degree in learning disabilities and education of the hearing impaired from Teachers College, Columbia University. Ms. LaCerva is a doctoral candidate in community education. She is also a National Fellow for the Humanities, focusing on the study of democracy in education, a 1989 graduate of the East Side Institute for Short Term Psychotherapy Training Program, and an adjunct faculty member at the East Side Institute, where she teaches the social therapeutic approach to education. Prior to her work at the Barbara Taylor School she taught in special education in the public school system for 10 years.

Diane M. Lee is an assistant professor in the Department of Education, University of Maryland, Baltimore County. She teaches courses in human learning and cognition and research design. Her B.A. degree is from Towson State University, Maryland, and her M.A. and Ph.D. are from the University of Maryland, College Park. Her recent publications include *Toward Curriculum for Being: Voices of Educators*, written with others.

Eleanor Linn is associate director for gender equity concerns at the Programs for Educational Opportunity, located at the University of Michigan, where she has developed materials, model programs, policies, and workshops about sexual harassment and other gender-related issues for school districts throughout the Midwest. She holds a bachelor's degree from Brandeis University, an M.A.T. from Harvard University Graduate School of Education, and an M.Ed. from Lesley College. Ms. Linn previously taught at the elementary, junior high school, and high school level and was the supervisor of a university teacher-internship program and director of a grass-roots counseling center.

Debian Marty is an M.A. candidate in women's studies at Ohio State University. Her areas of interest include feminist and postmodern issues in the historiography of sexuality as well as pedagogical strategies regarding the politics of diversity.

Lynn Phillips is a doctoral candidate in social psychology and human development at the University of Pennsylvania's Graduate School of Education. She has worked on issues of violence against women for the past 9 years as an advocate, educator, and researcher. She is currently writing her dissertation, exploring how young women's experience/understandings of desire, power, and violence fold into the construction of their sexual subjectivities.

Mara Sapon-Shevin is a professor in the Division for the Study of Teaching at Syracuse University. She obtained her B.A. and Ed.D. from the University of Rochester and her M.A. from Western Michigan University. Her research interests include the politics of special education and gifted education, mainstreaming, and cooperative learning. She is actively involved in university and community peace activism as well as discrimination/prejudice reduction activities.

Charol Shakeshaft is professor and chairperson of the Department of Administration and Policy Studies at Hofstra University. She received her B.S. at the University of Nebraska and her M.S. and Ph.D. in educational administration at Texas A&M University. A prolific writer, Dr. Shakeshaft's most recent book is *Women in Educational Administration*.

Jonathan G. Silin is an AIDS education and policy specialist who holds an M.S. from Bank Street College of Education and Ed.M. and Ed.D. from Teachers College, Columbia University. He has taught at Bank Street College and Colgate, Columbia, Adelphi, and Long Island universities. A former director of education and public information for the Long Island Association for AIDS Care, Dr. Silin has pioneered the development of progressive AIDS education programs and policies. He is a consultant to Bank Street's Project Healthy Choices and the Nassau-Suffolk Hospital Council's HIV/AIDS Education Project for Physicians.

Nan D. Stein, a former teacher, counselor, and educational equity specialist with the Massachusetts Department of Education, is known nationally for her work in sex discrimination and sexual harassment, and for her leadership role in national organizations involved with sex equity in education. She is the author of a variety of print and audiovisual curriculum materials about student-to-student sexual harassment. Dr. Stein holds a B.A. in history from the University of Wisconsin, an M.A.T. from Antioch College Graduate School of Education, and a doctorate in education from Harvard University Graduate School of Education.

Bambi W. Sumpter currently serves as health education consultant for the South Carolina State Department of Education, where she provides exhibit-oriented training and instruction to teachers and students. She holds a doctorate in health promotion and education from the University of South Carolina, a master's degree in physical education and health from Tuskegee University. Dr. Sumpter's area of specialization is family life and sex education and HIV/AIDS. She is co-author of a supplemental health text for college instruction, *Added Dimensions in Fitness*, and a contributor to several journals.

Jill McLean Taylor is a research associate at the Harvard Graduate School of Education and project manager for a longitudinal study of a diverse group of at-risk adolescents attending an urban high school. Dr. Taylor is a graduate of the New Zealand School of Physical Therapy and the University of Massachusetts and holds a master's degree in education and a doctorate in human development and psychology from the Harvard Graduate School of Education. She is the co-editor of *Mapping the Moral Domain: A Contribution of Women's Thinking to Psychological Theory and Education*, with Carol Gilligan and Janie Ward. Dr. Taylor's research interests include the psychosocial development of adolescent mothers and the development of adolescents from diverse racial and ethnic backgrounds.

Bonnie K. Trudell is an assistant professor at the University of Wisconsin–Madison, with a joint appointment in curriculum and instruction and women's studies. She has an M.S. in child and family studies and a Ph.D. in curriculum and instruction from the University of Wisconsin–Madison. Her research raises critical questions about the unintended consequences and dilemmas that school programs designed to address wide social problems such as sexual abuse and teenage pregnancy can pose for students and teachers.

Janie Victoria Ward is an assistant professor of education and human services and coordinator of the Human Services Program at Simmons College. A 1990–91 recipient of the Rockefeller Research Fellowship at the Center for the Study of Black Literature and Culture, University of Pennsylvania, Dr. Ward is a graduate of New York University and holds a master's in education and a doctorate in human development from Harvard Graduate School of Education. She is the author of several articles and is the co-editor of *Mapping the Moral Domain: A Contribution of Women's Thinking to Psychological Theory and Education*, with Carol Gilligan and Jill Taylor. Dr. Ward's research interests include the psychosocial development of adolescents of color, particularly African-American and Latino youth.

Mariamne H. Whatley received her A.B. in English from Radcliffe College and her Ph.D. in biological sciences from Northwestern University. She is currently an associate professor at University of Wisconsin–Madison, with a joint appointment between the Department of Curriculum and Instruction and the Women's Studies Program. Her research interests include evaluation of health and sexuality texts and curricula from a feminist perspective, feminist critiques of science, and women's health issues. She has co-edited *Women's Health: Readings on Social, Economic, and Political Issues* and *The Ideology of Images in Educational Media*.

James A. (Tony) Whitson teaches in the Department of Curriculum and Instruction at Louisiana State University in Baton Rouge. He received his undergraduate degree from Harvard College and his law degree from the University of Wisconsin. After practicing public interest law in Madison, Wisconsin, he earned a Ph.D. in education at the University of Rochester. Professor Whitson's books include *Constitution and Curriculum: Hermeneutical Semiotics of Cases and Controversies in Education, Law, and Social Science* and, with other authors, *Preparing Teachers as Professionals: The Role of Educational Studies and Other Liberal Disciplines.*

Index

Abbey, A., 332
Abortion, 243, 247, 295; and current state of education, 7, 8, 9; fear of as topic in education, 79, 172; and goals of education, 7, 16; and needs of students, 10, 81, 295; and progressivism, 40–41, 42–43, 44; and radical Freudianism, 47; and sexual knowledge/learning, 212, 218, 222, 237–238; and South Carolina curriculum, 304–305, 306, 309, 310, 311, 316, 320, 322
Abrahamse, A. F., 286
Abramson, Allen, 142
Abramson, P., 28n1
Abstinence, 222, 268, 272; and goals of education, 10, 16, 17; and ideology, 39–40, 41–42, 45, 79; and South Carolina curriculum, 303, 307, 309, 319–320; and victimization, 22. *See also* "Just say no"; Sex Respect program
Adams, S., 307, 311
Administrators, 74–75, 178, 328–335
African-Americans. *See* Race
AIDS: concern about, 7, 8, 173, 185; and a critically based education, 148; and culture, 192–193, 214, 251–252, 268, 270, 276–277, 279; and current state of curriculum, 7, 8; as an epidemic of signification, 274–278; and gender, 280n2; and goals of education, 17; and ideology, 39, 45–46; and language, 274, 279; and mandating education, 8, 61; and philosophical basis of education, 255; and politics, 270, 272; and power, 276, 277; prevalence of, 268; and problems in education, 186; and safe sex, 267–280; and sexual knowledge, 214, 216, 251–252, 253, 280n2; as taboo, 244, 311. *See also specific topic*
AIDS Coalition to Unleash Power (ACT UP), 223
Ajzen, S., 256
Alan Guttmacher Institute, 8, 9, 186, 212

Alcoff, L., 167
Alexander, C., 9, 11
Alliance Against Sexual Coercion, 115–116
Alternative high schools, 289–290
Altman, Meryle, 20–21
American Association of School Librarians, 316
American Educational Research Association, 136
American Family Association, 308
American Federation of Teachers, 74
American Library Association, 74
American Orthopsychiatric Association, 136
American Psychological Association, 136
American Society of Sanitary and Moral Prophylaxis, 38
Anyon, J. M., 230, 314, 315, 318
Anzaldua, G., 159, 160
Aoki, T., 288
Apple, Michael W., 1, 35, 227, 239, 300, 301, 315, 316, 317, 318, 323–324
Aries, P., 25
Armstrong, W., 16
Arons, S., 62
Asian Women United, 159
Association for Supervision and Curriculum Development, 149
Association for Women in Psychology, 136

Baetz, R., 158
Baker, Robert, 19, 109
Banks, J., 185
Barbara Taylor School (Harlem, NY), 86, 124–125, 129–134, 135, 239n1
Bardige, Betty, 237
Barrett, Michele, 140–141, 158
Barthes, R., 234
Basch, C. E., 268
Bass, E., 215
Bauer, D., 168
Beales, R., 25

Beck, E. T., 158, 159
Becker, M., 256
Belenky, M., 195
Bell, T. A., 253
Bennett, William, 16
Benvenuti, A., 149
Berg, A., 163
Berlet, C., 86, 134–136n2
Berlin, G., 285–286
Berman, L. M., 23, 252, 255, 289, 297
Bernstein, B., 227, 272
Berscheid, E., 257
Best, J., 24, 26
Best, Raphaela, 89, 171, 331
Biesta, G., 136
Biographies/autobiographies, 85, 90–98, 149, 152, 158, 292
Biology, 12, 14–15, 36, 56, 99, 167, 168, 176, 182, 183, 184, 192, 212, 223, 243, 303
Birth control, 9, 269, 277, 279, 288, 309; and censorship, 66, 316; and current state of curriculum, 9, 10, 12; and progressivism, 44, 45; and race, 12; and sexual knowledge, 10, 212, 221–222; and sexual learning, 237–238; and South Carolina curriculum, 304, 306, 308, 309. *See also specific type of birth control*
Blasius, M., 27
Bleich, D., 163, 230
Bleier, Ruth, 14, 18, 19
Blos, P., 184, 195
Body concept, 257–259
Bogart, K., 114, 175, 333
Booth, W., 173
Bottom, F. J., Jr., 253
Bowers, C., 86
Brandt, A. M., 272–273
Brant, O., 159
Brick, P., 258, 271
Brinkerhoff, D., 140
Brogan, P., 291
Brongersma, E., 26
Brooks-Gunn, J., 186, 187, 192–193, 268, 288
Broughton, J. M., 135
Brown, P., 135
Brunner, Diane, 12, 149, 182, 247–248, 279
Bullough, R. V., 301, 312
Burress, L., 59, 74
Butts, Peter, 239n

Calderone, M. S., 256
Campbell, D., 10

Campbell, P. B., 172–173, 174, 177
Campbell, T., 10
Cannon, Lynn Weber, 163
Carlson, Dennis, 5, 18, 71, 80, 276, 305
Carrera, M. A., 256
Categorical thinking, 150–152
Censorship: and administrator-teacher conflicts, 74–75; and advocacy, 244–245; and a critically based education, 148; and culture, 82; dealing with, 73–75; and definition of "educator," 65–66; and disruption in schools, 61–62; and educational level, 61; and fear in education, 79, 303, 308–309, 313, 315–316, 317–318, 319–322, 323; and feminism, 71; impact of, 75; justification for, 6; legal cases about, 6, 18–19, 59–64; and legal ideology, 6, 64–70; and needs of students, 82; and power, 61, 64–73; and prophylactic curriculum, 72–73; self-, 79; and sexuality and warfare, 69; theoretical perspectives about, 70–72; and traditionalism, 40. *See also specific topic*
Center for Population Options, 267, 268
Centers for Disease Control, 185, 253, 304
Center for Sex Equity in Schools, 117–118
Center for Women's Studies (Ohio State University), 158–167
Champion, V. L., 257
Charest, P., 271
Child abuse, 24–27, 111, 112–113, 114, 173–174, 224n3
Children's Defense Fund, 1
Childress, Alice, 66–67, 68, 229–230
Chilman, C., 186, 192
Chipouras, S., 261
Chism, N., 148–149
Chodorow, N., 126–127, 144, 184
Churchman, C. W., 284
Citizens for Decency, 7, 16, 17
Clark, D. L., 173
Clark, Kenneth, 142
Cleveland, S. E., 257
Cochran, S. D., 197
Cohan, A., 333–334
Cohen, I., 37, 47
Cole, T. M., 261
Comas-Diaz, L., 195, 197
Communication: and culture, 12, 197; ground rules for, 102; with parents, 12, 95, 100, 212; and philosophical basis of education, 255; and a reconceptualization of sexuality education, 252; and sexual harassment, 108–109; and sexual scripting, 95, 98, 100, 102–104; and social prob-

lems, 287, 288; and South Carolina curriculum, 323
Condoms: and AIDS, 7, 272, 278, 280n2; and culture, 192; and progressivism, 44, 45; as safe, 152; and sexual knowledge, 213–214, 221–222, 223; and South Carolina curriculum, 306, 310, 320, 321; as taboo, 8, 244
Conlon, F., 160
Conservatism: and a critically based education, 147, 148; and current state of education, 8, 242, 243, 245, 246, 248; and family planning, 45; and fear in education, 79, 83; and feminism, 242, 243, 245, 246, 248; and goals of education, 16; and progressivism, 45; and sexual learning, 262; and sexual scripting, 104; and South Carolina curriculum, 300, 303, 305, 306, 309, 318, 320, 321; and teenage pregnancy, 23, 28n3
Constructionism, 86, 157, 158, 167, 168, 182, 183, 184, 277
Contraception: and AIDS, 269, 277; and censorship, 316; and culture, 12, 192–194; and current state of education, 8, 12; fear of as topic in education, 79; and gender, 193; and goals of education, 17; and needs of students, 10, 295; and progressivism, 40–41, 42–43, 44, 45; and a reconceptualization of education, 56; and sexual knowledge, 11, 213–214, 221–222; and sexual scripting, 99; as a social problem, 288; and South Carolina curriculum, 303, 304, 307, 310–311, 316; as taboo, 79, 243, 295
Cormier, Robert, 229–230
Counterculture, 46, 48–50
Cowan, John, 38, 39
Cremin, L., 37, 41
Crimp, D., 274
Critically based education, 145–152
Critical theory, 300, 313, 318
Croteau, J. M., 279
Cruikshank, M., 158, 160
Crumpacker, L., 163
Cuban, L., 13
Cultural studies, 5–6, 35, 56–57, 59, 71, 80–81
Culture: and acculturation, 187–188; and changing student populations, 184–186; and current state of curriculum, 11–12; and gender, 12, 82, 86, 139–153, 191–192, 193, 194–196; and multiculturalism, 181, 186–198, 245–246, 248–249; and

needs of students, 11–12, 181; and parents, 189, 197–198; and personal sexual histories, 152; and a reconceptualization of education, 252; and stereotypes, 187, 191–192; and student voices, 248; and talking about sex, 129. *See also* Popular culture; *specific topic*
Culvershouse, R., 65
Cummins, J., 185
Cvetkovich, G., 13, 193

Daly, Mary, 143, 158
Daniels, Susan, 261, 262
Das, A., 256
D'Augelli, Anthony, 152
Davenport, W., 141–142
David, M., 23, 28n3
Davis, J. E., 73–74
Davis, L., 215
Davis, S. M., 12
Dawson, D., 9–10, 11
de Anda, R., 12
De Cecco, J., 167, 168
Deconstruction, 56–57, 129–130, 158–159
Delamater, J., 36
Delany, H., 289, 296
Delaport, F., 274
de Mauro, D., 9, 17
D'Emilio, J., 159, 276
Democratic society, 147–150
Desire, 22–23, 129, 223, 224n1, 243, 244, 277, 278, 295
Development, human, 41, 126–127, 128–129, 152, 181, 184, 195–196. *See also* Socialization
DeVito, J., 148
Devor, H., 158
Dewey, John, 37, 103, 273
diAngelis, T., 136
DiClemente, R. J., 280n2
DiLapi, Elena, 150
Dillon, C., 149
Diorio, Joseph, 17, 277
Doll, W. E., Jr., 256
Double standard, 19–20, 82, 107, 176, 184, 196–197
Dryfoos, J. G., 286
Duncan, L., 195
Dutile, F. N., 74, 147

Eagle Forum, 16, 307
Eakins, B. W., 109
Eakins, R., 109
Earls, Ruth, 28, 252

Eckland, J. D., 272
Eco, U., 234
Eder, D., 89
Edgar, T., 270
Edwards, L., 286–287
Ehrenreich, B., 21
Ellis, Albert, 94
Ellsworth, Elizabeth, 215, 224n
Emont, N. C., 285
Engels, Friedrich, 47, 130
Engler, R. K., 279
Epstein, S., 158, 167, 277
Equal Employment Opportunities Commission, 110
Equal opportunity, 115, 116, 173–174
Equal protection clause (Fourteenth Amendment), 112–113, 115, 174
Erdman, J. I., 292
Erickson, R., 193
Erikson, E., 184, 195
Espin, O., 187, 197
Essentialist sexual pedagogy, 276–278
Ethnicity. *See* Culture
Eugenics, 41, 43–44, 45
Existentialism, 251, 254–255
Eyerly, Jeanette, 229–230

Family, 36, 44–45, 47, 50
Family life education, 41, 44, 57, 60–61, 187, 302–303, 304, 306, 312, 316
Fanon, F., 135
Farganis, S., 143–144
Fausto-Sterling, A., 14
Faye, C., 18
Fazio, R. H., 256
Fee, E., 273
Feldman, Margaret, 171n, 172
Feminism: and advocacy, 248–249; concerns of, 242, 277–278; contributions of, 157; and culture, 181, 182, 192; and gender issues, 20, 86, 174; and scientific approach, 14, 28n1. *See also specific topic*
Ferguson, A., 182
Fernandez, M., 193
Ferree, M. M., 177
Feshbach, N., 226
Fine, M., 1, 22, 27, 40, 171–172, 182, 191, 204, 210, 223, 224n1, 277, 295
Finkelhor, D., 24, 114
Firestone, Shulamith, 18
First Amendment. *See* Censorship
Fishbein, M., 256
Fisher, M., 55

Fisher, S., 257
Fiske, E., 45
Fiske, J., 83
Flannery, P. J., 253
Flavell, J. H., 237
Flax, E., 39
Flax, J., 167
Flora, J. A., 271
Flynn, S., 86
Fonow, Mary Margaret, 86, 151
Forrest, J. D., 8, 9, 10, 12, 139, 254, 268
Foucault, M., 18, 35, 36, 70–71, 143, 182, 226
Fourteenth Amendment, 111, 112–113, 115, 174
Fox, D. M., 273
Fox, G. L., 20, 253
Francoeur, R., 55
Fraser, J. G., 304, 307, 310
Fraser, K., 270
Freedman, E. B., 276
Freire, P., 135, 152, 230, 301–302, 313, 323
Freud, S., 35, 36–38, 41–42, 46, 48–49, 135
Freudianism, 34, 41, 46–50, 56, 128
Friedberg, J., 257
Fulani, Lenora B., 127, 135, 136
Furstenberg, F., 11, 186, 187, 192–193, 288

Gagnon, J., 89
Galda, L., 230
Gallup, A. M., 173
Gardner, R., 24
Gay, G., 185
Geist, C., 141
Gender: definition of, 85; equity, 172, 174, 175, 176–178, 223; fears about in education, 79; historical aspects of, 172; need for concern about, 171–179; and needs of students, 81–82, 145; and sexual arrangements, 19–22; and social problems, 295; and stereotypes, 174. *See also specific topic*
Gerard, Kent, 142
Geronimus, A., 186
Gibbs, J., 187
Gilchrist, L. D., 287
Gilligan, C., 116, 126, 128, 129, 184, 195
Gingiss, P., 10
Giorgi, A., 135
Giroux, H., 1
Goettsch, S., 21
Goldman, Juliette, 25–26
Goldman, Ronald, 25–26

Goldstein, J., 259
Goldstein, M., 143
Goodman, Jesse, 22, 85, 102, 175–176
Gordon, P., 271
Grahn, J., 158
Gramick, J., 141
Grant, C., 185
Green, L., 256
Green, R., 153n2
Green, V., 141
Greenberg, S., 172–173, 174, 177
Greene, M., 255
Grote, B., 193
Growing Healthy (curriculum), 271
Grudin, R., 292
Grumet, M. R., 71
Gunn, P. A., 159

Habermas, J., 135, 255, 300, 302
Haffner, D. W., 8, 173
Hall, E. R., 253
Hall, G. Stanley, 37
Hallinan, M., 89
Hallman, C., 196–197
Hamilton, R., 10
Hansot, E., 172
Haraway, Donna, 247
Harding, Sandra, 71, 126–127
Hardy, B., 148–149
Haring-Hidore, M., 176
Harmony Middle School (Bloomington, IN), 101–104
Harper, A., 187, 192
Harris, M. B., 12
Hart, E., 149–150
Hass, A., 253
Hayes, C. D., 286, 293
Heilbrun, C. G., 295
Hekma, Gert, 142
Heller, Joseph, 69
Henri, R., 292
Henriques, J., 127
Herek, Gregory, 107, 161
Herz, E., 11, 20
Hester, N. R., 256
Hetrick, A. D., 148–149
Hetrick, E., 148–149
Hewett, G., 149–150
Hidden curriculum, 13–15, 28, 85, 145–146
Hingson, R., 253
Hipple, T., 149
Hiring practices, 252, 319, 329–331
Hirt, M., 257

Hispanics, 11, 12, 67, 68, 185–186
History, 5–6, 56–57, 71, 80–81
HIV education, 267–280
Hoang, G., 193
Hocquenghem, G., 276
Hofferth, S. L., 286
Holistic learning, 5–6, 251, 253–263
Holland, N. H., 230
Holmes, K. K., 253
Holzman, L., 126–127, 130, 131, 135–136
Homophobia. *See* Homosexuality
Homosexuality: and administrators, 333–334; and AIDS, 139, 277; and categorical thinking, 150–152; and censorship, 8, 62–63, 65, 316; and child abuse, 26; and "coming out" letters, 159, 162; and a critically based education, 146, 147–152; and culture, 142–143; fear of as topic in education, 79; and gender, 141, 142–143, 175; and ideology, 79; legal cases about, 18; and lesbian panels, 160–167, 168; materials for teaching about, 153n4; and moral issues, 151; and needs of students, 10–11; and organizational climate, 333–334; and parenting, 164–165; and philosophical basis of education, 255; and radical Freudianism, 47–48; and sex equity, 176, 177; and sexual harassment, 107–108, 175, 177; and sexual knowledge, 212, 215–217, 222; and sexual rights, 56; and sexual scripting, 91–92, 94; and socialization, 127, 141, 153n2, 158; and social order, 144–145; and social therapy, 133–134; and South Carolina curriculum, 8, 309, 311, 316, 321, 322; and stereotypes, 151, 161, 164, 167; as taboo, 8, 9, 243, 309, 311; as a threat, 175; and traditionalism, 36. *See also* Sexual identity
Homosexual rights movement, 174
Howard, M., 16–17
Hubbard, Ruth, 192, 227, 238
Hughes, John, 82
Hulsizer, D., 73–74
Hutchinson, M., 257

Ideology, 15–24, 28n3, 35, 86, 127, 139–153, 305, 323, 324. *See also specific ideology*
Illich, I., 272
Imber, M., 38
Information-based education, 269–270, 278
Institute for Neighborhood Academic Development, 229–239

Instructional materials, 21, 72–73, 99, 148, 149, 223, 228, 254; and South Carolina curriculum, 303, 308, 309, 311, 313, 315–316, 317–318, 320, 321, 322
Instrumentalist approach, 7, 16–17, 27, 28, 251, 272–273, 278
Interamerican Society of Psychology, 136
Irvine, J., 14
Iser, W., 230, 234

Jacklin, C., 126
Jackson, P., 301
Jackson, S., 21–22, 26
Jacobus, M., 295
Jaggar, A., 126–127
Janeway, Elizabeth, 108
Jay, M., 135
Jemmott, J., 193
Jemmott, L., 193
Jenkins, C., 149, 153n4
Jenkinson, E. B., 59, 73–74
Johns Hopkins Self Center (Baltimore, MD), 286, 287
Johnson, V., 5–6, 35, 53–54, 56
Johnson, W. R., 259
Johnston, R., 279
Jones, E. F., 186, 253
Jourard, S., 257
Journals, 230, 236–237, 292
Juhasz, A. M., 10
"Justify My Love" (Madonna), 82, 83
"Just say no," 17, 22, 23, 39, 79, 145, 216, 221, 224, 224n4, 268, 271, 295, 320

Kahn, J., 7
Kantner, J., 187
Kantor, K., 256
Kaplan, R., 173
Kaser, J., 114, 115
Katz, J. N., 167, 277
Kauffman, L. A., 168
Kelley, K., 86
Kelly, T., 103
Kempton, W., 259
Kendrick, M., 24
Kenney, A. M., 8, 9, 98-99, 254, 267–268
Kerr, D. L., 268
Kinsey, Alfred, 5–6, 26, 51–53, 94, 194
Kirby, D., 1, 174, 186, 187
Kirkendall, Lester, 42
Kisker, E., 189
Kitzinger, C., 145
Kitzinger, J., 26

Klein, M., 279
Klein, S. S., 1, 19, 20, 25, 86–87, 171–172, 174, 175, 176
Koch, P., 204, 251, 253, 257, 258, 259
Kolata, G., 268
Koop, C. Everett, 7, 186
Kotasek, A., 310
Krantz, M., 257
Kurtz, R., 257

Lacan, Jacques, 71
LaCerva, Christine, 86, 136, 239n1
Language: body, 54; and gender, 19, 22; and sexual arrangements, 19; and sexual knowledge, 218–219, 228–239. *See also specific topic*
Language arts, 12, 228–239, 279
Larson, J. R., 319
Lather, Patti, 246
Learning: holistic, 251, 253–263; observational, 226. *See also* Sexual learning
Lee, Diane M., 23, 252, 284, 289
Lee, P., 273
Lees, S., 196
Legal ideology, 6, 18–19, 64–70
Lehrman, N., 53–54
Leo, J., 14
Leont'ev, A. N., 135
Lerner, G., 144
Lerner, J. V., 257
Lerner, R. M., 257
Lesbian panels, 160–167, 168
Levi-Strauss, Claude, 143
Liberal arts. *See* Cultural studies
Libertarianism, 34, 35, 46, 50–55, 56
Life-adjustment education, 44, 57
Life Skills Counseling Program, 287
Lifton, Robert Jay, 69
Linn, Eleanor, 21, 85
Literature, 12, 20–21, 182, 228–239
Lockheed, M., 89
Lorde, Audre, 160
Lubeck, S., 238
Lucey, H., 126
Luria, Z., 89

McCabe, J., 16–17
McCarthy, J., 186
Maccoby, E., 126
McCrate, E., 186
McDade, Laurie, 27–28, 28n3
MacDonald, A., 150, 151
Macdonald, J. B., 300

McGee, E. A., 304
MacKinnon, Catharine, 19
McKusick, L., 256
MacLaury, S., 153n4
McNeil, L., 211, 219, 227
Macquarrie, J., 293
Macrina, D. M., 256
Madonna, 82–83
Mahaffey, J., 321
Maiman, L., 256
Mangan, K. S., 270
Manpower Development Research Corporation (New York), 289
Maran, Meredith, 160, 161, 167
Marcuse, H., 5–6, 18, 35, 46, 48–50, 135
Marek, E., 288
Markusen, E., 69
Marshall, J. D., 1, 256
Marsiglio, W., 9, 11
Martin, A. D., 148–149
Marty, Debian, 86, 151
Marx, Karl, 130
Massachusetts, 114, 115–116, 117, 120, 121n3, 188–190
Mast, C. K., 79
Masters, W., 5–6, 35, 53–54, 56
Masturbation, 9, 42, 52, 100, 101, 146, 212, 226–227, 243, 247; and South Carolina curriculum, 307, 308, 320
Mays, V. M., 197
Mbiti, J. S., 195
Meacham, J. A., 285
Mead, M., 141–142
Meaning-making, 12, 182, 228–239, 242–249
Medina, C., 187
Melby, C., 332
Menstruation, 93, 99–100, 101
Mentally retarded children, 251, 259–261
Mentoring, 176, 252, 288–289
Merleau-Ponty, M., 70
Miedema, S., 136
Miel, A., 291
Miller, J. B., 184, 195
Miller, P., 89
Millett, Kate, 26, 27
Mitcham, J., 303
Moglia, R., 256
Mohr, Richard, 151
Money, J., 153n2, 153n3
Moore, K. A., 304
Moraga, C., 159, 160
Moral issues, 15–16, 151, 237, 255, 273

Morey, R., 153n4
Morgan, S., 185, 279
Morishima, J. K., 195
Mosbacher, B., 306
Mosher, D., 23
Mott, F., 9, 11
Muhammad, Rashidah Jaami', 239n
Muraskin, L., 203
Myers, Walter Dean, 229–230
Myerson, M., 1, 21, 99

Nass, G., 55
Nathanson, C., 23, 28n3
National Association of Social Workers, 136
National Center for Health Education, 271
National Coalition of Advocates for Students, 185
National Council of Teachers of English, 73–74
National Education Association, 74, 149
National Gay Alliance for Young Adults, 149–150
National Institute of Education, 9
National Research Council, 45
National Right to Life Committee, 45
Navarre, M., 279
Nettles, S. M., 280n2
Network Publications, 214
Neuman, R. P., 25
New Alliance Party, 135, 136
"New Left," 48–50
Newman, Fred, 86, 130, 131, 135, 136
Newman, L., 126, 130, 135–136
"New Right," 23, 79, 83, 182, 242, 243, 246, 248
Newton, D., 150
New York City Board of Education, 270
New York (state), 8, 269–270, 333–334
Nickel, P. S., 289, 296
Nietzsche, Friedrich, 38
Noddings, N., 288, 297
Nordheimer, J., 24
Norris, C., 257

Oakley, Ann, 142
Offer, D., 184
Ogbu, J. U., 238
Ohio State University, 151, 158–167
Organizational climate, 252, 329, 331–332, 333–334
Orgasm, 18, 52, 53, 54, 226–227
Orlandi, M., 188

Orr, M. T., 9, 98–99, 205, 212
Orton, B. B., 304

Pacific Center for Sexual Minorities, 161
Pagano, J., 71
Paley, Julia, 198n
Paludi, M. A., 176
Parenti, Michael, 108
Parents, consent of, 8, 18–19, 22, 81, 286, 311. *See also specific topic*
Parmeter, S. H., 160
Parrot, A., 172
Patriarchy: and AIDS education, 277; definition of, 144; and gender, 36, 53, 86, 139, 144, 174–175; and ideology, 36, 47, 50–51, 53; and sexual abuse, 26, 27; and sexual arrangements, 19; and sexual identity, 86, 144; and sexual knowledge, 205, 223–224; and sexual scripting, 97, 98; and South Carolina curriculum, 305–306, 313; and teenage pregnancy, 23–24; victims of, 27
Patton, C., 278
Penelope, J., 158
People for the American Way, 73–74
Permeable curriculum, 278–280
Petchesky, R. P., 295
Petras, J., 36
Pharr, S., 166
Phi Delta Kappa, 73–74
Phillips, Lynn, 182
Philosophy, existential, 254–255
Physical disability and sexuality, 251, 261–262
Physiology, 5–6, 9, 10, 56
Pigg, R. M., Jr., 286
Pinar, W., 1
Pittman, K. J., 9, 205, 212, 284
Planned Parenthood, 7, 16, 17, 44, 45, 103, 244, 320
Pleasure principle (Freud), 37, 48–49, 50
Plummer, Kenneth, 26, 143
Polit, D. F., 289
Politics: and a critically based education, 147; and culture, 246; and feminism, 242, 248; and gender, 277–278; and needs of students, 246; and a reconceptualization of education, 252; as taboo, 243–244. *See also specific topic*
Polk, H., 130, 135–136
Pollis, C., 21, 28n1
Popular culture, 20–21, 81–82, 91, 92, 94,

159, 173, 178, 182, 214, 226, 227, 276–277
Pornography, 111, 277, 309, 311
Powell, R., 148
Power/control: and advocacy, 249; and culture, 139, 181, 183, 184; and discourses about sexuality, 35; and fears in education, 79; and gender, 19–22, 37–38, 53, 81, 128, 139, 174–175, 177, 234; and needs of students, 81; and reconceptualization of education, 57, 252; and social problems, 295. *See also* Patriarchy; *specific topic*
Pregnancy: and AIDS, 276, 277; and censorship, 63; and culture, 172; and evaluation of education, 16; historical aspects of, 172; and needs of students, 10; and progressivism, 41; and race, 12, 186; and sex equity, 176; and sexual knowledge, 11, 223; as a social problem, 286; and South Carolina curriculum, 304, 310–311, 312, 316, 320, 321, 322. *See also* Teenage pregnancy
Preschool-age children, 251, 257–259
Presidential Commission on the Human Immunodeficiency Virus Epidemic, 272
Preston, J., 279
Procter and Gamble Company, 99–100
Programs for Educational Opportunity, 117–118
Progressivism, 18, 34, 40–46, 55–56, 86, 273, 305–306, 309, 313
Project 10 (Los Angeles, CA), 148
Project Charlie (curriculum), 271
Project Redirection, 289
Psychology, 18, 36, 41, 129, 134–136n2, 181, 195–196, 251, 256

Quackenbush, M., 279

Race: and AIDS, 185, 280n2; and birth control, 12, 43–44; and censorship, 66–68; and culture, 11–12, 186–198, 238; and current state of education, 10–12; and double standard, 20; and parental communication, 12; and sexual harassment, 119; and sexual identity, 162; and sexual knowledge, 11, 223–224; and sexual learning, 228, 237, 238; and South Carolina curriculum, 304, 305; and teenage pregnancy, 11, 12, 23, 185–186, 304.
Radical Freudianism, 34, 46–50, 56
Rains, P., 193
Raker, S., 173

Rape, 111, 177, 255, 302, 316, 333
Rationality, 7, 12–13, 14, 41
Reality principle (Freud), 37, 49, 50
Recapitulation theory, 37, 195
Reich, Wilhelm, 5–6, 17–18, 35, 46–48, 135
Reis, E., 11, 20
Reis, J., 187
Relationships: and culture, 183, 192, 194–196; negotiating, 54–55; and sexual harassment, 107, 113, 115, 116, 303, 309; and sexual knowledge, 203, 204, 253; and sexual learning, 226–227, 261–262; and sexual scripting, 92–93, 95–96, 97–98; and social problems, 288–289, 294–295
Religion, 45, 59–62, 69–70, 74, 79, 147, 148, 246; and South Carolina curriculum, 305–306, 308, 309, 310, 319, 320
Republican Policy Committee, 16, 17
Reti, I., 160
RHETTA (South Carolina program), 303–304, 308
Rich, Adrienne, 277
Riessman, C. K., 23, 28n3
Riley, Richard, 304, 305
Roberts, Elizabeth, 226–227
Robinson, Paul, 51, 53–54
Rodman, H., 55
Rogers, J., 311
Role models, 91, 133, 148
Role reversals, 141–143
Rosen, F., 126–127, 135
Rosenblatt, L. M., 228, 230
Ross, M., 153n2
Ross-Reynolds, G., 148–149
Rothenberg, P., 126–127
Rowe, Mary, 121n4
Rubin, Gayle, 26–27, 182, 277–278
Ruddick, S., 192
Rudolph, J., 153n4
Rury, J. L., 172
Russell, Steve, 113

Sadker, M., 28, 172, 178
Safer sex practices, 9, 223, 255, 267–280
St. Lawrence, J., 256
St. Paul Ramsey Adolescent Health Service Project (Minnesota), 286–287
Salazar, M., 195
Sandfort, T., 26
Sapon-Shevin, Mara, 21, 85, 175–176
Scales, Peter, 14, 23, 187, 204

Schau, C. G., 174
Scheffler, I., 292
Schlafly, P., 308
Schneider, M., 149
Schofield, J., 89
Schofield, M., 194
Schott, Robin, 71
Schubert, W. H., 1, 254, 255, 291, 300
Scientific approach, 7, 12–13, 14–15, 36, 99. See also Biology
Scott, C., 187, 193
Scott, J., 167
Scott-Jones, D., 11, 187, 280n2
Search Institute, 79
Sears, James T., 1, 5, 27–28, 78, 79, 140, 147, 148–149, 153n4, 158, 175, 177, 204, 256
Seattle Institute for Child Advocacy, 24
Sebestyen, Ouida, 229–230, 231–233, 234–237
Secord, P., 257
Sedgwick, E. K., 167
"Semen theory of power," 37–38
Sex-equity, 114, 115, 176–178, 223
Sex Information and Education Council of the United States (SIECUS), 173, 253, 254
Sex Respect curriculum, 17, 39, 79, 145. See also "Just say no"
Sexual abuse, 252, 253, 255, 259–261, 302, 333–334, 335
Sexual assault, 111, 214–215, 255, 333
Sexual decision making, 9, 10, 12, 194–196, 268, 287–288
Sexual diversity, teaching for, 147–150
Sexual feelings, 10, 21–22, 38, 99, 152, 191, 258, 307
Sexual harassment: and administrators, 330, 333; and child abuse, 114; and communication, 108–109; concern about, 173; cover-ups of, 113–114; and culture, 108–110, 119, 120; definitions/etymology of, 109, 113–115, 121n1, 175; effects of, 85, 106, 116, 120; enforcement of regulations concerning, 111; and feminism, 110–111, 115; and gender, 21, 107–108, 115–116, 119, 173, 175; and hidden curriculum, 85; and hiring practices, 330; and homosexuality, 107–108, 175, 177; and ideology, 144; and language, 108–109; and law, 111–113, 174; management/prevention of, 110, 111, 118–120; and organizational climate, 333;

Sexual harassment (*continued*)
and peer relationships, 107, 113, 115, 116; pervasiveness of, 111, 115–118; policies about, 119; and power/control, 85, 106–110, 119; and race, 119; reporting of, 111–113, 121n3; and sex equity, 177; and sexual assault, 111; and sexual knowledge, 223; and sexual scripting, 85; and silence, 118–119; and status, 107; and stereotypes, 109–110; and theory development, 109–110; and touching, 114–115; and trust, 107, 114, 116, 119; types of, 111; victims of, 119, 121n2, 175

Sexual hygiene, 38–39, 56

Sexual identity: and AIDS, 277; and biology, 167, 168; controversy about, 172; and culture, 139–153, 159, 184; and equal rights, 166; and feminism, 86, 151, 157–170; and gender, 86, 126–127, 139–153, 173, 175; and ideology, 86, 139–153; and language, 142; and lesbian panels, 160–167, 168; and needs of students, 295; and politics, 86, 160; and power, 86, 139, 144, 165, 168; and race, 162; and role reversals, 141–143; and sexual knowledge/learning, 161, 223, 226–227; and socialization, 86, 126–127, 158, 166, 172; and stereotypes, 161, 164, 167. *See also* Homosexuality

Sexuality: characteristics of, 253; deconstructing, 128–129; definition of, 85; historical aspects of, 172; need for concern about, 171–179; and concerns of students, 145; and politics, 159–160; as victimization, 191

Sexuality education: adolescents' perceptions of, 190–198; basic assumptions in, 7, 12–13; and changing attitudes, 17; conceptual framework/organization of, 7, 9, 242; current state of, 8–15; definition of, 56–57; and democratic education, 245, 246–247, 248–249; effects of, 145, 171, 174, 186–187, 277, 307; fundamental questions about, 8; goals of, 12–13, 15–17, 28, 176, 251, 254, 308; and ill-structured problems, 284–297; instructional time for, 9, 284, 313–315, 320; mandating of, 8, 61, 79–80, 173, 205, 300–324; as a modular curriculum, 7–8; need for a reconceptualization of, 5–6, 56–57, 59, 71, 104, 125–126, 198, 242–249; and concerns of students, 8–9, 80–83, 190–192, 244, 289–290; and permeable curriculum, 278–

280; philosophical basis for, 254–255; prevalence of, 186; and priorities, 295–297; problems with, 186–187, 253; prospects for a "thoughtful," 6; quality of, 148; relevance of, 9–13; timing of, 9–10

Sexual knowledge: and concerns of students, 211–212; construction of, 203–224; and culture/values, 11, 204, 205–211, 218; and current state of education, 11; and examinations, 212–214; and feminism, 223; and gender, 11, 205; implications of limitations on, 217–219, 222–224; intra-/interpersonal, 294–295; and a lived sexuality curriculum, 221–222; and parents, 214, 253; and personal asides of teachers, 219–220; and power, 223; and race, 11, 223–224; and simplification of complex issues, 214–217; and South Carolina curriculum, 303, 311, 313–315; students' roles in constructing, 206–207, 209–211; and teaching strategies, 211–220. *See also* Sexual learning; *specific topic*

Sexual learning: beginning of, 253; and birth control/abortions, 237–238; and culture, 12, 227–228, 230, 237, 238; and feminism, 6, 228; and gender, 234, 257; goal of, 255–256; and holistic experiences, 256–263; and language, 218–219, 228–239, 257–258; and needs of students, 227–228, 234, 238, 256, 262; and politics, 230, 262; and power, 12, 226, 227–228, 234, 238; and race, 228, 237, 238; and sexual identity, 226–227; and teaching, 255–256

Sexual liberation movements, 46

Sexually transmitted disease (STD): and culture, 192–194; and current state of curriculum, 9, 186; and goals of education, 7, 15–16, 17; and ideology, 38–41; and philosophical basis of education, 255; and a reconceptualization of education, 56, 251–252; and sexual knowledge, 212, 213, 221, 223, 253, 280n2; as a social problem, 185, 286; and South Carolina curriculum, 302, 310, 311, 312, 316, 321, 322. *See also* AIDS

Sexual pleasure, 146, 277–278

Sexual politics movement, 46–48

Sexual rights, 51, 54–55, 56

Sexual scripting, 21, 85, 86, 89–105, 141, 174, 175–176

Shakeshaft, Charol, 252, 329, 332, 333–334

Shapiro, L., 239n1

Sherbine, D., 307, 309
Shively, M., 167, 168
Shor, Ira, 230
Shornack, L., 13, 23
Shrum, W., 89
Silence, 89–104, 118–119, 146, 171–172, 181, 184, 242–249, 295, 301
Silin, Jonathan, 251, 271, 272, 279
Silverman, J., 8, 9, 10, 12, 139, 254, 268
Simon, K., 256
Simon, W., 89
Sims, Rudine, 235
Sin, 38–39, 45–46, 303, 307–308, 310
Skills-based approach, 270–273, 278
Slater, A., 316
Slater, B., 148–149
Sleeter, C., 185
Smith, B., 159
Smith-Rosenberg, Carol, 159
Snitow, A., 20
Social class, 10–12, 23, 25, 44–45, 46, 47, 54, 184, 227–228, 305
Social engineering, 41, 43–44, 45, 55
Social hygiene movement, 15–16, 276
Socialization, 86, 126–127, 140–145, 153n2, 158, 166, 172, 182, 203, 329, 331. *See also* Social scripting; Social therapy
Social therapy, 86, 129–134, 135–136
Society for the Scientific Study of Sex (SSSS), 14, 16, 28n1
Solomon, Robert, 13, 14
Somerville-Cambridge (MA) Teen Pregnancy Prevention Coalition, 188–189
Sonenstein, F. L., 9, 205, 212, 284
Sontag, Susan, 273–274
South Carolina: AIDS in curriculum of, 311, 317, 321, 322; and censorship, 8, 139, 303, 308–309, 313, 315–316, 317–318, 319–322, 323; language issues in, 309, 310, 311–312, 316; legislature in, 252, 301, 302–312; local implementation in, 252, 301, 314–315, 316, 317, 318–323; parental authority in, 303, 308, 309–310, 311, 321; power in, 300, 301, 309, 313, 317–318, 324; religious issues in, 305–306, 308, 309, 310, 319, 320; state agencies of, 252, 301, 303, 304–305, 310, 312–318, 320, 322
Spender, Dale, 234
Spener, D., 185
Spiller, Hortense, 165–166
Stanley, Julia, 109

Status: and sexual harassment, 107; of sexuality education, 313–315, 317–318
STD. *See* Sexually transmitted disease
Stein, Nan, 114, 115–116, 117, 120, 121n4, 175, 333
Steinberg, C., 271
Storr, A., 292
Strickland, G., 127, 131, 135, 136
Strong, B., 38
Strunin, L., 253
Stubbs, M. L., 178
Students: and administrators, 332–335; changing populations of, 184–186; voices of, 81, 245, 247–249, 290, 321
Sublimation theory (Freud), 41, 42, 46–47, 48–49, 50, 52
Sue, S., 195
Sullivan, J., 39
Sum, A., 285–286
Suransky, V., 25

Talamini, J., 142
Taxel, J., 230
Taylor, Jill, 12, 136, 181, 228, 278–279
Teachers: classroom observation of (Mrs. Warren's class), 204–224; personal asides of, 219–220; physical education, 320; student time with, 335.
Teacher training, 178, 254, 301, 311, 313, 314, 317–318, 319, 323
Team building, 329, 331, 335
Teenage parenting, 247, 289–290, 292, 293, 304
Teenage pregnancy, 212, 243, 271, 277; concern about, 8, 22–23, 173, 185; and culture, 188–190; and current state of curriculum, 8; and goals of education, 7, 16, 17; and ideology, 22–24, 28n3; and needs of students, 311, 312; and power, 23–24; and progressivism, 40–41, 42, 45; and race, 11, 23, 185–186, 304; and a reconceptualization of education, 251, 252; and sexual knowledge, 11, 217–218, 221, 253; and sexual learning, 228, 231–233, 234–237, 238; as a social problem, 23, 284, 287, 291, 292, 293, 295–296, 297; and South Carolina curriculum, 302, 303–306, 307, 311, 312, 319
Thelen, H. A., 255
Thomas, L. L., 303
Thomas, Piri, 67, 68, 72
Thompson, S., 22
Thoresen, C. E., 271

Thorne, B., 89
Thorstad, D., 26
Tolman, Deborah, 198n
Tomboys, 141, 175
Traditionalism, 18, 34, 36–40, 46, 55, 56–
    57, 227, 276, 305–306, 311, 319
Treichler, P. A., 274–275
Tremble, B., 149
Trudell, Bonnie, 11–12, 24–25, 79, 80, 99,
    173, 181–182, 196, 203, 212, 215,
    224n3, 226–227, 247, 278–279
Trussell, J., 303
Turner, S., 11, 187
Tyack, D., 172
Typer, K., 259

University of Michigan, 117–118, 121n4
Upchurch, D., 186
U.S. Agency for International Development,
    44, 45
U.S. Bureau of Education, 38–39
U.S. Department of Health and Human Ser-
    vices, 39
U.S. Office of Adolescent Pregnancy Preven-
    tion, 304
U.S. Surgeon General, 38–39

Valentine, S., 158
Values: clarification of, 83, 303, 308; and a
    critically based education, 146; and cul-
    ture, 243, 245; neutral, 99; and philosoph-
    ical basis of education, 255; and social
    problems, 285, 294, 295; and value-free
    discourse, 243. See also specific topic
Valverde, M., 28n2, 167
Vance, B., 141
Vance, C., 20, 158, 279
Vander Haegen, E. M., 163
van Manen, M., 71
Van Wyk, P., 141
Ventura, S., 186
Verhoeven, C., 294
Victimization, 22, 40, 191, 277, 334
Villarreal, S., 279
Vincent, M. L., 303, 304
Vinovskis, M., 22–23

Vonnegut, Kurt, 69
Vygotsky, L., 126, 130, 135

Walden, J. C., 65
Walkerdine, Valerie, 71, 126, 128–129
Ward, Janie, 12, 181, 228, 278–279
Warfare, sexuality and, 69
Watzman, N., 104
Weis, L., 238, 300, 301
Weisstein, N., 126–127
Werner, L., 45
Wertsch, J., 135
Wexler, P., 227
Whatley, Marianne, 6, 10–11, 14–15, 21,
    24–25, 68, 79, 81, 99, 173, 176, 177,
    215, 223, 224n, 224n3
Whatney, S., 275
White, E. F., 167
White, L., 140
Whitehead, Harriet, 143
Whitlock, Katherine, 150
Whitson, James, 6, 18–19, 63, 65, 79, 80
Whitty, G., 227
Williams, Jacqueline, 143, 151–152
Williams, L., 271
Williams, R., 227, 234, 235
Williamson, Kay, 151–152
Willis, P., 238, 318
Wilson, D., 148
Wilson, W., 285–286
Wolfe, S. J., 158
Women's studies course (Ohio State Univer-
    sity), 86, 151, 158–168
Wood, P. K., 284
Worth, D., 192–193, 197

Yard, Molly, 177
Young, E. W., 256, 257
Young, R., 272

Zabin, L., 9, 10, 13, 187, 247, 286, 287
Zandy, J., 159
Zane, Nancy, 189
Zaretzky, E., 144
Zelman, D. B., 259
Zelnick, M., 187